Waterfront Archaeology

Waterfront archaeology

Proceedings of the third international
conference on waterfront archaeology
held at BRISTOL 23–26 September 1988

edited by G L Good, R H Jones
and M W Ponsford

1991

CBA Research Report 74   Council for British Archaeology

Published 1991 by the Council for British Archaeology
112 Kennington Rd, London SE11 6RE

British Library Cataloguing in Publication Data
International Conference on Waterfront Archaeology (3rd;
  1988, Bristol, England)
  Waterfront archaeology: proceedings of the Third
International Conference on Waterfront Archaeology held at
Bristol 23–26 September 1988.
  1. England. Archaeology
  I. Title II. Ponsford, M. W. II. Good, G. L. III.
Jones, R. H. (Robert Hugh) *1949–* IV. Council for British
Archaeology
  942

ISBN 1-872414-05-2

Printed by the Alden Press Ltd, Oxford

Contents

List of figures

List of tables

List of Contributors

B S Ayers, Norfolk Archaeological Unit, 17 St George's Street, Norwich NR3 1AB, England

D P Bowler, Scottish Urban Archaeological Trust Ltd, 55 South Methven Street, Perth PH1 5NX, Scotland

C E Brown, Department of Conservation, City of Bristol Museums and Art Gallery, Queen's Road, Bristol BS8 1RL, England

P Chitwood, City of Lincoln Archaeological Unit, The Lawn, Union Road, Lincoln LN1 3BL, England

R Daniels, Cleveland Archaeology, PO Box 41, Southlands Centre, Ormesby Road, Middlesbrough TS3 0YZ, England

G Egan, Department of Urban Archaeology, Museum of London, London Wall, London EC2Y 5HN, England

P W Elkin, Department of Technology, City of Bristol Museums and Art Gallery, Queen's Road, Bristol BS8 1RL, England

A Gołembnik, Institute of Archaeology, ul Widok 10, PL-00 023 Warsawa, Poland

D M Goodburn, Department of Urban Archaeology, Museum of London, London Wall, London EC2Y 5HN, England

R A Hall, York Archaeological Trust, 1 Pavement, York YO1 2NA, England

C G Henderson, Archaeological Field Unit, Royal Albert Memorial Museum, Queen Street, Exeter EX4 3RX, England

I P Horsey† and J M Winder, c/o K Jarvis, Archaeological Unit, Museum Service, 4 High Street, Poole, Dorset BH15 1BW, England

R H Jones, Department of Field Archaeology, City of Bristol Museums and Art Gallery, Queen's Road, Bristol BS8 1RL, England

J Lindh, Riksantikvaren Utgravningskontoret for Tønsberg, Nedre Langgate 30E, N-3100 Tønsberg, Norway

G Milne, Department of Urban Archaeology, Museum of London, London Wall, London EC2Y 5HN, England

S Myrvoll, Riksantikvaren Utgravningskontoret for Bergen, C Sundtsgt 64, 5000 Bergen, Norway

C O'Brien, Archaeological Unit for North East England, Department of Archaeology, The University, Newcastle upon Tyne NE1 7RU, England

G Potter, Department of Greater London Archaeology, Museum of London, St Lukes House, 270 Sandycombe Road, Kew, Richmond, Surrey TW9 3NP, England

V E J Russett, Berkeley House, Hythe Bow, Cheddar, Somerset BS27 3EH, England

C R Salisbury, 165 Tollerton Lane, Tollerton, Nottingham NG12 4FT, England

J M Steane and M Foreman, Oxfordshire County Museum, Fletcher's House, Woodstock, Oxfordshire OX7 1SN, England

Acknowledgements

The organisation of a conference and the publication of its proceedings rely heavily on people whose names do not appear on the title page. The editors are pleased to acknowledge the kind assistance of Mrs Jane Lake, Domestic Bursar, and her staff at Clifton Hill House, Bristol University, for their tolerance and apparently effortless hard work during the conference; Sir John Kingman, Vice Chancellor of the University of Bristol, and the Lord Mayor of Bristol, Councillor Derek Tedder, and their staffs for providing two excellent welcoming receptions; Professor Charles Thomas, whose entertaining introductory talk set the tone for the conference; the speakers and session chairmen who did their best to stick to time and the publication timetable; Pip Jones of the City of Bristol Museum for secretarial help and taking on the burden of typing the first draft; our colleague, Ann Linge, for editing and revising the drawings when necessary and providing advice; Henry Cleere and the CBA Publications Committee for agreeing to go ahead with the research report; Dr Julie Gardiner for final editing and seeing the book through the press; the indexer; Brian Hobley for initial advice and Gustav Milne of the Department of Urban Archaeology, Museum of London, for ongoing advice; the delegates without whose presence there could not have been a conference; all our colleagues, especially those in the Field Archaeology section of Bristol Museum who assisted in setting up the conference; and finally, Martyn Heighton, Director of Arts, City of Bristol Council, who agreed that the time of his staff might be spent in this way.

Abbreviations

Cal Close Rolls	Calendar of Close Rolls	LRO	Longleat Record Office
Cal Inq Misc	Calendar of Inquisitions Miscellaneous	MHWN	mean high water neap
		MHWS	mean high water spring
Cal Pat Rolls	Calendar of Patent Rolls	MNI	minimum number of individuals
DGLA	Department of Greater London Archaeology (Museum of London)	MSC	Manpower Services Commission
		OD	Ordnance Datum
DUA	Department of Urban Archaeology (Museum of London)	PEG	polyethylene glycol
		PRO	Public Record Office
Dur Acct Rolls	Durham Account Rolls	RCHM	Royal Commission on Historical Monuments
HBMC	Historic Buildings and Monuments Commission, England		
		SoRO	Somerset Record Office
KBA	Kingston Borough Archives	SuRO	Surrey Record Office

Introduction

The Third International Conference on Waterfront Archaeology was held in Bristol 23–26 September 1988. If the proposed sequence had been followed the conference should have been held in 1987 at the intended location of Bremerhaven, but this was not possible. Although the Bristol conference was held a year later and out of phase, it is to be hoped that the momentum and enthusiasm of the first two conferences, at London and Bergen, have not evaporated and that these valuable four-yearly gatherings will not be abandoned by default in the future.

If there was any doubt of the importance of waterfront archaeology, this was soon dispelled by the consensus reached at the conference. It was agreed that its main function, as always, was to provide an on-going academic forum by bringing together those involved in current research in any relevant branch of scientific and historical studies, including settlement archaeologists of all periods, nautical archaeologists, artefact researchers, dendrochronologists, historical geographers, environmental archaeologists, other scientists, and anyone interested in the study of the interface between the sea and ships on the one hand, and the shore and waterfronts on the other.

Although in the first two conferences there was an undoubted emphasis on urban waterfront sites, mainly due to the fact that most of the work had been carried out there, it is inevitable that the onward transport of commodities and the inland dispersal of much of the evidence for the landing and marketing of goods should encourage an investigation of smaller landing places and use of the shoreline. During the course of preparation for the Bristol conference the 'town' element was dropped so that the conference need not be bound by urban topics alone. This is not to say that urban ports and harbours are less important, indeed the contrary is the case, but that the hinterland should also receive attention: towns cannot exist in isolation; they rely on an economic and distributive base which is probably far more complex than is yet understood.

It is possible to say, therefore, that waterfront archaeology is continuing to evolve, and that archaeologists are beginning to look at 'causes and results' as Dr Herteig encouraged them to do in 1983. In terms of urban archaeology the extent of the material of the waterfront is often breath-taking compared with dry-land data. Waterlogging provides an extra dimension to the evidence without which urban studies would be very much the poorer.

There is still a need for comparative studies to collate this mass of evidence more directly and there is a great potential for review papers on the many topics already broached in these (now three) waterfront volumes. In this there has been little movement since 1983, perhaps because the publication of the data is ongoing, for example in London and Bergen, and synthetic papers may not yet be achievable.

The Bristol conference saw the presentation of 22 papers on the accustomed wide variety of themes. Would-be contributors had been urged to consider aspects either not previously covered in detail or needing further exposure, particularly the effects of sea-level change, fishing, waterfront trades and industries, and the use of waterfront buildings. Many papers covered several topics since they were about one settlement and what was known about it. It was therefore difficult to thematize this volume and thought best to offer it as a unified whole.

Two papers bear the name of the late Ian Horsey of Poole Museums Service whose tragic death was reported weeks before the conference. These two papers are published in his memory. At about the same time we heard of the sad death of Alan Carter, another supporter of previous conferences, whose enthusiastic excavations and research had done much to transform our knowledge of King's Lynn and Norwich. Brian Ayers of Norwich has acknowledged Alan's substantial contribution to his paper in this volume.

The first three papers in this volume describe the evidence for trade and industry in major English towns. It is not surprising, given the commercial interests of medieval England, that much of the information is about the cloth industry, but other trades, such as leatherworking, are also evident in the excavation record. The two papers on Bristol describe the curious problems which early mariners had to solve if they were to use a defensibly safe but navigably dangerous tidal river. Papers on Newcastle and Hartlepool emphasise not only the difficulties of frontier life with the Scots but also interests similar to those of their southern neighbours when it came to trading in such commodities as coal and fish. At Poole and Perth, the development of the harbours are correlated with cartographic evidence. A large collection of ship's timbers from Poole forms an additional topic of current interest.

A paper on the small ports and landing places of Somerset shows that there may be considerable evidence for pre-Norman Conquest and later regulation and trade to be found in the landscape and documents. At Tønsberg, Norway, the effect of topography and sea-level change on the settlement there are discussed as well as the evidence for fish-processing. The fishing theme is pursued in a paper about fishweirs which may be among some of the most ancient and fragile of waterfront structures. Fishing equipment is then described, enabling a better understanding of some waterfront finds. A ubiquitous find on many waterfronts is the oyster shell and the large middens from Poole, their significance, and date are considered.

No waterfront conference can move far away from boats or ships and some recent important finds near London are assessed. Similarly, timber revetments are omnipresent and the importance of some London techniques of river-front carpentry to the overall study of vernacular timber building is examined. The preservation and recording of such structures can often present problems, and current views on the conservation of wet wood are always salutary but very relevant to the study of waterfronts. This forms the subject of another paper from Bristol.

The excavation, interpretation, and ultimate display of a quayside building forms the main content of a paper from Exeter. A medieval bridge from Kingston-upon-Thames, another important waterfront structure, is then described in detail.

Two papers from Bergen show that there is still much to do in that famous city of waterfronts and that methods of investigation need to be adapted to the variety of rescue situations.

Finally, two contributions expressing hope for future work in Lincoln and York, two of England's most im-

portant Roman and medieval cities, describe the rich potential for waterfront archaeology there.

It is appropriate lastly to discuss briefly the future of waterfront archaeology conferences as this volume goes to press. Both secretaries of the original standing conference on Waterfront Archaeology have now left public archaeology: Dr Herteig has retired and Mr Hobley has become a consultant. We wish to acknowledge the help of both over the years. The whereabouts of the next conference is by no means established but should be held, hopefully on an appropriate European theme, in 1992. There have been many suggestions about a venue and about how large the conference should become, *ie* whether continental or intercontinental, but rather fewer about who will organise it. Having now discharged our duty on the publication of this book, we hope that this is not the last of the series but one of several more to come.

1 From cloth to creel – riverside industries in Norwich
B S Ayers

Abstract

This paper combines archaeological and historical evidence with regard to industrial activity along the river Wensum from the Saxon period. It discusses industry *beside* the river (such as cloth-finishing) and *of* the river (such as fishing) as well as industries which *used* the river (such as transport). Identifiable industries include tanning, skinning, dyeing and fulling. The river gravels were exploited for small-scale ironworking. Placename and documentary evidence is used to suggest the location of various industries along or close to the waterfront.

The title of this paper is not intended to convey the impression of a chronological development of industrial activity along the river Wensum in the city of Norwich. Rather it is an alliterative reference to the two main areas of industry to be discussed: industry *beside* the river which used the river as part of its processes (the cloth-finishing trade being a major example of such an activity); and industry *of* the river, extracting raw materials either for industrial purposes or retail sale (fishing being the most obvious example). A third aspect of use of the river can also be discerned in, to employ a modern term, service industries which *used* the river to provide services and which in turn made money.

All three of these aspects can be observed in Norwich in the medieval and post-medieval periods. Regrettably, however, they cannot always, as yet, be observed in the archaeological horizons. Thus much of this paper is necessarily based on historical sources and forms a statement of archaeological potential.

While it remains true that the geographic position of Norwich, especially in relation to the river, made the settlement, it is as true that the city made itself in terms of urban topography, in large part because of dependence on the river. Industrial activity, while a secondary consideration in the origins of the settlement, provides nevertheless a convenient window through which to observe how the river remained central to the economic well-being of this inland city for much of its history.

Norwich has its origins in the middle Saxon period, probably at the beginning of the 8th century. Several small nucleated settlements on either bank of the Wensum appear to have grown gradually in size and importance so that, by the 11th century, a major town of between 5000 and 10,000 people occupied the site.[1] The Norman Conquest, while devastating in the short term,[2] was of long-term economic benefit. By the 13th century Norwich was a prosperous city dominating its region. This prosperity, although fluctuating, seems to have continued throughout the medieval period, only fading in the 16th century. It was revived by a revitalised cloth industry in the later 16th century which enabled Norwich to be regarded as England's second city by 1700, relative wealth only deserting it with the Industrial Revolution.

The early industrial output of Norwich can only be revealed by archaeological excavation. Pre-Conquest documentation for the city is very poor and certainly does not mention industrial activity. It is also difficult to observe early industrial practice in the surviving topography, other than in the possible Anglo-Saxon origin of the great medieval and post-medieval extractive industries of chalk and flint mining. The major archaeological evidence for a pre-Conquest craft industry, however, concerns pottery manufacture. While this was centred on the area of Bedford Street/Pottergate (Atkin *et al* 1983) the portage of raw materials and the export of finished products was almost certainly effected, at least in part, by the river. Thetford-type ware products had a wide distribution over East Anglia and further afield and the use of the river is thus to be expected.

Such usage, however, is very much secondary to activities which utilise directly the proximity of the river to provide water as part of the industrial process. The evidence is, as yet, slim for such activity before the Conquest but, increasingly, excavations across the city are revealing evidence of a number of craft industries, such as leatherworking, which were often located close to the river. Evidence for shoemaking and cobbling has been recovered from the area of Whitefriars' Bridge (Ayers & Murphy 1983) and the tanning of leather at the riverside can be postulated. The shoemaking finds are probably 11th century in date.

More directly, it is possible that flax seeds recovered from deposits at Whitefriars' Bridge may represent retting of flax at the river's edge in the 11th century. Hemp seeds from the same site could be an indication that hemp underwent a similar process and stakes and posts recorded within the excavation may have been used to tether submerged bundles of stems (Ayers & Murphy 1983, 42).[3]

While it is thus true that direct evidence for the establishment of pre-Conquest waterfront industries is currently slender (as is that for craft activity in much of the settlement), likely areas of industrial work can be suggested. Early settlement was concentrated on that part of the Wensum between large river bends west and east of the city (Fig 1.1) and, although commercial activity probably took priority over industry (as seems

Ayers

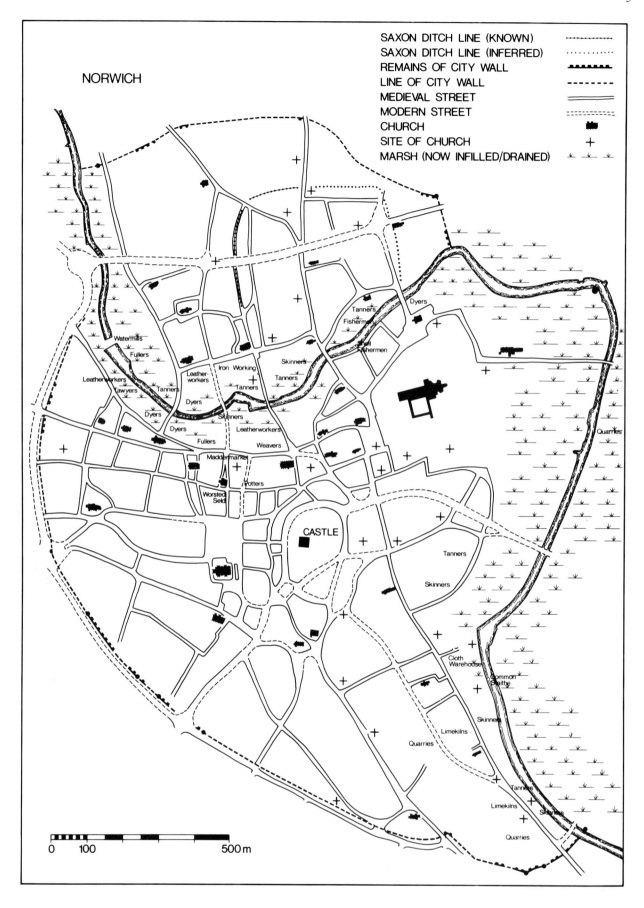

Fig 1.1 Norwich: plan of the city showing the location of major riverside industries in the medieval period

to have been the case at St Martin-at-Palace Plain; Ayers 1987a), small-scale tanning, skinning, retting, and quite possibly brewing were probably conducted along parts of Oak Street, Colegate, Fishergate, Quayside, and Palace Plain. If these trades have yet to be recognised in the archaeological record, other industries of the river are more visible.

Milling is the most obvious such activity. Several mills are mentioned in Domesday Book (Brown 1984, 116b, 117b). Their location is unknown although three quarters of one mill was attached to the church of St Simon and St Jude in the central part of the city on the south bank of the river. It does not follow that a mill was located here and indeed it has been suggested that the mills were situated upstream of the city, close to known later medieval mill locations (Campbell 1975, 7b).

Fishing was certainly a major pre-Conquest industry in Norwich. It may be that it was concentrated on Fishergate on the north bank of the river from an early period. The first record of the place-name dates from the 13th century although clearly the name could be much older. Recent excavation on the street has located significant quantities of fish-hooks and net-weights in contexts generally of the 11th century (Ayers forthcoming a). There is little doubt that the herring trade was important to Norwich by the time of the Conquest. Among other references, a last of herring was owed to the Abbey of Bury from its Norwich property. The importance of Norwich as a distribution centre, again using the river, can be seen here. It has been pointed out that 'fish, like pottery and iron-ware, was a basic commodity needed, but not produced, in every village' (Campbell 1975, 12a).

The evidence for Saxon industrial processes in Norwich is therefore sparse and requires much further work. The situation improves with a consideration of the aftermath of the Norman Conquest which stimulated industry in Norwich, even if this was most manifest in the building trades employed at the cathedral and castle. These, however, had to use the river to transport stone, much Caen and Barnack material coming to the city by water. The river was of such importance to the cathedral that a canal was cut from the Wensum into the Close, presumably to facilitate the transport of stone. It remained visible, as a 'stinking ditch', until the late 19th century when it was infilled (Ayers forthcoming b).

It is perhaps appropriate that the Norman period, initiated in England by the grandson of a tanner, should contain the earliest oblique reference to working with skins, a trade traditionally located close to the river. It occurs in connection with St William of Norwich, the boy saint reputedly martyred by the Jews about 1132, who was apprenticed to a skinner (William thus being the earliest recorded apprentice in English history; Campbell 1975, 10a).[4] Skinners, or parmenters, may have been grouped in Mountergate, or Permountergate, at this time, downstream of much of the settlement. The place-name suggests as much although later documentation does not indicate a concentration here, perhaps implying early and subsequently largely abandoned use of the site (tanners were grouped on Mountergate by the early 14th century, *below* p 5). Excavation of this area, a possibility in the near future, will clearly be extremely valuable.

The exploitation of hides is only to be expected in a growing city which needed much meat from the surrounding hinterland, most of it brought in on the hoof and slaughtered in the city.[5] The noxious trades of tanning and skinning were thus probable early polluters of the city's environment.

The cloth industry in Norwich does not appear to have been of such antiquity as that associated with cities such as Lincoln. There is little to suggest that the trade was at all important in the 12th century save for an obscure reference in a French chronicle which explains the sack of Norwich in 1174 by the Flemings as a result of Norwich men being 'for the most part ... weavers, they know not to bear arms in knightly wise'. The homely cameo this conjures up of peace-loving cloth manufacturers is perhaps given some substance by an entry in the Pipe Roll of 1202; citizens of Norwich were apparently trading in dyed cloth and had been doing so for some time (Hudson & Tingey 1910, xii).

Weaving and cloth finishing on at least a limited scale is therefore implied in 12th century Norwich and the possibility that at least one of these activities was taking place next to the river is supported by the results of excavation at St Martin-at-Palace Plain in 1981. Here, in deposits dating to the first two thirds of the 12th century, significant quantities of *Reseda luteola* seeds (or Dyer's Rocket) were found. *Reseda* produces a yellow dye and the abundance of the finds 'is thought to provide firm evidence for the use of this plant' (Murphy 1987, 133b). A dyer's workshop can thus be postulated some two or three generations before the earliest documented examples but in exactly the location that could be predicted for such an establishment.

The same site produced evidence of small-scale iron-working, probably utilising iron extracted from the river gravels. A possible roasting hearth was excavated, surrounded by stakeholes which may have represented successive positions of a portable anvil (Ayers 1987a, 22, 169). The process was comparable to that uncovered north of the river at Alms Lane in 1976 where, in the 13th and 14th centuries, roasting hearths and smelting furnaces were excavated as well as quarries for nodular ores or iron-pan (Atkin 1985, 152, 242–4 and fig 4). Contexts of the 10th and 11th centuries at Fishergate produced smithing slag, and a fragment of 'heating tray' probably for small-scale refining or cupellation was recovered (Budd forthcoming).

Other activities are occasionally recognised by excavation. The most obvious of these is hornworking, where horn-cores are discovered as discarded material after steeping in pits to remove the tine. Late 12th and early 13th century examples were recovered at Westwick Street in 1972 (Carter & Roberts 1973, 460) and, in 1985, pits of 14th century date were excavated on Fishergate (Ayers forthcoming a).

While the evidence for Norman Norwich is thus little better than that for its Saxon predecessor, it is now possible to suggest that industries known to be important later in the medieval period were in existence by the 12th century. Quantification is impossible although it is likely that some topographic change was being effected by industrial activity. Archaeological deposits at Palace Plain showed encroachment on the river. The same can be expected off Mountergate, and excavations upstream off Westwick Street showed encroachment on the river marsh by the end of the 12th century (Carter & Roberts 1973, 459). As, in subsequent centuries, much of these areas were given over to industrial activity rather than domestic occupation, it is reasonable to assume that precursors of documented tanners, skinners, and dye-workers were occupying the sites.

In the 13th century the available documentation improves dramatically. It now becomes possible to isolate individuals and groups working throughout the city (Fig 1.1). The Norwich Enrolled Deeds are particularly useful in this respect and, while they do not necessarily reflect the actual place of work or domicile of people involved in property transactions, they do at least enable a broad picture of areas of industrial activity to be drawn. In this way it is possible to see a notable concentration of dyers and fullers clustered near the river in the western part of the settlement while tanners and skinners seem to have been especially active in the east (Kelly 1983, 23).

The cloth-finishing industry is the most visible of the medieval industries of Norwich. The city was probably not much of a cloth-manufacturing centre in the Middle Ages (only fourteen weavers are mentioned in the Enrolled Deeds between 1285 and 1311; Kelly 1983, 24) but it held the monopoly of searching and sealing worsteds, wherever they had been made; all cloths 'were to be shorn, dyed, coloured and calendered in Norwich' (Salzman 1923, 237). Of the cloth finishers, dyers have left a colourful legacy in the place-name of Maddermarket, immediately north of the church of St John and close to Letestere Row or Dyers' Row at the eastern end of Westwick Street (Letestere Row being recorded in 1307/8; Hudson 1889, 52). This area formed the greatest concentration of dyers in the city (two thirds of those mentioned in the Enrolled Deeds *c* 1300 are found here) although they are also known to have been active elsewhere along the river. Immediately downstream of Whitefriars' Bridge, for instance, a John le Lytestere held a property in 1327. This property was subsequently sold to another dyer; a neighbouring property belonged to a dyer; and a third property was bought by a dyer in 1397 (Tillyard 1987, 143, 145).

The dyers in the area of Letestere Row are also well-documented. Galfrid le Teinturer (or Dyer) had a property there in 1257 and Kirkpatrick, an 18th century historian of the city, states that many others are recorded from the reign of Edward I (Hudson 1889, 52). The most dramatic evidence, however, has been revealed by excavation. Work by the Norwich Survey in 1972 on Westwick Street uncovered a dyer's workshop, complete with furnaces, stoking pit, well, and drain. The building, originally constructed in the late 13th or early 14th century, was adapted to dyeing use slightly later in the medieval period, the furnaces presumably supporting dyeing vats. The structure was kept clean until it was abandoned in the 16th century (Carter & Roberts 1973, 460–1). Among a number of documentary references, the will of Reginald Cobbe in 1384, in which he bequeathed to his widow the 'capital messuage with appurtenances in which I now live with all lead vessels built therein and all other vessels, tools for cloth making, goods and chattels', may well refer to this property (Sutermeister 1973, 467).

Riverside sites were clearly valuable, with a property boom evident in the 14th century. As much as £70 was paid for a property near St Lawrence's Well in the later part of the century and it is clear that a good return was expected on a sale – when the capital messuage inheritance of Reginald Cobbe's widow was to be sold on her death, Cobbe's son was to receive £30 from the profits (Sutermeister 1973, 465, 467).

Dyers needed raw materials and these had to be brought to the city or grown nearby. It is known that madder was grown in the Cathedral Close; the monks had 'a piece of Ground near the Churchyard of St Mary in the Marsh, where they sold 24 Beds of Madir for 48s ...' (Hudson 1889, 580). In 1286 Norwich reached an agreement with woad merchants of Amiens and Corbie over the supply of woad and weld (Hudson & Tingey 1910, 209). One of the woad merchants, Peter le Mouner, purchased a house in St Clement's parish (probably on Fishergate near Fyebridge) in 1287 with the river to the south. After his death he was referred to as 'Peter le Mouner, citizen of Norwich' (Hudson & Tingey 1910, lxxviii, 4–5). Six woad merchants are mentioned in the Enrolled Deeds of 1285–1311 (Kelly 1983, 25).

It is possible that pressure of space at the waterfront off Westwick Street forced other industries away from the river. Very recently work on the south side of the street by the Norfolk Archaeological Unit (Fig 1.2) has uncovered an area of industrial working with many pits and slots, and a single hearth in a lean-to structure. These levels date from the 13th and 14th centuries and are probably associated with the cloth trade, an activity such as fulling being perhaps as likely as dyeworking.[6] Fullers were certainly also concentrated upstream in the city, presumably for clean water and space for tenting frames (large tenting grounds were available in St Giles' parish just to the south). All ten individuals in the Enrolled Deeds around the turn of the 14th century were located here (Kelly 1983, 25). Cleanliness of the water must have been relative in many cases as 'Le Fulleres holes', 'a streit Lane [which] runs down North to the River' and probably so called 'from their [the Holes] grat descent' (Hudson 1889, 55), was recorded downstream of Letestere Row in 1322/3. John de Bastwyk is mentioned here in 1359/60 when he granted his capital messuage in Fullershole to William Gerard together with 'all his utensils, Leads, Fullyngstokks etc.' The grant also included a piece of ground in St Giles with a cottage and tenters (Hudson 1889, 55).

Fulling, which was also practised north of the river, as was dyeing, was originally a hand process but subsequently was carried on in mills. Two mills are recorded as disused *c* 1410 (Campbell 1975, 15a) but by 1429 water-powered fulling was taking place at the New Mills off Westwick Street (Kelly 1983, 25) and Kirkpatrick, referring to mills in the 1720s, could state that 'many Stuffs of Norwich make were fulled within the Memory of Man ...' (Hudson 1889, 56).

Fullershole, which was still called that in the early 18th century, lay in the parish of St Gregory, off Shearing or Charing Cross. A little further east was Le Bleckstershole, recorded in 1296/7, after blekesters or bleachers, those who bleached woollen cloth. This lane lay immediately upstream of the palace of the Dukes of

Fig 1.2 Norwich: view of the 1988 excavation at Westwick Street. The church of St Lawrence is in the background. Part of the site was owned by dyers at the end of the 13th century. Photograph: K Laws-Chapman, Norfolk Archaeological Unit

Norfolk, constructed in the 16th century, the situation of which was described in 1681 as 'a dunghole place ... pent up on all sides both on this and the other side of the river, with tradesmen's and dyers' houses who foul the water by their constant washing and cleansing of their cloth' (Kent 1932). It is perhaps little wonder that the Dukes of Norfolk were never noted for their attachment to their Norwich property.

It is clear, therefore, that there was a concentration of the cloth-finishing process in the western part of the city. Dyers, fullers, and bleachers lived close to their common major resource, the river, but also near support facilities such as tenting grounds and the shearmen of Charing Cross. These latter trimmed the nap on cloth after it had been fulled and stretched and, of eight such men recorded in the 1285–1311 Enrolled Deeds, most were present in this area (Kelly 1983, 25).

Such a concentration of activity inevitably engendered problems and the city records have numerous references to the state of the river. Individuals were prosecuted, such as John Long, dyer, in 1390/1 who

was 'wont to throw and lay muck, cinders, and other refuse by the stulps and stakes [presumably of his staith], wherof much falls into the King's river, to the obstructing of the river ...' (Hudson 1892, 73). By the 16th century the Assembly was actively discriminating against gross polluters. In 1532 it decided to assess inhabitants for the work of cleansing the river and recorded that 'barkers, dyers, calaundrers, parchement-makers, tewers, sadelers, brewers, wasshers of shepe, and all such gret noyers of the same rever tobe ffurder charged than other persons shalbe ...' (Hudson & Tingey 1910, 115).

Lists such as these give a useful indication of the importance of the river to industrial practice in late medieval Norwich. They emphasise relatively small-scale work such as parchment making which is less obvious than a major industry such as cloth finishing. Even the cloth trade, however, was overshadowed in numbers of people working by the leather trades which dominated waterfront activity throughout much of the city.

The Enrolled Deeds evidence of the late 13th and early 14th centuries suggests that leatherworkers formed the largest industrial group in the medieval city. Some 18% of the known trade population, 173 men, came from this group (only ecclesiastics accounted for more – representatives of an industrial activity of a kind and also noted for its use of water but perhaps not relevant here) (Kelly 1983, 19–22). After shoemakers, the largest sub-group of leatherworkers was the tanners (50 persons). More than half of these occupied riverside premises on the north bank of the Wensum, probably also utilising two major streams here, the Muspole and the Dalimund; Muspole Street survives as a place-name. They were also found in the east of the city in Conesford where Barkers Dyke is mentioned in the reign of Edward III, a reference to another stream or cockey used by tanners.

Skinners were also located in Conesford in the early 14th century although few seem to have worked on Mountergate where the place-name suggests them. Rather Mountergate had a group of tanners around Barkers Dyke while the skinners were at the southern end of Conesford (or King) Street. Tawyers or leather-dressers had premises on the Westwick river frontage (Kelly 1983, 23), intermixed with dyers and fullers. As with all trades, individual leatherworkers would be found elsewhere. A tanner, for instance, is recorded at St Martin-at-Palace Plain in 1397 (Tillyard 1987, 144).

The river also served domestic industrial purposes such as clothes washing. At St Ann's Staith off King Street in 1421 Robert Clark, a carpenter, and others were licensed to make a staith to wash 'linnen cloaths'. The city paid 10s in 1456/7 for damming at this staith, presumably to improve its efficiency, and a new quay of stone was built in 1546/7. In 1614 it was reiterated that the staith must be used for washing, not for loading or unloading goods (Hudson 1889, 8).

The foregoing paragraphs may give the impression that many of the industries of medieval Norwich were concentrated in areas particular to a craft or group of crafts. While this was true to an extent the variety of waterfront activity is also reflected by close study of riverside locations. One such area is Fishergate where

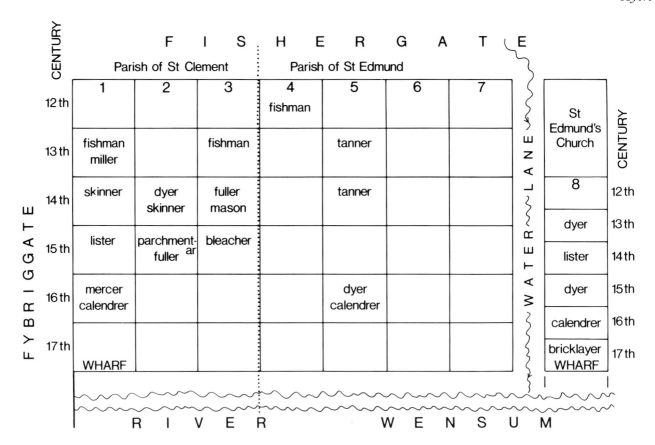

Fig 1.3 Norwich: diagram of documentary evidence for river-side properties on the western part of Fishergate in the Middle Ages (information researched by Margot Tillyard)

recent documentary research of that part of the street between Fyebridge and Water Lane has indicated a variety of occupations for owners and tenants of tenements, nearly all of whom would have been reliant upon the proximity of water for the successful prosecution of their trades (Tillyard forthcoming). The occupations are tabulated on Figure 1.3 where the implication is also clear that fishing on Fishergate was a declining trade by the 14th century.

Industrial activity beside the river was thus intense, although it was localised to certain areas of the city. The greatest density was in the central part of the city where both banks could be utilised and indeed it has been argued that the business of these areas partly explains the necessity for medieval Norwich having as many as five bridges (Campbell 1975, 11b–12a). Downstream, the east bank was outside the city and thus less utilised; much of the west bank lay within the area of the Cathedral Close or the Great Hospital, and much of King Street was occupied by affluent merchants.

These merchants were engaged in commerce, which is outside the scope of this paper, but one building should be mentioned as it seems to be a rare survival of a great cloth hall, a warehouse for much of Norwich's textile products. The Old Barge or Dragon Hall was constructed as a first-floor hall in the mid 15th century above earlier ground-floor walls. Although on the street frontage, its working facade was that to the river, where an arcade still survives encased in later additions, and a great arch afforded access into the ground-floor of the structure with winches presumably hauling material aloft. This was the grand face of Norwich's industrial power, using the river to distribute its goods.

The river was used, of course, by other trades as well. Stone for the successive building campaigns on the cathedral was still brought upstream (as in 1288/9 when Caen stone was trans-shipped in Yarmouth before being brought upriver; Fernie & Whittingham 1972, 54–5) and, in 1398/9, the construction of the Cow Tower required the carriage of bricks and hurdles by water to the site (Ayers 1987b, 20). Flint mining and chalk quarrying was an extensive Norwich industry, much material leaving the quarries by water. In 1561 the loading of lime was prohibited at Mrs Bulwer's staithes in King Street as 'the people cannot wasshe there onles they should moche hurte thos clothes that they shoulde so wasshe there' (Hudson & Tingey 1910, 135). Peat was brought from the Broads by water, the Cathedral Priory using 410,000 turves in 1326 alone (Campbell 1975, 14b). Wool exports, as well as those of cloth, were important, Norwich being a staple on several occasions.

This use of the river for industrial activities was complemented by extractive industries based on what the river could offer. The most obvious such activity was fishing. As early as the reign of Henry III an order had been made to the prior of the cathedral to permit the citizens a free fishery in the river (Hudson & Tingey 1910, 214). The state of the fishery continually exercised the authorities. Men of Surlingham (a village outside Norwich) were fined in 1292/3 for catching fry in nets contrary to the assize (Hudson 1892, 42). In

Fig 1.4 Norwich: Quayside in the early 19th century, the medieval shell-fishermen's wharf. The 15th century warehouse at the extreme right (the New Star Inn) was demolished in 1963. Artist unknown. Copyright: Norfolk Museums Service (Norwich Castle Museum)

1545 it was complained that the river was over-fished and 'every fisherman should be compelled to keep a dog to kill the otters' (Hudson & Tingey 1910, cxxx).

Herring were particularly important to Norwich, herring pies being tendered to the Crown from the 13th century and probably earlier. The practice survived until the early 19th century and a medieval recipe is recorded in the city archives (five herrings to a pie with ginger, pepper, cinnamon, cloves, long pepper, grains of Paradise, and galingale; Hudson & Tingey 1910, 208). Fishing boats certainly landed on Fishergate, most probably in the inlet formed by the outflow of the Dalimund and now followed by Hansard Lane. Shell-fish boats landed on Quayside, downstream of Fye-bridge (Fig 1.4). In 1963, following demolition of the New Star Inn, a 15th century warehouse, small-scale excavation by the Norfolk Research Committee recorded a layer of oyster shells 18in (0.46m) thick (Wilson & Hurst 1964, 267).

A more curious industry involved harvesting on islands within the river. In 1290/1 William Bishop appropriated an island near New Mills which ought to have been common (he was fined 2s) and stopped people mowing grass there in 1292/3 (when he was fined half a mark) (Hudson 1892, 37, 45). Water extraction was refined in 1583 when John Foster and Alexander Peele,

citizens and plumbers of London, 'erected buyled and sette up at or nere New Mylles, a mylle with all thinges thereto belongeng to dryve and conveighe water by and throughe certaine pypes to lead lyeng and beeyng in dyvers streets and churchyardes to the Market Cross ...' (Hudson & Tingey 1910, 392–4).

Water provision was a service industry as was that provided by boats. Three boatmen are mentioned in early 14th century enrolled deeds. A late 15th century cooper at the river frontage of St Martin-at-Palace Plain owned three boats (Tillyard 1987, 145b) and a ferry was in existence at the watergate to the Cathedral Close by the 16th century. Boats were used for nefarious activities such as the forbidden practice of conveying muck (Hudson & Tingey 1910, 84, 392) or crime. In 1570 the Assembly limited the number of passage boats between Norwich and Yarmouth to three 'as it was alleged that the river was a means of bringing in undesirable persons and aided their escape after their misdeeds' (Hudson & Tingey 1910, cxxxii).

Much of this survey of the medieval period has necessarily relied upon documentation as archaeological evidence is, as yet, unavailable. The scope for research is clearly great, especially as most of the riverside industrial areas are located on sites where a degree of waterlogging can be expected, an unusual situation in

Fig 1.5 Norwich: Colegate, showing distinctive dormer windows for weavers' lofts. Photograph: K Laws-Chapman, Norfolk Archaeological Unit

Dyeworkers thus continued to be of importance, waterfront dyeworks surviving into the 19th century. Leatherworking was to become increasingly important in the 18th century (Green & Young 1981, 27b) while brewing, widespread if small-scale in the Middle Ages (as observed, for instance, at Alms Lane in the early 14th century; Atkin 1985), became a major riverside industry with two large 19th century breweries being constructed on Westwick Street and Barrack Street. In 1801, 20,000 barrels of beer were brewed by Patteson's (Green & Young 1981, 27b). Even ironworking retained its local importance, a very large iron foundry being established on the north bank of the Wensum. Riverside timber-yards do seem to be a post-medieval introduction with water communications increasing their viability. The mustard industry was introduced next to the river soon after 1800. Service industries flourished by the river from the 18th century. Mr Bunn's Spring Gardens off King Street were very fashionable at this time.

One final aspect of industry should be mentioned, albeit one difficult to recognise within the archaeological record. This is the vexed problem of industrial espionage for, in 1478, 'two Aldermen were commanded to dismiss their two alien domestic servants whose parents were merchants in far distant lands, and had sent their sons ... to spy out the methods of the local trade ...' (Hudson & Tingey 1910, lxxviii). Such vigilance was clearly beneficial, given the success of Norwich in the market place.

well-drained Norwich. The wealth of industrial activity is easy to enumerate; as yet little is known of the mechanics of industrial production in the city.

The strength of the industrial infrastructure that was created during the Middle Ages is underlined, however, by the continued importance of traditional Norwich industries in the post-medieval period, of which the most significant was the textile trade, revitalised with the help of immigrant Dutch weavers in the late 16th century,[7] and which came to dominate the local economy. John Evelyn wrote in 1671 that 'the fabric of stuffs ... brings a vast trade to this populous Towne' (Priestley 1985, 183) and later visitors such as Celia Fiennes and Daniel Defoe endorsed this view. The urban fabric was changed by this trade as weavers, usually working in groups of two or three, created workshops in attics lit by distinctive dormer windows, which still survive in many parts of the city, but which were particularly dense in riverside parishes where weavers were close to the traditional sites of dyers and other finishers (Fig 1.5).

Notes

1 The process is summarised in Carter 1978. A further summary can be found in Green & Young 1981. There is little dispute over the probability of this osmotic development although the actual mechanics need much more study and authorities differ on the size, importance, and location of the nucleated settlements.

2 Domesday Book. 1320 burgesses recorded before 1066; only 665 English burgesses are recorded for 1086 (Brown 1984, 116b).

3 There is more conclusive evidence for retting of flax at the middle Saxon site of Brandon in Suffolk (Carr *et al* 1988), which leads to speculation that such activites were also present in Norwich.

4 Blomefield (1806, 27) states that St William was apprenticed to a tanner.

5 Documentary evidence for this is late although it has been tentatively suggested that marine plant macrofossils from the 1979 excavation at Whitefriars' Bridge could have been imported to the city on the hooves or in the guts of stock pastured on the rich marshland east of Norwich (Ayers & Murphy 1983).

6 Excavation ceased on 23 September 1988. Summary in Gaimster *et al* (1989, 203). Final report in *East Anglian Archaeology*.

7 The number of immigrants was extraordinary. In 1568 there were 1471 in the city; in 1583 the number had risen to 4670 (Rickwood 1967, 7). It is likely that the population of Norwich increased from about 12,000 to about 18,000 in some 20 years, most of the increase being accounted for by 'Strangers'.

2 Industry and economics on the medieval and later London waterfront

G Egan

Abstract

The published sequence of land reclamation at Trig Lane is compared with the wider picture of riverside develop-ment established from excavations at other waterfront sites in London. Fuller sequences beginning in the Roman period are discussed, with particular reference to Swan Lane. Evidence from several excavations suggests major programmes of land reclamation in the 12th and 13th centuries. At Swan Lane a large number of industrial hearths with associated fuller's earth in three adjacent properties represented the first use of land reclaimed at this date. It is suggested that the plant was used for cleansing cloths, perhaps in preparation for dyeing. Leaden cloth seals and fuller's earth from a 17th century well indicate post-medieval dyeing of provincial cloths here. Finds of thousands of cloth seals along the London waterfront, including a 17th century group excavated at Trig Lane, are interpreted as industrial evidence from a series of late medieval – 19th century riverside dye houses, reflecting the internationally important trade in cloths dyed in London. Archaeological and documentary evidence together demonstrate the continuation of textile finishing in the Swan Lane area for upwards of half a millennium.

The basic pattern of the reclamation of new land from the river Thames in London that has now been revealed by excavation on a large number of sites has become familiar from an extensive literature. The usual sequence can be briefly summarised: the natural pre-Roman river-bank was located to the north of modern Thames Street; within a few years of the founding of Roman London, the first of the remarkable succession of timber quays was built (Milne 1985b, 55, 57); these mark the stages of the gradual process of reclamation from the river through almost 2000 years; today the river wall lies at some points over 120m south of the original natural river-bank. Thus the entire strip of land to the south of Thames Street is a man-made extension to the available land space of the city. Reclamation still continues in the 1980s, when the annual ratable value of land (new or old) in the City is in the region of £22 per square foot,[1] and an extra couple of feet of floorspace along one side of a multistorey building can, over 25 years, bring in an additional rent of about £1 million. This paper looks at the development of the medieval waterfront, trying from some aspects of the excavated evidence to suggest how similar considerations may have been important in a period for which comparable information is incomplete and its implications uncertain. It also considers the Thames-side textile-finishing industries against this background and into the post-medieval period.

The evidence from Trig Lane (Fig 2.1) has been published in detail (Milne & Milne 1978, 84–104; Milne & Milne 1982), but the reclamation sequence in the area excavated there did not give the complete picture for the medieval period.[2] In isolation, this evidence may be somewhat misleading if it is taken to be typical of the waterfront as a whole. The excavated sequence on the site started in the 13th century: the earliest revetments were superseded by one which was replaced on the same alignment sometime before, and again a little after, 1300. This was followed during the 14th century by a further revetment at a property on the west, and two in succession on adjoining properties on the east. The subsequent stone river wall to the south was construct-ed in the 15th century, and the modern river wall some 10m to the south of that completes the sequence. This last 10m represents the reclamation over the past 500 years. Overall this suggests a relatively simple sequence of one or two phases of reclamation per century in the later middle ages, with a different rate of progression southwards for each individual property; on average over 13m of new land was reclaimed over each of the 13th, 14th, and 15th centuries, followed by a markedly slower rate of advance in the post-medieval era (Milne & Milne 1982, 62–4 and figs 4, 44; cf Milne 1985b, 18-19, fig 7).

That this is not typical of the London waterfront as a whole was suggested by evidence from other excava-tions, notably that at Billingsgate lorry park (down-stream of London Bridge, Fig 2.1). Here the early part of the post-Roman sequence was recorded in detail, though the constraints imposed by the developer did not allow adequate clarification of the structural sequence in the southern two thirds of the site during the subsequent watching brief (Youngs et al 1985, 173, site 44; for a summary of a narrow trench at the Seal House site, located just upstream of the bridge, see Schofield & Harrison 1975, 54–7, and Richardson 1977, 36). At the Swan Lane site to the west (Fig 2.1), by contrast, where the developers (Sir Robert MacAlpine & Sons) were helpful within the constraints of their work programme, it was possible in 1981-2 to build up a composite plan over most of an area c 4000m square, from a series of observations. Briefly stated, the sequence recorded here (Fig 2.2) was as follows: to the north of the site, on the other side of Thames Street,

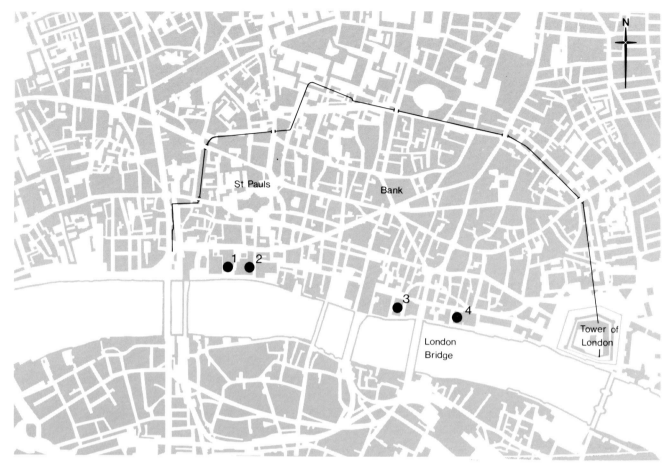

Fig 2.1 London: location of sites mentioned in the text:
1) Trig Lane; 2) Sunlight Wharf; 3) Swan Lane; 4) Billingsgate (lorry park)

were the natural pre-Roman river-bank and the presumed early Roman quays (as observed by Miller at a redevelopment site just to the east; Milne 1985b, 16, 55, 57, and figs 5, 34). At the extreme north of the redevelopment site itself, on the west side, was a 2nd century quay, a typical squared box-construction of massive oak timbers with dovetail jointing. The later Roman quays were far less substantial vertical-post and horizontal-plank constructions, with a north-south drain marking an apparent property boundary. The latest quay from the Roman period had very substantial baseplates (these were the largest timbers recorded on the site, c 7m by 0.5m, with a series of mortices for the removed vertical members along the tops). These latest Roman timbers mark an important division – to the north is Roman made land, and to the south reclamation is medieval or later.

The next major riverside structure was a Saxo-Norman clay river-bank, which has now been observed on several sites (Vince 1985, 158–60). Reclamation of

new land from the river recommenced, probably in the late 12th century, with the first of a remarkable series, over the next couple of centuries, of at least nine revetments which accompanied the creation of over 50m of new land – half of the total area reclaimed in the post-Roman period at this point. The importance of the late 12th to 14th century reclamation is clear at the Swan Lane and Billingsgate sites. At Trig Lane it was far less marked. It probably differed in detail at all points along the river frontage.

The post-and-plank form of revetment, with angled front braces on the river side, was very widespread in London and elsewhere at this time. Figure 2.3 shows the remarkable scale of one particular late 13th century revetment of this form. It was 4m in height, and must have represented a large capital investment. The timbers were so large that the braces were tapered towards the top, possibly because otherwise their sheer weight might have made the structure liable to collapse, though it would probably have been difficult to find

Fig. 2.2 (opposite) London: Swan Lane, land reclamation sequence showing the positions of the successive quay frontages: solid line = alignment recorded precisely; dashed line = alignment observed but less accurately recorded; dotted line = alignment inferred
Ceramic phase nos (6–12) indicate suggested finds-dating for reclamation of each block of land: 6 = c1150–c1200; 7 = c1200–c1230;   8 = c1230–c1260;   9 = c1270–c1350;   10 = c1330–c1380;   11 = c1350–c1400;   12 = c1400–c1450

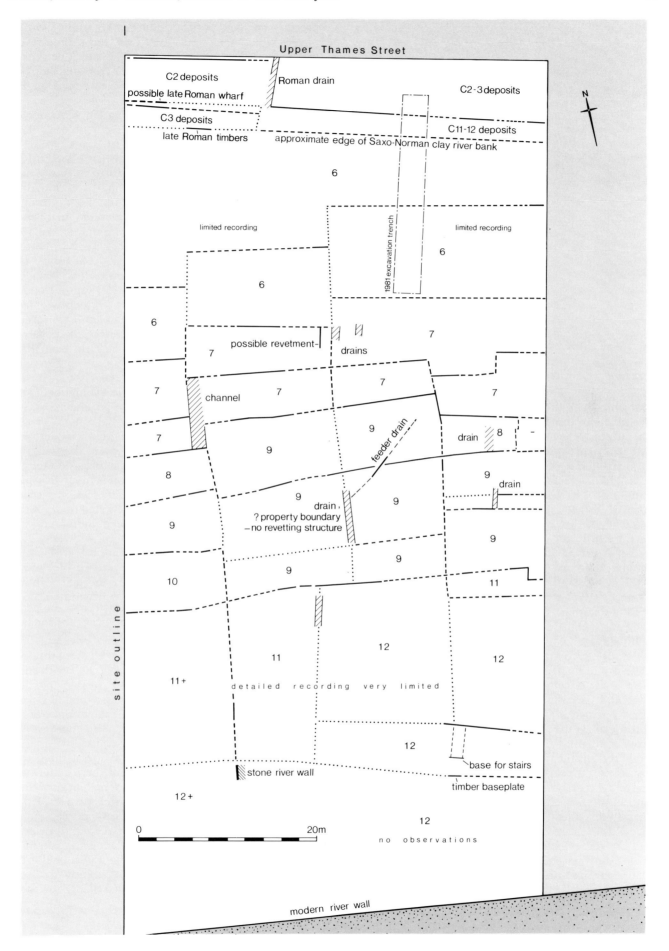

Upper Thames Street

C2 deposits

possible late Roman wharf

Roman drain

C2-3 deposits

C3 deposits

late Roman timbers

C11-12 deposits

approximate edge of Saxo-Norman clay river bank

6

limited recording

limited recording

6

1981 excavation trench

6

6

6

7

possible revetment

drains

7

7

7

7

7

channel

7

7

7

9

feeder drain

drain

8

9

8

9

drain

drain,

? property boundary

—no revetting structure

9

9

9

9

10

11

12

12

11+

detailed recording very limited

11

12

12

stone river wall

12

base for stairs

timber baseplate

12+

0   20m

12

no observations

site outline

modern river wall

N

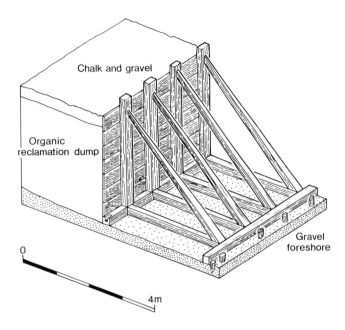

Chalk and gravel

Organic
reclamation dump

Gravel
foreshore

0

4m

Fig 2.3 London: Swan Lane, late 13th century front-braced quay-revetting structure (reconstruction after T Brigham)

parently non-functional cladding of scantling and thin planks which ran vertically.[5] Two stave-built revetments towards the south end of the site (one with a dendrochronological date of *c* 1393 from one timber) were the only structures it was possible to record in that area.

Completing the recorded reclamation sequence on the site was a ragstone riverside wall of early 15th century date, similar to that at Trig Lane (Milne & Milne 1982, 38–42, figs 31, 32). This left between 12m and 17m of reclamation up to the present river wall over the past 600 years, again emphasising by contrast the flurry of riverside expansion in the high medieval period. Stone riverside walls seem often to mark a slowing down of the reclamation process, in the 15th century in London, but as early as *c* 1300 in Dublin (Wallace 1981, 117 and 110, fig 107). They were undoubtedly more expensive and more robust than the wooden structures (a river wall at the Tower of London in 1389 cost £9 13s 4d for every 16.5 square feet; Salzman 1952, 469–70, appendix B no 42). There seems to have been less inclination to abandon or demolish an investment of this magnitude than with the timber revetments.

The sequence of the structures associated with reclamation which was recorded on the site highlights the 12th and 13th centuries (a period of general expansion in the national economy), but to make more of this aspect it is necessary to turn inland and to consider what was happening on the new land beside the wharves. This might provide a more specific explanation for the apparent boom in medieval development in this particular part of the river frontage. The 1981 controlled excavation trench turned out to be located over a series of late 12th – early 13th century industrial-scale hearths, most of which were about 3m wide (Fig 2.4). The majority were keyhole-shaped in plan, with a kerb of roof tiles and/or ragstones, and pitched tiles in the centre which retained traces of a mortar burning-surface. Some yellowish material concentrated along one side of the best-preserved hearth (Figs 2.5 and 2.6A, no 1) has been identified as montmorillonite (fuller's earth), which was found throughout the sequence. In all, 31 hearths were excavated, running the full 22m of the excavation trench (Fig 2.4), with three replaced burning-surfaces and 19 further possible hearths represented by traces – giving a total of at least 50. The section (Fig 2.7, *cf* Fig 2.8) shows most of the hearths that were nearly complete, on the slope down to the river. They included a vertical sequence of six. Just how many of the hearths might have operated together at any time is open to question, but there could have been a north-south row of eight or more. Not all of them were of exactly the same form. Hearth 2 was a small oval one, inserted next to no 1 (Fig 2.6A), perhaps to be operated in some kind of subsidiary capacity, prior to the construction of no 3, which was a replacement of no 1 on the same scale. Hearth 29 (Fig 2.6B), one of the latest hearths in the sequence, was apparently of rectangular form, with pitched tiles aligned diagonally. This

uniformly thick timbers of this length. Most London revetments of this form are a little over 2m in height. The successive medieval quay structures recorded were principally of oak timbers, the cost of which (even if reused from elsewhere) must have been quite considerable. The payment for constructing a wooden revetment at Broken Wharf in London in 1347 was £20 for example (Salzman 1952, 434–5 appendix B no 16). The frequency with which the successive wooden wharves were built at the Swan Lane site through the late medieval period (there would perhaps have been a dozen in all in just over 300 years) shows that there was clearly a substantial, sustained investment in developing an area that was not obviously a prime part of the city's waterfront. Coastal and international shipping trade might explain a similar phenomenon downstream at Billingsgate, but at this particular point upstream of the bridge such trade is not attested. Inland riverine trade would be perfectly possible here, but it does not seem from documentary sources to have been prominent. It is necessary to look for another reason for this investment (*cf* Milne 1981, 33–6).[3] In the majority of instances at the Swan Lane site, the land reclamation process involved the abandonment of seemingly perfectly serviceable timber structures, after an average of just 25 to 30 years' use at the river's edge, to burial under the material that was used to make up the new land in the next stage of reclamation.[4] One early 14th century revetment recorded on the site appears to be a blend of the common post-and-horizontal-plank type and the vertical-stave type that is generally, but by no means universally, later. The structural horizontal planks on the south face that would have been seen from the river were in this instance hidden behind an ap-

Fig 2.4 (opposite) London: Swan Lane, industrial and possible industrial features (cf Fig 2.2): F = fuller's earth; stippling = hearth (accompanying numbers indicate total recorded in vertical sequence)

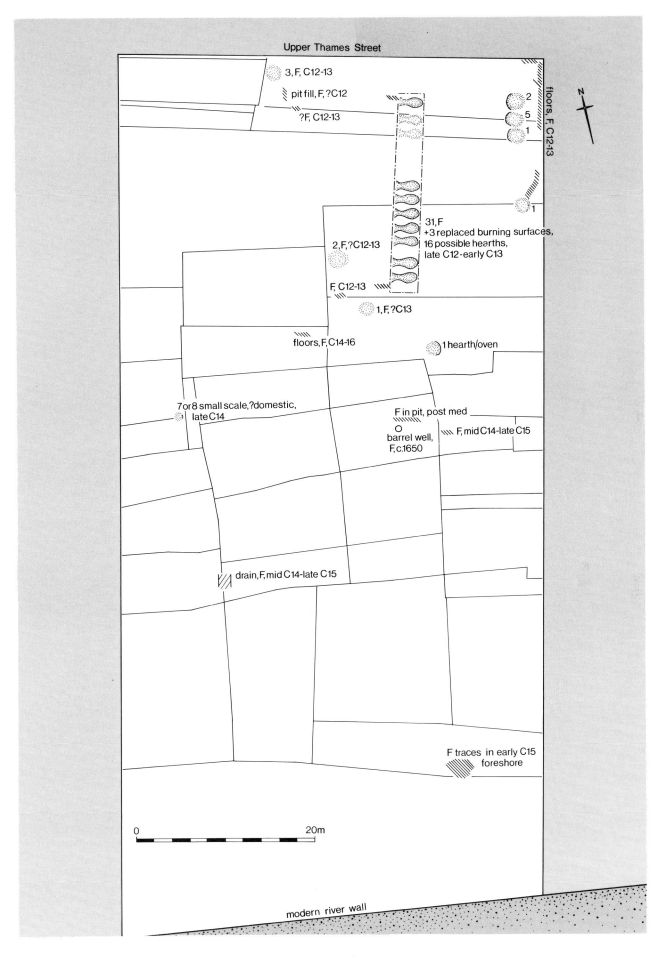

Upper Thames Street

3, F, C12-13

pit fill, F, ?C12

?F, C12-13

2
5
1

floors, F, C12-13

N

1

31, F
+3 replaced burning surfaces,
16 possible hearths,
late C12-early C13

2, F, ?C12-13

F, C12-13

1, F, ?C13

floors, F, C14-16

1 hearth/oven

7 or 8 small scale, ?domestic,
late C14

F in pit, post med
O
barrel well,
F, c.1650

F, mid C14-late C15

drain, F, mid C14-late C15

F traces in early C15
foreshore

0   20m

modern river wall

Fig 2.5 London: Swan Lane, late 12th/early 13th century industrial hearth (no 1) with fuller's earth (scale totals 0.5m). Photograph: T Hurst

large-scale industrial plant was apparently (as implied by the sequence of six) replaced very frequently over a period of at most a century. The reasons for this and for the diversity of form are unknown.

Fuller's earth is a natural clay with exceptional properties of absorbency, which led to its widespread use as a cleaning agent.[6] The excavated evidence for the industry represented on the site is limited to the hearths themselves and the associated cleanser. The scale of the plant makes it unlikely to have been a laundry at a time when women and servants would have cleaned the clothes for individual households, and so there would not have been a need for such an intensive commercial enterprise. The most probable function of fuller's earth in an industry of this scale is the eponymous one – to clean the natural lanolin out of newly woven cloths, and this is supported to some extent by the discovery of a large amount of grease in a sample submitted for analysis.[7] The connection between heating and fulling is not immediately clear;[8] it might speed up the basic process, but with the non-mechanical foot- (or, for hats, manual-) fulling that seems to have been the norm within the city of London (Carus-Wilson 1967, 186–8, 207), the most likely explanation is the simple, humanitarian one – that it made an otherwise very chilly occupation somewhat less unpleasant. Alternatively, or perhaps additionally, cloths might have been cleaned in large numbers in preparation for dyeing, so that the colour would take fast and evenly through the piece. No trace of dyes has been found by the limited analysis that has so far been carried out on samples, and there was certainly nothing like the very obvious highly coloured or botanically identifiable dyeing agents that have been

A

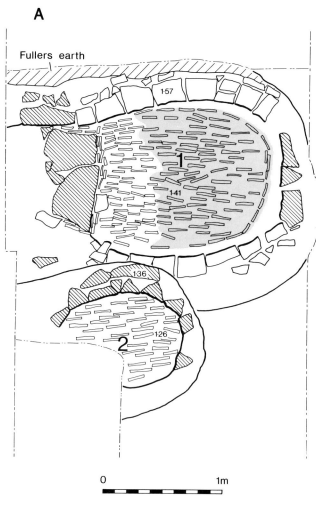

0   1m

B

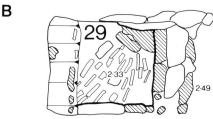

Fig 2.6 London: Swan Lane, industrial hearths: A) large keyhole-shaped hearth and smaller (?)subsidiary (nos 1 and 2); B) rectangular hearth with pitched tiles aligned diagonally (no 29)

uncovered in excavations in Bristol and in York (Jones & Watson 1987, 154; Hall & Tomlinson 1984, 21).

The large number of frequently replaced hearths invites comparison with those (not yet fully published) excavated at the Brooks site in Winchester, which were in the phases preceding the well-known 14th century channels that brought water into adjoining premises, including that of Richard Bosynton, who is known as a fuller from contemporary records, and who also carried out dyeing (Biddle 1967, 260–2, 264–7; 1968, 259–63, 266–7; 1969, 304–5, 310–12; 1970a, 298–302, 305–9; 1972, 102–3, 107–11; partly summarised in Biddle 1970b, 250–5; Keene 1985, 760–1, 765, nos 432, 435). The riverside location in London and Norwich (Ayers,

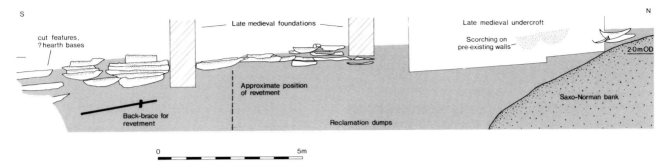

Fig 2.7 London: Swan Lane, section through industrial hearths excavated in 1981 trench

this volume), like the brookside location at Winchester, was appropriate for the cloth-finishing industries, which need large quantities of water. In London, some documentary evidence seems to suggest that those who called themselves 'dyers' concentrated their work premises on the block of riverside land south of Thames Street, while those who called themselves 'fullers' tended to work somewhat further inland, to the north of Thames Street.[9] Dyers' workshops might produce more obviously noxious or unpleasant-looking effluents, which could explain this possible difference in location at a general level, but both branches of the textile-finishing trades were active at or near the waterfront in the Swan Lane site area in the late medieval period, as other documentary research shows,[10] and (as in Winchester) both processes might have been carried out on one set of premises. The industry excavated at Swan Lane was clearly the first use made of the newly reclaimed land, since the hearth sequence immediately overlay the bulk reclamation dumps (Fig 2.7).

The watching brief covering the rest of the site revealed further, similar evidence: fuller's earth and hearths in several other areas (Fig 2.4). The indications are more patchy, but there seems to have been another north-south row of hearths, frequently replaced, to the east (perhaps in the next property) and, less clearly, the same kind of evidence to the west as well. It can reasonably be suggested that there were three adjacent properties, all apparently using the new land from the outset in the late 12th/early 13th centuries for textile finishing. The location would be convenient for the cloth market at Candlewick Street (modern Cannon Street), a couple of hundred yards to the north (Salzman 1923, 219 – the references given are from the 14th century). Hurry (1930, 75–6) cites a contemporary reference to the 'woad merchants of Candelwykstrete'.

The presence of a dyeing industry at Swan Lane in this early period is completely speculative, but (despite the lack of evidence of vat bases as found at Redcliffe in Bristol (Jones this volume) and elsewhere) this does fit better with the present notion of what large hearths might be used for in the textile industry (Biddle *op cit*; *cf* Keene 1985, 760–1, 765).[11] Early illustrations of dyeing include a French 15th century example in which

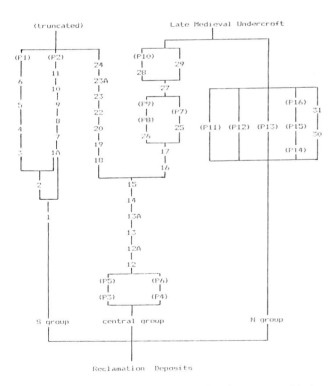

Fig 2.8 London: Swan Lane, matrix of sequence of industrial hearths: P possible hearth; A replaced burning surface (cf Fig 2.7)

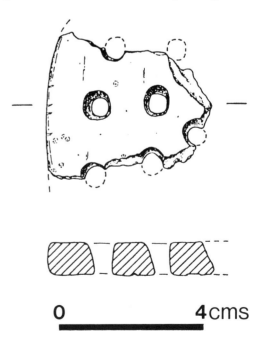

Fig 2.9 London: Swan Lane, fragment of pierced ceramic tile, 12th/13th century

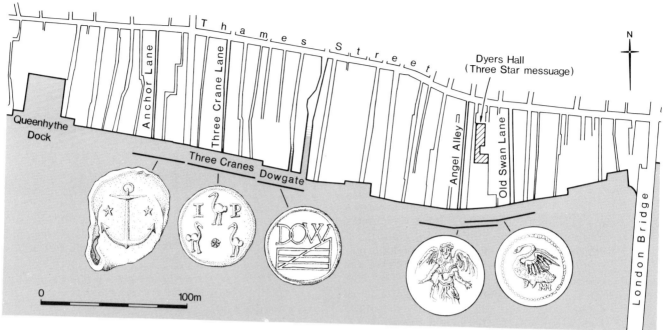

Fig 2.10 London: central waterfront area, with devices from 17th century leaden cloth seals excavated in the locations indicated (street plan and selected place-names are taken from 1676 Ogilby & Morgan map)

horizontal lines on a hearth that supports a metal vat in which a cloth is being coloured might represent tiles (*cf* hearth 1 in Fig 2.5); tiles are almost certainly shown in an Italian depiction of a dyer's furnace from 1540 (the former is reproduced by Robertson (1986, 99, fig 36); for the latter see Hübner (1913, 350–1, fig 3). There were virtually no finds at all from the industrial deposits at Swan Lane, but reused among the tiles from which the hearths were built were a handful of distinctive fragments, apparently from multiply pierced discs (Fig 2.9) that would originally have been about 0.15m (6 in) in diameter (Pritchard n d, section 14, page 15, and fig 7 nos 24–6). These are not known from any other site, though the fabric is one local to London. They could perhaps have been some kind of coarse filters for large-scale industrial drainage in another part of the complex. It cannot be demonstrated archaeologically, and it is certainly not going to be true of reclamation along the whole of the London waterfront, but it is possible to speculate that the great expansion in this particular area was specifically to cater for the developing textile trade.

Further south on the site were deposits of fuller's earth in 14th century contexts (including some in a pit), traces in a 15th century foreshore, and more in a mid 17th century barrel well (Fig 2.4). Also in the well were half a dozen of the objects which provide another major strand of evidence for riverside textile finishing in the later period – leaden seals which were attached to cloths. One or more of these seals was attached to each traded textile from the late 14th to the early 18th century as part of a complicated system of industrial regulation and quality control (like hall-marking on precious metals). The information stamped on the seals relates to the specifications, provenance, and the individuals who processed each cloth (Endrei & Egan 1982; Egan 1985). Thousands of these seals have been found along the river frontage on both banks of the Thames. Those from the well on the Swan Lane site indicate textiles woven in Essex (a Colchester seal for a

bay cloth) and Lancashire.[12] It is significant that this evidence for provincial cloths coming to London from definable parts of the country was found together with a hint of one of the finishing processes (see below, on seals from Trig Lane).

In the 16th and 17th centuries the hall of the Dyers' Guild was located in the north-east corner of the Swan Lane site (Fig 2.10). On the foreshore at the south of the site was a concentration of cloth seals, mainly dating from the late 16th to early 18th centuries. Among these (along with seals from textile-producing counties all over England) were a few with legends showing that they are early 17th century dyers' issues, including some which depict a swan. This is a specific reference to the location (Fig 2.10). An engraving from 1647 by Hollar shows 'the Old Swan' at this part of the waterfront, and a building to the west which has newly dyed cloths hanging from an upper storey, drying in the riverside breeze (Daynes 1965, pl 1), and presumably from time to time dropping the odd seal into the river below. Although no 17th century horizontal deposits survived for excavation on the redevelopment site, all this evidence – the seals and fuller's earth in the well, the seals on the foreshore, and the Hollar engraving – can be put together with Dyers' Hall to suggest that, in addition to its central administrative function in the regulation of the trade, there was a dyeing industry in this area in the later period. Samuel Scott's mid 18th century painting of London Bridge from the south-east (Somerset House 1977, no 25) shows another way that seals might have been lost during processing at the waterfront; in the river is a floating platform from which a freshly dyed red cloth is being rinsed in the water. There are earlier references in documents to similar installations ('put galleys') used by dyers (Jones 1955, 497–8).

At the Trig Lane site, some excavated late medieval oven-like bases could possibly be further evidence of dyers' plant. Alternative interpretations are possible, eg baking and brewing, since the latter is another industry which would benefit from proximity to a major source of water (Milne & Milne 1981, 36, fig 7). A 17th century brick drain on that site produced over a dozen cloth-seals, including some from Devon and Yorkshire, others indicating the reign of James I, and an unused blank.[13] Further seals from this group have the initials IW on one side, indicating an individual who was a dyer, because the other sides specify different colourants – one is inscribed 'cochineal', and another has W for 'woad' together with G perhaps for 'grain'.[14] These are presumably some of the tiny proportion of seals that must have been accidentally lost by Mr IW from provincial cloths being coloured at his dyehouse, and which, in this case, ended up in the drain leading to the river.

Other 17th century dyers' seals that have been found at different points along the waterfront appear, like the ones with the swan, to refer to specific localities (Fig 2.10). Some of the seals from the Swan Lane area have stamps with three stars that may be a reference to Dyers' Hall.[15] In all these areas, concentrations of various seals have been found, from some twenty counties in all. The dyers' issues are the key that these concentrations are evidence for local *industry*, rather than just a manifestation of the river's role as the principal dustbin of the city.[16] Provincial cloths passed into the capital at the rate of over 100,000 in some years in the 16th and 17th centuries (Fisher 1950, 153). This trade was worth over £1 million annually during part of this period (Ramsay 1982, 39, 53). The cloths passed on to the market to be used in London or to be traded across the country and to most parts of the known world. Only a small portion would have been dyed in London.

0   1cm

Fig 2.11 Stamp from 18th century cloth seal of the South Seas and Fisheries Company excavated in Texas; similar to examples found in London (Gilmore 1973)

A few of the seals found at London's waterfront can be identified as having come from cloths being dyed on the riverside for various trading companies. Their stamps provide indications of the intended final destinations of the textiles from which they became detached. From the Swan Lane area are seals of the Royal Africa Company (trading to West Africa in the late 17th century) and the South Seas and Fisheries Company (trading to southern America – see Fig 2.11),[17] and there are a large number of East India Company seals found in several areas (Egan 1990). The latter came mainly from the south bank of the Thames; in the 18th century the dyehouses became concentrated

there, while the city side was used for warehousing rather than industrial processing. London dyers' seals have been found in an early 17th century wreck off the coast of Norway (Molaug 1980, 173–95) and elsewhere in continental Europe,[18] and one was recovered from the wreck of the Dutch ship *Batavia*, which was driven on to the cliffs of Western Australia in 1629.[19]

It is a long way from 12th century reclamation in London to transatlantic trade and Australia, but this paper has tried to draw together some archaeological evidence to suggest that the important textile industries played a continuing key role on London's waterfront – in the Swan Lane area for upwards of half a millennium – and that the prime reason for the presence there of these activities was the basic resource, the water of the river Thames.

Acknowledgements

I am most grateful to the following for their help connected with the preparation of this paper: Ron Harris, Trevor Brigham, Dick Malt, Jez Reeve, Mark Taylor, and the rest of the Swan Lane excavation team; to the members of the Society of Thames Mudlarks and Antiquarians for retrieving many of the site finds for the Museum of London and reporting seals found elsewhere; to Julie Carr and Wendy Northcott for drawing the figures, and to John Maloney for finding the money to make this possible; to Alan Vince for information on ceramic dating; to Brian Spencer for support on several fronts; to Joan Barker for typing the script and thus bringing it to a state of legibility; to Philomena and Reg Jackson for their kind hospitality during the conference.

Notes

1 The figure is that for the Museum of London (information Barry Mason the Museum's house manager).

2 More recent excavation at the adjoining Sunlight Wharf site (Fig 2.1), supervised by Dick Bluer, has now added further perspective to the results from Trig Lane.

3 The stimulus for land reclamation at the Swan Lane site, as argued in this present paper, corresponds with Milne's reason A [to win land]. This is unlikely to have been the sole motive.

4 In a few instances revetment timbers were apparently retrieved for reuse after their primary function at the waterfront had ceased. Once superseded, buried revetments could provide a firm support for the foundations of later medieval buildings among the unstable organic refuse deposits which constituted most of the material making up the new land; eg the revetment recorded in sections 50 and 51 at Swan Lane (*cf* Milne & Milne 1982, 18 fig 8b and pls 14, 18; Milne & Milne 1981, 33–4, fig 4). This does not appear to have been a standard practice, but the opportunity was sometimes exploited.

5 Structure comprising timbers 1800A–L. After the angled front braces (almost flying buttresses) of some earlier revetments, a kind of perpendicular style comes to the quayside – here almost a cosmetic afterthought. Links between dry-land architecture and revetment types are considered elsewhere in this volume, and are far more complex than it is possible to bring out in this paper. The analogy with architecture in stone is ultimately unconvincing, since detailed consideration reveals some important chronological discrepancies between the two traditions.

6 The *ménagier* of Paris recommended it at the end of the 14th century for removing stains from cloth (Power 1928, 214). See also Robertson (1986) for a recent historical survey of this material and its uses.

7 The initial suggestion that the excavated waxy material (originally thought actually to be a kind of wax) was fuller's earth was made on the site by Dick Malt, who also arranged for its analysis by Dr Paul Henderson (Mineralogy Dept, Natural History Museum). Dr Henderson writes: 'X-ray diffraction shows the sample to be montmorillonite with a small admixture of quartz. The chemical analyses show the marked similarity of the two samples [ie that from Swan Lane, and one from a commercially exploited source of fuller's earth, Beechcroft Pit at Nutfield in Surrey]. The suggestion is that [the former] could have come from deposits in Surrey, but the limited data precludes a more definitive statement' (letter to the present writer 1 June 1981). Details of the analytical results have been published (Robertson 1986, 97–8, table 2). Fuller's earth was also used in the past to clarify beer (Robertson 1986, 350). Commercial brewing might provide an alternative explanation for hearths and associated fuller's earth, but the scale of the plant seems excessive at such an early stage in the development of the alehouse (cf Clark 1983, 21–4, 29–31), and no reference to this use for fuller's earth at such an early date has been traced. For fuller's earth in a late 13th/early 14th century deposit, apparently in a domestic context, see Ketteringham (1976, 9). Pits excavated in Southwark have been tentatively interpreted as fulling plant (Dean 1980, 371), but the evidence is unconvincing.

8 Heating for fulling is recorded in Italy in the 15th century (Patterson 1979, 215). Mechanical mill-fulling appears to have been confined in the London region during the medieval period to peripheral areas such as Stratford.

9 Information J Schofield, based on survey of evidence from late medieval tradesmen's wills proved in the London Commissionary Court between 1374 and 1488. Outside London, those who referred to themselves as dyers tended to be the capitalist entrepreneurs of the textile industries (Carus-Wilson 1967, 222–38); Carus-Wilson indicates a measure of independence for the weavers of coarse woollen burels in London, but evidence relating to fine dyed cloths there is lacking (cf Keene 1985, 303–6 for similar evidence from Winchester). A 16th century reference, also from Winchester, to 'fuller's woad' (*fullys wodd*) is indicative of continuing combinations of the finishing processes (Keene 1985, 306). If the evidence of the relative wealth of the dyers is applicable at London in the early period, it might have been their capital which actually financed land reclamation in the textile-finishing area.

10 In the 14th century, among other trades and tradesmen recorded at the waterfront within the area of the 1981–2 redevelopment site, was a dyer (*tinctuarius*), who held a tenement with shops, a wharf, and other appurtenances from 1331; a tenement probably for dyeing (*de teynture*) along with a wharf and houses on Thames Street was held by a draper from 1373 (information V A Harding, based on her unpublished PhD thesis *The port of London in the fourteenth century*, University of St Andrews 1983, 461–3).

11 Derek Keene is not convinced that the multiple 12th century hearths were connected with textile processing (pers comm). For further excavated evidence elsewhere, see Carter & Roberts (1973, 461–2, 464–7), furnaces and drain from 14th to 15th century; Williams (1981, 14–22), hearths and vat bases from late 13th century to late 14th century; Youngs *et al* (1983, 185–6) site 65, and (1985, 188) site 106 – 12th/13th century buildings at Beverley with several hearths, drains, a wooden vat, and floral evidence for dyeing; Coppack (1986, 56–62), evidence from the Cistercian Abbey: water channels and ashlar tubs for a fulling mill, mid 13th

to early 14th century, and stone tanks, water pipes, and furnaces which 'may relate to the working of cloth and perhaps dyeing', early 14th to early 15th century).

12 Museum of London, Department of Urban Archaeology (DUA), SWA 81 layer 1272, finds nos 1296, 1293, and 1295. Another seal in the well is dated 1650.

13 Museum of London (DUA) TL 74 layer 78, finds nos 3066, 3036 and 3086; 3037 and 3070; 3082. It was necessary to rely on the oral tradition to establish the exact circumstances of discovery of the Trig Lane seals (the site archive includes three separate deposits, each designated layer number 78 on a different document – none of them appears to be a drain fill). I am most grateful to Jon Cotton, Cath Maloney and Chrissie Milne (all of whom worked on the site at the time of recovery) for their independent but unanimous recollection that this group of seals came from the fill of a brick drain running north-south.

14 TL 74 layer 78, nos 3069 and 3074; nos 3080, 3081, 3085, and 3096 also have the initials IW, but the other stamps are difficult to read in each case. WG could indicate blue and red dyes combined in one cloth to give some kind of purple. Alternatively woad might have been a base to which other colours were added - another dyer's seal found in London reads 'woaded for green'. For the use of woad in combination with other dyes, see Hurry (1930, 47–8), and cf Egan (1985, 4, fig 19).

15 From the middle of the 16th century the guild's hall occupied part of a plot known as a 'Three Star Messuage', which extended from Thames Street to the river frontage (Fig 2.10) (Daynes 1965, 16; cf Guildhall Library (Manuscripts Section) MS 15.463). Another dyers' hall was located in c 1470 in Anchor Lane near Three Cranes (British Library, MS Harley 541, reference provided by J Schofield).

16 Blank, unused seals have been found in most of the areas where there are concentrations of stamped examples. The former, together with two of the stone moulds in which they were cast (Museum of London acc nos 81.234 and 83.61) are further evidence for industrial processing and regulation in the waterfront area. A shearman's hook (Egan 1979, 190–2) found in the Three Cranes area may derive from the local shearing of cloth. A 17th century dyer's seal with a sun stamp has been found near the Sunlight Wharf site (cf Fig 2.10).

  Similar evidence might be sought in other urban waterfront areas. Cloth seals (now in the Bristol City Museum) were recovered from the Floating Harbour in Bristol in the last century, and a number have recently been found in the river Avon at Salisbury (Salisbury & South Wiltshire Museum collection). Despite the large number of seals recovered in Amsterdam, apparently no significant groups have been found in Verwers Gracht, the eponymous dyers' area (information J Baart and W Krook).

17 An Africa Company seal is in the Museum of London (acc no 85.803). Two South Seas Company seals similar to those found at the London waterfront have been excavated in Texas (Gilmore 1973, 60 and fig 26 b and e), and a slightly different one found in a wreck off Tierra del Fuego has been reported by the Archivo Nacional de Buenos Aires in Argentina.

18 A seal probably found in Bruges is in the archaeological collections in the City Museum there, no 0.2911 XXIII.

19 The intended destination was Java. This seal (Western Australia Maritime Museum, Fremantle, BAT no 7056) is probably the earliest identifiable London-made object recovered in Australasia.

3 Industry and environment in medieval Bristol
R H Jones

Abstract

Extensive redevelopment in the Redcliffe area has allowed for excavation of various waterfront features within an important medieval settlement. Complex reclamation works in the harbour area have been revealed, the nature of waterfront development being largely dictated by the very high tidal range of the river Severn and the difficulty of navigation. At Dundas Wharf, 12th century quay walls were extended in the 13th and 14th centuries. Elsewhere, more extensive reclamation was needed, culminating in the construction of a substantial 14th century river wall. The docks faced problems of silting and pollution from household, farmyard, and industrial refuse — archaeobotanical evidence is supported by a series of city ordinances relating to hygiene and refuse disposal.

Shipbuilding was a major medieval and post-medieval industry and evidence for tanning, fulling, horn- and clothworking, and soapmaking is recorded. Remains of dye-vats have been recovered and evidence suggests that industrial and domestic buildings were interspersed.

Introduction

Waterfront archaeology has been a major part of Bristol City Museum's excavation and research programme for the last ten years (Fig 3.1). This paper will look at the environmental conditions which prevailed in Bristol, as revealed by recent waterfront work, and which were the major influences upon the way the harbour was developed. Recent work also sheds light on the immediate, usually man-created, environment of the harbour area, particularly its industrial nature.

The results of the waterfront excavations undertaken before 1983 have been summarised or published elsewhere (Ponsford 1981; 1985; Good 1987; Williams 1981; 1982). Extensive redevelopment of the important medieval settlement of Redcliffe, lying south of the river Avon and originally a rival to the growing town of Bristol on the north side, has meant that much of the work has been concentrated in this once-thriving trading and manufacturing area.

The excavation at Canynges House (6 on Fig 3.1), a site so called since it is traditionally thought to be on the site of the house of the great 15th century merchant William Canynges, one of the richest men in Bristol at that time, represents the most recent waterfront project in the Redcliffe area. The site was first occupied in the 12th century, but large-scale expansion in the 13th and 14th centuries meant the construction of major harbour facilities, until by the 15th century there was clearly a major dwelling on the site, quite probably Canynges' home (Jones 1986).

The topography of the harbour

All the waterfront excavations have revealed complex reclamation works, the common denominator of which was primarily the creation of suitable deep-water berths. Successive encroachments upon the river course, however, markedly accelerated the rate of sedimentation, by as much as 8–12 times according to one recent estimate, thereby creating greater impetus for further expansion (Jones & Watson 1987, 141).

In the Severn estuary the tidal range is 13m, reducing to 10.3m at Cumberland Basin, about 2km downstream from the city centre sites under consideration. The modern Mean High Water Spring Tide (MHWS) in the city centre has been estimated at 6.95m above OD. The medieval MHWS has been estimated at Dundas Wharf (5 on Fig 3.1) by measuring the level to which fluvial clays have accreted as 6.4m above OD (Jones & Watson 1987, 139). A similar exercise at Canynges House suggested a level of 6.6–6.7m above OD. It would appear, therefore, that the medieval MHWS level may have been within 0.5m of its modern value. The modern Mean High Water Neap Tide (MHWN) is at 3.65m above OD. It is suggested here that a similar difference occurs between the modern and the medieval MHWNs, placing the medieval MHWN at around 3.2m above OD. At the lowest level of water, 3m below OD, all river traffic ceased until the onset of the next high tide.

The tidal range of the river dictated the nature of waterfront development. The dual factors of the extreme tidal range and accentuated silting were to cause problems throughout the history of the port until the creation of the Floating Harbour in the early 19th century. Thus Bristol was made an exception to an Act of 1559 which ordered that no vessel was to load or unload during the hours of darkness since 'the port of Bristowe is so dangerous and low of water, except it be at spring tides, that great ships laden cannot come nearer than 4 miles, because the water ebbs and flows suddenly for loading and unloading...' (Vanes 1977, 5).

At Dundas Wharf the quay walls were built to utilise the large tidal range to maximum effect. Around the mid 12th century, two walls were constructed well down the slope of the bank (Fig 3.2). The upper wall (W80) had been truncated and its height is difficult to determine, but it would appear to have been above an

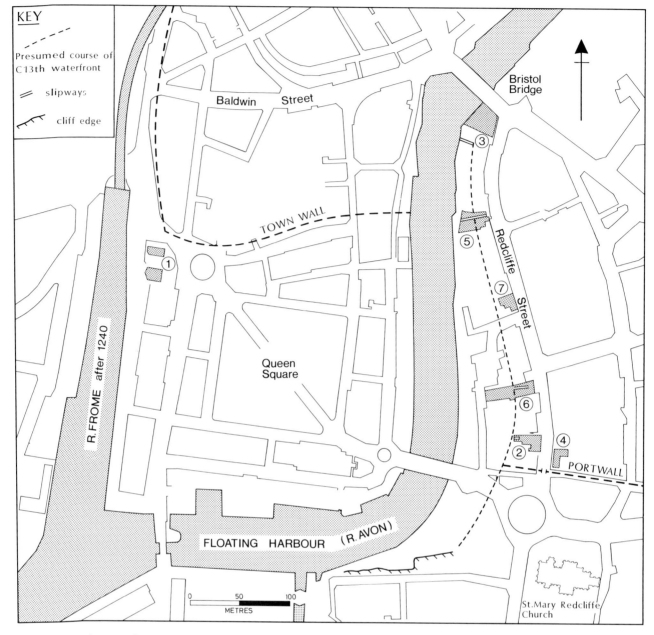

Fig 3.1 Bristol: waterfront excavations, 1978–1986

effective level at the medieval MHWN. It could, however, have functioned at tides above this level, possibly as high as the medieval MHWS. Contemporary with it was a wall further down the slope of the bank (W89). It was also reduced in height but probably existed at least to the height of the medieval MHWN and formed a corresponding low-water wall. The timbers between may have functioned as the base of a connecting stair between the two walls.

In the 13th century the waterfront was extended forward with the construction of a wall (W37), well above the level of the medieval MHWN, and a corresponding low-water wall (W14a) was built, probably again to take full advantage of the neap tides. From the 14th century, the property was subdivided. By this period the frontage had probably been extended far enough into the river channel to render the construction of two contemporary river walls unnecessary.

The evidence from the Canynges House excavation suggested a somewhat different development sequence although still with the same objective in mind (Fig 3.3). The relatively shallow slope of the bank here meant that the construction of two walls, one for utilising the spring tides and one for the neaps, would have needed extensive reclamation. In the 13th century, for example, it would have required about 10m of further reclamation from the main river wall to construct a major low-water wall. Indeed, the relatively large area reclaimed over about 250 years, 60–70m compared to about 30m in the same period at Dundas Wharf, is another indication of the shallow slope of the river bank at this point.

A simple wattle revetment constructed in the 12th century represents the first attempt at stabilising the river-bank. It would have formed a rudimentary landing place, although the adjacent foreshore would

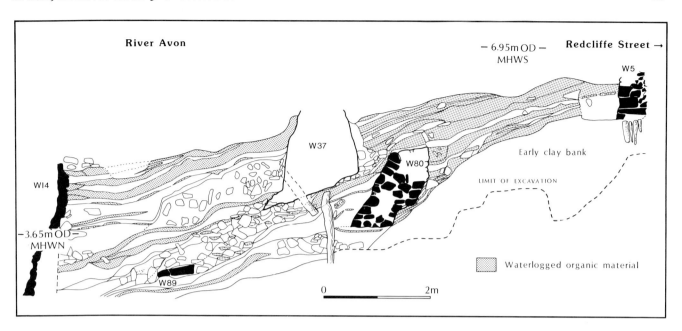

Fig 3.2 Bristol: Dundas Wharf, south-facing section through medieval waterfront deposits and associated quay walls (after Jones & Watson 1987)

have been dry at the conjectured MHWN. It was in the 13th century, however, that major riverside reclamation took place. The 13th century river wall stood only to about 6m above OD, but had almost certainly been partly demolished for later structures above. It was presumably as high as a contemporary roughly paved surface found on its landward side, at 6.5–7m above OD. The effective base of this wall was at 5.3m above OD, above MHWN level, but providing a sufficient draught at the higher tide levels. Contemporary with this river wall was a stone-lined slipway (Fig 3.4). It connected with a stone-paved jetty along the front of the river wall. The jetty could not be excavated in its entirety, but it was found as low as 3.8m above OD. It is likely that the slipway and jetty provided access to the river for loading and unloading at all high tides and possibly at low water as well. Many of the slipways may also have served as ferry terminals, as in the much later example, near Cumberland Basin, of Rownham Ferry, which replaced a medieval ferry further downstream (Elkin this volume, fig 4.2).

The 14th century extension of the river frontage (Fig 3.3) entailed the construction of a substantial river wall, surviving to about 6.2m above OD but certainly higher originally, probably at least as high as 6.7m above OD since traces of contemporary timber structures were found from that level on its landward side. The successive docks which were dug initially beside it and later forward of it would have been usable at all high tides and represent the first recognisable attempt at docking bow or stern first.

The harbour works can be seen primarily as an attempt at harnessing to economic effect the large tidal range. While river traffic certainly ceased at low water, it is nevertheless likely that some provision was made for cargo handling. It remains an aspiration to excavate in its entirety one or more of the slipways which formed such a common feature of the Bristol waterfront.

The environment of the harbour

The natural sluicing action of the river was probably sufficient to clear much of the waste which the inhabitants of Bristol deposited into the river. Increasing indentation of the river bank, however, meant that much was trapped within docks or against protruding harbour works. Analysis of diatoms from the Dundas Wharf excavation suggested a significant rise in nutrient input into the Avon from the period of the first quays (Jones & Watson 1987, 146). Drains and garderobes frequently issued directly into the river (Fig 3.5) and, with the casual dumping of household and industrial refuse, contributed to the rise in effluent levels and the associated insanitary conditions. Available hollows, such as infilled slipways and docks, were used as an easy means of disposing of frequently unpleasant debris. Concentrations of fly pupae, as have been found in the organic layers filling a dock by Bristol Bridge, or in a similar dump within the 13th century slipway at Canynges House, suggest a rotting mass of organic matter close to the contemporary quay and houses.

Detailed studies of plant macrofossils from the Dundas Wharf excavation (Jones & Watson 1987, 146–55) have indicated a rich assemblage of plant remains. These include both plants imported from areas outside the walled city in dung and straw, and as foodstuffs, and plants which were indicative of the native environment of the river frontage. Species of disturbed ground or waste, untended areas were found throughout the stratigraphy. Stinking mayweed, for example, while associated with arable land, may originally have been widespread in the high nutrient environment of medieval towns. Stinging nettle, chickweed, black nightshade, and others all thrive in the nitrogen-rich conditions which exist near dung heaps and in the farmyard-type conditions which probably existed not only by the waterfront but in the town as a whole.

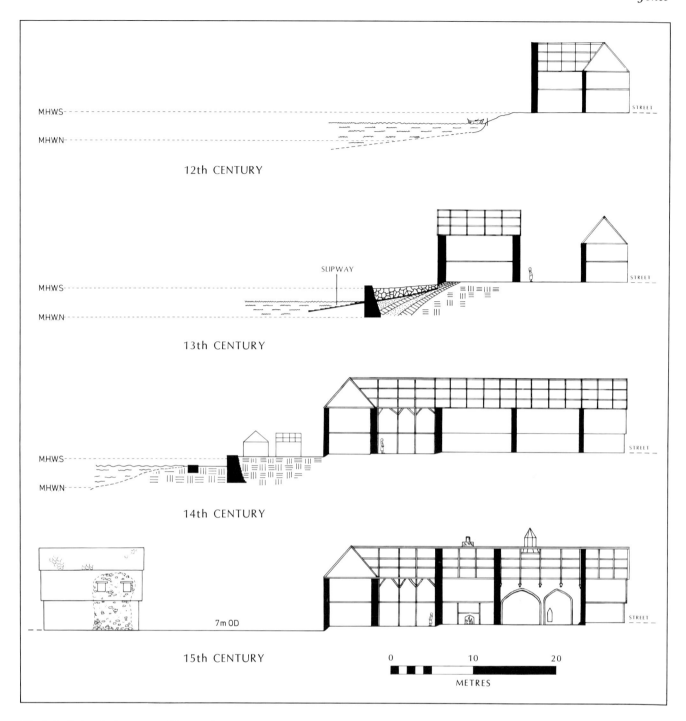

MHWS
MHWN

12th CENTURY

SLIPWAY

MHWS
M.HW.N

13th CENTURY

M.HWS
MHWN

14th CENTURY

7m OD

15th CENTURY

0   10   20

METRES

Fig 3.3 Bristol: Canynges House, development of the river bank in relation to medieval river levels, 12th to 15th century

Within close proximity of the main harbours were areas of almost rural quality. The area now occupied by Queen Square, for example, was known as the Marsh until it was built up from the 17th century. It would have provided good pasture during the summer months. Canon's Marsh on the west side of the Frome was used for the cultivation of hay by the monks of St Augustine's Abbey in the 15th century (Beachcroft & Sabin 1938, 28).

Successive ordinances by the City Council indicate the problems caused by rubbish disposal and the inhabitants' apparent disregard for hygiene. It was forbidden to cast dung or rubble at the Quay or the Back,

except at assigned places (Veale 1933, 142). Walking through the streets was a hazardous occupation since it was necessary to issue an ordinance preventing people throwing urine or 'stynking water' out of the windows or doors (Veale 1933, 142). Livestock such as pigs, dogs, and ducks could be found wandering loose and regulations were required to curb this (Veale 1933, 144; Bickley 1900, 32). The repetition of such regulations which occur throughout the documentary record shows that they had little effect on the ways of the inhabitants who continued to follow human nature by disposing of rubbish in the most convenient way possible. In 1646 a Corporate minute says that the main thoroughfares

Fig 3.4   Bristol: Canynges House, 13th century river wall and slipway, from the west

were 'full of dirt, soil and filth and very dangerous in this time of infection' (Latimer 1900, 212). The banks of the two rivers, especially the Frome, were particularly bad at low water because of the outflow of sewers and the casting of rubbish. In 1621 it was ordained that no soapmaker was to cast soap ashes into the river (Nicholls & Taylor 1881, 282). In 1700 an Act of Parliament was required which empowered the Corporation to impose fines on glassmakers, copper smelters, and others for throwing refuse into the two rivers which were apparently the receptacles of most of the ashes and filth of the city (Jenkins 1942, 165). The situation was clearly worsening in the late medieval and post-medieval periods. The city was still largely confined within its medieval walls until the 18th century, and the rise in population and associated overcrowding must have aggravated the situation.

Such insanitary conditions were no doubt contributory to outbreaks of the plague throughout the medieval period, while flooding appears to have presented a problem in the immediate riverside areas. Occupation levels during the medieval period in the area immediately adjacent to the river have been found at about 7–7.5m above OD, above the level of most tides, but reports of flooding during the medieval and post-medieval periods are reasonably common, especially the great flood of 1607 when Redcliffe, St Thomas, and Temple were inundated to several feet (Latimer 1900, 32).

Riverside trades

Shipbuilding was a major industry in medieval and post-medieval Bristol, located mainly outside the historic town centre in the Marsh and later in Canon's Marsh (Sherborne 1965, 17). Two post-medieval docks have been excavated at Narrow Quay, outside the town wall (1 on Fig 3.1; Good 1987). An ordinance of 1475/6 forbade anyone to break ground anywhere in the town to make a ship or ships without licence from the mayor (Veale 1950, 113–4). The stone-built dock at Bristol Bridge and the successive 14th century docks excavated at Canynges House may have been used in shipbuilding, although there was no evidence for this. They were probably used simply for the repair and maintenance of vessels while lying in dock.

Fig 3.5 Bristol: rear of houses on St James' Back, showing overhanging privies. City of Bristol Museums and Art Gallery, Braikenridge Collection M 2912/5

Fig 3.6   Bristol: Redcliffe Street excavation, 1980, remains of dye-vat base

The noxious nature of some of the industries sited by the river contributed to the sometimes unpleasant conditions of the harbour area. The river was an obvious attraction for several groups of craftsmen as a convenient means of waste disposal as well as being the

point at which their raw materials and finished products could be loaded and unloaded. Dyers, tanners, fullers, hornworkers, clothworkers, and soapmakers are all known to have been located near the river in the Middle Ages. Weavers, dyers, and fullers in particular were concentrated south of the river Avon in Redcliffe and Temple (Lobel & Carus-Wilson 1975, 10). Traces of the tenter racks where the cloth would have been stretched out to prevent shrinkage have been found in the Temple area, and by the 14th century Bristol was pre-eminent as the leading exporter of finished wool cloth. The range of imports into Bristol during this period also shows the importance of cloth finishing in Bristol's economy. Woad, from Picardy and later from Toulouse, was the second most important commodity reaching Bristol after wine. Custom accounts also show madder from the Low Countries and alum from around the Mediterranean coming to Bristol throughout the medieval period.

The activities of dyers in Redcliffe Street have been clearly indicated by recent archaeological findings. Studies of plant macrofossils at Dundas Wharf have demonstrated the presence of the dyestuffs madder, dyer's greenweed, weld, and possibly woad (Jones & Watson 1987, 154). The presence of madder was first recognised by its distinctive purplish red colour. It has also been recognised at the Bristol Bridge excavation (3 on Fig 3.1), and more recently at the Canynges House site where it was found in the infill of the 14th century dock. A detailed examination of wool fibres was carried

Fig 3.7 Bristol: Dundas Wharf, remains of wooden barrels

out and showed a variety of colours from red and blue to black.

Excavations in 1980 at the southern end of Redcliffe Street (2 on Fig 3.1) revealed what may be the remains of dyeworking premises (Williams 1981, 17–22). Three possible dye-vat bases were found here (Fig 3.6). It is not certain whether they were connected — there may have been a pair of dyeing workshops — but they were contemporary, dating to the 14th century. Clean water would have been easily obtainable from a supply by St Mary Redcliffe church. Drainage was certainly efficient. A pit which may have contained a water tank for the washing of cloths was connected to a pair of drain chutes which fed into a substantial main drain leading directly to the river Avon.

At the front of one of the buildings were two parallel gullies with post-holes at each end and very tentatively identified as the bases of a horizontal loom. It is possible, therefore, that several clothworking processes were being carried on within the same premises.

Further north, at the Canynges House excavation, a 13th century keyhole-shaped oven may be the remains of another dye-vat base. A circular stone feature adjacent to it and contemporary with it may perhaps be the base of a water trough. Both these features were likewise beside another substantial stone-lined drain with which they were probably linked. Six 14th century circular ovens were also found, most of them linked to the main drain by connecting drainage channels. Although they certainly had an industrial function, it is debatable whether they were used in the dyeing process.

Tanning was another industry known to have been carried on in the riverside area. Like the dyers, tanners needed not only a ready water supply, but also the convenience of the river for rubbish disposal. Two barrels found at the Dundas Wharf site may have been used in this process (Fig 3.7). Both contained lime residues at their base and could have been used in the initial immersion process. At a small site to the south of the Canynges House excavation, there may have been two further barrels, represented there merely by circular slots which may have housed the barrel bases.

All these trades appear to have been fairly randomly distributed in the riverside areas, although the street name Tucker (= Fuller) Street indicates a concentration of fullers to the east of Bristol Bridge. Also notable is the juxtaposition of these trades with the private residences of wealthy merchants. It was not until the beginning of the post-medieval period that the southern suburbs of Redcliffe and Temple declined in status and became predominantly industrial areas, with the cloth industry still represented and the glass industry coming into prominence from the end of the 17th century.

Acknowledgements

I would like to thank my colleagues in the Field Archaeology Section, City of Bristol Museums and Art Gallery, particularly the directors of the various excavations, Les Good and Bruce Williams. Julie Jones advised on the environmental aspects of the paper and commented on the initial draft.

4 Aspects of the recent development of the port of Bristol

P W Elkin

Abstract

This paper discusses the importance of Bristol's old harbour in relation to its location on the river Avon and the peculiar difficulties presented by its topography. Bristol is unique amongst Britain's ports in the severity of its tidal conditions and the hazards presented by them. Methods of navigating the channel and the perils involved are described. Although Bristol prospered in the medieval period, mercantile trade declined during the 18th and 19th centuries when larger vessels preferred the longer route to London or Liverpool rather than face the dangers of the Avon. Attempts to revitalise the docks during this period are discussed from historical sources. Current efforts to preserve and record sites in the dock area are described.

Bristol has always been a port; the Avon Gorge provides shelter from prevailing south-west winds in the Severn estuary and, once mastered, the high tides of the river Avon could be used to advantage to bring vessels some seven miles inland to a defensible anchorage. Although archaeological evidence (Boon 1949, 187) suggests that the pill (tidal creek) near the modern village of Sea Mills, was chosen during the Roman occupation as a convenient dock and ferry point to south Wales, there were strategic advantages in bringing sea-going vessels several miles further upstream to the landward side of the gorge to where the tidal river Avon could be conveniently crossed and was more accessible by land to the south of the region in what is now south Avon and north Somerset. This encouraged the development during Saxon times of the main trading settlement of the region, Brycg-Stow (Bridge Place).

The enterprise of its citizens in exploiting its geographical advantages as a centre for trade has been remarked upon over the centuries. Ireland remained a 'prop of Bristol's prosperity', nurturing the skills of both its sea-faring and merchant communities in the early Middle Ages and preparing the city for its increasingly important role in later years as the major trading link between England and its developing colonies across the Atlantic, away from the traditional overseas markets of the Baltic, Flanders, and Mediterranean lands. By the mid 14th century, the town's principal export trade was in English manufactured woollen cloth and, since this particular commodity escaped the punitive tariffs applied to raw wool handled primarily by rival English ports, Bristol prospered whilst Southampton, Boston, or Lynn, for example, had a difficult time. By 1500, Bristol was established as the second seaport of England, after London (Ross 1955, 179–82).

The modern port utilises man-made, deep-water docks at the point where the river Avon joins the Severn estuary (Fig 4.1). The first of these, at Avonmouth, was completed in 1877, followed two years later by Portishead Dock, two miles to the south. Both came into municipal ownership in 1884. The Bristol Corporation carried out a major extension of the Avonmouth system in the first decade of the 20th century, which resulted in the eclipse of the Portishead Dock in commercial terms. The latest dock development, a 70 acre container terminal, Royal Portbury, is located between Avonmouth and Portishead and can accommodate six vessels of 70,000 deadweight tons, the largest ships now in general use for international trade.

Bristol continues, therefore, as a major port even though the old inland harbour has ceased commercial sea-going activity, with the exception of sand-dredging and small-scale shipbuilding. The modern docks are less than a mile from the M5 motorway, which has encouraged the associated industrial area, now known as Severnside, to develop as a major road transport distribution point for a huge hinterland in the south and west of England, continuing a pattern established by railway transport in the previous century. However, to appreciate fully the historic significance of Bristol, it is necessary to study the location and working of the old port some seven miles to the east of the modern docks.

Apart from its inland position, there are other puzzling aspects about Bristol's old harbour, particularly in relation to its significance in terms of trade by the late Middle Ages. Viewed from the famous vantage point of the Downs on the north side of the Avon Gorge, the river Avon appears to be little more than a dismal, muddy stream rather than a major navigable waterway; the river ebbs and flows with frightening speed and ferocity through a massive tidal range (Fig 4.2), and is quite obviously too narrow for any sail-powered vessel to navigate without assistance. Harland (1984, 199–202) describes the surprising variety of techniques that could be employed to work a vessel, even in meandering tideways, both with and against the tide. Study of these techniques reveals, however, that to be successfully applied a vessel would inevitably be required to travel considerable distances broadside with the tide and be free to turn to and fro across the navigable channel, utilising its sails to power it both forwards and backwards at appropriate moments, in order to negotiate bends. Whilst some elements of these manoeuvres might be applied to navigating the lower

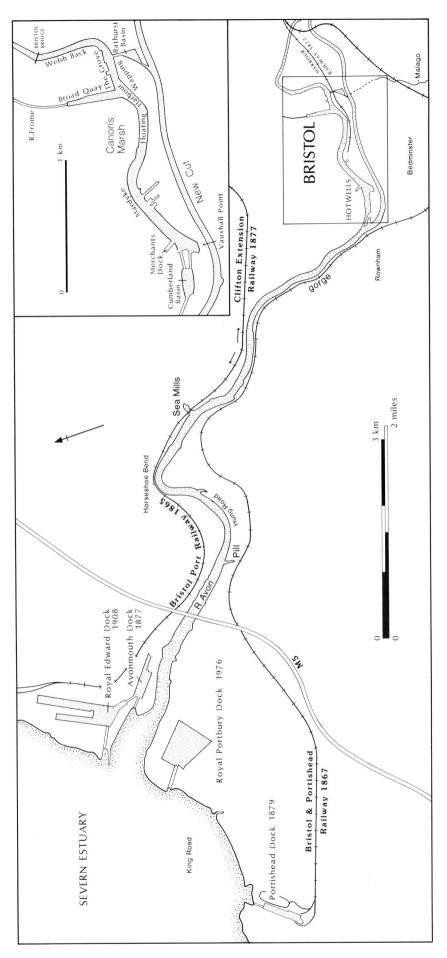

Fig 4.1 Bristol: plan of the Port of Bristol docks and river Avon

Fig 4.2 Bristol: the ferry at Rownham Mead, one of at least twelve in Bristol which crossed the river and the Floating Harbour. This photograph of 1900 emphasises the ferocity of tidal conditions in the region and the height and steepness of the river banks

reaches of the Bristol Avon, its tide and narrowness rendered it far too dangerous a waterway for any large vessel even to attempt to reach further upstream; any sizeable vessel travelling broadside in the river Avon was almost inevitably moments away from disaster.

The range of spring tides in the Thames at London is around 5.3m (Greeves 1980, 3) and here, as in any historic seaport, mariners have had to understand and utilise local sea and weather conditions and the ebb and flow of tides. Bristol is unique, however, amongst Britain's historic ports for the severity of the tidal conditions and the hazards which they presented to the stranger or the unwary. The tidal range of the Severn and its tributaries like the Avon and Frome which flow through Bristol, are indeed the largest of any major navigable waterways in the world — some 13m off Avonmouth and still a notable 7m in the centre of Bristol at the medieval quays at Broad Quay, the Grove, Welsh Back, and Redcliffe Back (Williams 1962, 143).

It is the narrowness of the river Avon, however, which combines with this large tidal range to create the danger. At high tide, there is an illusion of a wide expanse of safely navigable water; local artists have tended since the 18th century, perhaps in the interests of good public relations for the port, to depict the old harbour in this way whenever possible (Fig 4.3). However, the river is barely 120m wide and unexpectedly deep because of the huge volume of water flowing in the Severn estuary; every tide, therefore, scours the river-bed into a deep trench with underwater banks that slope steeply to the very edges.

Observing a modern motor vessel navigating the Avon with comparative ease can obscure the fact that, before the advent of steam-power, no vessel of any significance could normally sail unaided along this narrow, winding river between the old port and the anchorage called Hungroad, barely two miles upstream from the river mouth (Fig 4.1). Every ship had to wait for the tide and rely on hobblers in rowing boats to tow the vessel round bends in the river and to counter cross-winds and currents that would, in moments, drive it off course from the narrow navigable channel and aground on one of the steeply sloping banks. Even the judicious use of topsails to help power a larger vessel along straighter reaches of the river, as often depicted by local artists, was fraught with difficulties further upstream, where the tide and the towing power of the hobblers were the only satisfactory means of reaching the quays (Fig 4.3). Smaller vessels might use animal power working from towpaths through the Avon Gorge, but this was a strictly limited alternative, given the local topography. Use of the hobblers was mandatory for a cargo-carrying vessel of any consequence.

The inhabitants of Pill, a village on the south bank near the mouth of the river, traditionally rendered service as hobblers. With the introduction of steam-powered tugs their role changed somewhat; most of the tug crews came from Pill and in the later years of commercial navigation on the Avon, a hobbler would often be carried on board larger vessels as pilot and helmsman specifically for the voyage up or down the Avon. Hobblers also became responsible for the

Fig 4.3 Bristol: etching and watercolour of 1781 by Nicholas Pocock illustrating the Grove (left) and Wapping (right). Note the use of a single hobbler skiff to tow the coastal barge downriver; larger vessels utilised five or more boats propelled by at least 50 oarsmen. City of Bristol Museums and Art Gallery, Mb 5089

securing of mooring lines and the Pill Hobblers Association continues to supply quayside workers to the Port of Bristol Authority to dock and moor vessels, providing an interesting link with the past.

The timing of the voyage between Bristol and the mouth of the Avon was, and still is, absolutely critical for any vessel; it was dangerous for larger classes of vessel to be navigating the Bristol Avon more than two hours before, or even a relatively short time after, high water as the risk of grounding and capsizing was considerable. The narrow and fast flowing tidal channel left no room to manoeuvre; the slightest mistake or hesitation and any vessel, large or small, would be in difficulty. Of the many accidents to ships which have occurred in the Avon over the centuries, one of the most spectacular happened comparatively recently, in 1929, when fog blanketed Sea Mills Reach causing several vessels to collide or be run aground (Fig 4.4).

It was particularly dangerous for sailing ships leaving the port, since their voyage, in the days before steam-tugs, had to be timed to start as soon as possible *after* high water, in order to be carried downriver on the ebb; later steam-powered and motorized vessels could leave well ahead of high water thus gaining a valuable margin of safety by steering into the tide and travelling in the river with a rising tide. Any sailing vessel, however, which prematurely grounded as it travelled with the tide was inevitably swung broadside in

moments; the rapid fall in water level (as much as 5ft (1.5m) in one hour) gave no time to free the ship, which would begin to list down the steep underwater bank within minutes. Hobblers in rowing boats or the crew could do nothing under these conditions to haul or warp the vessel free. A loaded ship would be, at the very least, severely strained, requiring costly repairs; as the waters ebbed away almost completely, some might capsize or be broken in half, their remains blocking the approach to the port for weeks, until the wreck could be dismantled where it lay (Fig 4.5). In later years, massive insurances against such an eventuality were required of the owners of any vessel trading into the old harbour by the port authorities, even though it was the inadequate port facilities that were to blame!

Contending with these particularly difficult tidal conditions, Bristol's mariners refined their skills of seamanship to a high degree and local shipbuilders constructed rugged and heavy-timbered vessels better able to withstand the stranding which even the best-managed vessel could expect to encounter whilst operating to and from the port. The traditional phrase 'shipshape and Bristol fashion' alludes to this combination of seamanship and solidly built craft which, in practical terms, was nothing more than a virtue born out of necessity.

However, one factor which tended to compensate for the difficulties of the Avon was the prevailing south-

Fig 4.4 Bristol: the Bristol City, *a North Atlantic cargo steamer based at the City Docks, and other craft stranded at Sea Mills after being trapped by fog in the river Avon on the night of 1/2 November 1929*

westerly wind that blows squarely along the Bristol Channel. An outward-bound vessel, once clear of the Avon, could tack back and forth across the Bristol Channel and expect to reach the Atlantic relatively easily. Similarly a Bristol-bound ship could expect to run before prevailing winds and, providing the final passage up the river Avon was expedited without delay or mishap, reach port and be unloading some days, or even weeks, before a rival vessel making for London had negotiated the English Channel and the Thames estuary.

Bristol was also unusual for the length of time which a vessel spent out of the water against the quays, owing to the extreme tidal range of the Avon. A fully loaded merchant vessel with a draught of 15ft (4.6m) could be taking the ground within an hour, or two at most, of high water and remain so for at least ten or eleven hours. Because the waters of the river Severn and its tributaries contain huge quantities of silt, mud rapidly accumulated in drifts against the harbour walls and jetties, further shortening the time larger vessels remained afloat and obstructing access to even the main quays. Shiercliff's Guide to Bristol (1793, 61) refers to this problem:

Notwithstanding the great accommodation of the wharfs, and other conveniences, for loading and unloading vessels at the *Quay-walls*; complaints have frequently arisen that ships of burthen, by lying aground, (although in a soft bed of mud), when the tide is out to discharge their cargoes, have had their timbers so strained, that it was found necessary to send them into dock, to repair the damages sustained thereby.

Similarly, the preamble to the Act of Parliament of 1803 for the reconstruction of the harbour illustrates that the tidal conditions had become a deterrent to foreign ships using the port:

Whereas Ships and Vessels lying at the Quays in the Port and Harbour of *Bristol*, are by the Reflux of the Tide left dry Twice every Twenty-four Hours, which prevents many Foreign Vessels, and others of a sharp Construction, from frequenting the said Port and Harbour, and occasions great Injury and Damage to Vessels using the said Port.

These references to visiting ships and 'others of a sharp Construction' alludes to the fact that local ships were able to cope rather better, perhaps, than some vessels from other ports. But every ship using Bristol's old tidal harbour suffered regular and sometimes costly damage as vessels jostled two or three deep alongside

Fig 4.5 Bristol: the 690-ton steamship Gypsy *plied regularly between Waterford and Bristol City Docks, but broke her back when stranded in the Avon at Black Rock Quarry on 12 May 1878; dynamite was used for three weeks to demolish the wreck and clear the river*

busy quays, and neighbouring hulls would chafe dramatically as the tide ebbed and flowed with characteristic speed. Every ship needed to be very securely moored since any that broke free would be swept with the tide causing damage to themselves and neighbouring ships and invariably finished up blocking the approaches to the harbour at great cost and inconvenience to all concerned.

The risk of fire was another cause for concern aggravated by the particularly long period when all classes of vessel were immobile. The loading dock for an adjoining powder house at Hungroad can still be seen as evidence of the precautions taken to reduce the hazards of fire on board ships in the port (Buchanan & Cossons 1969, 17), but nothing might be done to move a stricken vessel once aground against the quays.

Bristol had prospered because of the overall advantages of its westerly location and the creation of extensive quays alongside a deepened channel excavated for the river Frome in the 13th century. This had been a major piece of civil engineering for its time and probably the crucial factor in Bristol's emergence as England's second port and city. It enabled local merchants to operate substantial fleets of the largest vessels for their time, and thereby establish Bristol as an international entrepôt (Ross 1955, 182). However, as the size of merchant ships increased over the years, the other drawbacks of the tidal harbour gradually came to outweigh any advantages Bristol might have had, certainly compared with London and subsequently Liverpool. By 1700, the fearsome reputation of the river amongst the country's merchant and sea-faring classes was having a detrimental effect on the city's mercantile trade and the Avon, source of medieval Bristol's prosperity, had become the major obstacle to further development. The crisis deepened throughout the 18th century and lingered throughout most of the 19th century. Today the approaches to the city's modern docks via the Severn estuary present no serious obsta-

cles to bulk carriers, whereas the Avon may only be navigated with extreme caution by vessels a fraction of their size.

To relocate the entire port of Bristol to the mouth of the river Avon in 1700 would have required construction technology, land transport systems, and a level of capital investment beyond anything that was practical for almost two centuries. As it was, considerable resources were expended during the 18th century, by the Society of Merchant Venturers, in attempts to improve the harbour facilities and maintain the port's position, particularly in the face of growing competition from Liverpool, which applied a far lower scale of harbour tariffs; Bristol had become notorious during this period not only as one of the most dangerous ports in Britain, but also as one of the most expensive.

The town had developed mainly to the north of the river Avon; the community of Redcliffe to the southeast was distinct in medieval times and only gradually absorbed as a southern suburb of Bristol. In the main, land to the south of the town remained undeveloped commercially until the mid-19th century. Much of it was low-grade marshy ground as the name Wapping from the Saxon *wapol*, meaning a marsh, testifies. Maps indicate use for grazing pasture, brickfields, lime-burning, and for shipbuilding and repair.

Where streams like the Malago and Ashton brooks in Bedminster flowed into the Avon, deep tidal creeks (pills) were scoured out; the process may be observed today at any place in the tidal river. Farr (1977, 4–5) describes the use of these creeks, as recorded towards the end of the 15th and beginning of the 16th centuries, for building, repair, and fitting out of ships. By 1742 plans of Bristol clearly depict a series of dry and wet docks to the south and west of the town at Wapping, on the west bank of the river Frome in Canon's Marsh, and at Mardyke, which derives from Marsh Dyke, the name for the westerly portion of an earth embankment, the Sea Bank, thrown up around the southern fringes of Canon's Marsh to prevent flooding at high tide (Fig 4.1). At Wapping, two dry docks and a floating (wet) dock are depicted in outline by John Rocque on his map of 1742 and confirmed more precisely by Benning's map of 1780. The pioneer transatlantic paddle-steamship *Great Western* designed by Isambard Brunel was launched from this site in 1837 and the dry and wetdocks remained in use for shipbuilding and repair until filled in during the construction of the Bristol Harbour Railway, opened in 1872.

Prompted, perhaps, by the construction of London's first major enclosed dock, the Howland Great Wet Dock of 1703 (Greeves 1980, 1) a Bristol merchant Joshua Franklyn and 32 partners financed the construction, in about 1712, of a substantial wet-dock located at Sea Mills (Fig 4.1), some way nearer to the mouth of the Avon, specifically for cargo handling. This represents the first recorded attempt to overcome the tidal difficulties of the port; it failed because all cargo and supplies still had to be trans-shipped between the city quays in barges, which was no advantage, as larger vessels, particularly those from foreign ports, had been resorting to this expedient for many years, anchoring off the mouth of the Avon in Kingroad or a short way upstream at Hungroad to avoid the risk of navigating the rest of the way to Bristol. A further disadvantage of the dock for incoming ships was its location upstream of the notorious Horseshoe Bend. So although Sea Mills Dock was a forward-looking attempt to overcome the port of Bristol's problems, since it was only the third such enclosed dock intended for cargo on record in the country, it was remote from the traditional port centre in an age when land transport was indifferent and expensive, and therefore stood no chance of succeeding in commercial terms for more than a century until the railways had been developed. It was used for some years as a depot for Bristol privateers and for a small fleet of whaling ships, but was reported in 1794 as 'long disused' (Farr 1939).

The year following the winding up of the Sea Mills Dock Company in 1761 saw the start of construction of another, more substantial floating dock (wet-dock) at Hotwells (Fig 4.1), much closer to the medieval quays, less than a mile upstream; a dry-dock (which still exists) was also constructed alongside, together with slipways for shipbuilding. Financed by William Champion, a patentee of metallic zinc manufacture and a leading Bristol merchant and industrialist of the time, the dock seems to have been intended for the safer discharge of cargoes (Farr 1977, 8), although Williams (1962, 145) considers its purpose was primarily for the fitting out of ships, as hitherto all the other local wet-docks had been; certainly it could be, and was, used for either purpose and is described in 1793 by Shiercliff as 'a wet dock, wherein forty sail of large vessels deeply laden may at all times securely lye afloat' (Shiercliff 1793, 60).

Champion became bankrupt and was forced to sell his 'Great Dock' to the Society of Merchant Venturers in 1770, after which it was referred to as the Merchants Dock. It remained in existence until 1966 when it was filled in; houses were constructed on the site in 1982. Both Sea Mills Dock and the Merchants Dock demonstrated that such limited schemes alongside the tidal river were of little commercial value to Bristol and considerably greater investment was required to improve the port. Williams (1962) carefully documents more than 50 schemes that were put forward between 1765 and 1900 for this purpose, culminating in the Royal Edward 'Ocean Dock' at Avonmouth completed in 1908 (Fig 4.1). Throughout the second half of the 18th century, the Society of Merchant Venturers commissioned and debated several dozen schemes to create a non-tidal harbour for Bristol that would incorporate the previously tidal stretches of the Avon and Frome alongside which the established quays were located. Smeaton made the first proposals in January 1765, but 37 years were to elapse before a plan by William Jessop was finally accepted and a Bristol Dock Company was formed to build and operate the new harbour. Even then, many prominent Bristol shipowners and merchants objected to the cost and withdrew.

However, between 1804 and 1809 a deep trench, one and a half miles long, called the New Cut, was excavated, utilising, so legend has it, the forced labours of the many French prisoners-of-war billeted in the area. It still runs about a quarter of a mile to the south of the old river-bed, carrying the tidal flow of the Avon (Fig 4.1). By constructing a rubble and earth dam across the Avon at Vauxhall Point, Jessop created a large area

of water stretching some two miles through the centre of Bristol and transforming the traditional quays along St Augustine's Reach, the Grove, and Welsh Back, and well beyond Bristol Bridge into a non-tidal 'Floating Harbour'. The name was derived locally as if to emphasise that Bristol had overcome all the difficulties of its tidal port which, of course, it had not; the notorious river approach to this new harbour remained unchanged and it would never revive the failing fortunes of the old port.

Nevertheless, as Neale (1968, 2) emphasises, 'There should be no underestimation of the scale of this scheme. To provide a dock with some 80 acres of non-tidal water space is an achievement by any standard at any time'. Cumberland Basin, the largest of the three systems of entrance locks and tidal basins provided as part of the original scheme, remains in use. The overall layout of the Floating Harbour also remains unchanged since this major development was completed in 1809. The following year, the Kennet and Avon Canal linked the ports of London and Bristol for inland barge traffic for the first time, and for a while the prospects of the port looked better.

The land on either side of this new harbour was intensively developed for commercial use during the 19th century. At its peak there were 17 firms of boat and shipbuilders around the harbour and, later in the century, a multiplicity of factories, warehouses, and railway installations. Bristol retained much of its traditional medieval street pattern until after the Second World War, and some districts displayed an amazing mix of residential and commercial or industrial accommodation until well into the 20th century, although the move to fashionable residential suburbs by the majority of the well-to-do was under way before 1830. It is, however, this retention of domestic accommodation at the heart of many of the central districts adjoining the harbour that has given Bristol its interesting character and placed it ahead in the process of late 20th century urban renewal. The 'backs' denoted on late 17th century maps as the name of several areas of quayside or an adjacent street testifies to this close interrelationship that once existed between the merchants and shipowners and their trade; vessels moored on quaysides at the backs of houses which frequently incorporated large cellars functioning as warehouses. The final traces of these are only now disappearing with late 20th century redevelopment.

The Floating Harbour, known in later years as the City Docks, has undergone considerable changes since 1970 when commercial shipping was effectively at an end. The water area is now dedicated to leisure boating and water-sports. Many dock buildings have been adapted for leisure, housing, and service-industry office use; few remain in use as industrial premises. The fires of planning controversy seem to have rekindled in the late 1980s, as some particularly heavy-handed redevelopment schemes obliterate dockside buildings and lengths of quayside walling (Fig 4.6).

Preservation and recording of sites of historical or archaeological significance for the old port have been taking place for some years, but are still piecemeal. Several sites around the harbour have been the subject of detailed archaeological study, invariably prior to

Fig 4.6 Bristol: the changing face of the old harbour in January 1990; the construction of a new office building for Lloyds Bank is well advanced on the former site of quayside transit sheds and multistorey tobacco warehouses. The quayside in front of the building is being lowered to create a waterside amphitheatre with the base of a steam-crane as its focal point

redevelopment that would destroy the remains beneath. Standing structures are recorded by individuals and organisations ranging from local residents with a life-long interest in the port and its shipping to commercial businesses and the Port of Bristol Authority. One element to emerge has been the definition of sites of potential interest along the waterfront which might be examined by future generations; several wet- and dry-docks and shipbuilding sites, denoted on old plans and maps, fall into this category.

A number of buildings and quayside structures remain as preserved historic features. A 35-ton steam-powered crane on Prince's Wharf built in 1875 by the Bath-based firm of Stothert & Pitt, now maintained by the Bristol Industrial Musm as part of the City Museums and Art Gallery collections, is a prime example, as is the nearby Industrial Museum building itself. Opened in 1978, the Industrial Museum and an adjoining Lifeboat Museum, occupy transit sheds L and M, constructed in 1952 and the last large quayside buildings to be constructed in the City Docks.

The lengths of quayside established in medieval times remained basically the same until the mid 19th century. Only minor works and alterations were carried out from time to time; the Floating Harbour absorbed the medieval quays, obliterating only the site of the Trin tide-mill for the construction of one of the harbour entrances, Bathurst Basin (Fig 4.1). However, the 1865 Parliamentary session passed the first of a long series of Acts that empowered the Bristol Corporation and the Great Western Railway Company to create lengths of quayside furnished with railway tracks and the new style of warehouse, the transit shed, so typical of large dock installations of the late Victorian era everywhere. The site occupied by the Industrial Museum typifies this later phase of harbour development.

The demolition of transit sheds Y and Z on the opposite side of the harbour on Canon's Marsh, high-lights the conflict that now exists in Bristol, London, and traditional ports elsewhere, when the pressure for urban renewal is fuelled by a rush by developing agencies to acquire sites overlooking the former commercial waterways. Only a few years previously these were dismissed as unsightly and unsellable. At the time of writing, demolition of existing structures that stand at or near the water's edge is assumed to be a prerequisite to redevelopment. Y and Z sheds of 1903 were probably the earliest surviving examples in England of Mouchel-Hennebique steel and concrete buildings but, sadly in the view of the author, are being demolished to make way for an office development (Fig 4.6). With this happening, the future of the Industrial Museum in its architecturally undistinguished transit sheds — the last to remain *in situ* surrounded by the essential elements of the working dockside, cranes, capstans, and railway sidings — becomes a critical aspect of the battle to retain significant features of Bristol's post-medieval and more recent port, the fabric of which is fast disappearing.

5 Newcastle upon Tyne and its North Sea trade
C O'Brien

Abstract

This paper considers Newcastle mostly in the 13th and 14th centuries and its position on the river Tyne, in terms of its institutions and infrastructure; its competitive position in relation to other interests on the river; the trade in which it engaged; and the effects of changing conditions after the onset of the Scottish Wars in 1296. The topography of the riverside is described and the history of the town and its burgesses' fight to enforce a monopoly of shipping on the Tyne discussed. The effect of the Scottish Wars and their outcome on the economic life of the port are assessed. Wool and hides were prominent commodities traded through the port which had trading contacts as far afield as the Low Countries and the Baltic, but there is evidence for a wide range of goods. Coal was shipped from the Tyne from the 13th century and, after a series of disputes, Newcastle eventually became the principal port for handling coal.

Introduction

In the eyes of the mariner, Newcastle was not the most suitable site for the port on the river Tyne. For whereas good harbourage was to be had close to the river mouth, the journey to Newcastle took ships 15km along a river which was narrow and twisting and, until it was dredged just over 100 years ago, in places shallow (Fig 5.1). Fishweirs encroached on the channel and caused sand banks to add to the difficulties. 'Will our Lord the King and his Council please order hasty remedy' appealed the Mayor, bailiffs, and commons of Newcastle in 1368 (Fraser 1966, no 225). It was to be another 500 years before there was really effective remedy.

In the town, the mariner was not the primary concern. For Newcastle was, before all else, a fortified river crossing: fortified and bridged first by the Emperor Hadrian, and fortified for a second time in 1080 by Robert Curthose, son of the Conqueror, with the eponymous new castle, and bridged again in the

12th century. For both Hadrian and Robert, Newcastle was a northern frontier stronghold, yet before 1300 it had evolved to become the principal port of north-east England. How did this come about?

The Laws of Newcastle, formulated before the mid 12th century, established the rights of the burgesses with certain monopolistic privileges: a monopoly of trade in the staple commodities of wool, hides, and cloth; the sole right to buy goods from a vessel lying at anchor in the mouth of the Tyne; and the right to insist that all cargoes be unloaded at Newcastle, save for salt and herring which could be sold on board ship (Fraser 1961, 135). Here then was the institutional underpinning of the privileged trading base in Newcastle, and by the beginning of the 13th century it had already become a port of some prominence, for we find that in 1203–4 when King John imposed a tax of one fifteenth on imports and exports, £158 5s 11d was raised in Newcastle, some 3.2% of the national total and the eighth

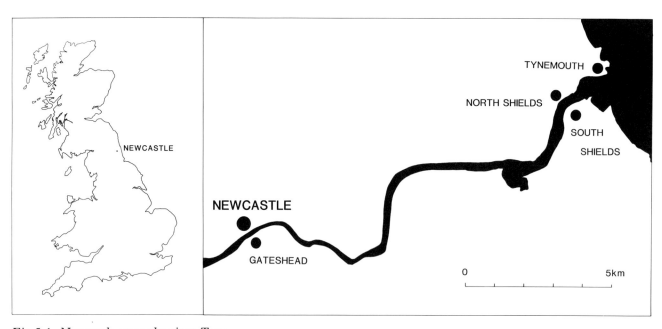

Fig 5.1 Newcastle upon the river Tyne

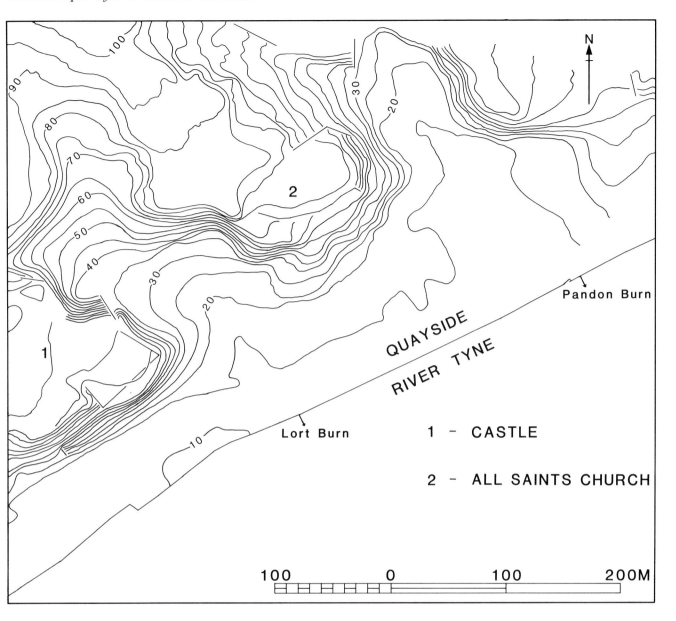

Fig 5.2 Newcastle upon Tyne: waterfront topography, contours at 5ft (1.5m) intervals

highest sum (Lloyd 1977, table 1). At about the same time a transformation of the riverside began as the town developed a waterfront infrastructure to support its maritime trade.

The riverside topography

It is a steep descent from the town and castle on the hill to the waterfront along the Tyne, and the extent to which the riverside forms a discrete topographical unit is emphasised in a contour map (Fig 5.2). Two tributaries, the Lort burn and the Pandon burn, break the lines of the cliff edge. Both are now culverted, but the gorges which they formed are still evident to some extent in the modern-day landscape, and throughout the medieval period both were open watercourses with the Lort burn splitting the town in two and the Pandon burn separating Newcastle from Pandon. At the foot of the cliff is a level platform leading to the quay wall up to 100m

forward from the cliff. This is an artificially raised platform built out across the foreshore.

The infrastructure which was developed on the platform can be summarised in diagrammatic form (Fig 5.3). The two tributaries (1 and 2) were bridged behind the cliff, and the Sandhill (3) immediately upstream of the Lort burn was the site of the Tyne bridge. Three lengths of river frontage were divided by these natural features. Above the Lort burn (4) there was no public quay; the Close was parallel to the river, just below the cliff, with houses and private wharves between the road and river. The principal thoroughfare for the western half of the town led down beside the castle to the Close and the Tyne bridge on the Sandhill which was the nodal point for communications. Between the burns (5) and below Pandon burn (6), a public quay, the Quayside, drew the whole waterfront into a unified system. Narrow lanes led back from the quay and were linked together by a road on the cliff and thence to Pilgrim Street, the principal street in the western part

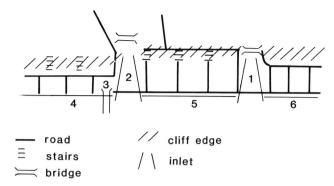

road — road
Ξ stairs
≍ bridge
// cliff edge
/\ inlet

Fig 5.3 Newcastle upon Tyne: diagrammatic view of the waterfront infrastructure

of the town. This is a familiar form of medieval waterfront development, elements of which can be matched in other English and Continental ports of the North Sea (O'Brien *et al* 1988, 155–9 for further comments). There have been changes to the street plan in modern times, particularly those brought about by the fire of 1854, and where there was one bridge until 1850, now there are six, but much of the original lay-out remains intact.

The principal evidence for the chronology of the waterfront development is from the excavations carried out between 1984 and 1986. The main area studied was midway between the two burns, at the back of the riverside platform, taking in two of the streets, Fenwick's Entry and Broad Garth, and the space between (O'Brien *et al* 1988).

The stratigraphic sequence, which was nearly 6m deep, began with a retaining wall along the river-bank, and piers consisting of clay platforms faced with sandstone projecting forward towards the river, with open space for docking in between the piers. These were constructed in the first half of the 13th century, and were in use for only a short time before being filled in and covered over by an episode of dumping on the foreshore in which a large volume of material was brought to the riverside from elsewhere.

This dumping was the key event in the evolution of the waterfront, for by this means was created the continuous platform of raised ground which lasts to this day. Once the ground had been built up sufficiently, streets were set out and building started, with the street surfaces directly above the now-buried piers, and the buildings enclosing what had previously been open docking space. All this happened before the end of the 13th century. Between then and the 20th century the ground level was built up another 3m with no change in the positions of the streets and a succession of buildings occupying the same sites, with the walls of earlier, partly demolished buildings serving as foundations for later constructions.

East of the Pandon burn, the initial stage of riverside development took a different form with a stone quay wall some 50m behind the modern frontage. This was covered over in the same episode of dumping which created the continuous riverside platform (O'Brien *et al* 1989).

The only element of the developed waterfront which may not have been in place by the end of the 13th century is the Quayside itself; there are arguments for placing that in the latter half of the 14th century (O'Brien *et al* 1988, 156–7). This would mean that for a period of 100 years or so each of the streets had its own watergate and landing stage before the continuous quay emerged.

The town's investment in its riverside infrastructure was considerable. The total amount of reclaimed land brought into use on the riverside was some 70,000m^2, 11% of the total area contained within the town walls. It is possible that the Lort burn and the Pandon burn inlets were used for harbourage from the earliest days of the town (though it has not yet been possible to test this in excavations), but the development of a waterfront along the river Tyne lifted the town's capacity to support a maritime trading base on to an altogether higher level. The excavation results show that this happened in the 13th century as a secondary development in the town, and that once begun it progressed quickly with most of the elements in place before the year 1300.

Competitive forces

Newcastle's development as the port on the Tyne was not only a matter of investment in infrastructure. For whatever the Laws of Newcastle may have said, others had interests on the river, and these included men of power. The Prior of Tynemouth, whose monastery occupied the headland on the north side of the river mouth, held a considerable asset in the form of the first natural harbour within the river, North Shields, where since 1225 a fishing community had been established. Such was the threat in the eyes of the burgesses of Newcastle that in 1267 the mayor, Nicholas Scot, led a band of men who seized a boat moored at North Shields laden with hides and coal, burned the houses, and beat up the prior's men. Their satisfaction was short-lived, for the Abbot of St Albans (Tynemouth's mother house) prosecuted and the burgesses were fined £300 (Craster 1907, 285–6).

They did not make the same mistake again. Next time it was the burgesses who went to the law, arguing in 1290 that contrary to the Laws of Newcastle and the royal rights of prisage, the prior was trading at North Shields, which had once been just a place of huts for storm-driven sailors, but was now a great township where they bake and brew to the detriment of Newcastle (Fraser 1966, no 207). This time judgement was given in Newcastle's favour on the grounds that the prior was attracting trade beyond the needs of his house. Henceforth no ships were to load or unload at Shields; no provisions were to be sold there to merchants; and all wharves below the high tide mark were to be removed. So ended the prior's first attempt to establish a trading community at the mouth of the Tyne (Craster 1907, 287–8).

Thirteen years later the burgesses of Newcastle were again successful in thwarting the prior who, enjoying the patronage of Queen Margaret, was granted an annual fair in Tynemouth at the feast of St Oswin. When the burgesses pointed out that ships laden with fish, wine, and other merchandise would in these circumstances go to Tynemouth and not to Newcastle, and thus the king would lose prisage, murage, and other customs, the grant was revoked (Gibson 1846, 138).

In the Bishop of Durham the burgesses faced an altogether stronger opponent who, through his manor of Gateshead, faced them across the length of the Tyne bridge. They suffered a rebuke in 1314 for having forced the bishop's men to bring their goods to Newcastle. Further, allegations were made in 1336 that contrary to the liberties of the Church in Durham, the burgesses were forcing the fishermen of Gateshead and South Shields to bring their catch to Newcastle; that the Prior of Durham was not allowed to unload his own wool from Holy Island on the south bank of the Tyne; and that Newcastle was monopolising all the revenues of the Tyne bridge, even though its southern end was on the bishop's land. In 1342 when Edward III restored the liberties of Newcastle he warned that this should not be held as being prejudicial to the rights of the bishop (Fraser 1961, 143–4).

In 1383, by which time coal export had a prominent place on the Tyne, we find Bishop Fordham complaining to the king that, whereas his predecessors had derived great profit from the coal on their land, he was gaining none at all because the men of Newcastle were blocking him (Fraser 1981, no 127). The king at first warned off the burgesses, but they in turn appealed to the king's interests using the same sort of argument which they had successfully deployed against the Prior of Tynemouth. Did he not realise that they held the town and its customs in fee farm for £100 per year and that he had granted the bishop rights to load and unload without payment of tolls or customs? No tax, customs, or tolls would be payable to the king in Gateshead, whereas they in Newcastle paid as much as the city of York, all but 40 marks. If this was how it was to be, they would leave and go to Gateshead and enjoy their burghal rights without the tenths, taxes, customs tolls, and other royal obligations, and the king would lose his annual farm of £100. On this occasion the king was not persuaded (Fraser 1962, 218; 1966, no 230). But that was not the end of the matter; arguments rumbled on, even to the extent of two attempts by Newcastle in the 16th century to annex Gateshead.

Imports and exports

What was the trade which Newcastle was so keen to monopolise? The murage toll first levied in Newcastle in 1265 lists the rates on a wide range of commodities. While there is undoubtedly an element of standard formulae in these tolls, comparison between towns points up the differences (Fraser 1969). Newcastle was one of a small number of places where sea-coal was taxed. Salmon were expected in large quantities, being charged at 1d per 20 at Newcastle, Berwick, and Durham, but per single fish elsewhere. Herring and cod were listed at Newcastle as well as sea-fish by the cart load. Woad, alum, and fuller's earth were all charged and these indications of clothworking bring to mind the petition of 1278 against the granting to the Carmelite Friars of a spring used by the fullers and dyers (Fraser 1966, no 85).

There are a few ships which can be identified individually (Fraser 1969, 53–5). John, son of Roger, a Newcastle merchant, was captured by pirates in 1277 and lost nine bolts of cloth as well as money, silver, and jewellery. At about the same time a Norwegian, Tjodrik, who was in Newcastle carrying fish, had his ship stolen, loaded with coal, and taken to King's Lynn (Fraser 1966, no 203). This ill-fated voyage combined English coastal travel and a North Sea crossing. Nicholas Scot in 1342 exported from Newcastle ox hides, horse hides, and sea-coal, and in 1336 three Newcastle merchants loaded their ship at St Valery on the Somme with cob-nuts, herrings, cockles, apples, woad, and a carpet and coverlet. Robert de Castro of Newcastle shipped wool, wool-fells, and hides in 1333–4, and he also stocked Rhine wine and Eastland boards. These latter suggest business with Germany and the Baltic ports, and in the Newcastle tolls some evidence of the importance of the Baltic connection can be seen, for board is charged not simply by the 100 as is usual, but pine board, maple board, and Eastland board are all specified individually (Fraser 1969, appendix). In 1294 storms in the North Sea forced a number of Baltic ships en route to Flanders to take refuge in English ports. They were searched, and thus there is a good insight into goods being carried from the Baltic. Eleven ships from Lübeck, Stralsund, and Stavoren were driven into the Tyne, and these were found to be carrying hides of various animals: oxen, seals, calves, goats, lambs, and horses, and hare pelts, white herring and 'hard fish', some 20,000 boards, casks of ash, bowstaves, pitch and tar, rye, butter, and wax, many of which commodities are listed in the Newcastle murage tolls (Davies 1953).

The archaeological record for the 13th century, from the Quayside excavations, includes ceramics from Saintonge, Rouen, and Beauvais (Bown 1988), a textile fragment from Norway or Iceland (Walton 1988), and pottery from Scarborough which found its way to many of the North Sea ports in Britain and on the Continent (Farmer 1979).

The wool trade

Wool, wool-fells, and hides were the principal commodities exported from Newcastle in the later part of the 13th century. In 1275 it ranked sixth amongst the wool ports of England with 3.2% of the total exports (Lloyd 1977, 64). In five customs accounts from the period between 1281 and 1297 the ports of origin of the ships and the home towns of the wool merchants trading in Newcastle can be seen (Davies 1954): Middelburg in Zeeland, Bruges in Flanders, Calais and St Valery in France, and others as far afield as Hamburg and Lübeck in the Baltic; more than 40 foreign ports in all, and other English ports. There seem to have been close links with Picardy, based on an exchange of wool and woad. Newcastle had a merchant community of its own engaged in this trade. Henry le Escot, Roger Le Rus, Isolde de Pampeden, Peter Graper, Peter Sampson, and Gilbert of Cowgate were amongst the most prominent and we can trace them also in the Lay Subsidy Roll of 1296 (Fraser 1968). Nearly half of the wealth assessed for tax in that record was in the hands of exporters of wool and hides (most dealt in both), which gives an indication of the value of this business to the town at the end of the 13th century.

During the following 40 years Newcastle's fortunes fluctuated. In the favourable conditions early in the 14th century Newcastle prospered and gained an increasing share of the market nationally, but the establishment of an overseas staple brought a decline, though when this was abolished Newcastle recovered more quickly than the country as a whole so that by 1335/6 it had 5% of the total market (Lloyd 1977, fig 12).

The Anglo-Scottish wars

These figures, however, disguise the fact that already conditions were changing and working against Newcastle. One problem was that wool from the north was of poor quality. When the king instructed his agents to buy up wool in 1337 at fixed prices they paid 12 marks per sack for the best fleeces from Herefordshire, but only 5 marks for the northern wool (Fraser 1969, 56; *Cal Pat Rolls* 1334–8, 480–2; *Cal Close Rolls* 1337–9, 148–50). But the greater problem was the onset of the Anglo-Scottish wars in 1296 which disrupted the economy of Northumberland. In 1327 the commons of the county petitioned for pardon of debts incurred during the war, as there were 200 townships now deserted. Petitions reached the king from Bamburgh, Beadnall, Hexham, Holystone, Shorestone, North Sunderland, and Tynemouth (Fraser 1966, nos 156–60, 162, 167–8, 176), and also from Newcastle where in 1316 the commons asked for financial assistance because they had kept the town at their own expense since the beginning of the war, and fortified it with a wall and ditch. Those with lands outside were wasted by the enemy, merchants were unable to trade because of guard duties, ships had been captured at sea, and artisans had no work because the county had been devastated (Fraser 1966, no 155).

The war brought a new competitor within Newcastle's sphere of influence. Berwick-on-Tweed was a Scottish port until 1296, and a considerable one at that. In 1286 its customs revenue is estimated to have been over £2000, more than six times greater than Newcastle's at about the same period (Fraser 1961, 137). As a town in English hands after 1296 Berwick was in competition with Newcastle for the same Northumberland hinterland and to mitigate the costs of its defence it enjoyed concessionary treatment (*Cal Pat Rolls* 1313–7, 257, 671). In 1318 wool was being brought to Berwick from Northumberland and Durham with the result that the king was losing revenue of 30 shillings per sack, as the Newcastle customs collectors were careful to note (Bain 1887, 155; Fraser 1961, 141). From 1333 Berwick was once again under English control, and once again the Newcastle merchants protested that Northumberland wool was being exported through Berwick where customs due was lower, half a mark per sack as against the standard English rate of 40 shillings (Fraser 1961, 141). The king also took this problem seriously because in 1340 he ordered the customs collectors to seize Northumberland wool brought to Berwick to gain advantage of the different rates of duty (*Cal Close Rolls* 1339–41, 434).

The Newcastle merchants, ever resourceful, tried to use Berwick to their own advantage, for they too were shipping wool out of the Tweed to exploit the lower rate of duty. Feigning innocence they protested when the customs collectors began to charge the full English due on any wool which they brought into Newcastle from Berwick for trans-shipment (Fraser 1966, no 190). The following year, 1341, they threatened to desert Newcastle and move to Berwick to take advantage of the lower customs dues (Fraser 1966, no 194), as they were later to threaten a move to Gateshead.

The coal trade

In the longer term, war damage and the loss of its Scottish hinterland undermined Berwick's trading position, while Newcastle suffered from the combined effects of low prices for its wool and the expense and hazards of the journey to the staple port in Calais. In 1362 the mayor appealed for the lifting of the prohibition on coal exports on the grounds that there was no other common merchandise with which to trade and pay the fee-farm (Fraser 1966, no 222). Three years later the king agreed to allow aliens and denizens to export coal and grindstones, as well as woollen cloth and hides from Newcastle to any foreign ports (*Cal Pat Rolls* 1364–7, 90).

As we have already seen, coal was being shipped from the Tyne in the 13th century, and it was to become a source of dispute with the Bishop of Durham. Sea-coal, as it is usually known, outcrops along the banks of the Tyne and was easily exploited, and Newcastle found ready markets both domestic and foreign. It was widely used for lime-burning, with Tyne coal being delivered for building at Corfe, Berwick, Rochester, and Windsor Castles, and the Tower of London where the clerk of works was an important trader in coal in the 13th century and subsequently. Smiths used coal for smelting iron, and it was ordered for making weaponry and armour in Newcastle, Dundee, Berwick, and Westminster. Sea-coal, peat, and charcoal were amongst the materials bought for casting a bell at York Minster in 1371. Coal and other commodities were stored for defensive purposes at Dover and Calais which may have received regular shipments from Newcastle. In 1351 the Sheriff of Northumberland was commissioned to carry twelve shiploads of coal to Calais and in the following year Nicholas Rodom, a Newcastle burgess, agreed to deliver 720 chaldrons to the king's sergeants-at-arms there. Two hundred and thirty-two chaldrons were purchased at Newcastle in 1385/6 for provisioning at Calais. Monastic houses used it as a fuel. Holy Island, Jarrow, and Whitby all made purchases (Blake 1967, 2–9).

Newcastle had no formal monopoly of the coal trade during the Middle Ages, but enjoyed the greater part of it as demand increased, and came to supply many of the ports of England, Scotland, and western Europe. London was the principal home market, importing coal from early in the 13th century. The first ship which can be identified individually is the *Welfare* of Thomas Migg who in 1305 carried wine from London to Berwick and returned with coal from Newcastle. Numerous London merchants received licences to

Fig 5.4 Newcastle upon Tyne: the destination of Newcastle coal exports 1377–91

travel to Newcastle to buy coal, and Newcastle merchants were trading themselves. William Acton in 1337 sold 1600 chaldrons in London and the following year Elias Bulkham, John Denom, and William Hoton gained a licence to buy 3000 chaldrons for sale to London (Blake 1967, 11–12).

Four customs accounts for the years between 1377 and 1391 show detail of trade with Europe (Fig 5.4). Markets were in France and Flanders, with 78 sailings from Nieuport, Dunkirk, Heyst, and Sluys, half of the total amount for 1377/8. In the subsequent accounts the

ports of Holland and Zeeland are dominant. Kampen ships made a total of 53 sailings, more than any other port. Thirty-eight came from Veere with lesser numbers from Schiedam and Zieriksee. A smaller number of ships came from ports in the Baltic, with Danzig the main one in this area sending 15 ships, and lesser numbers from Hamburg, Lübeck, Rostock, Bremen, and others (Blake 1967, 17–21). The Newcastle Chamberlain's accounts of the early 16th century show the extent to which this trade had grown by the beginning of the Tudor period (Fraser 1987).

Conclusion

The town and its burgesses, on the strength of the Laws of Newcastle, strove to enforce a monopoly of shipping on the Tyne, challenging, sometimes with violence, sometimes with cunning, the Prior of Tynemouth and the Bishop of Durham, and by the end of the 13th century the frontier stronghold had emerged as a great port supported by an extensive riverside infrastructure. Wool and hides were prominent in a trading network which took in France and Flanders, Holland and Zeeland, and the ports of the Baltic and Scandinavia. Poor quality and low prices meant that Newcastle was never in the first rank of the wool ports and as a result of Anglo-Scottish wars from 1296 Berwick emerged as a competitor for the Northumbrian hinterland. But with coal in the ground, Newcastle had a resource which kept its economy buoyant and brought it to the forefront of the Industrial Revolution.

6 Medieval Hartlepool: evidence of and from the waterfront

R Daniels

Abstract

Hartlepool was a Norman foundation granted borough status in 1200. Excavations since 1981 have revealed a sequence of dock structures as well as much information about the rest of the town. The docks were constructed in the 12th century and additions, repairs and land reclamation continued into the 14th century when a new dock was built further into the harbour. The docks were only designed to handle coastal trade which boomed with the Scottish Wars in the 13th and 14th centuries, reaching a peak at the end of the 14th century. Fishing was an important part of the town's economy throughout its history, cod and herring being the predominant catches. Severe economic decline after the 15th century was only reversed in the Victorian Period with the building of docks and the railway for the coal trade. The port now prospers again.

The town and port of Hartlepool lies on the north-east coast of England, to the north of the mouth of the river Tees (Fig 6.1). It occupies an outcrop of limestone which is an outlier of the Durham Plateau. To the east and south this outcrop finishes in cliffs, while to the west the limestone dips down to a natural harbour in the lee of the ridge. A sandspit at the southern edge of the harbour offered further protection to shipping. Connecting the headland with the mainland is a low-lying area which was subject to inundation. Consequently, until the arrival of the railways, communication links with the hinterland were never good and this undoubtedly retarded its development as a major port.

The first major settlement on Hartlepool Headland was the Anglo-Saxon monastery, which was founded in the 640s. The monastic settlement lay on the ridge top and recent excavations have shown it to be an organised community of considerable importance in our understanding of early Christianity in Northumbria (Cramp & Daniels 1987; Daniels 1988). It is possible that a secular fishing community occupied the slope at the harbour edge, although no evidence of this has yet been recovered. Whilst there is a tradition that the monastery was destroyed by the Vikings, there is no clear archaeological evidence for this. Rather, excavations suggest that the monastery had gone into decline by the last quarter of the 8th century. By the beginning of the 9th century there may have been little more than a remnant surviving of the monastic community.

The period between the demise of the Anglo-Saxon monastery and the beginning of the Norman development of the town is as yet a virtual blank. There is evidence for cultivation on the headland, whilst to the south of the church, a cemetery excavated in 1972 may date to this period (Hinchliffe forthcoming). Scandinavian influences are suggested by two fragments of hogback tombstone in the church. The monastic church may well have survived up to this time, but there is no evidence for substantial settlement. Hartlepool's natural advantage as a haven probably meant it would have played a part in maritime activities, but its poor communications inland retarded development as a port.

The Norman conquest of England marked one of the most turbulent periods in the history of the north as Normans, Scots, and native Northumbrians strove to establish control over the region. Eventually, but not without difficulty, the Normans imposed themselves on the region and set about its economic reorganisation. In this sense the development of Hartlepool can be seen as part of the broad-based economic development of the Tees lowlands, led by the activities of the Brus family and the Bishop and Prior of Durham. In addition to the establishment of the major economic centres, the rural infrastructure was reorganised, almost certainly giving rise to the large two-row villages which are still so much a part of the countryside. In short, everything possible was undertaken to realise the potential of the region in order to provide the economic powerbase necessary for ambitious Norman nobles and institutions.

It is against this background that the development of Hartlepool must be seen. In Hartlepool, as elsewhere in the region, the most crucial period, the late 11th century and the 12th, is that of which least is known. Probably by this time the town was laid out on the slope leading from St Hilda's church down to the harbour. The plan perhaps comprised two opposed rows of buildings, one along Middlegate, the other along Southgate/High Street, with a large open space between. As the town prospered this space was infilled and occupation moved outwards from this core along Northgate and Durham Street (Fig 6.1).

In 1200 the town was granted borough status with a weekly market and in 1216 an annual fair lasting three days was granted. This boost to the status of the town was accompanied by a boost to its economy in the form of the construction of St Hilda's church, which was financed by the Brus family. This impressive building embodied the ambitions the Bruses had for the town and was closely followed by equally impressive accommodation for the Franciscan friars (Daniels 1986a). These two structures provided a period of around 80 years of constant building activity within the town. During this early period of the town's development its

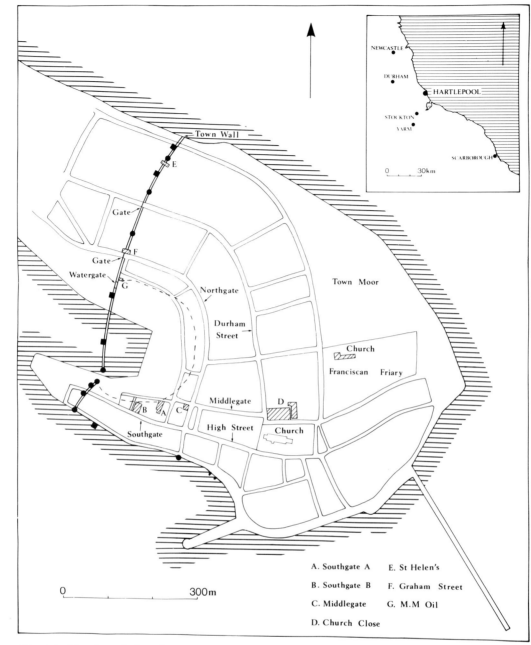

Fig 6.1 Hartlepool: location plan

inhabitants probably continued in agriculture in order to augment their commercial activities.

The harbour

The harbour comprises a natural bay protected from the worst of the tides by the headland and the sandspit, later to develop into Southgate. The first reference to the use of the harbour is in 1171 when Hugh, Earl of Bar, landed with an army of Flemings comprising 40 knights, their retinue, and 500 foot soldiers (Young 1987, 27); this force was also re-embarked at the port following the failure of the enterprise. Whilst these activities could have taken place on the foreshore it seems more likely that there were docking facilities.

Evidence of medieval docks was recovered from excavations on Southgate, where two different types of dock structure were recovered (Young 1987).

Southgate Area A (Fig 6.2)

Pre-dock construction (12th century)

A stone wall (I) formed the eastern limit of the excavated harbour installation. Only the west face of this was within the excavation area and it may have formed a quayside rather than a freestanding wall. At its northern limit there was an eastward return which presumably continued along the south side of the harbour perimeter to form a landing stage of some kind.

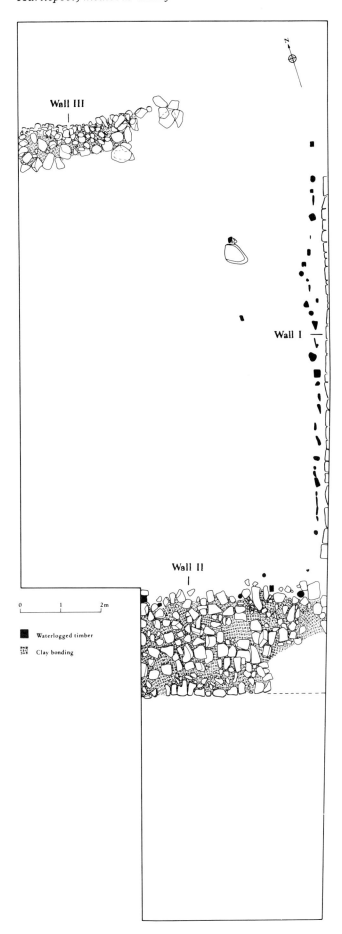

Fig 6.2 Hartlepool: Southgate Area A, dock

Construction of a dock (c 1213)

Wall II was added at right-angles to the south end of wall I to produce the south-east corner of a new dock. Five vertical timbers were integrated within the north face of wall II, which was open to the sea. There were no timbers on the south side, which presumably faced the dry land of the sandspit. Contemporary with wall II, a row of closely set vertical timbers was inserted in front of wall I. These comprised posts and planks and formed a protective fender between boats and the stonework of the wall. Most of the timber was oak and included five planks which were reused boat timbers. They provided evidence of caulking, clench nails, treenails, and diamond roves. The trunks and radially split timbers appear to have been obtained specifically for the construction of the dock and tree-ring analysis of four oak posts and two other timbers produced a felling date of the spring of 1212/13. Two posts were set some 2m from the face of wall I, and were probably mooring posts. The dock sustained severe damage and rubble was displaced from the face of wall I and fell behind the timbers.

Dock modifications and decline (mid 13th century)

A third wall (wall III) was built in the northern part of the area. It formed the northern limit of the dock and may have functioned as a breakwater. On both sides of the wall were alternating layers of sand and organic deposits. These deposits contained various pieces of cobblers' leather waste which had been thrown into the dock from the beginning of the silting. A mixture of domestic refuse and sands brought in by the tides filled the dock to the top of wall I, by which time wall III was completely covered.

The dock area was subsequently reclaimed in the late 13th century. Walls I and II remained as the boundary lines of this corner of the dock and were still in use, although decayed, in later periods.

Southgate Area B (Fig 6.3)

This lay to the west of the former area and probably represents an extension to the west of the harbour facilities, although there is no reason to suggest that the two areas were not contemporary.

Construction of the sea defences (12th–13th century)

Two walls, I and II, formed the south-west corner of this harbour installation. These walls probably formed the northern limit of the town docks and sea defences at this time. Both walls were constructed from limestone, roughly coursed with alternate layers of clay inside a box framework of timber and built on clean sand.

Wall I had three constructional elements within its timber framework. Firstly, a row of vertical timbers ran down the east and west faces of the wall and these supported horizontal planking, traces of which survived on both faces. In addition, four grooves for east-west tie beams were located. At right-angles and of the same

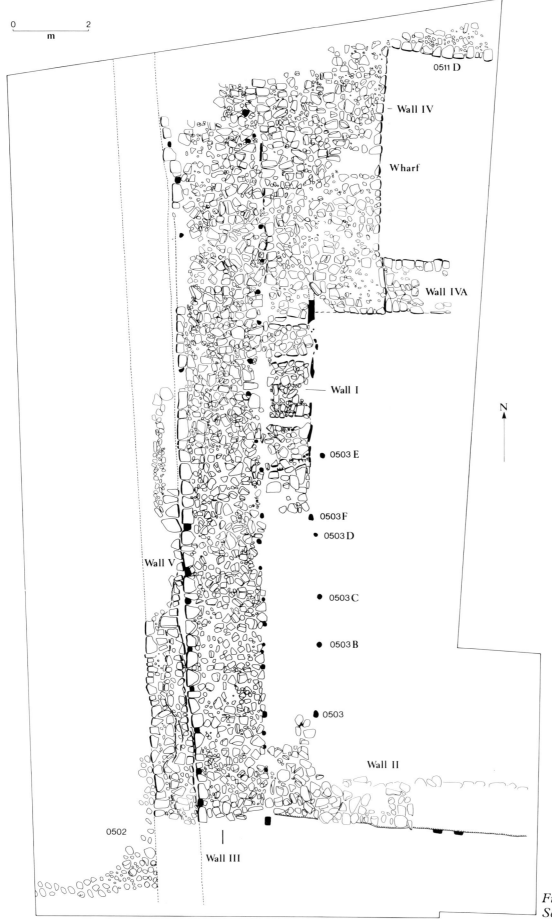

0 ___ 2
m

0511 D

Wall IV

Wharf

Wall IVA

Wall I

● 0503 E

▲ 0503 F
● 0503 D

● 0503 C

● 0503 B

● 0503

Wall V

Wall II

0502

Wall III

N

Fig 6.3 Hartlepool:
Southgate Area B, d⸺

build, was wall II, of similar construction with horizontal planking on its south side and closely set upright posts.

Rebuilding of the sea defences (13th century)

A major rebuilding of the sea defences took place when wall I was replaced by the more massive wall III. This was built to the west of the earlier wall and had deeper foundations. The south end of wall III stopped at the same point as the earlier wall and incorporated the east-west wall II into the rebuild.

Wall III was also constructed in a box of timber. Eleven upright timbers occurred on its west side. Their positions could be seen as voids in the stonework, and solid timbers were detected by probing. Horizontal planking was evident on both sides of wall III and at its south end, demonstrating that this was its original limit.

The wharf (late 13th–14th century)

Further modifications to the docks took place when a massive wharf was constructed in the late 13th to 14th century. The wharf was a solid construction of limestone blocks bonded with clay (wall IV), built against the east side of wall III over the remains of wall I. Stonework 0511D was bonded into the north edge of the wharf walling and formed a right-angled return to the east. This may have been another wharf, but little of it survived. The foundations consisted of a single offset course of stone which had been built directly onto natural sand. The original surface of the wharf was 1.2m above the sand and it survived throughout the medieval period, until at least the 16th century. During this phase this corner of the docks appears to have silted to such an extent that, like Area A, it was in desultory use as a rubbish dump for a short time.

Construction of a small dock (14th–15th century)

The addition of wall IVA to the extant wharf created a small docking area or berth to the north of the main dock, which had by now become defunct. As the docks moved to the west and north the land behind to the south was reclaimed, probably by the construction of stone-revetted dumps of material. As this was the seaward side it raises the question of the possibility of some form of substantial sea defence along Southgate. However, there is no evidence, archaeological or documentary, of such a defence prior to the construction of the town walls in the 14th century; indeed a document of 1300 records a beach immediately south of properties on Southgate.

Commerce

Calculations based on the modern tidal range indicate that the dock installations contained a depth of c 0.8m of water at Spring Mean High Water and would have been dry at Spring Mean Low Water (the bottom of the dock lay at 1.55m above OD, Mean High Water being 2.35m above OD). While the docks were deep enough to handle the smaller coastal vessels, larger vessels could not have docked and these must have been served by lighters. The minimal depth of water suggests that the port was expected to handle smaller rather than larger vessels, and that the type of trade envisaged was coastal rather than international. Both the archaeological and documentary evidence support this: there is a marked absence of identifiable north European imports in the town, a situation which contrasts markedly with the larger ports of Newcastle upon Tyne and Hull. This is not to suggest that there was no trade with the continent from the port; there are records of Hartlepool merchants trading abroad, and prior to the creation of the staple at Newcastle the town handled a volume of wool export. However, there is little to suggest that this trade was creating much wealth for the town.

From the end of the 13th century onwards the amount of coastal trade on the north-east coast increased dramatically, largely as a result of the Scottish wars. Hartlepool took full advantage of these increased opportunities and the 14th and early 15th centuries mark the peak of the town's economic prosperity.

Unfortunately, there is little evidence for the quayside structures of this period, with the exception of the wharf at the rear of the excavations on Area B at Southgate, outlined above. These lie beneath the present Fish Quay and its associated dock, excavated in the 19th century. However, it is at this period that it became worthwhile for the king to appoint a Collector of Customs to the town, and there are records of Hartlepool vessels and mariners being chartered by the government to carry supplies to Scotland.

In addition, there is evidence that many of the provisions were processed in the town. From the eight tenements excavated in the town to date all but one have had oven complexes which can only be described as commercial. These ovens have millstones and grindstones associated with them, and would seem to suggest the processing of materials into edible foodstuffs, such as bread and biscuits. Moreover, one oven encountered had a substantial deposit of herring bone associated with it, suggesting the small-scale drying of the fish (Daniels forthcoming). These oven complexes are spread throughout the town and not just concentrated on the harbour edge; they seem to indicate that a large section of the population took full advantage of the new financial opportunities.

Town walls

The Scottish wars also had a lasting effect on the appearance of the town and harbour (Fig 6.1). In 1316 the king was petitioned to allow the construction of walls around the town to enhance the defence offered by the ditch the townspeople had already dug across the peninsula. Permission for the construction of the walls was given and grants for their construction and maintenance were made throughout the 14th century (Daniels 1986b). The walls cut off the narrowest part of the peninsula, following the same line as the ditch. They then ran across the harbour, continuing up Southgate to finish at the cliffs to the east. The harbour entrance was guarded by two large circular towers which had a boom chain slung between. To the north of these there was a

Fig 6.4 Hartlepool: a cobble. Photograph by courtesy of Hartlepool Borough Council

watergate which was large enough to allow the fishermen to pass through with their cobbles. Only that stretch of wall along Southgate survives and this contains the Sandwell Gate, a later insertion into the wall. This may date from the late 15th century, when a pier was first constructed. The construction of the pier would have protected the area of beach in front of the Sandwell Gate and enabled the beaching of boats and the transference of cargoes at the gate, a procedure saving the journey around into the harbour, and still used in the 19th century. The gate may therefore have been built as a commercial convenience rather than as part of the defensive arrangements of the town, and this would explain a construction date as late as the 15th century, after the murage grants had ceased.

Fishing

Whilst the port handled many items, it is clear from both documentary and archaeological sources that fishing was probably the most important single item in the town's maritime economy. Extensive finds of fish bone from most excavations within the town confirm the predominance of cod and herring in the catch. Documentary records indicate that a large proportion of the catch was destined for the city of Durham and its ecclesiastical bodies. By 1325 there was a 'great herring house' in the town, at the harbour edge. This was built by the Brus family and later passed to the Prior of Durham, and it is worth considering whether there was

a compulsion on the fishermen to take their catch to the lord's herring house rather than dry it themselves. The lord of the manor also had the right to buy a proportion of the catch at a price he could determine. These two factors serve to show the importance the authorities placed on the town's fishing; the prior's accounts indicate the large quantities of fish being made available (*Dur Acct Rolls* I and II). The account rolls record the purchase of salted and fresh cod, whiting, and mackerel, but salted and dried herring predominate by far and the priory could consume as many as 2000 and 1900 fish in consecutive weeks. This attests either a remarkable appetite for herring amongst the monks, or good storage facilities! In order to purchase the fish, the prior employed a bursar within the town, supplying him with robes. The prior also purchased and hired fishing boats in order to be certain of fish for the Feast of St Cuthbert.

The fishing was relatively local and there is no suggestion of Hartlepool boats going as far as the Icelandic fisheries or the Dogger Bank. This must be a reflection of the boats used and the relatively small scale of the fishing industry, which could not rival that of Scarborough, one of the first ports to exploit the Icelandic fisheries on a large scale (Heath 1968). As far as can be ascertained, the vessel used was the cobble and in this the fishermen ventured up to 30 miles offshore. The medieval cobble probably did not differ much from that which is in use today, typically measuring 25ft by 5ft (7.5m by 1.5m), and weighing 3 tons (Fig 6.4). The

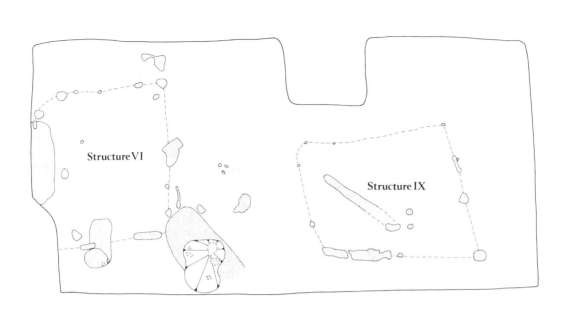

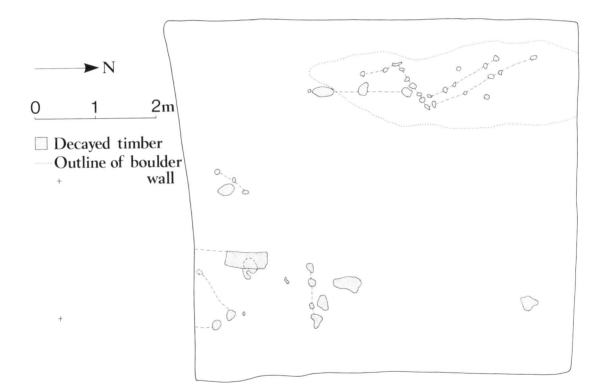

Fig 6.5 Hartlepool: Middlegate, shoreline structures

catch was probably sold on the beach, straight from the cobble, and could be bought by the cobble-load.

In addition to the fish bone, fishing hooks and possible weights have been recovered archaeologically, as have piles of mussel shells. The mussel was used to bait the lines with which the majority of fish were caught. Traditionally it was the job of the women to take the lines home and bait them, hence deposits of mussel shells beside a number of the buildings. Moreover, excavation at Middlegate revealed a series of shoreline timber structures of probable 13th century date which may relate to marine exploitation (Fig 6.5). They comprised a series of light timber fencelines forming a number of small subrectangular structures, perhaps used as holding tanks for crustaceans. They were succeeded by a boulder wall, parallel with the shoreline and made of igneous rocks, probably derived from ballast. This represented the first phase of reclamation of the shoreline and was contemporary with the reclamation on Southgate, both of which raised the land level by up to 1.5m. The area was then occupied by buildings (Daniels & Robinson forthcoming).

Later history

By the 14th century, the harbour facilities were pushing further north and west and the associated quayside activities would have followed. This resulted in the semi-industrial features which originally characterised Southgate giving way to a more polite residential area. With the end of the Scottish wars the economic impetus died out. By the beginning of the 16th century, there were large areas of waste within the town and it had long disappeared from the custom accounts. The harbour was slowly silting up and was enclosed for cultivation at the beginning of the 19th century (Sharp 1816, 151). However, with the construction of the railways for the coal trade the town began a new lease of life and the excavation of the Victoria Dock brought shipping back into the harbour. The Tees and Hartlepool Port Authority now constitutes the third largest port in the country, handling over 33 million tons of cargo annually, and current proposals for a marina should ensure Hartlepool's continuing links with the sea. The fishermen of the Headland have, of course, never disappeared.

Acknowledgements

Cleveland County Archaeology Section has undertaken an extensive series of excavations in Hartlepool since 1981. These have been funded by the Manpower Services Commission, Historic Buildings and Monuments Commission, and Cleveland County Council. The generous help of officers of Hartlepool Borough Council, in particular John Mennear and his staff at the Gray Museum and Art Gallery, cannot go unacknowledged. In addition my thanks go to Pip Robinson for allowing me to use the Middlegate material ahead of publication. The text was typed by Tracey Harper and Wendy Howells and the illustrations were produced by Peter Allison and Louise Hutchison. Blaise Vyner kindly read and commented on the text and permission for the reproduction of Figure 6.4 was given by Hartlepool Borough Council.

7 Poole: the medieval waterfront and its usage

I P Horsey†

Abstract

The commercial nucleus of medieval Poole lay between St James's Church and the Great Quay. Documentary sources suggest a timber quay during the 16th century, probably replaced by a stone quay later in that century. Maps of the 1630s suggest that part of the quay was little more than a shoreline. A new quay was constructed in 1618. Remains of another, less substantial, quay area have been excavated to the south and at the Poole Foundry site a jetty of oak piles and chalk blocks was recorded. Stacks of oak timbers representing a medieval boatyard's store of *c* 1500 undergoing wet seasoning were found. Some of the timbers had been salvaged from boats. Documentary evidence points to trade in a variety of commodities to north-western France and the Channel Islands.

Medieval Poole was virtually an island cut off from the heath of the mainland by a boggy and tidal dyke. Today the area of old Poole, *ie*, the area below the dyke and excluding the Baiter peninsula, occupies some 36.5 ha of which it can be estimated that 16.5 ha or 45% have been reclaimed since the late medieval period.

Poole is not mentioned in the Domesday Book: if any settlement had existed here (for which there is no evidence) it would have been included in the entry for Canford Manor. The first documentary reference to the town is dated 1196 × 1226 when the lord of the manor granted Canford church with its dependent chapel of St James at Poole to Bradenstoke Priory (Penn 1980, 78–83). The origins of the town are further considered below (Horsey & Winder, Chapter 13).

The present church of St James is a rebuilding of 1821. That the area between the church and the Great Quay formed the commercial nucleus of the medieval town is indicated by the building record. It is argued elsewhere (Horsey forthcoming) that the first constructional phase of the wool-house can be dated to *c* 1300 and that it may have formed part of a larger stone-built, L-shaped complex in association with a similar building whose foundations were excavated on the Thames Street frontage (Fig 7.1). On the corner of Sarum Street and Thames Street, Machin salvage-recorded a large first-floor hall of indeterminate date (Machin forthcoming).

The wool-house itself lies immediately behind the Great Quay. A document of 1558 describes the 'Bounds of the Quay' placing it in relation to other topographic features. The Great Quay was 240ft (73m) in length, bounded at one end by James Mesurer's house and at the other by the quay head beyond which was the water of the river above Poole, now Holes Bay. It is interesting to note that on the map of 1642 and in subsequent documents Holes Bay is located immediately to the west of the Poole peninsula: not until later did the name transfer to the bay to the east of Poole, formerly known as Longfleet Bay. According to the Bounds of the Quay the low water mark was 48ft (14.6m) from the wool-house. This may imply the absence of a continuous stone quay wall. Indeed several mid 16th century

references suggest that part of the quay may have consisted of little more than a shoreline. In 1551 17 men received 'a groat a tide' for carting up the 'filth' at the east end of the quay by the quay stairs. The reference to the quay stairs, taken together with the many references for wooden piles and timber boards, suggest the possibility of a timber quay. In 1564 there is an entry: 'For repayryring and new bylldyng at pt of the kay being fallin downe in to the sea £50'. The high cost of rebuilding suggests a stronger stone quay. In 1620 masons were paid to make repairs 'about the oll keye'. There are a number of references to 'posts to moor ships by' and 'millstones for anchorage'. There are also many references to carts operating on the quay. It is possible that larger vessels were either moored or beached offshore and that the carts were used in the loading/unloading process.

Access to the water continued to be via the Great Quay and private jetties. The Chief Rent of 1563 records 162 buildings including 26 'houses and piles', *ie*, jetties. The medieval shore ran along Strand Street and behind Thames Street (16th century Quay Street).

Building accounts survive for the construction of the New Quay in 1618 at a total cost of £27 8s 0d. This reclamation of the Strand Street jetties preserved the jetty and property lines in the arrangements of the alleys which survive today. The town plan of 1634 shows this reclamation, but only partial colonisation. Parallels to the Strand Street reclamation may be found at other British towns. Where built on a level site the reclamation zone is often found between a sinuous street laid out over the original river bank or shore, and the present day waterfront. Such topography can be found at King's Lynn and Hull, for example.

There has been no excavation in the Strand Street area although site observations of timber piles and an examination of the stratification confirm the nature of the waterfront interface. On the other side of the town, perhaps in a less commercially commanding position, an excavation at Newports revealed details of land reclamation and a comparatively slight waterfront revetment. The cartographic evidence suggests that land to the east of the site was reclaimed between 1634 and

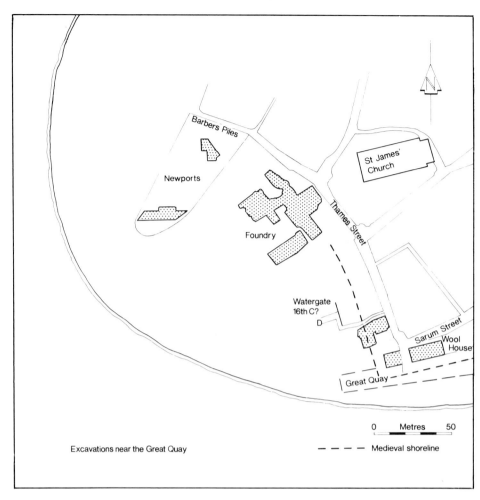

Fig 7.1 Poole: plan of excavated waterfront sites

1751. A layer of vegetation represented accretion at the water's edge sealed by black 'silts' during a subsequent phase of reclamation dated by pottery to *c* 1790. Barber's Lane could reflect late 17th/early 18th century reclamation of the 'piles' as similarly observed off Strand Street. The reclamation silts sealed evidence of the mid 18th century waterfront. A number of limestone slabs each measuring up to 1.75m × 0.75m were stood on edge in a row and revetted on the seaward side by timber piles. This appears to coincide with the high-tide line as marked on the map of 1751. Clearly this was not a substantial quay, but a relatively unsophisticated revetment designed for the mooring of small boats and to prevent the encroachment of high tides. The use of limestone slabbing is unusual and in marked contrast to many waterfronts excavated elsewhere. In London, for example, timber planking was the norm, sometimes featuring the reuse of boat timbers.

Excavations on the Poole Foundry site in 1987 produced evidence of a rather different kind, shedding important new light not only on the nature of the medieval waterfront and the urban topography, but also on the nature of land use on the foreshore. This rescue excavation was undertaken with two primary research purposes in mind: firstly, as the site is located only metres from Poole's only medieval church, it was hoped to find evidence of early settlement around the church; secondly, it was hoped to determine detailed evidence

for the nature of successive medieval waterfronts — based on the evidence from the Thames Street excavation, a linear sequence was expected.

The results of this excavation were, however, quite unexpected. Rather than the otherwise standard linear reclamation sequence, it was found that the area up to a wall extending at right-angles from the shore had all been reclaimed *c* 1500. On the west side of this wall an early post-medieval subrectangular jetty of oak piles and rough chalk blocks was uncovered. Dug into the pre-reclamation beach were over 60 substantial timbers, mostly of oak, found in stacks. These represent a medieval boatyard's store of timber which was undergoing wet seasoning in the tidal sands before being built into craft. The majority of timbers had been only roughly shaped and many still had bark attached.

The most important timbers were those that had been salvaged from built craft. A group of ten 'floor timbers' were found, cut to accept clinker planking and bored for the treenail fastenings. Another group of stem and stern posts included one with corroded iron fastenings still in place.

The evidence is that this timber stack dates to *c* 1500 or a little earlier. Other than from rare shipwreck sites, medieval boat timbers occur only occasionally reused in waterfront revetments; the only parallels to these Poole rough-outs are three 'knees', probably late medieval, found in a wicker pen on the foreshore at Kingston-upon-Thames (Potter this volume). The Foundry site is therefore important not only for the information it has provided on the medieval waterfront topography, but also because the timber store for a medieval boatyard is the first to be excavated. The reclaimed boat timbers are additionally important for understanding the nature of medieval coastal craft and methods of construction.

Indeed it is important when considering the nature and construction of medieval quays and wharves not to lose sight of their main purpose after containing and protecting the land; *ie*, they were also a means of providing deep-water berthing for shipping (but see Dyson 1981). Waterfront archaeologists must not lose sight of the trade which was taking place or of the ships which were engaging in that trade.

Maritime activities dominated Poole's character; besides commerce it was an important fishing town. During the late Middle Ages Poole, as a port of the staple, relied mostly on cloth for its exports together with smaller quantities of other products such as grain and beer brewed in Poole. It was, however, also importing a wider range of produce from Normandy, Brittany, the Channel Islands, and the Bay of Biscay, particularly wine, cloth, canvas, salt, and iron. Mr R Hairsine is currently analysing the customs accounts for Poole. Notwithstanding the incomplete nature of the documentary record, this will provide a statistical basis on which to analyse the town's trade in the late medieval period. We also need to know more about the ships, the carvels, the spinaces, and the balingers, recorded as entering the port.

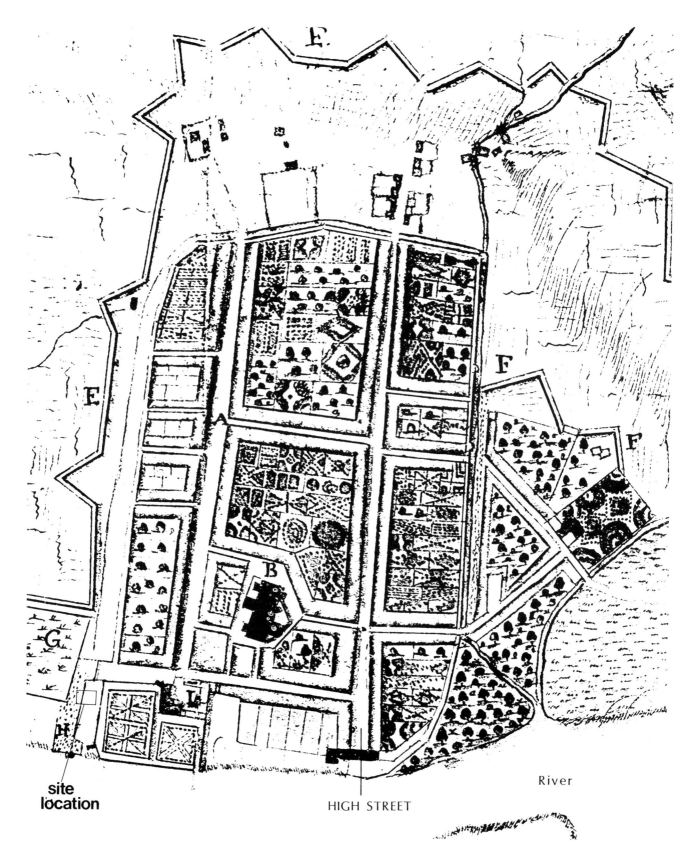

Fig 8.1 Perth: part of Louis Petit's plan of the Jacobite defences, 1715 (North is to the right)

8 The post-medieval harbour, Tay Street, Perth
D P Bowler

Abstract

Three harbour sites are known from Perth, which lies at the highest navigable point on the river Tay. The earliest originated in the 12th century and remained in use until the 19th. Excavation has confirmed the position of the second harbour, the New Haven, begun in the 16th century. The construction sequence for the main quay and harbour wall was examined. The robbed remains of two successive harbour walls, rubble built with ashlared faces, were recovered and a comparison of 18th century maps confirmed that the quay had been altered sometime between 1715 and 1774.

Introduction

During the autumn and winter of 1987/8, the Scottish Urban Archaeological Trust excavated a post-medieval harbour in Tay Street, Perth. The site had lain empty since the summer of 1984, when the Baptist church was destroyed by fire, and is now being redeveloped as sheltered housing.

Perth

Perth is on the eastern side of Scotland, at the highest navigable point on the river Tay. Until the 19th century, this was also the lowest bridging point. From Perth, the river valleys radiate, west up Strathearn towards Dunblane and the Forth valley, north up the Tay towards Dunkeld and the Highlands, and north-east up the Isla, through Strathmore to Forfar and Brechin.

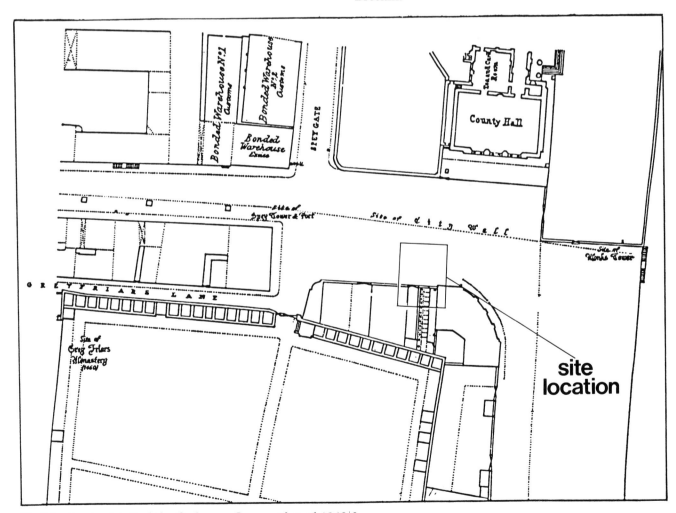

Fig 8.2 Perth: detail of the Ordnance Survey plan of 1862/3

Fig 8.3 Perth: view of County Hall from the east bank of the Tay showing the harbour basin being infilled. The low white building on the far left lies partly within the excavation area

Fig 8.4 Perth: view from the north of cobbled pavement built against the harbour wall, with 19th century foundations in the background

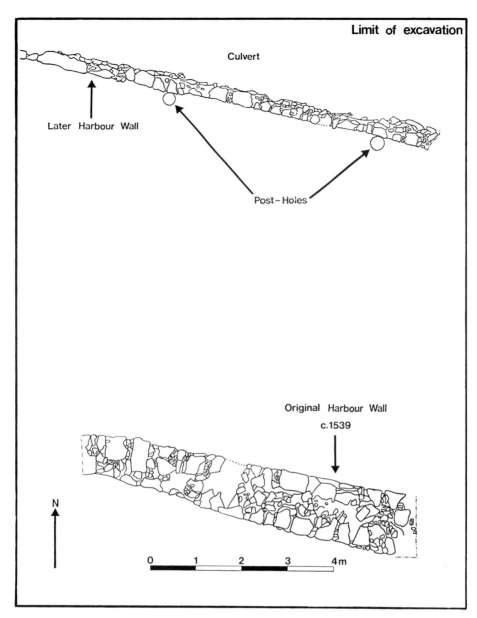

Fig 8.5 Perth: plan of harbour walls

The harbour

Three harbour sites are known. The earliest was close beside the bridge and was probably the original harbour of the burgh as founded by David I, just before 1127. It appears on the earliest map of Perth, of 1715, at the eastern end of the High Street, and remained in use into the 19th century (Fig. 8.1). There has been no controlled excavation here, but underpinning work beneath the council chambers has revealed timber structures nearly 5m below street level.

The second harbour is dated to 1539, when the Perth Guildry Book records that John Moncur of Balluny paid for the carriage of 200 ashlar stones for the New Haven by the Greyfriars. This harbour also appears on Louis Petit's map of 1715, up against the Greyfriars' burial ground (G on Fig 8.1). It is this harbour which was excavated by the Trust.

The third and final harbour site is at Friarton, about a mile down river. This superseded the first two in the

19th century, and like its predecessors, carries on a busy and growing trade with Scandinavia, the Baltic, the Low Countries, and the east coast of England.

The New Haven by the Greyfriars was built at the south-east corner of the town. Medieval Perth was bounded on the east side by the Tay and on the other three sides by a stone wall and wet ditch. The ditch was filled with water from the tail race of the City Mills, which stand just outside the north-west corner of the town. After leaving the mills, the mill lade divides in two. The northern branch flows straight along the northern boundary of the town and out into the Tay. The southern branch flows down the western boundary, then turns east, flows along the southern boundary, into the New Haven, and so into the Tay. The two branches of the lade remained open into the 19th century, when they were covered over with stone vaulted culverts and streets laid above them. The southern branch of the lade now runs underneath Canal Street.

Fig 8.6 Perth: the later harbour wall and post-holes from the east

The New Haven was formed by opening up the mouth of the southern lade, the canal, into a large basin, and building a stone quay on the south side of the basin, under the walls of Greyfriars. It was also known as the Coal Shore, and continued in use up to the 19th century. The canal was covered over by about 1806. After this, the basin was also covered over and filled, as shown on the Ordnance Survey plan of 1862/3, and also in an early photograph, but it was still possible to tie up ships along the Tay waterfront until the 1870s, when the Tay foreshore was embanked to form Tay Street (Figs 8.2 and 8.3). At the end of the 1870s an opera house was built over the site of the New Haven, opening its doors in 1881. The opera house was not a success, and was soon converted into a Baptist church, remaining in use until the fire in 1984.

The excavation

The excavation was placed so as to examine a strip extending from the basin across the harbour wall, into the make-up layers forming the quay, and up as close as possible to the walls of Greyfriars. The purposes were: to examine the construction of the harbour wall and quay, and anything sealed beneath them; to recover an assemblage of datable artefacts from the make-up layers; and to explore any links with Greyfriars adjacent.

The later structures were well preserved under the Baptist church. It was easy to recognise the foundations of buildings shown on the 1862/3 Ordnance Survey plan. These and a contemporary system of stone-built storm drains were cut into a very solid cobbled pavement. The pavement was set at an oblique angle, and built up against the top of what proved to be the harbour wall (Fig 8.4). The cobbles were set on end in a bed of clean sand and deeply ingrained with coal dust, a reminder that this was the Coal Shore. The outer, exposed face of the harbour wall had been robbed away. Springing from its foot was the barrel-vaulted stone culvert which now carries the canal under Canal Street and out to the Tay. Built into the vault were unusually long rectangular blocks, probably robbed out of the facing of the harbour wall.

When the cobbled pavement and its sand bedding were lifted, two large post-holes were found in a compacted layer beneath, hard up against the harbour wall (Figs 8.5 and 8.6). These seem to belong to mooring posts on the quay. The make-up layers behind the wall were more than two metres deep, mostly deep dumps of sand, clay, and shingle. At the back of the wall, the inside face was well built, but in rubble masonry, not squared blocks.

About 10m back from the harbour wall, close to the Greyfriars burial ground and the southern limit of the excavation, another wall was found, similar and parallel to the harbour wall (Fig 8.5). Again, the outside, northern face had been robbed away except at the very bottom, where one of the long rectangular facing blocks was still in place, while the southern inside face was built of rubble masonry. A careful comparison of Louis Petit's map of 1715 with the next oldest map, Rutherford's of 1774, shows that the New Haven was indeed altered between those dates (Figs 8.1 and 8.7). The quay seems to have been enlarged at the expense of the basin. It can be deduced that the southern, earlier wall is that shown by Petit in 1715, probably the original wall of 1539, with one of John Moncur's 200 ashlar stones still in place. The later, northern wall is that shown by Rutherford in 1774, which remained in use until the 19th century. The remaining 199 of John Moncur's stones were no doubt reused twice, once to build the new wall in the mid 18th century and again to build the culvert in the 19th century. Petit's map also shows a closure of some kind at the mouth of the basin, which is missing on Rutherford's. It was not possible to excavate the harbour mouth area to look for remains of this structure.

Conclusions

The excavation has successfully confirmed the location of the New Haven, and revealed an unexpected complication in its development. It has shown the significance of a previously overlooked variation in the map record. It has also provided a large and closely datable post-medieval artefact assemblage, in a town where this period is usually missing from excavated sites. The significance of this will emerge as the post-excavation process begins in earnest.

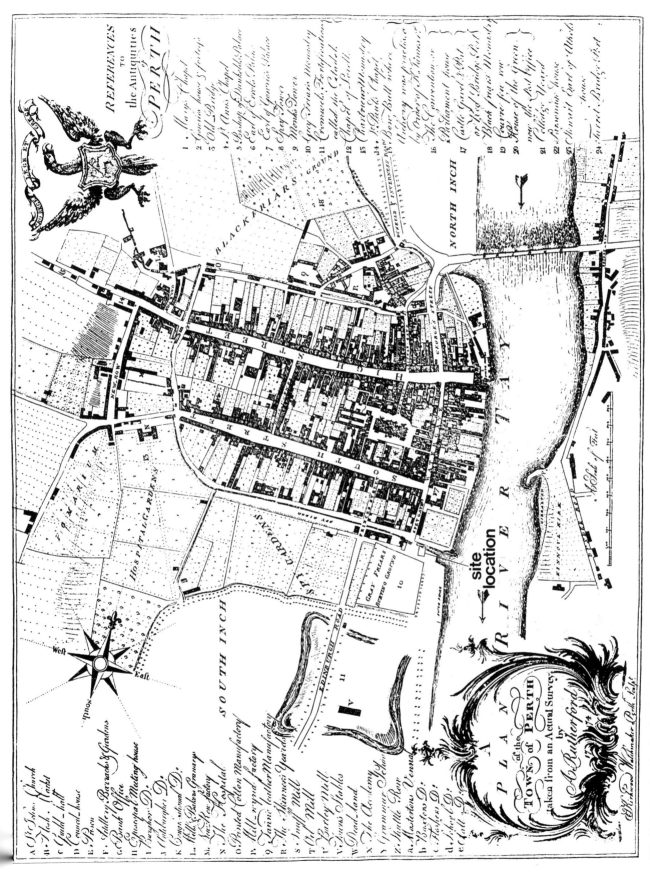

Fig 8.7 Perth: Rutherford's plan of 1774

9 Hythes and bows: aspects of river transport in Somerset

V E J Russett

Abstract

Major engineering works have substantially altered the course and flow of Somerset's major rivers. Much of this activity relates to drainage management of the Levels but the work has also affected the use of the rivers for transportation and the life of the county's ports. There are a number of small, mainly landlocked, ports but Bridgwater and Minehead achieved some status in the later medieval period. Bridgwater became a capital port in the 14th century and was able to handle sea-going vessels.

The ports of each of the major rivers are briefly discussed, with emphasis on those of the river Axe. Placename evidence for the location of other small rural landing-places is examined and the nature of possible archaeological remains described.

This study examines several aspects of medieval and post-medieval river transport in Somerset, broadly based around the following questions:

1 What is the evidence for river transport in medieval Somerset?
2 What goods were moved by water?
3 What was the relationship of Somerset's ports to the river trade?
4 What physical evidence survives of rural landing places and wharves?

Somerset is a large county in the west of England (Fig 9.1). It is rimmed by hills, the high moorland of Exmoor and the Quantocks on the west, the rolling hills south of the county in Dorset, and the hills of Mendip and Selwood to the east. Between the hills is the central low-lying area known as the Somerset Levels, an area of flat peat or alluvial deposits, lying less than 15m above sea-level and drained by the major rivers of Somerset.

The area has a complex settlement history. Its wealthy medieval monastic landowners, such as the abbeys of Glastonbury and Muchelney, and its other great landowners, such as the Bishop of Bath and Wells, and the Crown, contributed much to the formation of the current landscape. The major rivers have been substantially straightened, widened, and deepened, and even diverted from one area of the Levels to another. These immense water-engineering schemes were largely for the purposes of drainage for agricultural improvement, although the use of the rivers for transport was carefully regulated, especially by Glastonbury Abbey (Williams 1970).

Early maps of Somerset emphasised the river systems of central Somerset. Speed's map of 1610 shows that, while water transport was clearly possible in much of central and eastern Somerset, it was denied to the hillier upland districts of west Somerset which could only be served by road.

Goods arriving in the area from other parts of Britain (or further afield) arrived at the internationally important port of Bristol to the north of the county or at Bridgwater in its geographical centre (Fig 9.1). Until the middle of the 14th century, Bridgwater was a member port of Bristol. It then became a capital port in its own right, with jurisdiction for the Somerset coast between Brean Down and Porlock; the small harbours in the north-east of the county remained with Bristol. Bridgwater's small member ports were generally concerned with coastal trade, or with the Welsh and Irish trade. In 1540, for example, John Leland, King Henry VIII's antiquary, said of Minehead '...this town is exceding ful of Irisch Menne...' who were presumably there because of the town's trading links with Ireland (Bates 1887).

The village of Porlock has the tiny port of Porlock Weir attached, which probably only ever handled local traffic. Only yachts berth there today.

Minehead is a larger town, now a tourist resort, but still an active coastal port into the early years of this century, when it possessed a steam crane running on rails on the stone jetty which still survives (Binding 1983). The port was first recorded in the 14th century and weirage duties were regularly collected for the maintenance of the harbour. The Luttrell family developed the harbour at Minehead, probably to replace the small harbour on the river Avill at Dunster (Aston & Leech 1977) which seems to have been silting up. Even its location is today uncertain, although it has been suggested that it lay close to the south-west of the castle hill, a common position for wharves (as at Bristol and Bridgwater). Minehead's port was frequently damaged by storms throughout the medieval period, although a doleful but successful petition to Queen Elizabeth requesting a charter freeing the town from the manorial control of the Luttrells probably overstated its case when it said that the decay of the pier would very soon be the 'utter undowing' of the town (Hancock

60

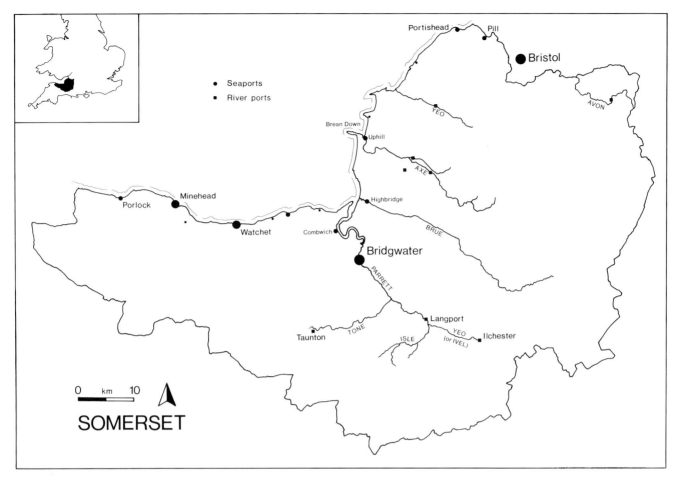

Fig 9.1 Somerset: location (inset), and ports and rivers of the pre-1974 county

1903). The imports and exports listed in the petition (cattle, sheep, woollen yarn and cloth, butter, stone and coal, oysters, salmon, and other kinds of fish) typify the materials passing through the ports at this date. They were largely a result of trade with South Wales at the time, although the Irish trade was still important.

Watchet was (and is) the other major port on the west Somerset coast. A victim of Viking raids in the 9th century, it was chosen as the site of a Saxon *burh*, thought to be at Daw's Castle above the town (McAvoy 1986). Its history is also full of destruction by storms, and spectacular photographs survive of the destruction of the last wooden jetty by the storm of 28 December 1900 (Wedlake 1984).

Harbours also existed at Lilstock, Kilve, and Combwich at various dates. These were much smaller, local harbours, although Combwich also served as the haven for local pilots guiding ships into Bridgwater, much as Pill did for Bristol (Elkin, this volume).

All the harbours of the west Somerset coast shared the fact that they were land-locked; none had a substantial river for trans-shipment of goods inland, unlike many of the coastal ports of central and north Somerset.

Many of the ports of northern Somerset were also small: Highbridge and the new port of Dunball have coal jetties today; Uphill was a trans-shipment port for the river Axe as well as a small port in its own right; and Portishead was always linked with Bristol and not really a Somerset port. The small harbours of Clevedon and Weston-super-Mare were never more than locally important, although as recently as the late 19th century attempts were made to establish a new harbour at Brean Down, near Weston-super-Mare. However, the grand opening ceremony and laying of the first stone was the farthest the project ever practically went. Like many of its predecessors in other ports along the Somerset coast, it was eventually wrecked by storms (Knight 1902).

It would not, however, have been necessary to have had huge and expensive stone harbours for all trade. Photographs exist of Welsh coal boats beached at Weston-super-Mare in the mid to late 19th century, with donkey carts being loaded up directly from the boat by shovel. It is likely that some informal arrangements of this kind always existed along the coast (information J Evans).

The biggest port of medieval Somerset was Bridgwater. A capital port from the 14th century at the latest, its very high tidal range allowed sea-going vessels to reach the town and the quay which lay below the castle. A long sequence of documentation exists for Bridgwater, much of it unpublished and only casually catalogued in the Somerset Record Office in Taunton. There are, for example, water bailiffs' accounts from about 1300 onwards, when the port of Bridgwater was still a member of Bristol, as well as many accounts of tolls on ships, coroners' enquiries concerning accidental deaths, and much other material concerning Bridgwater and its trade. These make it quite clear that the transshipment trade was very important and well-organised. There was, for example, a quay specially allocated to the boats plying the trade up the river to Langport. A post-medieval deposition recording an accident to one of these boats is revealing:

> The information of Benjamin Witts and Robt. Hartland both of Langport in the County of Somerset taken on their respective corporal oathes the twenty second day of September the year of our Lord 1743.....Who say that they these informants are employed by Thomas Biddle of Langport aforesaid, merchant, to Row conduct and Manage a boat or Lighter for carrying and transporting Goods and Merchandizes to and from the towns of Bridgwater and Langport aforesaid and Say that yesterday a ffair being held at the town of Bridgwater called Saint Matthews ffair these Informants fell down the river from Langport to Bridgwater aforesaid with the said boat or Lighter in order to get a ffreight of Goods and accordingly they took on board Diverse Goods belonging to several persons and the said Boat or Lighter being moderately loaden these Informants lay with the same in the river at the Back Key at Bridgwater.....near a place called Langport Slip there waiting for the coming in of the tide in order to proceed to Langport.....and say that about five of the clock yesterday in the Afternoon, the tide came in and no other boat being bound for Langport that Tide, a great number of people who had been at the said ffair to witt about 70 or 80 people crowded into the said boat just as the tide came in, and being in a great hurry and confusion at the going off of the said boat, all the said people run to one side of the boat, and the tide being very strong and rapid, the said boat suddenly overset... (SoRO D/B/la 32)

Saint Matthew's fair is still celebrated in Bridgwater but the transport of goods to and from the fair is now by road. The references to the commonplace transport of goods in the deposition are of interest in that sea-going vessels were prevented from travelling any further up the river Parrett than Bridgwater by the narrow arches of the medieval town bridge, while the Back Quay lies on the upstream side of the bridge.

The transport of materials inland from Bridgwater was a constant feature of its port activities. Salt, coal, millstones, ironmongery, and fine pottery are mentioned in the post-medieval accounts as imported through the docks (SoRO D/B/bw 1981), and wine, wheat, barley, beans, and peas in the 14th century (Dilks 1933), while wood ashes, corn, cheese, and manufactured cloth were exported. The huge commercial export trade in earthenware and rooftiles which was carried on in the 19th century resulted in the distribution of Bridgwater rooftiles to Europe; they are not uncommon in Brittany, for example (information M Batt).

Most of the dock facilities visible at Bridgwater today are 19th century in date, although traces of possible medieval structures have been seen during pipe-trenching in the town (Bridgwater 1977). Bridgwater has tremendous potential for further archaeological work and the possibility of preserved wooden waterfronts of traditional type is high.

The Parrett was also the key to trading further inland, to Taunton via the Tone (Fig 9.1). The river Tone was later supplanted by a canal, itself now derelict, but due in the near future to be restored for use. Ilchester was also reached, via the Ivel, and Roman wharves have been suggested on the course of the river

to the north of the present village (Leach 1982). Other smaller rivers like the Cary would have made it possible to pass even further inland with small vessels.

Gerrard has illustrated the distribution of Ham Hill stone, an easily recognisable yellow limestone quarried near the headwaters of the river. By plotting the occurrence of this stone in churches, he has been able to show a clear correlation with the line of the river Parrett, interesting secondary evidence for the transport of the stone by water (information C Gerrard).

The Brue was certainly used for navigation in the medieval period, although its present course is largely the result of centuries of alterations to the river's course. These began with its rerouting by the Abbot of Glastonbury away from the Panborough Gap, through which it had once flowed to join the Axe, and towards an eventual outfall to the sea at Highbridge. As this immense drainage scheme proved inconvenient for the abbey's water-transport, a new route was developed along the Pill Row Cut between the new course of the river Brue and Rooksbridge (Rookysmylle in the medieval period) (Williams 1970). Other users of these waterways are recorded. In 1500, for example, the churchwardens of St John's church in Glastonbury commissioned one Davit Carver of Bristol to make new seats for the church. They purchased them at a cost of £41 in Bristol and then, 'at the Back by Temple Friers' in Bristol, hired two 'great boats' to carry the seats to Rooksbridge, which cost in total 34s 4d. They were then trans-shipped to 13 smaller vessels from Meare, a small village near Glastonbury, and taken, presumably along the Pill Row Cut and the Brue, eventually to Maydelode bridge at Glastonbury for a further 15s 1d. The whole 70km trip by water cost a modest £2 9s 5d. In comparison, the cost of moving them the last 1km or so to the church, with a horse and wagon, was 9s (Daniel 1895).

The churchwardens listed other goods travelling by water, such as timber brought in 1458 along what must have been very narrow rhynes from Steanbow bridge at Pilton, 4km to the east of Glastonbury. The goods probably began their journey to Glastonbury at Steanbow for much the same reason as the sea-going ships in Bridgwater, that the bridge was too small to permit further progress. Glastonbury Abbey attempted to control the height of bridges over its waterways but the tiny bow bridges must have posed considerable problems for river users. It seems no coincidence that later bow bridges, for example at Hythe and Clewer in the Axe valley, lay immediately upstream of known boat landing places.

The Axe valley in central Somerset is typical of the river systems used for extensive trade during the medieval period (Fig 9.2). The small port of Uphill at the mouth of the river was documented in the medieval period and later; for example, when one Henry Moyle, out of Uphill, had piratically seized a large Scottish merchant vessel during the reign of Henry VIII (Hancock 1903). The port was certainly very active during the 16th and 17th centuries when the trade in Welsh cattle was at its height. These cattle were brought from South Wales to be fattened in Somerset, before being driven to the markets of Bristol (information J Bettey).

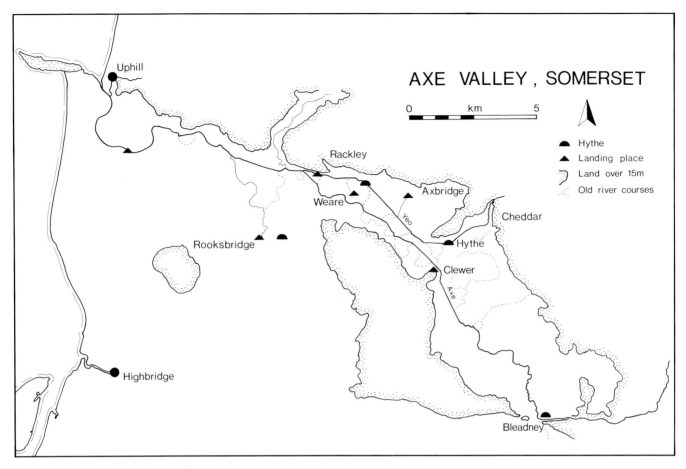

Fig 9.2 Somerset: the Axe valley

Inland from Uphill the river is almost entirely an artificial construction. The Axe rises in the cave at Wookey Hole, near Wells, and runs across the valley to Wookey and eventually to the Panborough Gap, where it was once greatly enlarged by a tributary bringing through the water of the Brue from the Brue valley. At the meeting point of these two rivers was the hythe documented at *Bledenithe* in 712 (when it was presented by Forthhere, bishop of Sherborne, to Glastonbury Abbey) and 1065 (Finberg 1964), which was at modern Bleadney, near Wells. The former site of the hythe has been discovered (information H Hudson) and it could have served the purpose of ferrying goods from the Axe (and, therefore, from the sea) to Wells and, centuries later, perhaps the Abbot of Glastonbury's grapes from the adjacent Panborough vineyard to his abbey. The journey through the Panborough Gap could still be made in 1276, when a court case at nearby Andresey (modern Nyland, near Cheddar) revealed that the Abbot of Glastonbury had a right of navigation in the river Axe. To improve the draught of the river, he had banks built on either side and had recently increased the height of one bank still further by building a 'wall' (the local term for a turf and mud bank). After a dispute between the abbot and some local worthies (including a local nobleman, Thomas de Baeuse, and Walter de Lawerton, the parson of nearby Rodney Stoke) concerning the grazing rights on the (old) bank, the commoners had taken the law into their own hands, demolished 103 perches of the bank (about 500m), and

blocked the river, causing extensive flooding of the abbot's lands in the manor of Andresey. During the court case that followed, the Jury decided

'... the bank is of old time, and that by the water channel alongside the bank, the abbot and his predecessors had a thoroughfare by their boats to go from their manor of Andredesye to the abbey of Glastonbury, carrying their corn, their stone and their lime to the abbey, and from the abbey to Andredesye and to other places.....because the bank was old and not worth repair, the abbot had rebuilt it entirely...' (Landon 1926).

In this way Glastonbury Abbey jealously maintained its rights in the waterways of central Somerset. In the Axe valley, however, the right of navigation along the river eventually took second place to the demands of agriculture. By the 14th century, the demands of a growing population for food were such that the draining of the Axe valley was undertaken. Both the river Axe and later its smaller tributary, the Yeo which flowed from Cheddar, were canalised and straightened. The old courses survive today in many places as small ditches, recognisable by their curvilinear shape among the straight lines of the later 18th century ditches of the Enclosure period. They are also frequently followed by parish boundaries, emphasising their early date.

The Axe was not closed to trade, however, and remained navigable to small sea-going vessels until the early 19th century, when a renewed interest in drainage led to the construction of lock-gates at Lympsham, near the mouth of the Axe, for better regulation of drainage.

Until this time, the river had remained tidal for many miles up its course.

Three recorded ports, albeit of modest size, lay inland from Uphill. The small port of Rackley is represented today by a single farm and a handful of small houses. In 1179, the Pope confirmed a charter to the Bishop of Bath and Wells concerning the village of Compton (Bishop) with the port of Radeclive (Rackley), which King Richard I affirmed by a further grant in 1189. Rackley was in decline at the latest by 1390 (Aston & Leech 1977). The port presumably failed to compete effectively with other ports on the Axe, such as Weare, and off it, such as Rooks Mill (present-day Rooks-bridge). The position may have been chosen for its proximity to the bishop's portion of the medieval town of Axbridge, or it may have been the position of Rackley which determined that the new course of the river Yeo would be cut to this point at some time in the medieval period. Although Rackley was probably never a large and thriving port, it was remembered as of former importance. When the watercourses of the Yeo and Axe were cleaned of vegetation each year to keep the drainage as clear as possible, Rackley was one of the specific points mentioned in the documents. Again, when the great storm of 1703 generated a flood that washed away the sluice gates from a drained area of the Levels in the moor at Cheddar, about six miles away, the moorwardens of Cheddar despatched a rider to Rackley to recover them (SoRO DD/SAS 212 for 1703).

Weare, another small medieval town, privately founded by the Gournay family around 1190, achieved some local status, and burgage plots were referred to in the town in the 14th century. The river Axe runs very close, and 'port' field names are recorded on the Tithe Map of 1840 on a relict course of the river about half a mile from the settlement. The Bristol to Bridgwater route, which ran through the town until the building of the M5 motorway in the early 1970s, may well have been the original reason for the original foundation. A well-known dispute between the Bishop of Bath and Wells and the Master of Gaunt's Hospital, Bristol, in 1316, concerned the blockage of the river by mills at Weare. This reflects concern not only about the drainage being impeded, but probably the passage of goods on the river (Baildon 1914).

Larger sea-going vessels could make the trip up-river to Rooksbridge as late as the 15th century. Edmund Whittok, from Cheddar, was in the year 1400 found to be in possession of items of armour from a sea-going vessel that had foundered at 'Rokysmylle'; other items, such as cloth and metalwork, were lost and in possession of other locals, and in the end, the Abbot of Glastonbury took in no less than £1000 worth of materials for safe keeping (*Cal Inq Misc*, 1399–1422, 163). The site of the wharf at Rooksbridge is not known. It may have been by the bridge carrying the modern A38 trunk road over the Pill Row Cut, where large quantities of sherds of late 16th century ceramic cream pans have been found in dredging operations [information R Myles]. The pottery was manufactured at Nether Stowey, some 25km away on the far side of Bridgwater. Since sherds of large ceramic vessels from this kiln source are very common on 16th and 17th century sites

in both rural Somerset and urban Bristol, it seems likely that any commercial load of this pottery would have travelled by water. The other major medieval and post-medieval pottery industries of Somerset (the 12th/13th century industry at Ham Green, near Pill, and the medieval and post-medieval industries of Donyatt in south Somerset, and Wanstrow in east Somerset) would probably have used water transport extensively. The large quantities of Wanstrow pottery used in Bristol in the 16th to 18th centuries, for example, are much more likely to have arrived via the Avon and Frome rivers, which lie within 2km of the kiln sites at Wanstrow and Truddoxhill, than by the tortuous overland route from Frome to Bristol (Good & Russett 1987).

In the Axe valley, there is some documentation for other landing sites besides those relating to the trans-shipment ports and small medieval towns.

The examination of place-names in the search for rural landing places is helpful, but must be carried out with care. The place-names 'port', 'wharf', and 'hythe' have been studied, with mixed results. Although Bledenithe was referred to as a *porta* in 712, the word has several meanings. The 'port' field-names at Weare may well refer to landing places, but the other Old English meaning of 'port' (a town, or object relating to a town) is very common in Somerset, hence the numerous 'Portway' names (= a road leading to the town), and perhaps field-names such as Port Meadow, of which there is a well-documented example at Oxford, meaning simply 'the town meadow'.

'Wharf' from the Old English *hwearf* was a more promising candidate. It certainly has the modern meaning of 'a landing place for boats or ships', as it has been used in this paper. The place-name Uphill Wharf on the Uphill tithe map of 1840 refers to the port, while the later canal ports, such as Chard and Taunton, used the word in that sense. There are many examples on local rivers such as Wick Warth at the mouth of the Congresbury Yeo, and Bleadon Wharf on the Axe. In cases like these, the name seems from local fieldwork to mean something like 'area of bank or artificially raised land next to a river'. Toller & Bosworth (1976) only quote this type of example; it may be that the 'landing-place' sense is a later development of the word.

The third name, 'hythe', which is fairly common in the east of England, has the precise meaning 'a (small) landing place for boats on a river', a meaning retained, at least in the west of England, up to the present. Gelling (1984) discusses the name, and refers to the groups on the Thames in London, and in the Cambridgeshire Fens. She points out that the place-names sometimes give information about the structures at such sites; for example, Stockwith in Lincolnshire suggests an association with tree-trunks, and there are various 'clay' and 'gravel' hythes.

Four of the six 'hythe' place-names recorded in Somerset occur in the Axe valley (information M Costen). These are Bleadney Hythe, as documented in the 8th and 11th centuries (above); Hythe House, at Cross, near Axbridge on the new course of the river Yeo, where it coincides with the old loop of the river Axe which also contains the Weare 'port' names; a 'hythe' field-name on the Badgworth tithe map of 1840 which may refer to Rooksbridge; and the simplex settle-

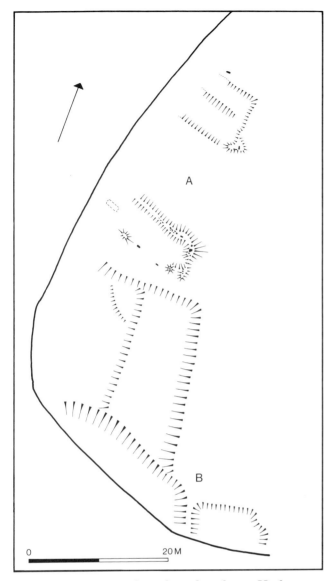

Fig 9.3 Somerset: plan of earthworks at Hythe, near Cheddar

ment name Hythe, near Cheddar, first recorded in 1212, but there extrapolated back to the 12th century (*Book of Fees* 1, 82). The earthworks at Bleadney Hythe are under investigation. Cross and Badgworth have yet to be looked at but Hythe has been intensively studied.

Although first recorded in 1212, disturbance of the occupation site at Hythe by badgers has revealed 11th century pottery in sufficient quantities to indicate settlement of pre-Conquest date. The 1212 record and all subsequent documentation until the final desertion of the site in the 18th century is concerned with agricultural matters. The hamlet is referred to as *La* Hythe until the 15th century (for example in the *Mendip Forest Perambulation* of 1219, Gough 1930) implying the existence of, or knowledge of, a landing place although the name becomes simply Hythe after that date.

A survey of the area (Fig 9.3) shows a few surviving but incomplete earthworks at Hythe, indicating the site of two buildings (A), and two low-level, apparently metalled platforms at the southern end of the site (B), next to a ditch and hedge which run along the line of an

abandoned river course. Documentary sources indicate buildings standing in this and the adjacent field until the 18th century (Verrey 1788); the name is now applied to two 19th century farms on the Cheddar to Wedmore road 500m away.

Around this central feature is an area of about 10ha of small fields surrounded by a low bank, all called 'At Hythe' (SoRO DD/WY Cheddar). No other name ever seems to be recorded for them; they may be the original infield of the settlement. Beyond and in an arc to the east are woodland clearance and wood-edge names (SoRO TPH/Vch/325) and beyond this, field-names indicate the existence of about 3km^2 of woodland called Hythe Wood in the medieval period.

To the west of the settlement, a large area of land in the alluvial levels, drained in the early 14th century, was named Hythe Ham (LRO Box 23 WMR). This area was later cultivated, and frequent medieval references were made to the 'Clyce' by which it was drained (*eg* SoRO TPH/Vch/324 1459); it was cut off from Hythe about a century later by the construction of the new watercourse of the Cheddar Yeo, as the field-names Hythe Load Batch in the area indicate (*eg* Highlode 1503 (LRO 5674), from the Old English *lad*, Middle English lode = an artificial watercourse). The other 'hythe' names in the area have not developed in this fashion, and the special status implied for Hythe by this is probably connected with the existence of the Cheddar Royal estate.

As Corcos (1983), among others, has pointed out, many very large middle Saxon estates existed in Somerset. Each possessed several settlements, which from place-name evidence are thought to have performed specialist functions within the structure of the estate, and the 'Shapwick' (= sheep farm) names of Somerset and Dorset are quoted as examples of this. Most settlements are thought to have lost their original names when the break-up of the multiple estates, along with the development of open fields and village nucleation and replanning, occurred in the 9th to 10th century. Hythe, with its evidence for Saxon occupation, a defined role recognised by its simplex place-name, and its location, may be one of the rare settlements that have not lost the original specialist name; if this was so, it would have fitted into a late Saxon estate at Cheddar similar to that in Figure 9.4.

The final question is whether it is possible to detect and examine any physical remains of the rural landing-places discussed in this paper.

In the Somerset levels, many of the major rivers have been extensively enlarged for drainage purposes over the last half-century, and any structures which once stood on or by them have probably long since been destroyed. Field survey of the known landing-place at Clewer on the Axe, for example, revealed no surviving structures, and merely a hint of activity in the form of pottery scatters in the adjacent field, perhaps derived from the known medieval settlement (Russett 1987).

It is a counsel of despair, however, to suggest that all evidence for these rural landing-places has been destroyed. At Glastonbury, for example, excavations by C and N Hollinrake have detected a possible waterside structure of upright timbers by the side of an artificial watercourse at Fairfield (information C Hollinrake).

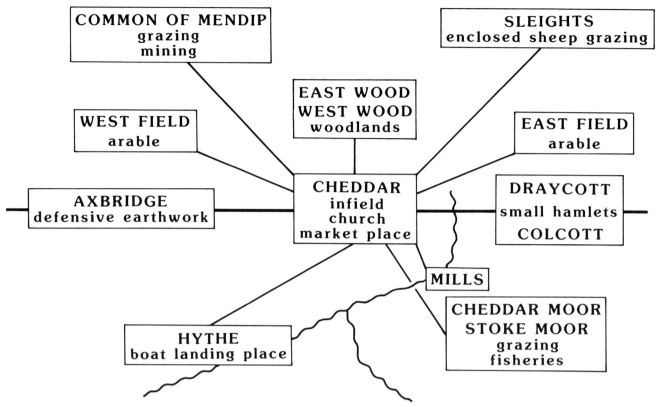

Fig 9.4 Somerset: hypothetical structure of the late Saxon royal estate at Cheddar

Further, Albany Major (1911) described the partial exposure of a wooden structure at Brinscombe near Weare, which may also have been a waterside jetty or other structure. The site is not identified closely in the report, but from the description it was certainly on the old course of the river Axe abandoned in 1317 when the New Cut was made from Clewer to Weare. No documentary evidence for its existence in the form of field-names seems to have survived, and Major was happy to have simply proved that the structure was not that of a boat.

At the simpler landing-places, a single stone may have been used as a mooring place on the bank of the river. This was the case at Rackley in the early 20th century, where a stone well-head of 19th century date had been buried on edge in the bank and used as a

mooring stone (Hack 1988); even an upright post or convenient tree may have sufficed at the smaller landing places, and clearly evidence for these will be almost impossible to find.

Any settlement that carries out the functions of a landing-place long enough to be given a name describing that function, such as hythe or staithe, will probably have had some structural adaptations to its role, such as revetments of the river-bank or metalling of surfaces. These should be detectable in the archaeological record. Accordingly, the line of research now being pursued is to attempt to identify possible landing places for boats on abandoned river-courses. If the survival of structures or environmental deposits at these sites can be demonstrated, then a strong case for full investigation of a rural waterfront can be made.

10 Aspects of sea-level changes, fishing, and fish processing in Tønsberg in the Middle Ages
J Lindh

Abstract

A project of waterfront excavation work is described in which three main sites have been excavated. A shoreline with beachside structures pre-dating the earliest known settlement (12th century) has been identified. Changes in the alignment of buildings suggest several phases of occupation. Problems in dating the foundation of the settlement at Tønsberg are discussed and the effects of known changes in sea-level on the medieval coastline considered. The main channel would have been very narrow, shallow and prone to heavy sedimentation, possibly making it impassable to boats. Dredging is mentioned in 13th century documents. Evidence for a jetty and possible ferry are discussed.

It is possible that the centre of medieval trade may not have been the site of the present town but situated outside the channel at the head of a bay. Work on the remains of about 20 small ships has revealed vessels which were worn-out and being stripped down. A possible shipbuilding yard has been identified. Abundant sea-water fish remains are recorded as well as fishing equipment and skewers and pins used in the drying of fish.

The town and its surrounding district

Tønsberg, on the western side of the Oslofjord, has a hidden but still strategic location by the Tønsberg fjord. The medieval town lay on the western slopes of the Tønsberg Peninsula (Fig 10.1) between the fortified hill to the north and a rock outcrop to the south (Fig 10.2). There are two barrows on top of the outcrop. These are undated, but are probably from the late Iron Age period. The south-west facing slopes are favourable for farming. In fact, many historians claim there were two or three farms there in the Iron and Viking Ages (Gjessing 1913, Johnsen 1929). Many traces of ploughing exposed in the excavations confirmed this. Soil samples from some of the ploughmarks have been dated by radiocarbon to periods earlier than the medieval. Many are of the Viking Age, but some date as far back as the Bronze Age (Brendalsmo 1986, 34). The fortification on the hill to the north, and the hill itself, are vital when it comes to discussing the premises for the rise of the town. From the hill the view is excellent and suitable for a military observation post with an outlook over the vital routes into the Tønsberg fjord. The importance of the hill and the fortification will, however, not be a subject for this paper.

Today there are two ways into the sheltered inner fjord where the harbour and the medieval quays have been excavated: from the south through the long and narrow Vestfjord, and from the east through the so called 'Kanalen', ie, the channel.

The sites within the project

The research of the last four years has been based on three large excavations located in the southern part of the medieval town (Fig 10.2):

A The Bank site

This contained remains — mainly buildings — dating from the early 12th to the late 15th centuries. The zoological samples referred to below were collected on this site (Lindh 1984).

B The Britannia site

As far as this paper is concerned, the finds from this site are, in this context, not comparable with the finds from the other two sites because of the difference in date of the remains that were excavated. Most of the finds here are late or post-medieval.

C The Long Trench

Located in Nedre Langgate, the remains of quay constructions and infilling in the fjord dated c 1250 – c 1400. The excavation uncovered more than twenty medieval boundaries in a narrow section through the buildings and passages, leading from the main street down to the waterfront.

The shoreline

On the Bank site, in the earliest phase, there were traces of what was believed to be a shoreline. There were also remains of a fence dividing the beach area, and postholes indicating buildings situated on the beach (Fig 10.3). A number of samples was taken, and the botanical analysis provided clear evidence of a shoreline, by the presence of *Ruppia* and *Carex*, two plants usually found in shallow water close to the shore (Griffin 1984). There was a remarkably large number of macrofossils of these plants in the samples taken from just below the present sea-level, +3.5m (c 11.5ft).

Fig 10.1 Tønsberg: the peninsula from the south-east. In the background is the Tønsberg fjord and the mouth of the river Auli; to the right is the Bay of Træla

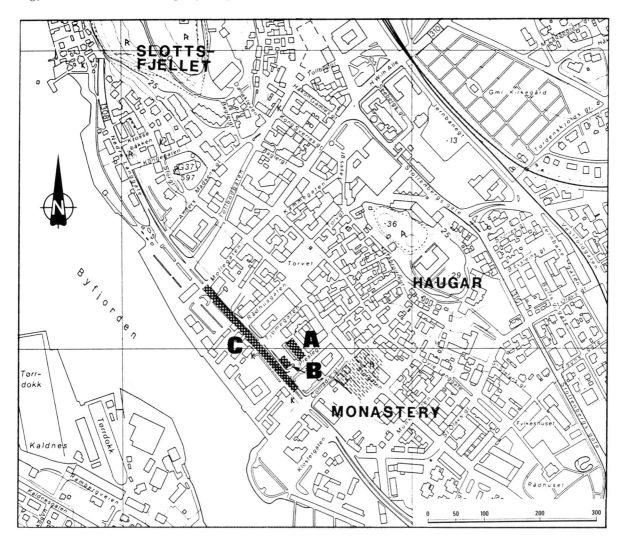

Fig 10.2 Tønsberg: map of the town centre and location of excavations A, B, and C. To the north is the fortified hill 'Slottsfjellet', and to the east the rock outcrop called 'Haugar', where the local Thing and coronations sometimes took place in the Middle Ages. South-east of the excavations is the location of the monastery of St Olav

The lack of finds associated with the shoreline phase was a problem. There was enough organic material in the sample for this to be radiocarbon dated, and from two of the samples a date of AD 1000–1050 was obtained. However, the finds from the period after the shoreline phase did not indicate a date earlier than the early 12th century. So it seems that the remains from the shoreline phase must belong to a period some time before the earliest settlement which could be called urban.

This theory is not based on radiocarbon dating alone. By looking at the structure of the first phase and comparing it with those in the later phases, a difference in the property alignments is found, particularly in their orientation (Fig 10.4). In the earliest phase the orientation of the fence was 67° from a north-south line, while there is an 8° difference in the alignments in the later phases. The orientation of the fence was at right-angles to the shoreline. It is not possible to say what the later orientation meant in relation to the shoreline, since, within the excavation area, no later quay or other frontage to the water was found.[1] However, the difference in the orientation of the alignment is most likely a

result of a change in direction of the shoreline, and it indicates that the intention was to have an alignment at right-angles to the water (Lindh 1980). The alignment, over the early fence, is found in the same place and through all the phases, even in today's building structure. This might not be unusual in itself, but the new property alignment, with the new orientation, had one aspect in common with the old one, namely the starting point close to the beach.

Since the change in orientation seems to have taken place some time before urbanisation, the point by the sea where the property alignment starts must have been of some significance in the period prior to any urbanisation. Perhaps it was the boundary between two of the farms on the peninsula, in which case the boundary and the ownership of the land was so important that the urbanisation process did not have any influence on it.

Sea-level change — the channel

A major question for archaeologists in Tønsberg is the age of the town. Patriots claim that Snorri Sturlason is to be trusted when he talks of Tunsberg as a *kaupstadir*

Fig 10.3 Tønsberg: the Bank site, showing the beach area in the first phase, with stake-holes indicating the fence

(a trade centre) even before the battle of Hrafsfjord, previously assumed to have taken place in AD 872 (Johnsen 1929, 38ff). However, the archaeological evidence for a town or urbanised settlement as old as that is lacking, at least in the central area of the modern town where most of the excavations have been carried out (Eriksson 1986). In 1988, however, a Viking Age cemetery was excavated in the southern part of the medieval town area and there are also other Viking Age finds from Tønsberg. In this context there is a key question to be answered. Is there any possibility that there was a *kaupstadir* here as early as is claimed, but perhaps located in another area of the peninsula? This is a question to come back to later.

In order to get a clear picture of the landscape and the 'seascape' of the Tønsberg peninsula, it has been estimated, on the basis of the plant remains and their habitat, that the water-level at the end of the Viking Age was *c* 4m (13ft) above present mean sea-level, *ie*, 3.5m plus the normal tidal fluctuation. Extreme high tide has not been taken into consideration, although a high tide of nearly 2m above normal sea-level is not unlikely.

The map (Fig 10.5) shows the coastline with a sea-level drawn in at +4m. It can be seen that Tønsbergfjord was more than double the size of the fjord today. Of course the depth of water must have been very shallow over large areas in the bottom of the fjord. However, this cannot have been such a large problem. The draught of an Oseberg-sized ship, for example, with men and cargo was not more than *c* 0.75m (2ft 6in) (Ellmers 1972, 256). The Saga tells that it was here, in the fjord near Tønsberg, that the fleet of warships (*Lei-*

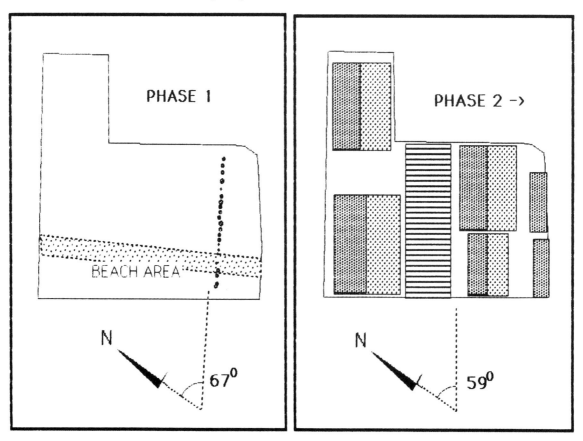

Fig 10.4 Tønsberg: the Bank site, the directions of the alignment in the pre-urban phase and in the later phases

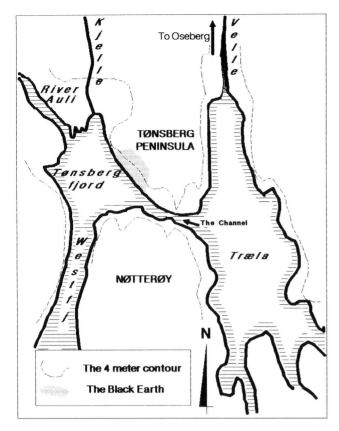

Fig 10.5   Tønsberg: the peninsula and surrounding district. The dotted line indicates the sea-level c 1000 years ago

dangen) was to gather together. The number of ships could be as many as 300–400, as mentioned in contemporary documents. The map also shows a deep bay east of the peninsula. The medieval coastline here runs halfway to the Oseberg barrow from today's coastline. The higher sea-level also means that the peninsula would have been narrower and therefore could easily have been protected from attack from the north.

A remarkable detail of the reconstructed medieval coastline is the wide strait between the mainland and the island of Nøtterøy to the south, remarkable because the medieval name of the strait — *Skjeljasteingrunn* or *Skjeljasteinsund* — indicates that it was both narrow and shallow. It is also known that King Håkon Håkonsson in the middle of the 13th century gave orders to dredge the channel so the '4m reconstruction' can hardly be trusted in this very special area. But it is not only the sea-level change that has made the channel less navigable, there is also considerable transport of clay and sand from the river Auli out into the fjord. The amount of sediment has been estimated to be *c* 27,000m³ (*c* 35,000 cu yd) per year (N I V 1966). In relation to the channel, this means that theoretically the sediment could fill the strait between the mainland and Nøtterøy in less than 7 months. Of course, only a small part of the total amount would have been deposited in the narrow

channel, but still, as today, there must have been a need for regular dredging operations if the channel was to be navigable.[2] As an illustration of the problem, it can be mentioned that many of the citizens of Tønsberg built their own jetties on the eastern part of the peninsula in the 16th century because of the overgrown and unnavigable channel.

As already mentioned, the changes in topography mean that today's contour cannot be followed uncritically and be expected to give a true picture of the medieval topography. With survey drillings on the peninsula it was hoped that more evidence could be gained, but close to the channel, changes caused by dredging, digging, and infilling in the area mean that this kind of survey will not give the required information. Therefore other signs must be sought to prove or disprove any theory concerning the actual topographical situation by the channel.

In the written sources (Robberstad 1923) there is information about a jetty belonging to the Premonstratensian convent of St Olaf at the south end of the town. The jetty is called *Farkarlsbryggjur*, interpreted as 'the jetty of commercial traders', an interpretation from which the writer dissents. Why place a traders' jetty on the outskirts of the town, and why at a monastery? What made this jetty so special that it deserved that special name? There must have been many jetties for traders in Tønsberg in the Middle Ages. The Old Norse word *Far* in *Farkarlsbryggjur*, however, also has the meaning of transportation on water of goods and people, *ie*, ferrying. It can surely be assumed that there was some kind of ferry between the mainland and island of Nøtterøy in the Middle Ages — maybe not in the meaning of regular public transport, but certainly there must have been some kind of service for those who did not have their own boat. But why was there a ferry from a monastery's jetty? The answer might be that the residence of the bishop, Teie, lay right across the channel on the Nøtterøy side, and the convent was favoured by both the king and the bishop, at least for a period. The right to run ferries might have been a privilege for them. So the jetty is likely to have been for local communication. Its location, away from the narrowest part of the strait, must therefore be seen in the light of the navigability of the channel.

If, as indicated, there is reason to believe that the strait between the mainland and the island was too narrow, shallow, and overgrown, and therefore impossible to pass in a boat, then it is likely that another place where a ferry-boat could land would have been chosen. The *Farkarlsbryggjur* has not yet been found, but was most likely situated close to the monastery, at a place where the distance between the peninsula and the island was short. The location of the jetty might be indicated by a short stone paving, exposed in recent excavation. By looking at the island of Nøtterøy, on the other side of the channel, it is found that the main road from the centre of the island to the channel terminated opposite *Farkarlsbryggjur* (Fig 10.6). This kind of information can hardly be used as proof, but it is an indication that the inner fjord in the early medieval period should be regarded as a deep cleft, a *cul-de-sac*, rather than a sheltered fjord that could be reached from two directions.

Fig 10.6 Tønsberg: map of 1832 showing the channel. G is the former main road from the centre of Nøtterøy to Tønsberg. The dotted line may indicate its original path. M is the main road today. F is the assumed location for Farkarlsbryggjur

An early settlement and its possible location

The earlier question — whether there is any possibility that there was a *kaupstadir* as early as Snorri Sturlason has indicated, but perhaps located in another area of the peninsula — must now be considered.

If the channel itself were unnavigable, the present site of Tønsberg could not have been as attractive to sea-farers because it would mean that, if approaching from the north, they would have to go round the island of Nøtterøy, and in from the south through the Vest-fjord.

Like the inner fjord, Træla (Fig 10.5), outside the channel, is sheltered behind a barrier of three islands

and a peninsula to the east. It is hoped soon to test the theory that the *kaupstadir* may have been situated *outside* the channel, perhaps at the head of a bay near the farm of Gunnarsbø, which is mentioned in medieval sources. Some minor survey drilling has been done in the area, but so far only humus has been noted in levels which, according to calculation, should hold pure clay. Further drilling and excavation are therefore desirable.

Ships and fishing

During the research programme a student of ethnology, Terje Olsen, was engaged to work on the finds connected with fishing and fish processing. This presentation is a summary of the results in his report (Olsen 1987).

Fig 10.7 Racks for stockfish in Lofoten, Norway. Photograph: Arthur Sand, Institute of Ethnology, Oslo University

In addition, Olsen has compiled a report on ship finds. He concludes that, within the south part of the town, there were remains from at least 20 vessels, covering a period of 250–300 years. Five or six of these seem to be from ships of about 30–35ft (9–11m) in length. A few, six or seven, are smaller, 15–18ft (4.5–5.5m). For the rest, the size of the vessel cannot be estimated. The finds were all parts of ships which were worn out, had been stripped down to be reused elsewhere, or had never been used. It is therefore natural to ask whether there had been a shipbuilder's yard — or rather a repair workshop — in the area. From the finds and their context, Olsen concludes that this was the case. From a period of 150 years he has identified many objects which confirm this theory.

In the second phase (approximately dated to the first half of the 12th century) many objects were found close to a structure, perhaps connected with the shipbuilding yard. There was a fireplace, surrounded by seven posts which might have been the supports for a roof. There were no signs of walls, so the construction seems to have been an open shed, as in modern examples. Use of fire or heat is normal in shipbuilding: hot tar is needed for the caulking between the planks, and hot water to make the planks more flexible. It was not possible for Olsen to classify the function of the vessels, but there is no reason to doubt that some of them could have been used for fishing.

The five main species of fish in the zoological samples from the excavation of the Bank site were cod, haddock, ling, herring, and ray. In addition mackerel, flounder or halibut, sea pike, whiting, coalfish, wrasse, garfish, perch, eel, and carp were found in the material (Lahtiperä 1984). There are few or no freshwater fish in the material; two or three species are brackish water fish, probably caught in the inner fjord. Since seals also used to be regarded as fish, finds which indicate sealing should also be mentioned. Seal bones were found in layers dating to the middle of the 14th century. There were no finds of shark, but the lack of finds is probably due to its skeleton of cartilage rather than to the fishing methods or the medieval diet.

Export of fish meant an enormous boom in the Norwegian economy. Perhaps there is a connection between the boom and Lenten fare since fish, whale, and seal were not banned during Lent. Although the products came mainly from west and north Norway, cod and haddock could also be caught in the south, and the written sources sometimes mention fish products for export from ports in the south of Norway. It is nevertheless obvious that fishing is to be regarded as a minor branch of the economy in the south, where wood and agricultural products played a more important role. For the household economy, however, fishing was probably very important for the population, at least for the non-farming section.

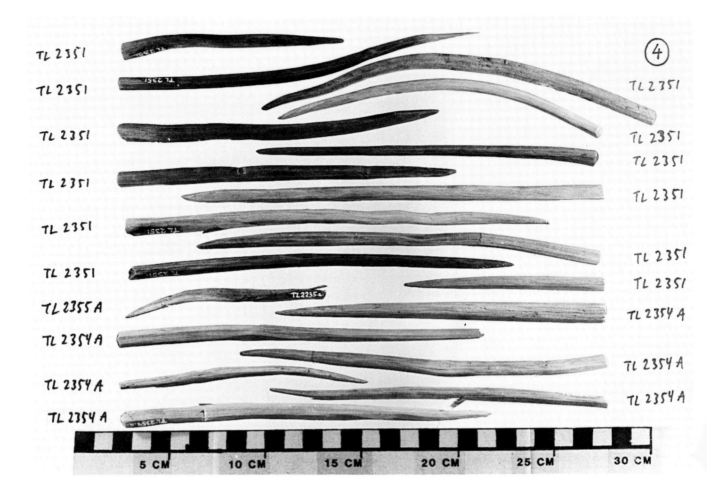

Fig 10.8   Tønsberg: 'sausage pins' from the waterfront area

Olsen found an obvious relationship between the frequency of fish bones in the zoological samples and the artefacts usually connected with fishing. Floats and sinkers for fishing nets were the commonest objects found, but there were net-making tools as well as other items associated with netting. Only a few fish-hooks were found in the material, but there were objects which could be connected with angling. The lack of hooks could, of course, be due to bad preservation conditions for iron or the fact that metal was recirculated to a greater degree than wood and stone. There have been only two finds of nets in Tønsberg. Both have the same width of mesh, 23-24mm, a size which, compared with modern fishing tackle, is suitable for herring. The frequency of fish bones in the material can, if the samples can be regarded as representative, give an indication of how extensive fishing had been over the period of 300 years. In the 12th and 13th centuries (to phase 6) the level of fishing was very much the same. Thereafter, in phase 7, ling, cod, and herring increase, and in phase 8 (late 14th and early 15th centuries) there was a boom in fishing, especially herring, and the connection with the enormous catches of this species in the North Sea in this period can be seen.

Although it was possible to preserve fish in salt, the best-known method of fish-processing was the production of stockfish. This was done by drying the fish on racks (Fig 10.7). The bodies were held open by wooden pins or skewers of various sizes. These skewers are flat, with oval or rectangular cross-sections, and pointed at both ends. Finds of skewers in Tønsberg indicate that stockfish were produced in the town, since they were always removed and kept for reuse before the stockfish was sold. The total number of skewers (not more than 40–50 from a period of less than 200 years in the south part of Tønsberg) indicates, however, that the production was not extensive. For comparison, in an inventory of a fisherman's equipment from the beginning of this century, some 20,000–30,000 skewers are mentioned (Hasslöf 1949).

Among the finds there were also an enormous number of round-sectioned wooden pins, pointed at only one end and often curved (Fig 10.8). These are usually called 'sausage pins' as wooden objects of this kind were (and still are) used for closing sausage skins (Weber 1981). These pins have been found mainly in the waterfront area and only a few of them in the upper parts of the town, well away from the waterfront. This is a distribution pattern also found in other medieval towns.

In the previously mentioned early 20th century inventory, so-called 'rump-pins' are mentioned, 4000 for one fisherman. There are also descriptions of how these were used. Stockfish could be prepared without

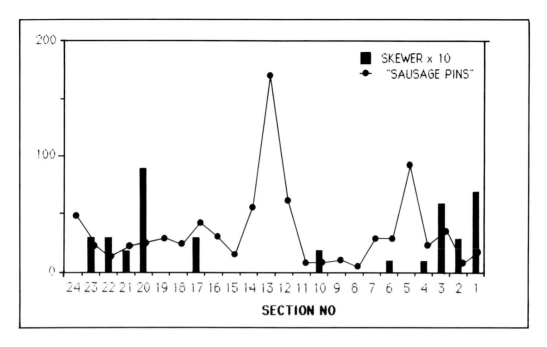

Fig 10.9 Tønsberg: the Long Trench. Graph showing the numbers of pins and skewers found within the different boundaries

using wooden skewers. Small fish could often be dried without having to hold the body open. A pair, held together with a pin through the tail, could be taken and hung over the rack.

There are differences in opinion about the main usage of these pins, but it seems to the writer that the connection with the sea and with fishing is obvious. The frequency of pins and the frequency of skewers within the 24 boundaries in the Long Trench were compared. Generally speaking it could be said that where pins are found, skewers are not (Fig 10.9).

The writer's interpretation is that there have been differences in the processing methods and, consequently, differences in the catch. Unfortunately this theory can neither be proved nor disproved from the analysis of the fish bones since no samples for zoological analysis were taken in the Long Trench.

Conclusion

This paper has tried to stress some aspects concerning Tønsberg in the Middle Ages relevant to the themes of

the conference. One of the most important questions that begs an answer is without doubt the hypothesis of an earlier settlement, a centre of trade as yet unknown to archaeologists. There is still more detailed research to be done into the topography and finds. The questions that have been raised here, and most certainly the attempt to answer them with plausible theories, must therefore be understood as steps on the way.

Notes

1 This was because of the change in sea-level and the dumping of rubbish into the bay, so moving the waterfront westwards out of the excavation area.

2 It can be assumed that the channel must have been important as a seaway and perhaps as an escape-route by boat for the population living by the Tønsberg fjord, even before there was a town or a trade centre here. King Håkon, therefore, might not have been the first to dredge the channel in order to improve communications.

11 Primitive British fishweirs
C R Salisbury

Abstract

This paper presents a summary account of a number of fishweirs, bank revetments and a mill-dam of Neolithic, Saxon and medieval date recorded from a small stretch of the river Trent. The different structures are described and compared with examples from elsewhere in Britain and Europe. The types and location of weirs used is seen to be partly related to the nature of the river bed and flow of the river as well as to the intended catch. Gravel quarrying at Hemington Fields has allowed a plan of ancient river channels to be made and revealed remains of several weirs. Several large, shaped stones were recovered which may be anchor stones, though other possibilities are suggested.

A fishweir is a barrier erected across a fish route in the sea or in a river to deflect the fish into an opening where they can be caught in a net or wicker basket. Various types of fishweirs are illustrated in Figure 11.1 and described in Table 11.1. Usually the barriers are in pairs to form a V with a small opening at the apex. The barrier may be a low wall of stones on the sea shore, or a line of posts supporting nets in a tidal race. In rivers and estuaries the typical construction is of wattle hurdles supported by posts driven into the river bed or wattle work woven between the stakes *in situ*. Sometimes, stone piers are used in the centre of the weir to support nets or pounds (Fig 11.1, nos 2, 5, 14, 24). The long axis of the V is parallel to the flow of water and the walls of the weir may be up to 400m long, reinforced by stones or wooden shoring. In estuaries the wide opening is usually upstream to catch fish on the ebb tide. In rivers, the wide opening may be either downstream to catch salmon swimming to the headwater in spring, or upstream to catch eels moving seawards in the autumn migration (Fig 11.1, nos 14–23).

The earliest fishweir known from excavation is a row of wooden stakes supporting wattling in an ancient river-bed at New Ferry, Lough Beg, Northern Ireland, dated to before 1000 BC (Mitchell 1965, 1). Its appearance was similar to Norman and Saxon weirs excavated at Colwick, Nottinghamshire (Losco-Bradley & Salisbury 1979; Salisbury 1981) and to eel weirs still in use on the river Bann, Eire (Fig 11.1, no 19 and Fig 11.2). A similar row of wattled stakes excavated in a gravel pit alongside the river Thames has been radiocarbon dated to the 5th century AD (information Bird) and wattle fencing, found during excavations in the river silts of the Witham at Lincoln, have been interpreted as fishweirs dating from the 2nd to the 10th century AD (Gilmour 1982).

The earliest illustration of a fishweir is found in a 1460–70 estate map in the archives of Westminster Abbey recording the fishing rights on the river Coln (Harvey 1980, 87). The earliest written references in Britain are from Anglo-Saxon charters, for Tidenham on the Severn estuary (Seebohm 1884, 152-4) which mentions the *haccwer* or hedge weir, and from Bewdley

where peasants had to 'make a hedge to capture fish' (Heming's Cartulary 1, 256, quoted in Doubleday 1901, 272).

The similarity of all these structures shows the timeless method of construction and emphasizes the relevance of the study of modern weirs to the understanding of excavated examples of ancient weirs. This applies particularly to the catching devices, which by their nature are ephemeral. Extensive surveys of the written evidence for fishweirs have been made for the British Isles (White 1988; Losco-Bradley & Salisbury 1988; Pannett 1988; Bond 1988) and worldwide (McGrail 1983, 35, 39–46). The classic work of Went and Mitchell in recording the dying fishweir tradition in Eire remains the most important source of information.

The wide, level, gravel-filled flood-plain of rivers such as the Trent encourages meandering, braiding, and oxbow formation. The redundant courses may slowly silt with fine sediments or fill rapidly with gravel and sand during floods. In either case, fishweirs, dams, or revetments will be buried under many metres of deposit and preserved by the waterlogged anaerobic conditions. Since gravel quarriers avoid the fine sediments, waterfront structures revealed by their extraction tend to be in the rapidly filled channels and are often severely damaged by the same flood that buried them. However, continuous surveillance of quarrying in portions of the parishes of Colwick, Nottinghamshire, and Castle Donington, Leicestershire, has revealed five medieval, and possibly one prehistoric, fishweirs as well as seven bank revetments and one mill-dam (Losco-Bradley & Salisbury 1979; Salisbury 1981; Salisbury *et al* 1984; Clay 1986; Clay & Salisbury forthcoming).

The Saxon fishweir at Colwick (Fig 11.1, no 15) has a calibrated radiocarbon date of AD 810–80. It lay 5m deep at the bottom of the gravel deposit and was made of a close double row of round-section posts including oak and hawthorn, but mostly holly. The posts were 115 to 140mm in diameter and about 1.4m long. Between the rows was a series of wattle panels to make a fence-like structure, the panels being mostly of hazel but with a little holly, ash, and willow (Fig 11.3). A 35m

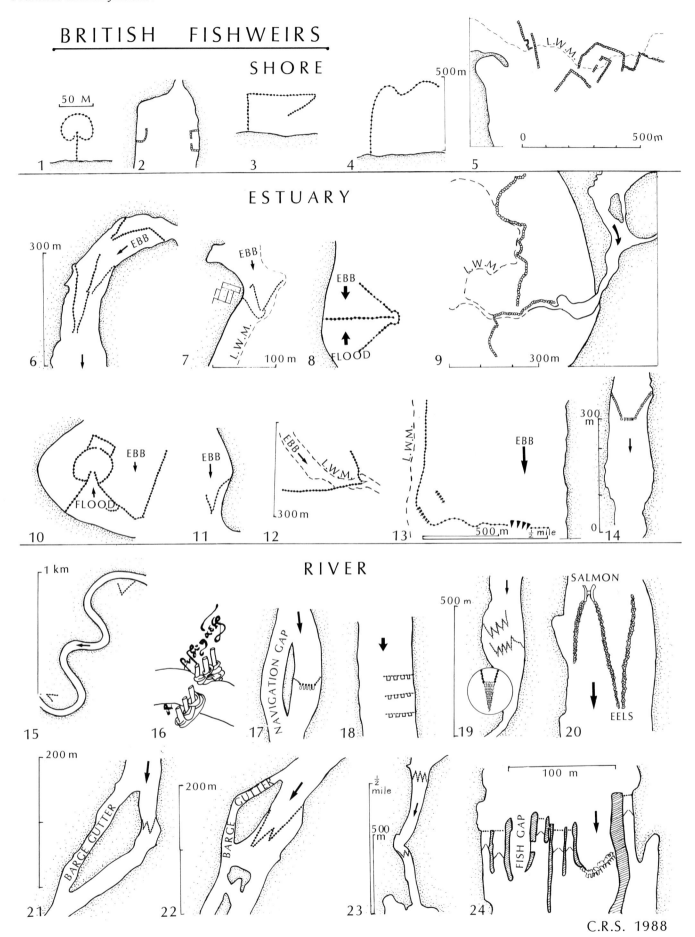

C.R.S. 1988

Fig 11.1 Types of fishweir in the British Isles (see Table 11.1)

Table 11.1 Summary of types of fish-weir in the British Isles (Fig 11.1)

	Place	Date	Situation	Fish	Construction	Catching Device	Reference
1	Dungeness, Rye & Dymchurch (England)	20th century	Sea	Sea fish	Posts & net	Pound of netting	Davis 1958, 32
2	Loch Broom (Scotland)	19th century	Sea	Sea fish	Rubble stone - a 'Galloway dyke' up to 1.75m high	Wattle barrier or net	Bathgate 1948
3	Beaumaris (Wales)	1448 to 20th century	Sea	Sea fish	Wattle & post	Pounded in the hook until low tide and then scooped out	Davis 1958, 28
4	Penrhyn (Wales)	20th century	Sea	Sea fish	? Stone	Pounded in the bends until low tide and then scooped out	Davis 1958, 28
5	Minehead (England)	Ancient to 20th century	Sea	Sea fish	Rubble stone	Nets placed over the apex. Fish caught as the tide ebbs.	Aston & Dennison 1988, 401
6	Corlea, river Erne (Eire)	19th century	Estuary	Eels	Post & wattle	Coghill net (see 19)	Went 1945, 219
7	Molona Abbey, river Barrow (Eire)	20th century	Estuary	Sea fish	Post & wire netting (previously wattled)	Coghill net (see 19)	Went 1969, 257
8	Thames (England)	12th century	Estuary	Sea fish	Posts	Probably a net pound	Davis 1958, 29
9	Doonbeg (Eire)	20th century	Estuary	Salmon	Rubble stone wall up to 1.75m high	Gratings in the wall to allow the tide to ebb. Fish scooped out of pools.	Went 1946, 190-2
10	Ravenglass, river Esk (England)	19th century	Estuary	Salmon	Wattled posts with nets above	Circular pound of wattled posts and netting roofed with netting against birds	Davis 1958, 30-1
11	Buttermilk Castle, Waterford (Eire)	20th century. Earliest record is 1684	Estuary	Salmon, cod, & herring	Wattled posts with a four-poster platform at the apex on which the fisherman stands	Coghill net (see 19)	Went 1946, 189
12	Castle Bellingham, Dundalk (Eire)	20th century. Earliest record is 1756	Estuary	Salmon, flatfish	Wattled posts	Conical 'purse' net	Went 1946, 186-7
13	Sheppardine, river Severn (England)	Ancient to 20th century	Estuary	Salmon	Wattled posts	Conical wicker baskets, either large and single (putts) or smaller and ranked on tiers (putchers)	Personal observation & Davis 1958, 47 Jenkins 1974, 45-6
14	Corry McGinty, river Erne (Eire)	20th century	Estuary	Eels	Rubble stone	Seven masonry piers built across the apex with Coghill nets between them (see 19)	Went 1945, 217-9
15	Colwick, river Trent (England)	Saxon & Norman	River	Eels	Double row of posts 0.5m apart braced by oblique posts and supporting wattle panels	Wicker basket or net	Losco-Bradley & Salisbury 1988
16	Hawton, river Devon (England)	Tudor	River	Eels	Wattled posts	This is not shown but there is a statutory two perches gap at the apex. When not in use for catching fish this would allow navigation.	Salisbury 1983, 57
17	Thames (England)	19th century	River	Eels	Wattled posts	Eel 'bucks' - wicker baskets lowered from an overhead gantry and raised to empty the eels.	Wheeler 1979, 28-9
18	Trent (England)	20th century	River	Eels	Wattled posts	Fixed square wicker baskets spaced along the weir	Information Mr Stokes
19	Portna, river Bann (Eire)	20th century	River	Eels	Posts 1.5-3m apart supporting wattle panels and braced by props. Posts may have metal tips.	A conical net held open by two posts set at the apex of a Coghill net	Mitchell 1965, 4
20	Coolnamuck, river Suir (Eire)	Modern, recorded in 1860	River	Eels & salmon	Wattled posts	Coghill nets (see 19). Salmon caught going upstream. Eels caught downstream.	Went 1956, 200-1
21	Montford, river Severn (England)	Modern. The navigation channel or barge gutter follows the parish boundary suggesting medieval origin.	River	Eels	Wattled posts supported by timber braces	Conical net draped over a frame at the apex of the weir.	Pannet 1988, 371-89
22	Preston, river Severn (England)						
23	Lough Beg and Toome, river Bann (Eire)	20th century. Fully established in 1835. Probably ancient.	River	Eels	Posts supporting	Coghill nets (see 19), wattle panels	Mitchell 1965, 6-7
24	Cutts, river Bann (Eire)	16th century	River	Salmon	Rock cut and stone walls	Fish pass upstream through the V made of flexible metal rods. This is a non-return barrier and further progress upstream is prevented by a fixed grating. The fish are scooped out.	Mitchell 1965, 18-9

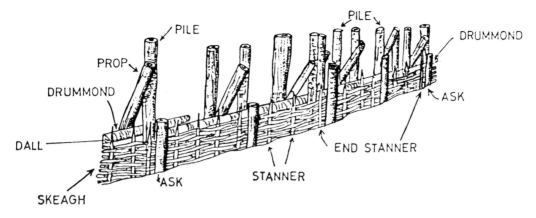

Fig 11.2 Part of a fishweir at Toome on the river Bann, Eire, showing wattle panels supported by vertical piles and diagonal props (after Mitchell). Not to scale

Fig 11.3 Part of the Anglo-Saxon fishweir at Colwick, Nottinghamshire

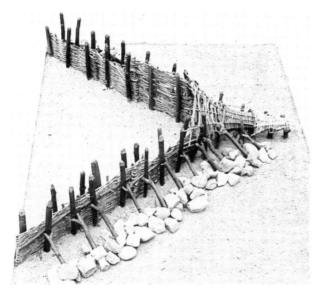

Fig 11.4 A reconstruction of the Anglo-Saxon weir at Colwick in the Canal Museum, Nottingham

Fig 11.5 Montford eel weir, Shropshire. Watercolour by F W Seville, 1897. Shrewsbury Museum (see Fig 11.1, no 21)

Fig 11.6   A modern fishweir at Molana Abbey, Eire. Wire netting has replaced the traditional wattle fences (Fig 11.1, no 7)

section of this fence was exposed, but both ends disappeared into the quarry face. The weir had collapsed and lay horizontally over a jumble of rubble-stones and posts, suggesting the reconstruction (Fig 11.4) based on the 18th century eel weir at Toome (Fig 11.2), at Montford on the Severn (Fig 11.5), and the modern eel weirs at Molana Abbey, Eire (Fig 11.6), and the Severn estuary (Fig 11.7).

No evidence for the catching device was found at Colwick, but this is not surprising given the conditions of destruction and burial of the weir. Conical baskets are used at the 'eyes' of fishweirs worldwide and are still in use on the Severn estuary (Fig 11.8 and Fig 11.1, 13) where they are made of 'withies' or willow rods tied to posts. Long, small-meshed baskets in the shape of an 'eel wheel' are fitted over the narrow end of the cone (Davis 1958, 46–7; Jenkins 1974, 45–65). The wheel is the traditional method of catching eels and was used especially in mill leats. Its earliest illustration is in the *Luttrell Psalter* (British Library, *Royal* 10.E.IV).

One kilometre upstream of the Saxon weir at Colwick was found a Norman weir with a calibrated radiocarbon date of AD 1070–1200 (Losco-Bradley & Salisbury 1979). It was buried beneath 4–5m of flood-plain deposit, the posts being driven into a gently sloping, ancient cobbled river bed. The V-shaped weir pointed downstream with one wing 30.8m long and the other approximately 100m long (Fig 11.9). It was built of a double row of oak round-section posts 0.5m apart, 100–150mm in diameter and up to 2.5m long. The posts

supported wattled hurdles of round-section rods and 12 double sails (Fig 11.10). Bound bundles of twigs lay at the foot of the hurdling to make the weir 'fish tight' (Went 1969, 254–60). Behind the fence were further lines of posts which probably were the remains of earlier weirs. At the 'eye' of the weir were layers of horizontal hurdles with vertical posts driven through them. These were probably to stop the scouring of the river bed. The large number of irregularly spaced post-stumps in this area may have been used to anchor catching baskets or to form the foundation of platforms for fishermen to tend their nets (Fig 11.11). They could also have been the stumps of frames to carry nets or baskets. From the evidence of modern examples, the position of the weir pointing downstream makes it certain that it was for catching eels.

Since 1986, gravel quarrying in the parish of Castle Donington adjacent to the Trent at Hemington Fields has allowed a more detailed examination of the geology of the flood-plain than was undertaken at Colwick. Hemington Fields lies near the centre of a flood-plain, 2.5 miles (4km) wide, built up by the confluences of the rivers Trent, Derwent, and Soar. The plain consists of about 5m of gravel and sand underlain by the Mercian mudstone group (formerly known as Keuper Marl) and covered by a metre of overburden of silts and clays which have accumulated since Flandrian times. The lower levels of the gravel were probably deposited after the maximum glaciation of the last Ice Age (Devensian) about 15,000–10,000 BC. A discontinuous pure clay

Fig 11.7 A contemporary fishweir on the Severn estuary

horizon about 3m above the floor of the quarry pit probably represents a time of maximum braiding and stagnation across the late Devensian flood-plain which allowed the clay to settle out. This clay deposit forms the upper limit of a number of frost cracks or proto-ice wedge casts, 17 of which have been identified in the gravel pit so far.

With the final disappearance of the ice and the onset of Flandrian times about 10,000 BC, the Trent shrank and settled into its present meander belt. During this time, it wound across the plain, often braiding or forming oxbow cut-offs and depositing another 2–2.5m of gravel. It is in this upper suite of gravel that all the channels containing archaeological material have been found, although at times major river courses have cut down deeply into the Devensian deposits.

Fig 11.8 Contemporary withy putches used for catching salmon on the Severn estuary

The Hemington Fields gravel pit lies between an old course of the Trent (a former county and parish boundary) and the modern line of the Trent (Fig 11.12). Between these waterways lay one Neolithic and three Norman channels, identified as silted river beds in the gravel. It seems likely that the old county boundary course of the Trent is associated with the complex of braided Norman channels and that the present course of the Trent represents an avulsion or violent change of direction during a catastrophic medieval flood.

One Norman channel was crossed by a Norman mill-dam which was excavated by the Leicestershire Archaeological Field Unit, directed by Patrick Clay and the author. Massive squared posts of oak, 180–220mm wide and up to 5m long, have been dendrochronologically dated by Robert Howard of the Nottingham Tree Ring Research Group. Within a 98% confidence interval their felling date was AD 1127–58. Their pointed ends had been driven 3m into an ancient river bed to form a double row of posts 3.6m wide and 50m long. Within the rows, the posts were 1.5–2m apart and linked by wattling. Between the rows, the core of the dam comprised quarry rubble, hand querns broken during manufacture, and broken, worn-out millstones (Fig 11.13). This is the earliest example of a traditional method of revetment and mill-dam construction used in the Trent Valley until the 19th century (Salisbury 1985) (Fig 11.14 A).

Beneath the dam and parallel to it was another flimsy line of round-section posts 0.5m apart and between 85–110mm in diameter. These were of birch, hazel, holly, rowan, and willow. The row joined, at right-angles, a similar line of wattled posts running beneath the core of the mill-dam. Wattle from this structure had a calibrated radiocarbon date of AD 1030–1215 and the

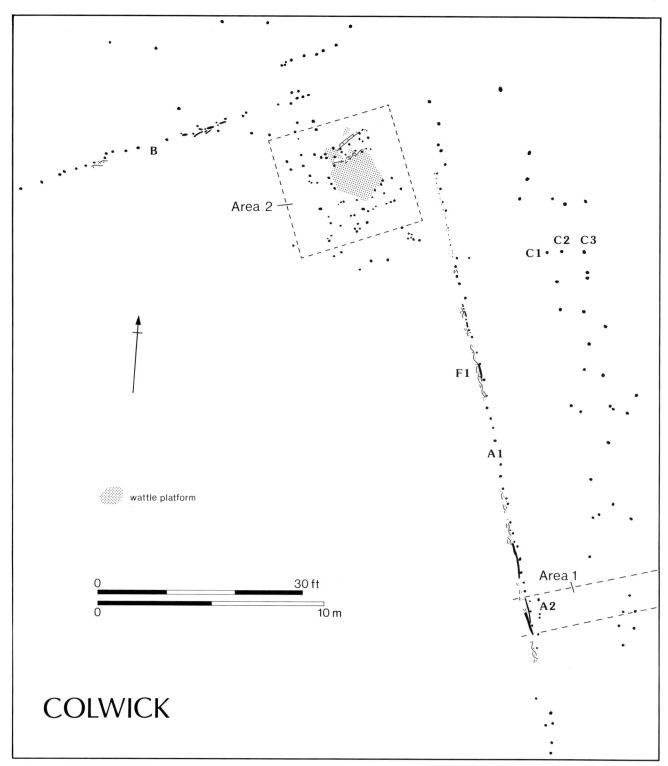

Fig 11.9 Plan of the Norman fishweir at Colwick, Nottinghamshire

Fig 11.10 A standing section of the Norman fishweir at Colwick, Nottinghamshire

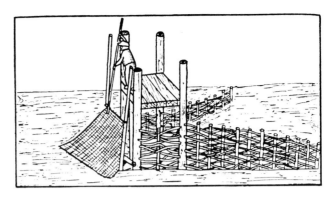

Fig 11.11 A fisherman tending conical (Coghill) nets from a platform set on the eye of an eel weir. 20th century Eire (after Went)

posts had dates of AD 793–983 and AD 1020–1125. This fragile line of posts is typical of a fishweir. The lack of wattling on most posts suggests it was ruinous when the massive mill-dam was built on top of it. Large beams and planks had been reused to repair the dam. Because the timbers had been trimmed and lacked sapwood, they could only be given an approximate felling date of around AD 1100. A wheel pit, bearing, paddle, and mall were also found (Clay 1986; Clay & Salisbury, forthcoming).

Examination of successive quarry faces allowed a plan of ancient river channels to be made (Fig 11.12). Two fishweirs were found in channel 4. At FW2, two vertical oak posts 1.7m apart seemed to be part of a row at right-angles to the quarry face and parallel to channel 4. Two metres away was a five-sail fragment of a hazel wattle panel, bundles of brushwood, and rubble stone. The calibrated radiocarbon date of the panel was AD 1016–1157, suggesting that this weir was part of the mill-dam industrial complex. At FW3 were two rows of oak posts 0.3m apart and parallel to the channel. The posts were 50mm in diameter, 0.2m apart, and were found in association with rubble stone and brushwood. The calibrated radiocarbon date was AD 695–820. This structure might have been a bank revetment or small mill-dam rather than a fishweir or, indeed, might have served multiple purposes. Fifty metres further downstream, two anchor stones were recovered.

Only one quarry face exposure of channel 1 was made and the danger of collapse made excavation impossible. A bunch of horizontal posts with a bizarre preponderance of purging buckthorn lay in the channel with a calibrated radiocarbon date of 3611–3361 BC. Only a nearby fragment of wattle panel raised the possibility that this was a fishweir. It could have been a random collection of wood, but all the stems, with one exception, were between 100 and 200mm in diameter. It could have been a beaver dam, but on balance it is likely to have been a fishweir.

The anchor stones

Although it was impossible to establish the relationship between channel 2 and the mill with certainty, channel 2 was probably the tail-race. The silting of this channel

can be roughly dated by an oak trunk, lying in the filling, revealed by quarrying. Dendrochronology gave a date for the outer-most heartwood ring of AD 1046. Taking into account some abrasion of the surface and an arbitrary 25 sapwood rings, the felling date would have been about AD 1075. Further quarrying in the immediate vicinity of the trunk and within a 15m length of channel 2, produced 12 large worked stones. These stones were mostly of rubble derived from local rocks, five being of Mercian mudstone and seven of Sherwood sandstone. They were characterised by V-shaped cuts on two or more sides, giving a waisted appearance (Fig 11.15). In many cases the chisel marks of the cutting showed no signs of wear although the groove had obviously been designed to hold rope. Three of the stones were of chiseled masonry that had been reused. The weight of the stones varied from 9kg to 50kg. One groove retained remains of a twisted band of split withy rods (skeins), with a calibrated radiocarbon date (at 95% confidence) of AD 1175–1410 (OxA – 2289).

Although similar to thatch weights and net sinkers, the size of the majority of stones suggested they were used for anchors. Many stone anchors have been found round the shores of the Mediterranean and France, but these are pierced by three or more holes to hold the rope and wooden flukes, and where the date is established they appear to be Bronze Age (Frost 1963, 4). Waisted stones have been used to weight wooden anchors or 'killicks' worldwide (Upham 1983, 10–11) until the present century (Fig 11.16), usually by poor fishermen who could not afford an iron anchor. The stones could have been used as simple weights but the bed of the Trent is shifting gravel and they could not have held a boat in times of flood. Alternatively, they could have been 'veer weights' and used as a drogue from the bows, slowing the downstream passage of a boat and allowing it to be steered 'backwards' by the rudder. Other possible uses for the stones would be as anchors for basket fish traps or for a pontoon bridge. The latter idea is attractive as the stones were all found close together, but this could also be accounted for by their being the cargo or ballast of a ship which foundered. By August 1990 72 anchor stones had been recorded in this gravel pit. It is strange that this type of stone has not been recognised in any other gravel pit in the Trent Valley, apart from two examples from the nearby channel 4

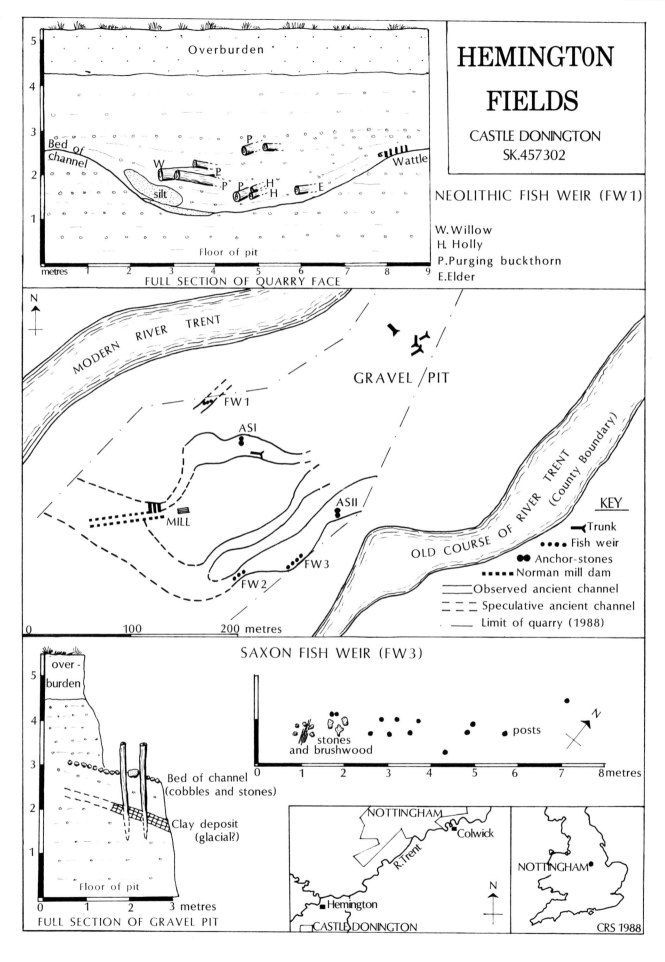

HEMINGTON
FIELDS

CASTLE DONINGTON
SK.457302

NEOLITHIC FISH WEIR (FW1)

W. Willow
H. Holly
P. Purging buckthorn
E. Elder

FULL SECTION OF QUARRY FACE

Overburden

Bed of channel

silt

Floor of pit

metres

MODERN RIVER TRENT

GRAVEL /PIT

FW 1

ASI

ASII

MILL

FW 3

FW 2

OLD COURSE OF RIVER TRENT (County Boundary)

KEY

Trunk
Fish weir
Anchor-stones
Norman mill dam
Observed ancient channel
Speculative ancient channel
Limit of quarry (1988)

0   100   200 metres

SAXON FISH WEIR (FW 3)

over-burden

Bed of channel
(cobbles and stones)

Clay deposit
(glacial?)

Floor of pit

FULL SECTION OF GRAVEL PIT

stones
and brushwood

posts

N

8 metres

NOTTINGHAM

Colwick

R. Trent

Hemington

CASTLE DONINGTON

NOTTINGHAM

N

CRS 1988

Fig 11.13 A Norman mill-dam at Hemington, Leicestershire. The double row of wattled posts holds a core of quarry rubble and millstone fragments. An earlier fishweir shows on the left as wattle and a line of small posts

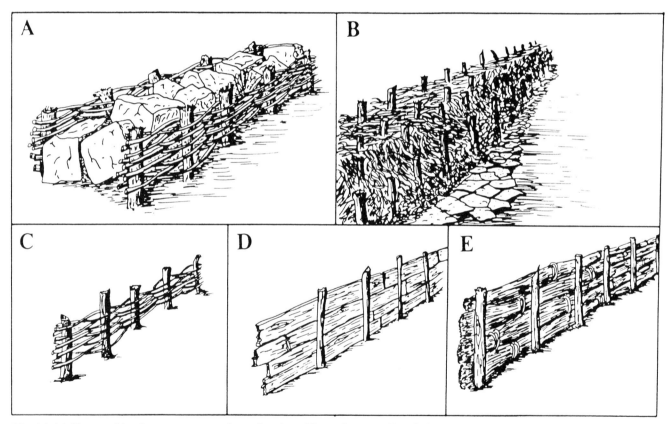

Fig 11.14 Types of bank revetment used on the river Trent from medieval times to the 20th century

Fig 11.12 (opposite) Silted medieval and prehistoric river channels revealed by gravel quarrying in the Trent flood-plain at Hemington, Leicestershire

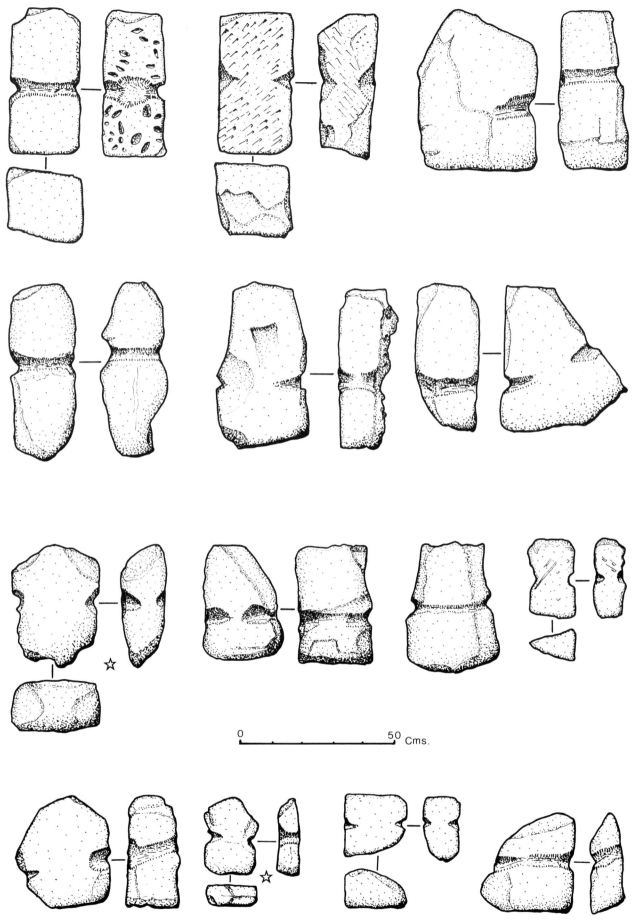

C.R.S. 88.

Fig 11.15 Stones found in a silted Norman river channel and probably used as anchors

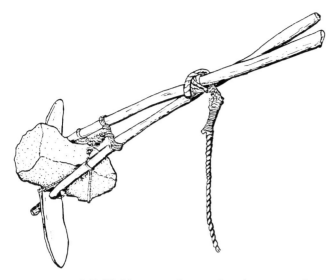

Fig 11.16 A 'killick' or wooden anchor from a modern Spanish fishing boat using a waisted stone (drawn from a photograph of the author's taken in the Barcelona Maritime Museum)

which is of a similar date to channel 2 (marked ★ in Fig 11.15). Similar stones in a Roman context have been found in Belgium (de Boe & Hubert 1977).

Conclusion

The finding of six weirs, seven bank revetments, and a mill-dam within the bounds of the two parishes, highlights the exciting possibilities of flood-plain archaeology. Fisheries are mentioned in Domesday for every parish bordering the Trent and the majority of these would have been of the fishweir type. The frequent silting of old courses means that weirs of every age will have been preserved, under the gravel, awaiting quarrying. The fragmentary nature of these remains, coupled with their rapid destruction by modern quarrying methods, means that constant surveillance is required if they are to be recorded.

The situation on the Trent contrasts sharply with rivers such as the Severn with much less gravel in their flood-plains. The meanders of these rivers remain unchanged for thousands of years (Pannett 1988, 378). Because the Trent weirs were opportunistically sited and their position frequently changed because of rapidly moving meanders they can only be found by excavation. However, on the Severn the position of the weirs is well documented and shown to be both constant and ancient by the invariable use of navigation channels (barge gutters) as parish boundaries (Fig 11.1, nos 21, 22). Any river with a flood-plain of deep gravel has great potential for the recovery of rural waterfront structures.

12 The archaeology of medieval fishing tackle
J M Steane and M Foreman

Abstract

This paper provides a summary of fish catching methods in medieval England. The principal methods and associated tackle are described with archaeological examples. Distinct regional fishing traditions are identified, the lack of overlap between these techniques possibly reflecting differences in the prey species available. The technology employed in coastal fishing is different again and its development seems to reflect changes in the economic importance of the fishing industry. Small-scale, essentially local, fishing with the sale of fresh fish at local markets was gradually replaced by large-scale fleet fishing in the late medieval period, accompanied by curing and salting processes.

The sources

Fishing is a comparatively sparsely documented industry (Heath 1968) and the archaeological information does not satisfactorily supplement the lack of written sources. There are several reasons for this. Much of the equipment was made from organic materials, and has not survived except in waterlogged deposits. A vivid reminder of this was given recently (Coles 1984) when the fishing equipment from the waterlogged Neolithic settlement of Traun in Switzerland was reviewed. Bark floats, and net sinkers consisting of pebbles wrapped and tied with bark were found. If there had not been exceptionally favourable conditions for their survival the evidence would simply have been scattered pebbles. Only in Norway, Poland, and Russia has the full range of medieval fishing tackle been found: floats, nets, lines, hooks, sinkers (Herteig 1975; Rulewicz & Zajdel-Szczyrska 1970; Artsikhovsky & Kolchin 1959).

Another difficulty arises from the fact that effective fishing methods were developed at an early period and thereafter continued with very little typological change for hundreds if not thousands of years. Consequently objects are difficult to date. On the other hand, recent material (such as the extensive collections in the Gloucester Folk Museum) may provide vivid insights into early fishing methods. Comparative anthropological material from other cultures (as in the Pitt Rivers Collections, Oxford) may also be valuable. Modern anthropological study of the lives of Norwegian fishermen is helpful (Kolsrud 1984) (Fig 12.1). It has recently been realised that literary evidence from all over medieval Europe shows that fishing for sport is older than previously thought (Hoffmann 1985). What emerges from a study of the fish remains themselves is that, throughout the medieval period, north European fishermen were becoming more daring and were venturing with their boats into deeper waters (Steane 1985, 261). Their boats were also becoming more seaworthy and bigger, and had storage compartments amidships with small holes to create a bath of sea water in the middle of the ship for the catch (Unger 1980).

Throughout this paper it is recognised that there were four types of fishing: that carried on in rivers and estuaries; inland fisheries, using ponds either natural or artificial; coastal fishing; and deep water fishing. The different methods used may be more appropriate to one or other or all four of these locations. The most valuable summary of fish catching methods is von Brandt (1984) and broadly speaking his classification has been followed.

Collecting by hand with no tackle

The simplest method of fishing is gathering by hand by wading fishermen or with the help of more or less trained animals such as dogs, otters, or cormorants. The most suitable areas for hand picking are those sea coasts which experience great differences in the rise and fall of tides. Here many species of shellfish can be collected or dug by hand from the wide muddy areas exposed twice a day. Rocky coasts with many small pools provide areas prolific for seaweed growth and cover for molluscs and urchins. The only tackle required is a supply of baskets or bags for carrying the collected material and perhaps an implement to help prise the shellfish. Medieval sites have produced evidence for this. Oysters, cockles, and common mussels were found at Castle Barnard (Donaldson et al 1980). Southampton produced quantities of marine bivalves (Platt & Coleman-Smith 1975). At Pevensey the molluscan species found included oysters, whelks, mussels, and cockles (Dulley 1967, 232). Oysters, cockles, and winkles were found at the palace of King's Langley in Hertfordshire (Locker 1977, 162), and at Oxford in the centre of England, finds of mussels, oysters, cockles, and limpets have been made (Wilson 1980). Doubtless they were transported live in barrels. Even an inland town like Bedford produced quantities of oysters, but very few mussels, cockles, whelks, and winkles (Baker et al 1979, 13).

Fish can also be grabbed by trailing the hands in the water behind boats. They can also be grasped by means of 'tickling' and by smearing the hands with bait. A crude but effective method was to drain ponds or pools and to pick the floundering fish off the exposed surface. This was much done in the 16th and 17th centuries.

Fig 12.1 Fair Isle fishermen c 1900. The methods these men used closely parallel those of medieval fishermen. Photograph: Shetland Museum and Library

Spearing, harpooning, and shooting fish

'Fishing by foot' means collecting fish food without a boat and without other gear. More important than equipment is the endurance and fitness of the collector; his legs would need to have developed resistance to the cold, and he would need good eyes and quick perceptive senses (von Brandt 1984). A fish spear has been found in interglacial deposits of the Early Pleistocene at Clacton-on-Sea which may be 300,000 years old (Dent 1984-5). Using such a spear is quite difficult. The refraction of light in water has to be allowed for; the fish seems to be higher and further away than its true position. To increase the effectiveness of aim, fish spears are often provided with several prongs. This also has the advantage of preventing the fish escaping by vigorous wriggling if speared by a single point. Medieval excavations at Novgorod have produced a fish spear with three prongs (Artsikhovsky & Kolchin 1959, 77).

One widely found freshwater fish, the common eel (*Anguilla anguilla* (L)) is so elongated and slender in shape that it requires a specialised tool for its capture. Eels gather in large concentrations, individuals being in constant shifting contact with one another (Tesch 1977). One solution was spearing by means of a head

fitted with many sharp tines close together, another was a comb in which the head was offset by some 15-20 degrees from the main axis. The 'glaive' was an implement with flat, blunt tines set close together and serrated on their opposing edges. Eels would be wedged between the blades without piercing.

Line fishing

The first tentative beginnings of sea fishing in Britain from boats using tackle including lines and hooks occurred towards the end of Mesolithic times on the islands and coasts of northern and western Scotland (Clark 1965). With the exception of the use of the primitive fish spear this is probably the oldest method of fishing (Holdsworth 1874).

There are two principal methods used at sea, hand line and long line, and both are very simple.

The *hand line* is composed of a line of a certain length, a sinker, a snood (a hook-carrying branch line) and at least one hook (Bridger 1981). The fisherman holds one end of the line and winds up the line on to a frame, or later, when it has been invented, a reel, feeling with his finger for the bite of the fish. To shoot the line the weight is dropped into the water where fish are

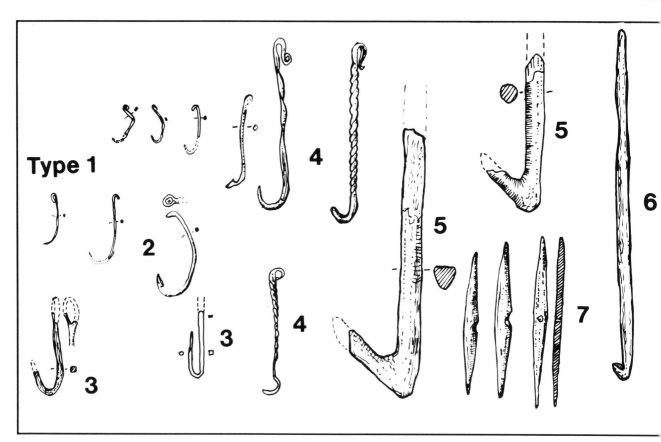

Fig 12.2 Wolin, Poland: medieval fish hooks of different types and materials, iron (3), bronze (1,2, and 4), and wood (5 and 6). Gorges are represented in 7. After Rulewicz & Zajdel-Szczyrska (1970)

expected. The line needs to be dropped quickly, perhaps with the aid of a stone, to prevent other fishes or crabs from gnawing away a slowly sinking hook. It also needs to be longer than the depth of the water due to the effect of currents and the drift of the vessel.

The *long line* can involve hundreds or today even thousands of hooks, each fixed to the main line by short lines called branch lines (or snoods, leaders, dropper lines, droplines, or droppers, gangion, or gangin). Bottom long lines with many hooks have been used in northern Europe and the Mediterranean area from earliest times (von Brandt 1984). The sea-bed needs to be fairly level, because projecting rocks may snag or break lines. Floats are needed to keep hooks and lines well clear of the bottom and in middle-depth waters where most fish are found. Sometimes one end of the line is tied to the beach, while the other is towed by a boat or an unmanned raft before the wind. A third method involves the vessel trailing the line — the so called troll line. Medieval spoons and hooks used in trolling have been found in Finland (Vilkuna 1975). Juliana Berners in 15th century England advised tying a short line with a hook to the foot of a goose and letting the hapless bird swim. Isaac Walton advised tying a line bait 'about the body or wings of a goose or duck and chase it over the pond' (Chevenix-Trench 1974).

The *gorge* was in use by the prehistoric Swiss lake dwellers (Clark 1965). This was a small piece of wood, straight and slightly pointed at either end, tied at the middle, where it narrowed, to the line and inserted lengthwise in the bait held parallel to the line. The gorge is swallowed readily by the fish, but when it swims away or the line is pulled the gorge takes up transverse position in the fish's throat or belly so it cannot spit it out. Gorges have been found in profusion in early medieval levels at Wolin (Rulewicz & Zajdel Szczyrska 1970), but have not so far been recognised in British medieval contexts (Fig 12.2).

The gorge is probably the prototype of the *bent hook* which is another and better-known device for holding the fish captive once it has taken the bait. The earliest fish-hooks are likely to have been made of wood branches with twigs sticking out at suitable angles were used. Sometimes hooks were made of small parts of plants such as thorns. Wooden hooks were found alongside metal ones at Wolin (Fig 12.2; Rulewicz & Zajdel-Szczyrska 1970). Compound hooks made of wood bone, and shell were made in primitive societies throughout the world (Hurum 1977), but were labour intensive. Most medieval European hooks were made of metal, either of bronze or, more frequently, of iron. The result of the use of metal was that the shape of the hook now became freer: iron hooks were often made bigger than bronze hooks but had to be treated with copper plating or tinning if they were to resist corrosion. They had to be neither too soft to avoid straightening out by pulling nor too hard to prevent their breaking under strain.

The hook consists of five parts (Hurum 1977): the point (1); the barb (2) may be immediately under the point or possibly at the rear; the hook is bent round (3) and straightens out to the shank (4) which is attached to

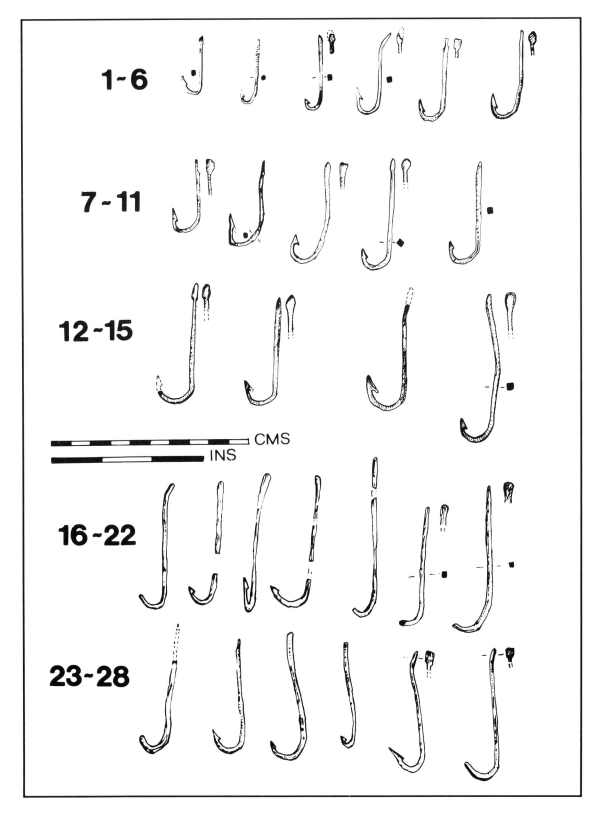

Fig 12.3 Medieval fish-hooks made of iron from London (1–15) and Great Yarmouth (16–28). Different sizes are explained by the fact that fishes of a great range of sizes were being sought

the 'snood' or the line by means of a thickening of the metal or by a ring or an eye (5). Very often in archaeological contexts the point, barb, and eye are missing leaving a piece of bent iron of ambiguous function.

The first bent hooks were barbless and indeed many medieval hooks now lack barbs, although it is likely that in some cases the barb has broken off. The barb performs three useful functions: it prevents the fish slipping off the hook; it holds the bait; and it can also prevent the point penetrating too far into the fish. Difficulties may arise once attempts are made to remove the barb from the mouth of the landed fish.

Fish-hooks found in British excavations vary considerably in size, a matter clearly related to the types of fish being sought. At Fuller's Hill, Great Yarmouth, where 45 fish-hooks dated between AD 1000 and 1200 were recovered (Rogerson 1976), their lengths varied from 54 to 75mm, with the exception of one which was 122mm long (Fig 12.3). The ends were either splayed (beaten flat) or thickened. All, in fact, are large and many have a distinct barb. They would have been fastened to a line by means of a short snood whipped onto the flattened spade end of the shank. Hooks of this size would have been used to capture the larger fishes represented in the fish remains, such as spurdog, conger eel, ling, cod, large haddock, turbot, and halibut. The other smaller species of fish are likely to have been caught by smaller hooks which have not survived or been recovered, or by nets (considered below).

The Coppergate site at York produced 10 fish-hooks. They are smaller than the Great Yarmouth ones, being 40–55mm long, and each has a square section. Half of them have barbed points. One has a flattened, bulbous end, and another has the end turned over sideways to form a loop. Fish remains at York included large marine fish like cod, haddock, flat fish, ling, the pelagic marine species, herring, and horse mackerel, while smelt, eels, and salmon may have been caught at sea, in estuarine waters, or in the rivers (Hall 1984).

Recent excavations at London have produced 23 fish-hooks (Fig 12.3). The medieval examples from Trig Lane, Billingsgate, and Custom House are all barbed and vary from 32 to 75mm in length with an average length of about 55mm. They have a flattened spade-like terminal for attachment to the line. A wide variety of river, estuarine, and marine fish were available to the citizens of London (Salzman 1923) and to the monks of Westminster (Black 1976, 170–6). Other fish-hooks have come from Hartlepool (information G A B Young), Pevensey (Dulley 1967, 228), and Sewer Lane, Hull (Armstrong 1977, 65). A contrasting group from medieval Wolin shows that the mainly freshwater fish inhabiting the lakes and estuaries of the south Baltic coast produced a different sort of challenge to the Slavonic fishermen. Hooks were small and curved while gorges were also used (Fig 12.2; Rulewicz & Zajdel-Szczyrska 1970).

The 15th century book *The Treatise on Angling in the Boke of St Albans* (Braekman 1980) describes in technical detail how to make fish-hooks. The author advises making them of needles.

The line was a crucial item of the fisherman's tool kit. None dating from the medieval period appears to have survived in Britain. A number of lines of different gauges have been recovered from the excavations at Wolin (Rulewicz & Zajdel-Szczyrska 1970). They were probably made of hemp or bast. The shorter lines used for recreational fishing and attached to rods were made of horsehair. Detailed instructions for making them of different colours to camouflage them from the fish in different seasons is given in the *Boke of St Albans* (Braekman 1980).

Bait hooks were used in a stationary position with rod and line from classical times. Roman wall painting show anglers fishing with springy rods (Chevenix Trench 1974). Rods are shown as an essential part of the angler's equipment in French medieval manuscript illustrations of the 13th century (eg, Bodleian Library MS *Douce* 118 f 12 v-13, f 128 v, f 127 v-8). Lady Juliana Berners (if she was the author) gives advice in 1496 about the making of composite rods from three different kinds of wood which seems sensible to the modern angler (Braekman 1980; Chevenix-Trench 1974). Her instructions about methods were sophisticated since she distinguished between bottom fishing with a weight but no float, for trout, bleak, roach, and dace; middle-water fishing with a float; and surface fishing 'without a float (but with a bait) for all manner of fish' (Chevenix-Trench 1974).

The reel was not used by medieval anglers. The hand frame for winding in hand lines was a piece of nautical fishing equipment in use towards the end of the period. The sailors who were aboard the *Mary Rose* in 1536 had hand lines, frames, and floats in their chests (Fig 12.4) to use for fishing to supplement their diet while at sea (Rule 1982).

Line fishing requires another item of equipment, the line-sinker. The tradition of making sinkers in stone goes back into the prehistoric period (Hamilton 1968). In the Viking period in Shetland three distinctive types of line-sinker were developed made either of steatite, a soft soapstone, or sandstone pebbles. They might be pear-shaped, on average 120mm long, with a medial perforation and an apical groove with a basal bored hole for the insertion of a wooden or bone plug for the attachment of the bait line. A second type consisted of an ovoid or spherical sandstone pebble with encircling groove along the major axis. A third type was sausage-shaped and had perforations at either end (Hamilton 1956, 3–4, pl xxxvii). The variation in sizes is accounted for by different fishing locations. A smaller cigar-shaped sinker with a medial and basal cord groove was probably used for surface fishing, the larger weights for fishing in deep waters. A decorated Viking Age stone line or net sinker was found in Clifford Street, York; it is obliquely perforated through both ends and is engraved with an interlace on the front and back (Waterman 1959, 97).

In the Middle Ages lead weights for angling or for hand line fishing were used in great numbers. Lead was readily available (Blanchard 1981). These sinkers could be made much smaller because of the greater weight of lead compared with stone. There was a great variety of shapes and sizes (Steane & Foreman 1988). They are found on the Thames foreshore in great profusion (Fig 12.5), doubtless lost by anglers sitting on the wooden waterfront structures (Milne & Hobley 1981, 1–38).

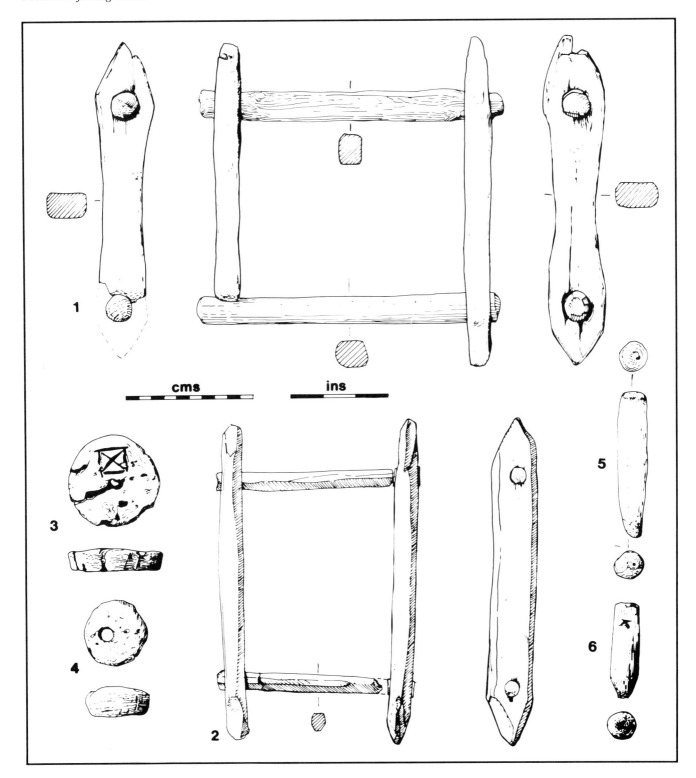

Fig 12.4 Hand frames, for winding in hand-lines, and floats found on the Mary Rose. The floats are of wood and cork

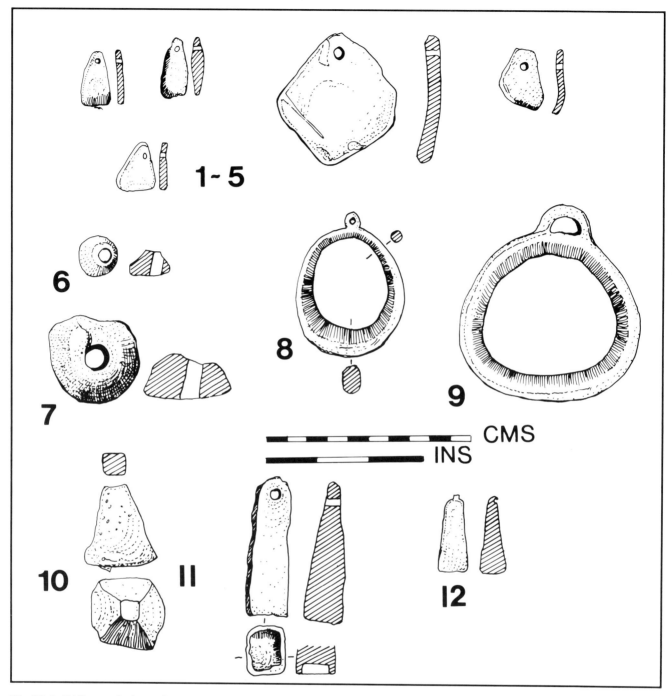

Fig 12.5 Different designs of medieval lead net weights and sinkers mostly from the Thames foreshore. After Department of Urban Archaeology, Museum of London

Fishing using nets

The most effective device for catching fish is probably the net and there is evidence that this had already been discovered in Mesolithic times, at least in its more primitive forms — the drag, sweep, or seine net which was devised for use in shallow waters to surround and enclose surface-swimming fish (Clark 1965). In favourable circumstances such as waterlogging, the evidence in the form of floats, weights or sinkers, and the nets themselves may survive as at Wolin (Rulewicz & Zaj-del-Szczyrska 1970) or at Borgund (Herteig 1975). Occasionally needles and mesh pins required for the

knitting or the braiding of the net are found (Taylor 1974), but usually only the evidence of the weights or the sinkers is left.

Three types of net were in use. The *seine net* is probably the oldest to be used in riverine or estuarine fisheries (Steane & Foreman 1988). Many of the smaller fish, notably whiting, plaice, small cod, and sole whose remains were found in early medieval levels at Great Yarmouth, were probably captured in a shore seine (Rogerson 1976). Here one end of the seine net was attached to the shore and the other was worked from a boat. The *drift net* was a major development of medieval

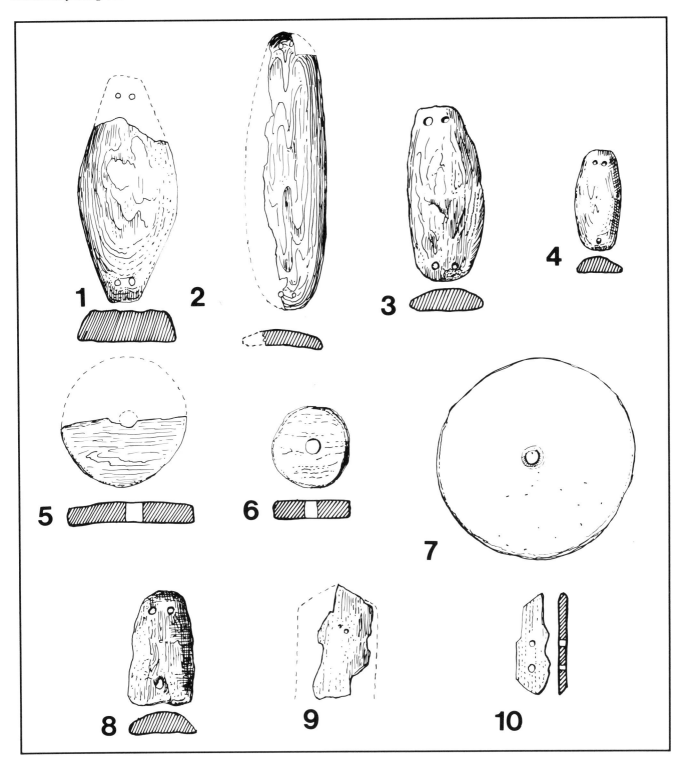

Fig 12.6 Wolin, Poland: floats of wood and bark. After Rulewicz and Zajdel-Szczyrska (1970)

fishing techniques. There is no clue as to the date or place of origin but undoubtedly large catches of herring from the North Sea vouched for in the archaeological and documentary records were made possible by the drift net (Hall 1984; Salzman 1923; Heath 1968). The nets form a perforated wall or barrier and shoals of fish in their endeavour to pass through the barrier force their heads into the meshes (Holdsworth 1874). They can be set near or on the bottom to catch demersal fish. They can be anchored, floating in the mid-water zone; they can be free, drifting gill nets to skim off the surface fish as well as the mid-water fish (von Brandt 1984). The third type of net which developed towards the end of the Middle Ages was the *trawl*. This was essentially a large bag, pulled over the sea bed towards the shore by two boats which kept its mouth open; the catch was

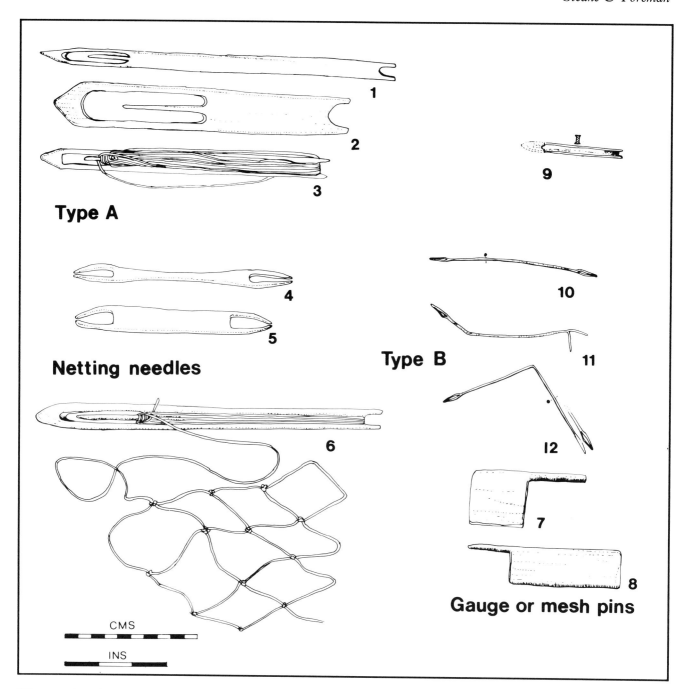

Fig 12.7 Netting tools from Gloucester (1–8), Wolin (9), and London (10–12)

spilled out onto the beach. By attaching a long wooden beam to hold the mouth open it could be operated by a single boat (Steane & Foreman 1988).

The physical remains of nets are difficult to come by in Britain, but nets, floaters and sinkers, have been preserved in Dutch, Norwegian, Russian, and Polish contexts. Some of the floats at Wolin are of wood, circular and perforated, and some are cylindrical with a notch out of the centre (Rulewicz & Zajdel-Szczyrska 1970, 370, 372, 376). Others, which appear to be made of bark, are oval with pairs of holes at each end (Fig 12.6; Rulewicz & Zajdel-Szczyrska 1970, 377-80).

Net making is one of the most ancient crafts and the fabric was normally made of hemp twine. The tools (needles and mesh pins) needed for knitting or braiding

the nets have been described (Taylor 1974). They were simply made of wood (Morris 1981) and were of two types (Fig 12.7). Type A is pointed at one end and has a large 'eye' into which projects a 'tongue'. The other end has two large open prongs. Type B has at each end two relatively long prongs curving inwards, until almost touching. Wolin has produced examples of type A (Rulewicz & Zajdel-Szczyrska 1970) and London has produced type B (information Brian Spencer, Museum of London).

The upper margin of the net is called the head and is carried on the head-line which is buoyed with floats. These are likely to have been made of wood or bark in the early Middle Ages, but cork was used towards the end of the Middle Ages (Gras 1918). The seamen of the

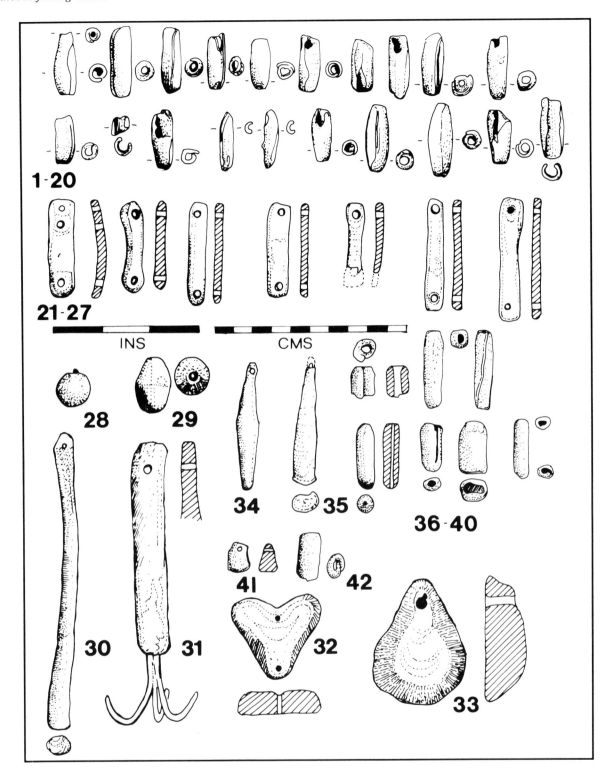

Fig 12.8 Lead net weights and sinkers. 1–20 from Meare, Somerset; 21–42 from London

Mary Rose used cork and willow floats (Fig 12.4) for attaching to their hand-held lines (information M Rule). The lower margin, the foot, is strengthened with a foot-rope which was provided with lead, stone, earthenware, or even iron sinkers or weights as necessary. Meare and Glastonbury lake villages in Somerset have produced pre-Roman Iron Age weights made of lead strip, rectangular, perforated, or rolled round the foot-rope in little, fat cylinders. Similar lead weights were found in the wreck of a 15th century vessel at Black-friars (Fig 12.8; Marsden 1971).

Fishing weights (Fig 12.9) from inland waters have been the subject of two recent surveys (Mynard 1979; Thomas 1982). Mynard dealt with weights from the midland Ouse, Nene, Tove, and Ouzel, and interpreted his weights as combination plugs and sinkers associated with basketwork fish traps. Thomas's article dealt with a smaller range of weights from the upper Thames.

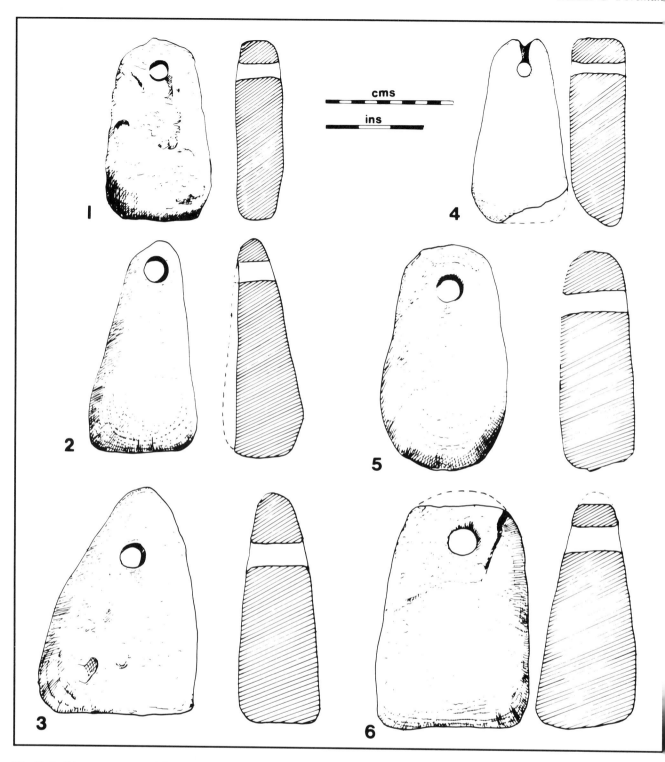

Fig 12.9 Limestone net weights from the river Thames, Oxfordshire. These were found in the upper Thames mainly above Wallingford. For distribution see Steane & Foreman (1988, fig 16)

This range has been greatly expanded (Steane & Foreman 1988). Both the Thames weights and Types 012 and 013 from the Ouse river system have the common feature of a hole towards the top which could facilitate the fixing of objects so that the bulk of the weight would hang down, stretching a net and holding it to the bottom of the river. The rounded forms of most of the weights were to protect the nets from snagging or tearing. A consistent size and weight for use on the same net seem to have been thought desirable. There is a remarkable uniformity in the brick types T9-T11 which betokens mass production. The brick types are found east of the Streatley-Goring gap in areas where limestone was not readily available (Firman & Firman 1967). Firm dating is not available but some are associated with 13th–14th century finds.

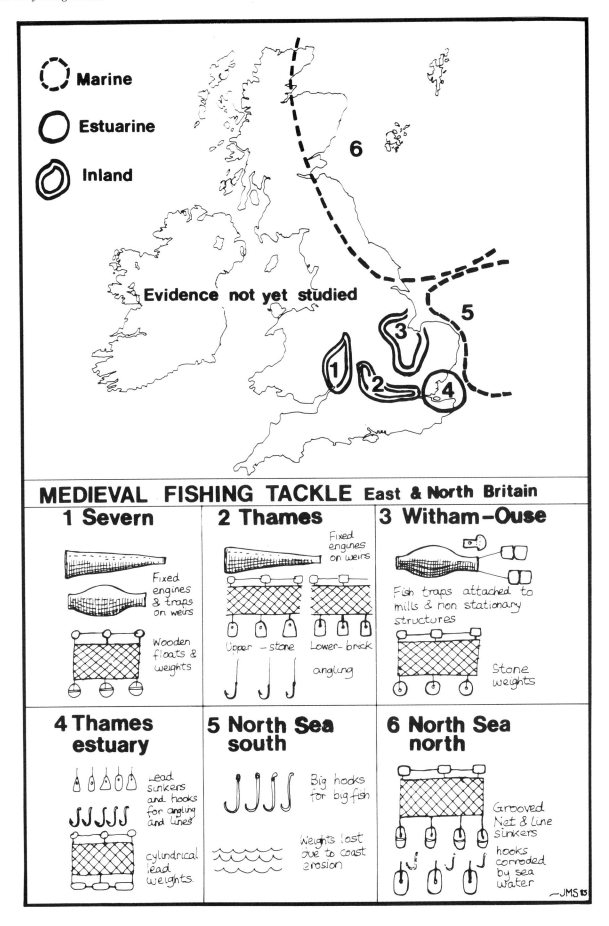

Fig 12.10 Summary of regional medieval fishing traditions as suggested by the variety of techniques and different fishing kits

Fig 12.11 The Haaf station at Stenness c 1880 with 'sixems' drawn up on the beach. Most medieval fishing boats would have dragged up beyond the reach of the tide and the nets dried. Behind are a series of fishermen's huts for storing gear. (Photograph: Shetland Museum and Library)

Fish traps and weirs

Steane & Foreman (1988, 170–8) have reviewed the evidence for these and it seems highly likely that Mynard's interpretation of a number of Ouse fishing weights (01-8) as plugs and sinkers for basketwork fish traps is correct. Further evidence from Salisbury's researches (Salisbury 1981) has shown that fishweirs survive as considerable structures. Where they do survive, other items of the fishermen's kit have been located, including net sinkers and curfew-shaped vessels used in smoking fish (White 1984).

Fishing baskets and scoop nets

Although the artefacts themselves rarely survive in archaeological contexts (Morris 1981), we must envisage medieval fishermen using a vast assortment of baskets for catching, handling, and transporting fish. A wooden skep with a woven rush base was found in the medieval fish tank at Washford (Gray 1969, 12). It may have been used to transfer fish fry from one tank to another. They were also used for handling or transporting fish, as are the landing nets of contemporary sporting fishermen (von Brandt 1984). Fishmongers employed baskets to transport and to hold and display their stock in the temporary market-place stalls which urban regulation insisted they use (Salzman 1923). Baskets were also used to filter water from wells (information B Dix).

Conclusions

The archaeological evidence cited suggests that in central and southern England there were a number of regional medieval fishing traditions, using a variety of techniques. The traditions within these regions did not greatly overlap. If we take the most commonly surviving artefact, the fishing weight, it seems that in the areas covered in the survey there were at least three such regions, each based on a major river system, the Ouse, the Thames, and the Severn (Fig 12.10). More extended studies of artefact distribution may suggest the identification of further regions. The reasons for the lack of overlapping in the techniques used may be connected with the different types of piscine prey available in them, demanding different methods of capture. The Severn fisheries, for instance, specialised in salmon, eel, and lampreys, and the river here was particularly suitable for the construction of weirs with fixed traps into which swift-flowing waters swept multitudes of fish. The rivers of eastern England, on the other hand, supported a more varied if less succulent fish population, which moved more slowly as befitted the quieter waters of their homes. Nets and fish traps weighted down on shallow river bottoms with stones were the consequent modes of capture in the Ouse basin. The Thames on the other hand offered possibilities for the capture of salmon, eels, and a whole gamut of freshwater fish. In the swift-flowing Thames, with its formidable outfall, weirs with fixed 'engines' (*ie*, not requiring weights) were *de rigueur*, a practice which left little trace in the artefactual record. The quieter waters of the upper reaches of the Thames were eminently suited to net fishing — hence the great quantity of stone weights. Towards the estuary and in the North Sea, line fishing involving quantities of lead sinkers clearly became a regular affair by the end of the Middle Ages. The seine net, weighted down by lead, was also in use but only so far proved at the end of the Middle Ages.

In marine contexts the technology changes. The great mackerel, whiting, and cod fisheries of the North

Sea and the stormy waters between Orkney, Shetland, and Norway involved the manufacture of line hooks and sinkers. The shaped and grooved sinkers have survived in large numbers where they were made of stone — as in the Shetlands, Orkneys, and northern English coasts. They have not apparently been found on East Anglian beaches so maybe indistinguishable beach pebbles were used — or possibly the sinkers were made of heavy wood. Perhaps the most likely solution is that coastal erosion has removed the beaches on which the nets were dried (*Observer*, 1 September 1985; Steers 1964) (*cf* Fig 12.11). Some hooks, however, have been found. Largely documentary evidence and the remains of the fish themselves demonstrate the widespread use of the drift net to catch immense quantities of herring, while improved methods of curing guaranteed a sale to the depleted populations of later medieval England. The frequent loss of such gear in the river or at sea has enriched the English language by contributing the expression 'hook, line, and sinker'.

Lastly, fishing had wider repercussions on the nature of society and the communities working within it. Jope (1963) postulated a series of regional cultures within English medieval society recognised by artefacts such as pottery with distinctive characteristics derived from various manufacturing centres and marketed within the region around. The present paper suggests that another group of artefacts, fishing gear, tells a different story. It was probably locally manufactured by members of the fishing community themselves. Most medieval agrarian and riparian communities were largely self-sufficient. The village blacksmith could easily forge the necessary hooks and the fisherman, helped by his wife, knitted or knotted his own nets. In the early Middle Ages the catch was difficult to preserve and so was largely transported live to market centres or eaten fresh. Fishing was on a small scale, the livelihood of scattered groups of riparian dwellers. Rivers crossed the boundaries of Jope's overlapping market centres, so the artefacts with the same stylistic characteristics have a long, winding, linear distribution.

Fisher communities serving a riverside borough like Oxford may have lived by selling their catch in the nearby market (Prior 1982) but it was only when improved methods of salting and curing fish were developed in the later Middle Ages that fish became a more substantial element in an improved rural and urban diet (Taverner 1600). The industry expanded in scale and the technology developed alongside. Great fishing fleets from the Cinque Ports began to exploit the shallow waters of the North Sea (Salzman 1923) thus competing with the herring *busses*, *hoekers*, and *doggers* of the Dutch (Unger 1980). Boat technology was thus stimulated. The aggressive English fishermen (they had a reputation for beating up their trading competitors) supplied smaller populations after the depletions of the Black Death with larger quantities of high protein food, thus contributing to the eventual recovery of the economy. So it can be suggested that any improvements in fishing tackle were less important than these other factors in encouraging the developing of the later medieval fishing industry.

Acknowledgements

We should like to thank the following: the staffs of the History Faculty library, the Bodleian Library, the Ashmolean Museum Library, and the Museum of Oxford; J A Bateman, C J Bond, and J Caton, Oxfordshire County Museum; J Clark and J Cowfill, Museum of London; B A L Cranstone, Pitt Rivers Museum, Oxford for allowing us to read a chapter of his book in advance of publication; R A Croft, then of Milton Keynes Archaeological Unit; B Green, Norfolk Museums Service; M Hall, Thames Water Authority; W Jones, Cleveland County Archaeological Service; A E Herteig, Historisk Museum, Bergen, Norway; C H Lewis, Great Yarmouth Museum; A MacCormick, City of Nottingham Museum; Dr S M Margeson, Norfolk Museums Service; Professor S McGrail, Institute of Archaeology, Oxford; J S McCracken, Museum of London; A McGregor, Ashmolean Museum, Oxford; S C Minnitt, Somerset County Museum, Taunton; C Morris, Gloucester Folk Museum; P Ottaway, York Archaeological Trust; J G Rhodes, Oxfordshire County Museum; Dr M Rule, Mary Rose Trust; Dr C R Salisbury; B W Spencer, Museum of London; D Tweddle, York Archaeological Trust; A J White, Lincolnshire Museums; A Williamson, Shetland Museum; G A B Young, City of Nottingham Museum.

13 Late Saxon and Conquest-period oyster middens at Poole, Dorset

I P Horsey† and J M Winder

Abstract

The investigation of massive medieval shell middens from urban contexts in Poole are described. Substantial middens were partly excavated at three sites where they could be seen to pre-date the town itself and to have provided a foundation for the 13th century wool house and adjacent hard for beaching craft. An estimate is given of the amount of oyster meat represented and methods for dating the material are discussed. The size of the middens and lack of other food remains incorporated in them might suggest commercial harvesting rather than collection for purely local consumption.

Introduction

Although the investigation of coastal middens is an established aspect of prehistoric archaeology, the investigation of similar middens in medieval, sometimes urban, contexts is a relatively neglected field. The discovery of an extensive midden beneath 13th century urban Poole led to a research programme to investigate the date and the nature of the deposit. The techniques used and the problems of dating oysters are likely to be encountered by workers elsewhere. It is to be hoped that this work will lead to the recognition of the importance of other similar deposits whether within urban or other contexts.

Attention was first drawn to massive oyster middens on the foreshore of the medieval port of Poole and on the Hamworthy peninsula opposite in 1981 (Horsey 1981). The location of the sites from which oyster shells were recovered is shown in Figure 13.1. The excavated sites include the interior of the Town Cellars building (PM11), the area of Paradise Street immediately in front of the Town Cellars (PM21), Thames Street leading off Paradise Street (PM9), nearby Pex Marine (PM24), and a borehole at the Shipwrights' Arms in Hamworthy (PM32). Watching-brief observations also recorded oysters at Poole Pottery.

Location of deposits

The Town Cellars is a medieval warehouse built directly on top of the shell midden which was sealed by layers securely dated by pottery to *c* 1300. The shell deposit covered the whole of the excavated internal area of the building and extended outside it in all directions. It consisted entirely of discarded oyster shells, thickening from 0.2m at the back of the building to 0.5m at the front, and increasing as the shells deliberately or inadvertently reclaimed the sloping foreshore outside, beneath Paradise Street, where it was not possible to determine the full thickness of the deposit.

At adjacent Thames Street the shells occupied a similar stratigraphic context to those from the Town Cellars but appeared as a discrete accumulation. On the Pex Marine site, only the top of the shell deposit, below later medieval rubbish dumped during foreshore reclamation, was sampled. A borehole through the foundations of the Shipwrights' Arms in Hamworthy revealed an oyster midden 3.4m thick.

Quantity of shell

Lack of data means that it is not possible to estimate accurately the full extent of these oyster deposits, but the archaeological evidence coupled with that from boreholes and observation sites may suggest that the midden on the Poole waterfront was continuous along the foreshore for a minimum of 100m. Its width is also difficult to estimate, but 40m may be average. Although the maximum depth of the deposit on the Poole side has not been determined, it would seem to average *c* 1m. There is a cluster of oyster observations, some on reclaimed land, in the Poole Pottery area.

The quantity of oyster shell represented by the Poole midden, based on the above size approximations, is enormous. Using the minimum and maximum estimates of length, and the number of individual oysters found in a measured volume of the midden (238 MNI oysters in a half-metre cube, PM21 502.206 sample 19), it is possible to calculate that the midden might contain between 3,808,000 and 7,616,000 oysters. The Ministry of Agriculture, Fisheries, and Food (Lowestoft) has provided unpublished data giving an average wet-meat weight of 7.5g for oysters. A Medical Research Council report on food values gives the value of 50 calories per 100g of oyster meat. Therefore, the midden could represent between 28.56 and 57.12 tonnes of raw oyster meat. If the average consumption in calories per day for a man is standardised at 2000, then the Poole midden would have provided 7140 to 14,260 man/days (between 19 and 38 man/years) of food. A man would have to eat 532 oysters a day to obtain the required energy level.

Dating of the oyster shells

Six samples of oyster shell were sent to the Harwell

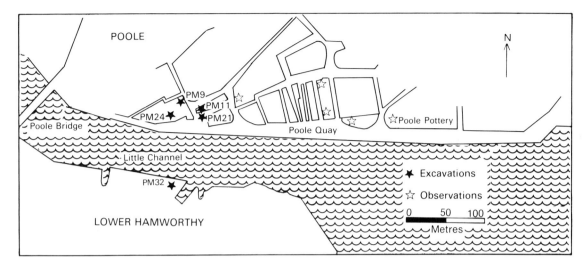

Fig 13.1 Poole: location of oyster deposits in Poole and Hamworthy

laboratory for radiocarbon dating. The problem of obtaining reliable radiocarbon age determinations from calcitic shells has been discussed by Burleigh (Preece *et al* 1983). The major problem is that the original carbon may have been replaced by more recent carbon, either by mechanical contamination where particles or solutions have entered the interstices and become absorbed, or by carbon isotope exchange between the shell and the environment. This recrystallisation by solution and reprecipitation (Craig 1954) can have an important effect on radiocarbon dating.

Shells from the samples PM11 (141) and PM32 (1D) examined by T Yates using acetate peels and a low-power petrological microscope showed them to be unaltered calcitic structures in which recrystallisation was unlikely to have occurred (information T Yates). There were, however, cavities in the samples, in one case occupying 15–20% of the section, and the growth layers were visible as deeply incised grooves immediately below the shell surface via which mechanical contamination could have taken place. The sample from PM24 (12) which came from immediately below a rubbish tip high in organic acids was considered likely to have been recrystallised (it was not examined microscopically).

The calculation of radiocarbon dates and the way in which results are expressed may vary at different laboratories (Mangerud 1972; Gillespie & Polach 1979). The Harwell figures were presented without the correction for 'apparent age', but this has been calculated using the formula presented by Harkness (Harkness 1985) and added to the results given in Table 13.1. Unlike terrestrial organisms which mainly utilise carbon containing relatively new carbon isotopes from the atmosphere, marine organisms tend to incorporate older, recirculated carbon from the oceans so that molluscs such as oysters have a radiocarbon age at death that can vary from 200 years to more than 2500 years according to the region of origin. In the United Kingdom the apparent age correction involves the substraction of 405 ± 40 (Harkness 1985) from the age given by the conventional radiocarbon dating for marine molluscs.

The dates for the Poole oyster shells range from AD 935 ± 81 for the lowermost layer from the Shipwrights' Arms core to AD 1385 ± 81 for the Pex Marine sample, which, as previously stated, could well have been subject to contamination by more recent carbon. The Thames Street sample dates to AD 995 ± 81 and therefore is contemporaneous with the middle layers of the Shipwrights' Arms core sample, but earlier than the other samples from the Poole side. The top of the Shipwrights' Arms core contained shells dating to AD 1075 ± 90 which is slightly earlier than the AD 1095 ± 108 dates obtained for both the Town Cellars and Paradise Street samples. The Shipwrights' Arms core deposit of 3.4m depth accumulated over a period of about 150 years.

Origin of the oysters

Preliminary analysis of the shells indicates that the oysters were not washed up naturally on the shore, but were deposited after harvesting from the sea (Winder forthcoming). The existence of the midden was fortuitous in providing both a firm foundation for the wool-house and an adjacent hard for beaching craft. The midden predates the founding of Poole. The group of radiocarbon dates for the Poole and Hamworthy oyster shells (excluding those from Pex Marine) places their deposition in the 10th, 11th, and 12th centuries. The occurrence of such large middens in the late Saxon and early medieval periods in this locality is enigmatic.

A parallel for waterside activity leading to a town's foundation could be Lynn in the 11th century (Owen 1979) where it is argued that salt-workings encouraged visits by merchants. The town itself was constructed on the piles of sand left by the salt-extraction process.

Although Hamworthy was a small port in the late Iron Age and early Romano-British periods, there is no evidence to suggest that the settlement extended beyond the end of the Roman occupation. Neither the documentary nor the archaeological evidence suggests an origin for Poole much before *c* 1200: neither Poole nor Hamworthy is recorded in the Domesday Book. Despite an intensive series of rescue excavations under-

Table 13.1 Radiocarbon dates for oyster (Ostrea edulis L) shells from Poole and Hamworthy sites (bp = before present (1950); years corrected to nearest whole number)

Lab No	Site	Context	Radiocarbon Age bp (Harwell figures)	Radiocarbon Age bp (Harkness formula)	Date
Har-2774	Town Cellars, Poole	PM11 (142)	1260 ± 100	855 ± 108	AD 1095 ± 108
Har-2775	Paradise Street, Poole	PM21 (58)	1260 ± 100	855 ± 108	AD 1095 ± 108
Har-3462	Pex Marine, Poole	PM24 (12)	970 ± 70	565 ± 81	AD 1385 ± 81
Har-3463	Thames Street, Poole	PM9 (6)	1360 ± 70	955 ± 81	AD 995 ± 81
Har-3464	Shipwrights' Arms, Hamworthy	PM32 (1D) Top sample	1280 ± 80	875 ± 90	AD 1075 ± 90
Har-3465	Shipwrights' Arms, Hamworthy	PM32 (11D) Bottom sample	1420 ± 70	1015 ± 81	AD 935 ± 81

taken by Poole Museums Service Archaeological Unit since 1972, no field archaeological evidence to alter this interpretation of the town's origins has been produced.

However, on the Foundry site excavated in 1987, a single sherd of pottery provisionally identified as an import from Quentovic was recovered in a residual context. This sherd is not closely datable although of post-Roman and pre-Conquest date. A sherd of 10th century English shell-tempered pottery was also present in a residual context on the Thames Street (PM9) site. These sherds seem to confirm the results of the radiocarbon dating without suggesting necessarily any permanent occupation – certainly not on any scale. If any small permanent settlement is implied it is best seen in relation to the 7th century ecclesiastical settlement and later Saxon *burh* at Wareham. The Poole area has double tides. Consequently, a sailing boat entering Poole Harbour on the incoming tide would probably reach Poole before the tide turned, and anchor. It would reach the mouth of the Frome on the next tide and finally reach Wareham on the third tide 18 hours later.

Oyster shells are frequently found on Roman and Saxon waterfront sites in London. At the Pudding Lane site, for example, analysis of the size, shape, and infestation of the shells suggested improvement of natural stocks by the Romans. One of the interpretations placed on the location of massive dumps of oyster shells beneath the openwork jetty was that processing of the shellfish may have taken place (Winder 1985).

Post-Roman middens have been recorded elsewhere, *eg*, at Bantham, Devon (Silvester 1981; Griffith 1986), and at Burrow Hill, Suffolk (Fenwick 1984). In the investigation of an 11th–12th century shell midden in Braunton Burrows (Smith *et al* 1983), the authors suggest that the midden represents a cooking or processing site for shellfish redistribution. However, there seem to be no middens comparable in scale to those at Poole. It is interesting to note that there are unsubstantiated reports of large oyster-shell deposits at Wareham. This town on the opposite side of Poole Harbour was in

existence before Poole. The silting-up of the Wareham channel and the advent of deeper-hulled boats is thought to have been one of the reasons for the establishment of a new port at Poole.

The massive oyster middens at Poole are an important additional strand of evidence for Dorset in the mid-late Saxon and early post-Conquest period, but without additional data it is possible only to speculate on the implications. Notwithstanding the difficulties of demonstrating post-Roman settlements, it is unlikely that the excavations at Poole would have failed to locate such settlement had it existed under the later medieval town. It is possible that, if a settlement existed, it could have been located away from the middens, either further along the waterfront, on Hamworthy which has not been extensively excavated since the 1930s, or on another part of the harbour. Probably any settlement was only small and could even have been seasonal.

The rapidity with which such waste from the exploitation of marine molluscs can accumulate is well demonstrated by modern parallels. Given the magnitude of the evidence from Poole and Hamworthy, and the fact that no other food remains are incorporated with the oyster shells, it could be that the middens do not simply reflect part of the diet of an as yet unlocated local population. It seems possible that the oysters were being harvested on an almost commercial scale, opened, and the meat salted or pickled in brine in the way documented in the 17th century (Philpots 1890).

Acknowledgements

This report is based on a first draft by the late I P Horsey. It has been prepared and revised by Mrs J M Winder who is conducting a detailed study of the Poole oyster deposits. Keith Jarvis kindly commented on the draft and advised on the most recent pottery and field evidence, and the interpretation of this evidence. David Hinton has also provided constructive comments on the draft and has suggested relevant literature.

14 New light on early ship- and boatbuilding in the London area
D Goodburn

Abstract

This paper presents an interim discussion on the evidence for shipwrightry from recent excavation of boat and ship timbers from the London waterfront area. The fragmentary finds from four sites are described. These examples serve to detail major changes in boatbuilding technology from simple logboats of the 10th century to complex, multi-decked ships of the 17th century. The tools and techniques of boatbuilding evidenced or implied by these finds is discussed and it is concluded that elements of local building traditions are discernible.

Introduction

This paper attempts a selective review of the evidence for early shipwrightry provided by some of the many recent finds of boat and ship timbers from London waterfront excavations (Fig 14.1). All were rescue excavations carried out by the Museum of London Department of Greater London Archaeology (DGLA) and Department of Urban Archaeology (DUA). Tribute must be paid to those who worked on the various projects mentioned here, often in extremely difficult circumstances. The quantity of boat and ship timbers that have been found from the winter of 1986 onwards is so large that many are still to be examined in detail. It will only be possible, therefore, to present a more detailed account of this material at a later date, and all the interpretations presented here must be viewed as provisional. The dating of the boat and ship timbers is also provisional, based mainly on initial finds dating, and will no doubt be rendered much more exact as the results of dendrochronological analysis become available. More detailed information about the finds mentioned here can be found with the site archive records.

Nature of the finds

All the recent finds, with one exception, are fairly fragmentary, unlike the relatively complete wrecks previously briefly published by Marsden (1981). However, as Christensen (1985, 197) has pointed out in his report on the Bryggen nautical timbers, the detailed recording and study of such relatively common finds can shed much new light on early shipbuilding, and provide a broader view of the evolving technologies concerned. The London finds vary between isolated, small, reused timbers to large, reused, articulated slabs of boat sides, which, to date, are the largest pieces of any vessels of the medieval period (c 1100 – c 1350) found in the whole of Britain (below, the Kingston no 3 boat). The relative paucity of medieval boat and ship finds from Britain means that any new finds are likely to add

detail to the existing corpus of knowledge. Though chronicling the craft of boat and shipbuilders in material terms, the study of these finds can also provide information of a social kind. Economy, social status, and the life history or changing use to which a vessel was put can also be investigated. The story presented by the fragments of ancient shipwrightry from London is a very human one, telling of the skills and daily life of waterfront communities in the Thames region. A working assumption has been made by the writer that all the recent finds derive from vessels which were built in the Thames region or another part of south-east England, as no evidence of foreign origins has yet been found. The larger ship fragments cannot, however, be so closely tied to the Thames region, but English origins still seem most likely. The dendrochronological analyses, yet to be carried out, may suggest foreign origins for raw materials which will cause the working assumption to be reassessed.

Documentary and iconographic sources for early shipbuilding

As yet little work has been done to investigate systematically the documentary sources which might shed light on the activities of early shipwrights in the London area. More work will clearly yield useful information, as can be demonstrated by a glimpse of the work of two early 14th century shipwrights. In 1311 a payment of 7s, as recorded in the Tower Accounts, was paid to one John Mitchell, shipwright, and 4s 8d to one William Litelwille for riveting together a gate (Salzman 1952, 309). This passage demonstrates that shipwrights, using rove nails, fastened together doors, and the difference in payments suggests that Litelwille was an assistant (journeyman) to Mitchell.

Another source often used, contemporary iconography, has yielded little evidence in London. The recent find of a badge (Fig 14.2), however, commemorating Becket's return from exile, and dated perhaps

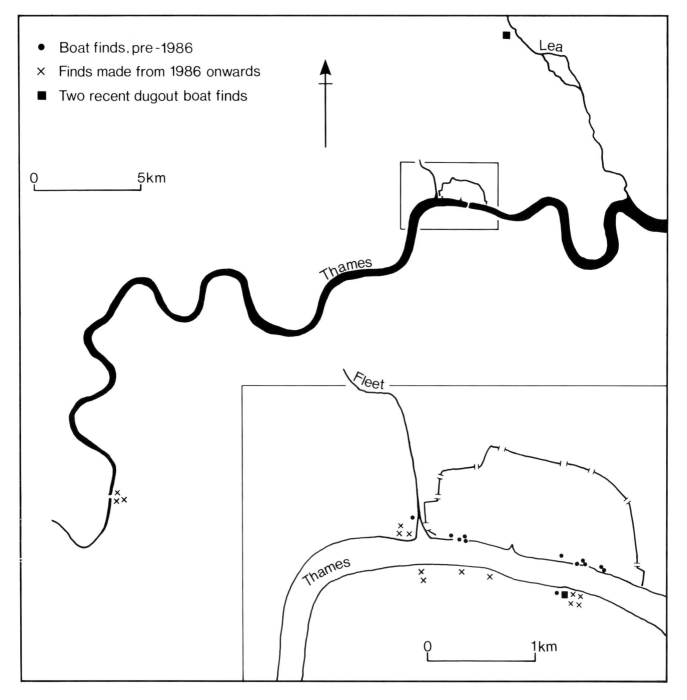

Fig 14.1 Plans showing the find-spots of Saxon to post-medieval boat finds in the London area

to the 14th century (information P Stott), shows what is usually referred to as a *hulk*, a type of later medieval trading ship with very upturned ends. Hulks are depicted rigged for sailing, but it has never been clear how the round-bottomed vessels obtained enough grip on the water to be able to do more than sail directly before the wind. This representation seems to show a projecting fin at the bow and stern which would have given the vessel more grip on the water to help counteract leeway (sideways drift). Similar fins or gripes were added to the bows of recent West Jutland fishing craft of a similar round-bottomed shape to the medieval hulk, to give them more grip on the water (Nielsen 1980). With these fins the hulks might actually be

considered practical sailing vessels, capable of crossing the North Sea. All previous depictions known to the writer omit these crucial details.

The Clapton logboat (dugout)

Description of the boat

Simple evolutionary models of the development of boatbuilding technology are inappropriate. This was underlined by the popular descriptions of the Clapton logboat as Stone Age when it was found by contractors and reported to the DGLA by the borough surveyor in late 1987. It lay in silt next to the river Lea. It was

Fig 14.2 Drawing of a c 14th century 'Becket's Return' badge recently found in London. It shows a hulk rigged for sailing, with a stern-hung rudder and what appear to be 'fins' (skeg and gripe) protruding from the bow and stern

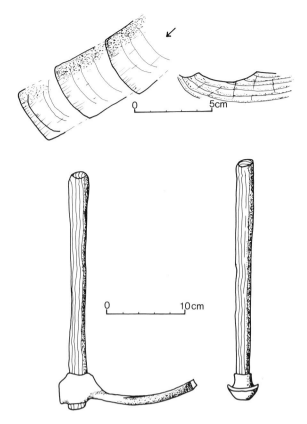

Fig 14.3 Top: scale sketches of gouge marks from the turn of the bilge inboard of the Clapton dugout. Bottom: a scale reconstruction sketch of a small gouge adze, probably used to finish the very concave internal surfaces of the hull

immediately clear from the tool marks surviving on parts of the hull that a very late prehistoric date was the earliest possible, as they had been made by metal tools. The vessel, of common oak (*Quercus robur* or *Q petrea*), was dendrochronologically dated by I Tyers to the latter half of the 10th century. A more exact date could not be given due to the lack of large numbers of sapwood rings (Tyers 1989).

The boat resembles a small round-bottomed punt in shape, with the angular chine at the bow and stern possibly simulating the appearance of larger contemporary plank-built boats (Marsden 1989). As the boat was moderately complete, with only the upper part of the wider presumed stern, and most of the starboard side broken off by the digging machine, it was possible to estimate its original dimensions. It was about 3.75m long with a beam of about 0.65m and a depth of side of about 0.41m. The squared off, narrower, presumed bow end had been split but was held together with a wooden tie treenailed down just in front of a larger open hole which may have accommodated a mooring pole. The boat had a distinctive ridge of solid wood left about midships, possibly for use as a thwart. The latter attribute, its general shape, and the presence of a tie at the end seem to be the characteristics of a local Saxon to medieval boatbuilding tradition peculiar to the river Lea, as three other similar craft have been found along its course (McGrail 1989). The original find will eventually go on display at Hackney Museum.

The recording of the tool marks, and the evidence for the woodworking techniques

The tool marks were examined during and after the cleaning of the boat by the conservation department of the Museum of London. Photographs were taken by P Marsden to record the general appearance of the marks. The largest and best-preserved examples of any particular apparent type were drawn at 1:1, and a plan record of selected blade-end impressions was made. Sketch cross-sections at 1:1 were also made to show the degree of concavity, if any, of the marks (Fig 14.3). Finally a three-dimensional record of the same facets was made by casting them with silicon rubber with the assistance of the conservation department. The casts were labelled and a sketch made of their orientation, so that the mode of use of the tool was recorded. The facets could then be examined in good light and more accurate measurements taken. They could also be used to make hard resin copies. It is important to note that erosion and the latest phases of working have removed many of the traces of the earlier stages of work (Goodburn 1989).

The tools and approach used to build the boat

It is possible to suggest a tool kit which may have been used to build the craft, composed of tools for which there is hard evidence and others which can be surmised, with reference to excavated tools of the period and practical experience. Listed below are the tools; with the exception of the first, all had left their marks on the hull of the boat.

1 A moderately large felling axe, for rough hewing and crosscutting.
2 A thin-bladed hatchet or small axe (possibly a side axe) with a blade 80mm or more wide, used for trimming the bulkhead and probably parts of the outside and upper inside of the hull.
3 An adze with a slightly rounded end to the blade, at least 70mm across, used to finish the flat middle parts of the bottom inside and possibly parts of the outside.
4 A gouge adze, or less likely, a large driven gouge with a concave flat-ended blade about 40mm across (Fig 14.3).
5 At least one auger, about 22mm in diameter, for boring the thickness-gauge holes and the treenail holes for the bow tie fastenings.

To the above can probably be added wooden wedges, levers, rope, and marking implements such as a knife or charred twigs. The gouge adze is not apparently otherwise known as an excavated tool type of the Saxon period.

The building of a replica

To investigate the technical problems involved with building such craft and to provide an educational display, the writer, together with the charity Marine Archaeological Surveys, and many volunteers, built an exact replica. Only hand tools closely similar to those above were used (Fig 14.4), and the work was fully documented (Goodburn & Redknap 1988). The project was a very useful learning experience, which tangibly demonstrated to all concerned the great effort and skills required to build even a simple boat. The vessel has been test-launched and though the original boat had been described as a one-man craft, the replica could carry four small adults in still water conditions, even in its heavy green state. It has now been displayed at two waterfront museums and will be systematically tested afloat.

The role of the original boat was probably varied, servicing the needs of a household of farming, fishing, and fowling folk living on the edge of the Lea or one of its tributaries. The wide expanse of wetlands would have made boats indispensable. Traces of beeswax and imported pine tar were found sealing one of the bunged thickness-gauge holes. The tar was probably exchanged for farm, fishing, or fowling produce and it is not difficult to envisage the Clapton boat carrying a small cargo of fish, poultry, or dairy products to the nearest exchange or trading place. The nearest recent parallels might be the small Norfolk Broads punts or farmers' milkboats from the Netherlands. Small dugout boats, such as the Clapton find, should clearly be viewed as an essential element of the rural economy, at least in the Saxon period, as several English river systems have produced groups of similar Saxon finds.

Fig 14.4 A gouge adze similar to that apparently used on the original Clapton dugout boat, being used to shape the concave bow of the Marine Archaeological Survey replica Ravensbourne

The clinker-built Kingston boat finds

In general terms, north European boatbuilding from AD 500 to AD 1700 is beginning to be well understood. The boats were most commonly built of oak except in the northernmost parts of Europe, where softwoods were used. The hull planks were sawn or cleft out, and attached to a backbone of keel and stem and stern posts; the planks were fastened together, overlapping along their edges, by iron rivets, treenails (wooden pegs with expanded ends), lashing or sewing. As a distinct second stage the crossways framing was fastened in, commonly with treenails, the shape of the planking which made up the strakes (run of planks) being the most important factor governing the shape of the boat. The boats and ships were often similar at both ends (double-ended).

Within this widespread system of nautical construction, there appear to be distinct variations relating to period, place, and function (see Goodburn 1986 for the English variants). Since many of the attributes of the finds about to be described are not paralleled in continental material, they are provisionally assumed to be elements of local traditions of construction.

The original building dates for the Kingston material should lie in the period c 1250–c 1300. Though small fragments of radially cleft, oak, small-boat planking 15mm thick were found, some of which appeared to derive from boats with treenail-fastened laps, the most substantial finds have been described as nos 1, 2, and 3 boats (Goodburn 1988). Importantly, some roughed-out shipbuilding timbers were also recovered, implying shipbuilding nearby. The scantling of these timbers suggests that they were destined for use in medium-sized craft, not small boats (Potter this volume).

The Kingston no 1 boat

For the sake of brevity, this reused boat find will be described in more detail than those which follow, where only attributes that differ will be the principal concern. The find consists of several slabs of articulated planking

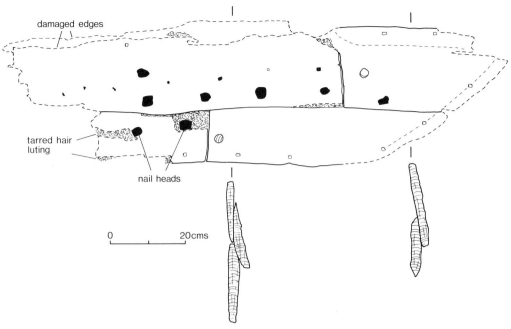

Fig 14.5 The outboard face of the planking from the stern of the Kingston no 1 boat, port side. Junction with the stern post to the right

reused as revetment sheathing. The largest is a slab of the port or larboard side of a vessel 9.3m long and about 0.8m wide. A section of port stern hood ends appears to line up with this, giving a length of 11m (Fig 14.5). The side of origin in the parent vessel is apparent from the consistent direction of the scarf slopes, cut so as to open aft, outboard (Fig 14.6). The original length of the vessel appears to be about 15m (50ft).

The planking was both radially and tangentially cleft oak averaging about 35mm thick. Some of it was quite knotty and must have required considerable skill to cleave out (it was often difficult to examine the cross-sections of planks). The knots, the presence of sapwood, and the reuse of sections of old boat planking, suggest that the choice of plank raw material was limited (Fig 14.7). There could be a number of other limiting factors, as well as raw material availability. The planking was held together at the laps and scarfs with iron rove nails (rivets), having square shanks and square, irregular, or diamond-shaped roves (washers). The luting in the laps and scarfs and under repairs consisting of cleft oak patches (tingles) was tarred hair

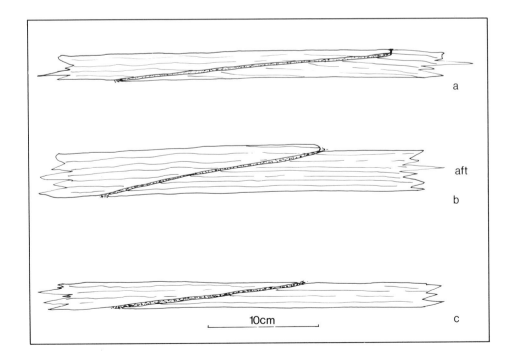

Fig 14.6 Longitudinal sections through a) the Kingston no 1, b) the Kingston no 3, c) the Abbots Lane watching brief boat finds (outboard faces top)

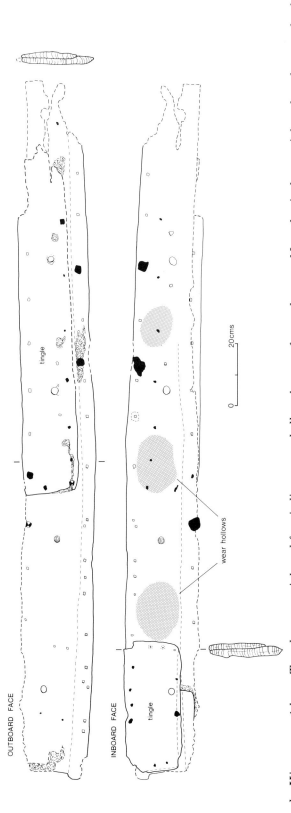

Fig 14.7 A plank from the Kingston no 1 boat. Toned areas on inboard face indicate wear hollows between frame elements. Note the tingles, one inboard, and one made of a reused boat plank outboard, as shown by the relict treenail holes

OUTBOARD FACE

INBOARD FACE

tingle

wear hollows

tingle

20cms

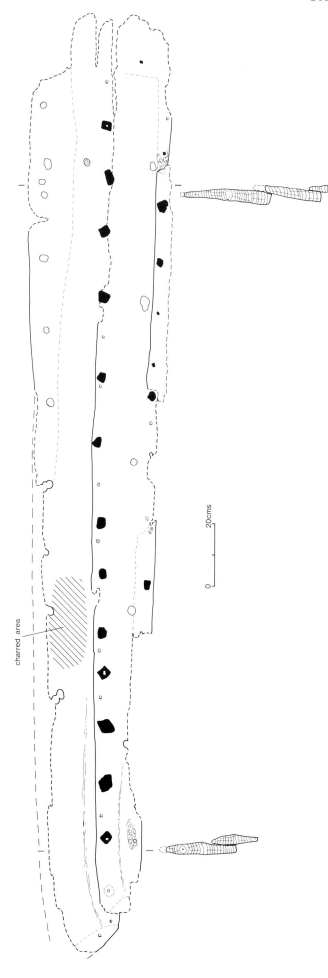

Fig 14.8 The inboard face of the possible sheer strake section from the Kingston no 1 boat. The holes between the roves (indicated by solid black) show either that the plank below the upper, sheer strake was reused, or that the sheer strake was a replacement, as the holes do not pierce it; the charred area (shaded), possibly resulted from bending the plank

charred area

20cms

laid in loose rolls. The tingles were laid in neatly dressed shallow hollows and were held on with twice-turned iron nails of square section.

The plank scarfs were very skilfully cut with an axe so as to have a strong 'nibbed' end outboard, and a slope of about 10:1 (Fig 14.6). The scarfs of this and other recent medieval clinker-boat finds from London appear to be very much longer than those of Dark Age craft, such as those in the late Saxon Graveney boat, which had a slope of 3 or 4:1 (Fenwick 1978). They required more skill and time to cut but were stronger, often being even longer than those used by modern British clinker-boat builders. The Kingston no 1 boat gives the impression of having been built and repaired by very skilled shipwrights who, however, often had to work with timber of varied and sometimes poor quality.

The frame elements were fastened in with bulbous-headed treenails originally of a soft smooth-grained wood, probably willow or poplar (*Salix* or *Poplus* sp). Some repair treenails were of oak. Where unabraded shadows of the frame timbers lay it was possible to record that they were at least 100mm (4in) wide.

The type of vessel from which the planking was derived is indicated by the relatively close spacing of the frame elements, at about 0.45m (centres) apart, and the tremendous wear on the planking inboard and outboard. These factors and the relatively thick planking, compared with that in the Graveney boat for example, suggest that the boat was a medium-sized merchant vessel, which, at least in later years, carried loose abrasive cargoes such as stone. The shape of the hood ends and the possible sheer strake section (Fig 14.8) indicate that the vessel did not have strongly upswept ends in the manner of the Viking stereotype. Very tentatively, it can be suggested that it would have resembled the coastal trader Kalmar no 1 and might fit into Crumlin-Pedersen's coaster class (Crumlin-Pedersen 1985). A less elevated function might have been as a river sailing barge principally engaged in stone carriage. The weight and size of the craft suggest that tides, sails, and poles, rather than oars, would have been used for propulsion.

The Kingston nos 2 and 3 boats

Two more large slabs of articulated reused clinker-boat side were found at the Kingston Horsefair site, apparently from two different parent craft. The no 2 boat consists of a slab, 13m long by *c* 0.9m wide, of the port side of a fairly large vessel. It includes part of the port side at the stern and is the largest piece of boat from the medieval period (*c* 1100–*c* 1350) yet found in England. As the strakes taper in towards the bow only slightly, an original length for the parent vessel of about 17m seems likely. The section is nearly five strakes wide, with planks about 45mm thick, where least abraded, and up to 0.3m wide. The significant differences from the no 1 boat are that the planks are thicker and the scarf type is a little shorter, with the outboard end overlapping and protruding about 8mm (*cf* Fig 14.6).

The no 3 boat consisted of a slab of the starboard side, just under 6m long, of what may have been an even larger vessel. The planking was on average about 50mm thick where unabraded and the widest was over 0.3m

wide. It was scarfed in the same way as the planks of the no 2 boat. The most significant feature of this section of planking was the presence of a D-section wale strake, possibly a sheer strake, 80mm thick and 0.25m wide. This rather knotty, tangentially faced strake had faint saw marks surviving on it in places. If a date of building of around 1300 is correct, this constitutes the earliest post-Roman use in Britain of sawn planking in boat-building. The limited use of the saw and tangential cleaving may have been adopted to make planking where particularly long and/or wide strakes were required, the wale in the no 3 boat being at least 5.9m in length.

The frame spacing, to centres, in all the larger Kingston finds was about 0.45–0.48m, where this was discernible. This corresponds to the writer's cubit or forearm (0.47m). This may have been a rough unit of measurement used when heavily built cargo vessels were constructed.

Though the three larger Kingston boats were all extensively and carefully repaired, their condition prior to break-up was totally unseaworthy. Even if they were only used as river barges or lighters, their condition implies that the safety of the crews was not taken very seriously.

The tool kit evidenced by the tool marks left on the planking of the medieval Kingston boats included various axes, some narrow-bladed adzes (used to cut hollow patch seatings between frames inboard), some kind of shave- or draw-knife for smoothing the laps, a variety of augers, a knife or gauge for marking laps and the occasional use of a large saw to convert specialised planks, though wedges and mauls would appear to have been the main plank-converting tools.

Clinker-boat finds at Hays Wharf

A large number of reused boat fragments was found during the DGLA Hays Wharf rescue project. One small group of reused, radially cleft, oak planks appears to derive from a very large vessel as they are about 60mm thick and pierced by bulbous-headed treenails about 36mm in diameter. These fragments constitute evidence of the largest clinker-built ship found in London to date. They have been provisionally dated to the late medieval period. The ends of some of the oak treenails were further expanded with square-sectioned wooden plugs, possibly as repairs.

Large fragments of articulated planking from the starboard side of a medium-sized 15th or 16th century vessel were found reused in a moat revetment. The parent vessel had been very heavily repaired and tingled inboard and outboard to such an extent that in places there was a total thickness of up to five planks.

Some of the other reused clinker-boat planking of about 16th century date were of elm (*Ulmus* sp) which, as it cannot be split into wide planks, must have been sawn out. This adoption of elm for plank stock in the post-medieval period parallels its increasing use in buildings, and indicates that sawn planking was now being accepted for some purposes by clinker-boat builders.

At 245 Blackfriars Road the DGLA found both reused clinker-boat planking and frame fragments of

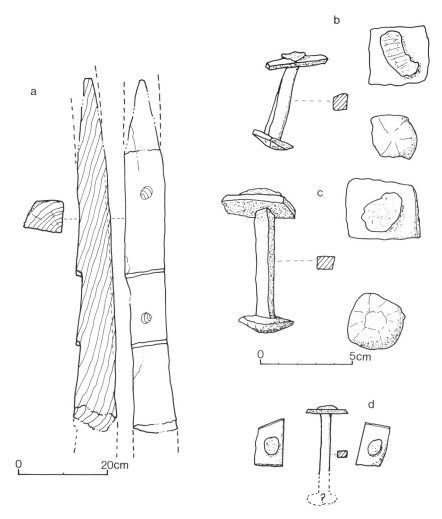

Fig 14.9 a) A clinker-boat frame fragment from the Blackfriars Road site, reused as a pile. Lap rivets (rove nails) from b) Kingston no 1, medieval, c) Abbots Lane watching brief, late medieval, d) Blackfriars Road, 17th century (note the reduction in size)

approximately 17th century date. The frame element fragments had been reused as piles, but the joggles (steps) cut to accommodate the stepped profile of a clinker-built hull were still visible (a on Fig 14.9). The frame-element fragments had been hewn out of small pieces of oak and much wane and sapwood were left on.

Two articulated, radial-faced, oak clinker-boat hull planks were found in which some of the iron lap rove nails were well preserved. Figure 14.9 shows how much smaller they are than the earlier medieval rove nails found in the Kingston no 1 boat even though the scantling is similar. This comparative reduction in size of the roves can be seen in other 17th century clinker boats, such as fragments from the City of London Boys' School, Blackfriars no 2, and the 17th century ceremonial barge in the National Maritime Museum at Greenwich. The change appears to mark a progress towards the much smaller rove nails used in recent times and may therefore be a datable characteristic.

The boat and ship timbers from the City of London Boys' School site

During a limited controlled rescue excavation in difficult conditions, and during later watching briefs, a collection of timbers was made from the City of London Boys' School site, which lay just to the west of the confluence of the rivers Fleet and Thames. What was very new, and initially confusing, about this material was that it was derived from carvel-built ships and boats, with the exception of some small very decayed clinker-boat planking. This was the first time such material had been found in London.

The developed carvel-building system involves the erection of an elaborate framework of timbers, which is then clad with planking placed edge to edge and flush, the seams being caulked by driving in a waterproofing material. The system was apparently introduced from southern Europe. Northern shipwrights, however, used to working by erecting the planking first, continued

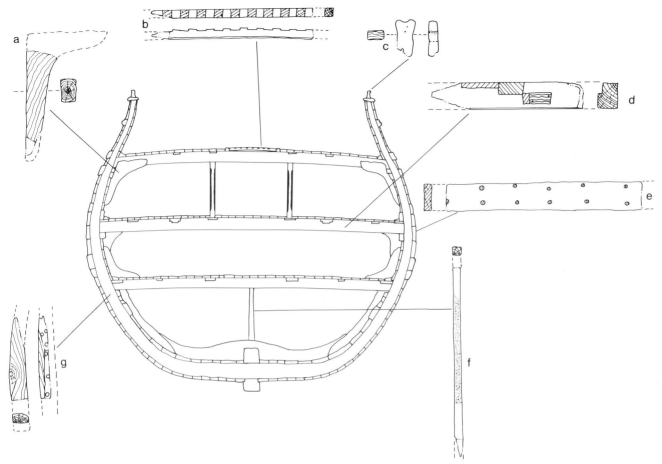

Fig 14.10 Diagram to show the probable points of origin of some of the reused carvel ship timbers from the City of London Boys' School site: a) knees; b) hatch grating beam; c) belaying timber; d) principal deck beam with a softwood blocking piece; e) hull plank; f) post or stanchion; g) section of resawn frame element

building at least the lower hull shell first, and then erected the internal framework as in the 17th century merchant vessel displayed in the Ketelhaven Ship Archaeology Museum. Though the evidence is not totally conclusive, it would appear that the smaller vessel or vessels represented in the collection of over 320 timbers was built at least partly shell first. This is suggested because the frame elements have no trace of the fastenings necessary for pre-erection.

The timbers were reused in three main ways: as closely spaced piles driven into the soft made ground by the waterfront; as a timber raft foundation for a large building, probably the Duke's Theatre which was built on the waterfront in the 1670s; and as cladding of the 1670s post-Great Fire revetment. The building of the parent vessels should date to around the mid 17th century, though this is provisional, based on finds dates for the reuse of the timbers. There are also technological parallels with, for example, the *Dartmouth* which was built in 1655 at Portsmouth (Martin 1978).

The collection of timbers was analysed by computer, and the timbers grouped into structural classes, such as frame elements, and ship planking. It very soon became apparent that the material fell into two broad sub-divisions, timbers deriving from one or more large carvel-built ships, and timbers deriving from what appeared to be a medium-sized roughly built vessel.

The finish, size of timbers, and fastenings were the main criteria used.

A wide variety of parts of the large vessel or vessels and the medium-sized craft was retrieved. Large ship fragments (Fig 14.10) include: major deck beams; minor beams or 'ledges'; stanchions; knees; deck planking; hatch coamings; hatch grating beams; belaying timber; moulded ribbands and other external decorative timbers; frame elements; sheathed and unsheathed hull planking; and timbers probably derived from internal cabins. Medium-sized ship fragments (Fig 14.11) consisted of: frame elements, some of which may be 'floors'; ordinary and wale planking; and belaying timber.

The timbers from the larger vessel are important for what they show about the painted upper works of a ship, as these parts rarely survive in wrecks. A clear demonstration of how social status and display are built into vessels is the elaborately planed, carved, and painted timber (Fig 14.12) which was also given a top coat of yellow ochre-pigmented paint (Tamm 1988). Though paints were being more widely used at this time to protect timbers from weathering, it is clear that a low-cost version of gilding was intended in this case.

The large deck-beam fragments (d on Fig 14.10) are comparable in size with those of the *Wasa*, and both indicate the size of the ship and chronicle one of the

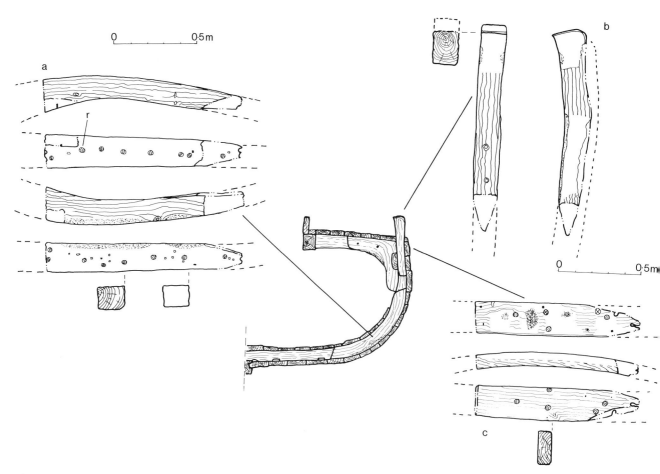

Fig 14.11 *Diagram to show the probable points of origin of some of the timbers from the medium-sized vessel or vessels represented in the collection from the City of London Boys' School site: a) a roughly hewn frame element (stippled area = sapwood, 'r' = pine repair treenail); b) a belaying timber with rope wear marks (blank areas = cream paint); c) a wale plank from near the bow or stern. The presence of tarred hair and iron spike shanks (shown as black dots) indicates that the plank was covered with another plank (doubled) (blank areas = cream paint). Note the cross-split outboard ends of the treenails on the upper face*

changes in the internal arrangements of the vessel made during its life. The blocked housing joints indicate that a carling (fore and aft beam) was removed and the deck layout remodelled, before the ship was broken up. From higher up in the vessel the elm belaying timber (c on Fig 14.10) carries traces of the wear caused by making rope fast around it, a relic of the working of the ship from which it came.

The roughly hewn grown oak frames (a on Fig 14.11) deriving from the medium-sized craft were made out of oak stems or branches as small as 0.2m in diameter. The one pine treenail was clearly evidence of the repair of the parent vessel. The 32mm diameter oak treenails and infrequent square-section spikes used to fasten internal and hull planking to these frames were also found in the oak wale-plank fragment (c on Fig 14.11). This seems to have derived from the bow or stern of a bluff-ended carvel-built craft perhaps something like the recent Humber Keel, and the oak belaying timber (b on Fig 14.11) closely resembles the shape of those used as mooring bollards in the same keels. It would appear that the medium-sized vessel was roughly and cheaply built and may have been something like a sailing barge or small coaster.

The new additions to the tool kit of the English shipwright, as evidenced by the tool marks found on these timbers and other technical features, are: planking saws, which were much more commonly used; larger adzes which were now essential for fairing frames and planking; small saws; chisels; planes; moulding planes and carving tools. This tool kit could be said to resemble more closely that of a 20th century wooden-ship builder. However, the technique used to bend heavy ship planks might shock a modern British boat-builder. It would appear that some of the 100mm (4 in) thick elm planking was subjected directly to fire, which resulted in a heavily charred surface. Up to about 10mm of charring is visible on the inboard face of the planking in the boldly curved stern of the *Batavia* replica being built in the Netherlands. A similar degree of charring was found on the inboard faces of fragments of elm ship planking from the City of London Boys' School site, probably implying the use of the same technique, the steaming of timbers for bending being a later development.

Conclusion

Although this review of the recently excavated evidence for early boat and shipbuilding in south-east England has been necessarily brief, some of the more general changes in boat and shipbuilding technology have been

Fig 14.12 Part of an elaborately carved and yellow-painted reused timber from the City of London Boys' School site which probably derived from above a stern quarter window in a large ship

outlined. The massive economic changes that culminated in the European expansion over, and domination of, the world, were clearly facilitated by the introduction of large multi-decked ships, such as is evidenced by the City of London Boys' School material. These very large, highly complex vessels contrast boldly with the simple technology used to build the Clapton boat, and demonstrate the social and economic dimension of nautical technologies. An attempt has also been made to outline what appear to have been elements of apparently local building traditions.

Acknowledgements

The presentation of a paper such as this would have been impossible without the considerable work of various Museum of London staff. Crucial help with recording the finds from Kingston was provided by G Potter (the site supervisor), and from the City of London Boys' School site by H White and R Bartkowiak. Thanks are also due to all the site staff and supervisors concerned, C Spence, A Thompson, J Hunter, N Shepherd, P Thompson, J Bowsher, and for the Clapton boat, P Marsden. R Gale carried out some of the wood identification. O Crumlin-Pedersen also commented usefully on the work during the conference, although he and all the above are not responsible for any errors the paper may still contain. Thanks are also due to all those involved with the Clapton dugout replica project, notably M Redknap and J Wallis, and Mr and Mrs Norman for providing the tree and building site. Thanks are also due to T Dyson for correcting the draft text.

15 Waterfront archaeology and vernacular architecture: a London study

G Milne

Abstract

The recording of well-preserved timber structures on waterfront excavations enables characteristics of the vernacular carpentry of a particular period to be identified and assessed. This is of crucial importance to the study of periods for which few or no examples of timber buildings survive on dry-land sites. This paper reviews evidence from the medieval London waterfront (examined in more detail in Milne 1985a, 155–76), arguing that the implications of such a study extend well beyond problems concerning the construction of riverside revetments. By way of an example, the date and manner of the initial introduction of fully framed buildings to London is examined.

Introduction

The process of reclamation or extension on the urban waterfront is now well known and the importance of the excavation of such sequences appreciated, as the proceedings of the first two waterfront conferences make clear (Milne & Hobley 1981; Herteig 1985c). Apart from the major topographical implications, work on the waterfront has provided other wider archaeological benefits, ranging from the recovery of large, closely dated finds groups to the study of changing styles of wharf construction (Milne 1987). It is an aspect of the latter subject that this paper attempts to summarise.

Intensive archaeological work on the London waterfront began in 1972 (Milne & Milne 1979) and is still continuing. A remarkable series of well-preserved timber structures has been recorded, ranging in date from the 1st to the 17th century (eg, Milne 1979; Milne & Milne 1982; Milne 1985b; Tatton-Brown 1974; Miller et al 1986). Although all of the riverfront revetments shared the same function, each was different. It is argued that the differences observed reflect changes in contemporary building practice, once the structural attributes particular to the waterfront situation are discounted. A study of the medieval waterfront installations of 11th to 15th century date may thus be used to illuminate the development of timber buildings in general, in a period which witnessed the change from earthfast post structures to box-frame buildings.

There is little evidence to suggest that London's riverfront revetment construction was the work of specialist carpenters. The only named carpenter known to have built revetments in the city is Richard Cotterel, who was employed not only to rebuild the timber face of Broken Wharf in 1347, but also to construct the jetty, fence, and sheds (Salzman 1952, 435). The three carpenters engaged to work upon a Southwark wharf in 1389 were required to rebuild two watermills and the millhouse as well (Salzman 1952, 467–9), while two carpenters employed to work on the roof of Westminster Abbey were also mentioned in a contract for a wharf at Vauxhall in 1476–7 (Woodward-Smith & Schofield 1977, 284).

The evidence from urban excavations where waterfront installations and contemporary buildings have been found supports the general proposition that the construction of both types of structure, although clearly different in function, utilised the same range of techniques. That this approach differs from the methods employed by other specialist carpenters, such as boatbuilders, is also apparent. The most cursory examination of the Scandinavian material makes this point emphatically: the solid lafted (half-lapped) block-house tradition of house building is obviously reflected in the form of the waterfront *kar* structures, and contrasts starkly with the graceful planked form of the contemporary shipping.

It is therefore argued that the waterfront installations in medieval London were erected by the same men who were responsible for timber building elsewhere in the city. Since so few examples of their craft survived the ravages of fire, the Blitz, and the pressures of urban renewal, one of the only ways that general changes in London's timber building traditions can be recorded, studied, and appreciated is through the waterfront material.

Vernacular timber building traditions in medieval London

Consideration of medieval London revetments and the reused timbers they incorporated demonstrates that three main techniques or traditions are represented: *earthfast post*; *stave*; *framed*. For convenience, the ensuing discussions will be conducted under these heads, but how discrete the techniques actually were in practice is a question that will be considered later.

Earthfast post building, in which the principal posts of the structure are set into the ground. On the waterfront or in well construction, the technique is recorded from at least the 11th century into the 13th century. The technique is also known to have been used in 10th–12th century buildings in the city (Horsman et al 1988), although the evidence for these only survives in the form of post-holes. The types of planked cladding

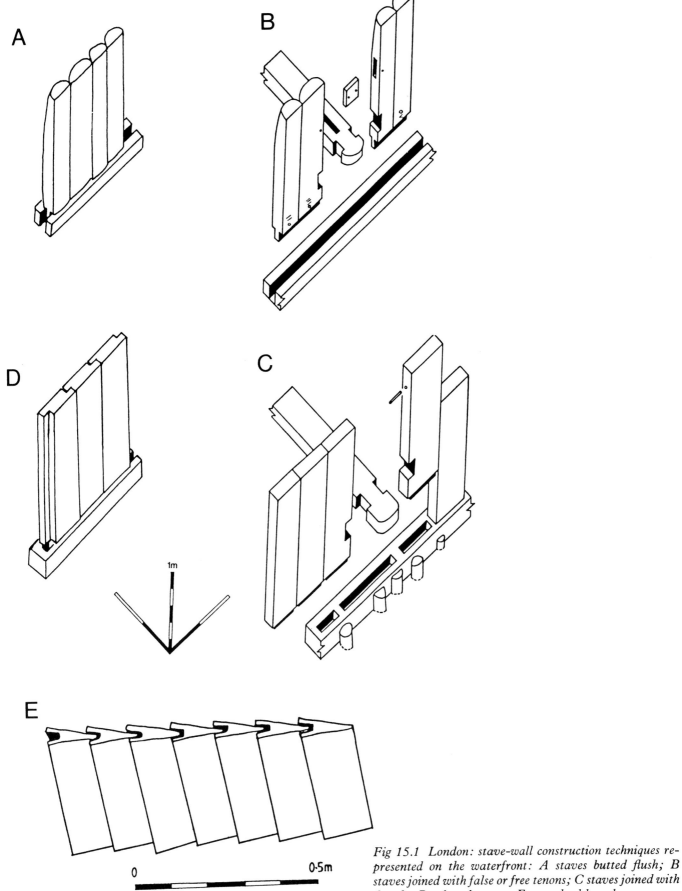

Fig 15.1 London: stave-wall construction techniques represented on the waterfront: A staves butted flush; B staves joined with false or free tenons; C staves joined with dowels; D rebated staves; E vee-edged boards

associated with the earthfast waterfront structures
include planks set in grooves cut into the edges of the
upright posts and planks fixed to the face of the posts
with wooden pegs.

Stave building, in which vertical timbering provides
both the structural rigidity for the building and also the
wall cladding (Fig 15.1). Examples of this technique
from the London waterfront date from as early as the
11th until the 15th century, and therefore represent a
technique of considerable longevity. Wall types
recorded include the use of vee-edged boarding; staves
butted flush; staves joined with dowels; staves joined
with false or free tenons; and staves joined with rebates
cut on opposing edges. All but one of the London
examples of stave walling incorporate a baseplate,
usually with a groove cut along its length into which the
feet of the staves were set. It is now clear that the
buildings incorporating baseplates which were constructed in London before the Norman Conquest were
stave structures, not fully framed buildings (Horsman
et al 1988).

Framed buildings, in which the structural carcass
comprises an integrated framework of timbers which
relies on its site for no more than the support of its
weight (Hewett 1980, 57). In buildings of this distinctive type, the principal posts are set in baseplates, after
which the wall-cladding is applied to, or infills the
framework. On the London waterfront, baseplates
accommodating vertical posts are introduced into revetment and river-stair construction in the early 13th
century, showing that the general technique would have
been in use elsewhere in the town by that date.

Introduction of framed buildings in medieval London

The introduction of the fully framed building could
only occur after the development of a number of specific
structural attributes, including:

a the use of timbers of squared, uniform scantling
b the introduction of well-cut, closely fitted joinery
c the use of a baseplate
d the adoption of the mortice and tenon with two
shoulders to form the basic articulation at the head
and foot of principal posts
e the adoption of the chase-tenon as the basic articulation for diagonally set braces integral to the frame.

Since none of these elements is required of necessity
in an earthfast structure, it could be argued that framed
buildings represent a new building tradition, imported
into London, fully developed, some time after the
Norman Conquest. However, a recent study of the
well-preserved riverfront structures allows a different
interpretation. It is suggested that the technique of
framed building was gradually developed following a
fusion of attributes taken from the otherwise quite
separate stave and earthfast traditions, which were
themselves developing independently. From the list
above, it seems that *c* and *d* were attributes taken from
the stave-building tradition, while the other attributes
(*a*, *b*, and *e*) were all being developed and used in
earthfast structures in the 12th and early 13th centuries.

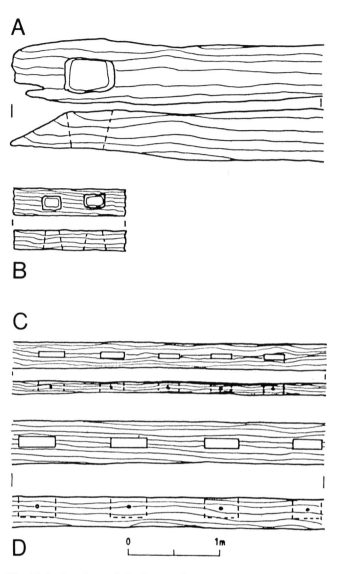

Fig 15.2 London: A & B pre-Conquest square through-mortices from the Billingsgate Lorry Park site (BIG82); C 13th century rectangular through-mortices (BIG82); D 14th century standard rectangular mortices, Trig Lane site (TL74)

Evidence to support this suggestion is found in a
number of hybrid structures of that date recently
recorded on the London waterfront. For example, at
Sunlight Wharf (site code SUN86), a stave wall was
found in which the staves were set in a series of baseplates separated by braced earthfast members; on the
Thames Exchange site (site code TEX88), massive
earthfast posts were braced with squared timbers
articulated with well-cut pegged joints, reminiscent of
the remarkable early 18th century hybrid of earthfast
post and framed building at Cedar Park (Hobley 1982,
fig 24).

The cutting of, and preference for individual joints
also changed. The standard mortice and tenon, the joint
which is basic to all fully framed building, is unknown
in London before the Norman Conquest. Square

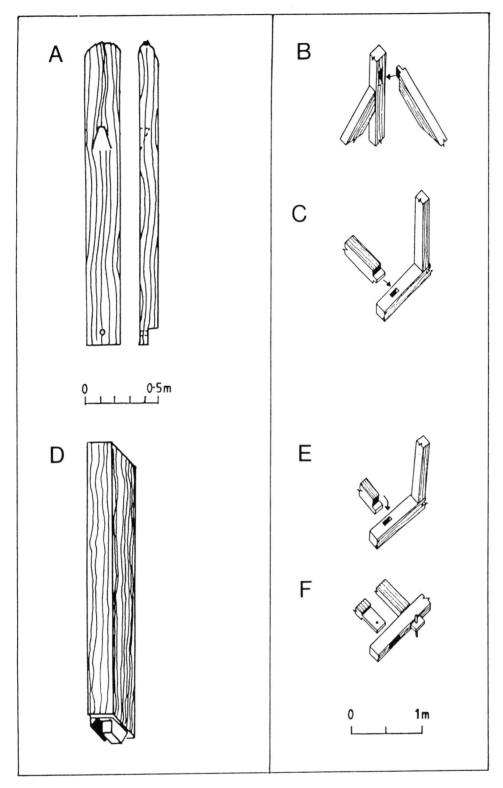

Fig 15.3 London: range of mortice-and-tenon types represented on the waterfront: A splayed recess (BIG82); B chase tenon (TL74); C standard tenon (TL74); D spurred tenon (TL74); E bare-faced tenon (TL74); F tusk tenon (TL74)

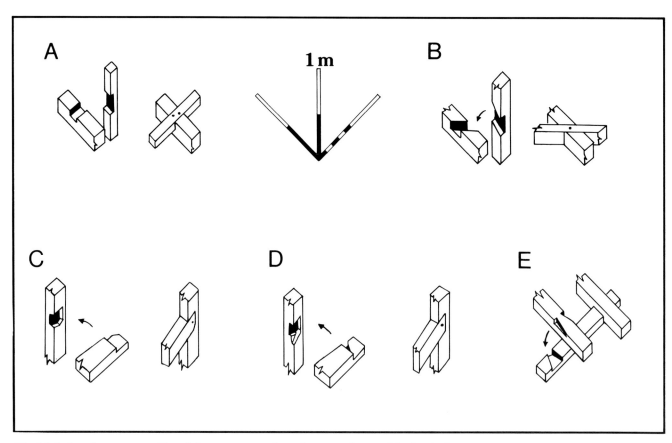

Fig 15.4 London: range of lap-joints represented on the waterfront: A halved (TL74); B diagonal (TL74); C notched (TEX88); D secret notched (TEX88); E lap dovetail (TL74)

through-mortices were used initially, and the stages through which the joint developed in the 11th and 12th centuries until it reached its more familiar form, can be traced (Fig 15.2). The front braces used in the earthfast revetments and the earliest baseplated structures articulate with the posts by means of a splayed recess, into which the crudely shaped head of the brace was wedged (Fig 15.3). By the end of the 13th century, the joint selected for such a position was invariably a well-cut chase mortice and tenon. Again, there is plenty of evidence for notched lap-joints from the 12th to the mid 13th century in situations where later the chase tenon would be used. Lap-joints can always be used in earth-fast building or similar structures in which the principal posts are raised first, and the bracing subsequently applied to them (Fig 15.4). However, in fully framed structures in which post and braces are raised in integrated units, such lap-joints cannot be employed, and the mortice and tenon must be used.

Conclusion

The recent study of well-preserved structures on the city waterfront summarised here has shown that the techniques used in the construction of the medieval riverfront revetments were varied and subject to considerable change. The significance of the changes recorded is considered to be wide ranging, for the structures represent a remarkable sample of truly vernacular building: as such they may be compared profitably with other studies based solely on surviving higher-status structures, such as tithe barns, cathedral roofs, and manor houses (*eg* Hewett 1969; 1980). It has been shown that there were two main traditions in evidence in London in the pre-Norman-Conquest period, earth-fast-post building and stave building. However, these two traditions did not exist in isolation, for not only was there development of a tradition, but there were also development between traditions (Milne forthcoming). As a consequence, the box-frame building was gradually perfected in London in the period between the mid 12th and the late 13th centuries. Although this new tradition completely superseded the earthfast technique, stave building continued to develop until at least the 15th century. How representative this picture is of developments in vernacular building elsewhere in the country awaits the excavation and study of similar large groups of well-preserved vernacular timber structures in other regions.

16 Conservation of waterlogged wood: a review
C E Brown

Abstract

The problems of handling and conserving waterlogged wood after their removal from primary archaeological contexts are discussed. There are simply not the facilities in Britain for coping with all the waterlogged wood which has been recovered and selective conservation is a necessity. Storage is a major problem as conservation is a slow and gradual process. Methods of temporary conservation on site and long term conservation in the laboratory are discussed and their relative merits assessed.

The initial conservation problems which archaeologists are likely to come across when dealing with waterlogged objects are those arising from the quantity of material involved and the expense, space, and facilities needed for treatment. Recording is obviously a priority, but consideration must be given to what happens afterwards.

Selection and rejection

Only a few centres in this country have facilities for freeze-drying or long-term impregnation treatment for large objects, notably Portsmouth, Dundee, York, and the National Maritime Museum. To illustrate the extent of this problem, it is worth noting that a good deal of the space in all of these centres is now taken up with material from the London waterfront excavations. From the thousands of timbers found on the Billingsgate site alone, only four pieces of revetments are being conserved. This is all that the time and facilities available will permit — everything else was recorded, sampled, and then discarded. This policy is not unique to London and indeed the Museum of London is currently reviewing the situation.

It is clear, then, that the extent of available facilities, time, and personnel have more impact initially than the ethical problem of how much and what is to be saved. The problem must be solved since valuable material evidence is continually being lost; records alone will not suffice and a valid collection policy for the artefacts themselves is clearly called for. Within these limitations, choices are obviously being made as to what exactly is to be preserved and the criteria vary greatly from region to region: a single ship's timber from a waterfront site in Cornwall would appear to be very important in its own context, though of little technological interest; such a piece excavated in a so-called 'major' urban waterfront site may be recorded and sampled only, before being discarded.

Another problem is the current lack of timber technologists. Most archaeologists or conservators coming into contact with a piece of excavated waterlogged wood would not claim to be suitably qualified to assess its importance. More specialists are needed, possibly working on a consultancy basis for English Heritage.

Funding could then be offered on the basis of their findings. At the moment, the only criteria for selection appear to be requirements for display and exhibition, though some centres are now building up reference collections demonstrating carpentry techniques. It is clear, therefore, that a national policy is needed to determine which pieces should be selected for conservation; reference collections of technologically interesting pieces should be given priority.

Storage and reburial

More temporary storage facilities are required; this would help provide valuable breathing space while sampling takes place and decisions are made over an object's suitability for preservation. Alternatives to the policy of recording followed by disposal do exist, but it is important to remember that long-term storage is not a final solution. Complete conservation should be carried out or else a serious attempt should be made to rebury.

In Northern Ireland, archaeologists routinely rebury the many dugouts that are excavated: a trench is dug, the canoe replaced, and a marker left. It must be understood, however, that the wood has not been returned to its former anaerobic environment and the effects of a partially aerated soil on excavated waterlogged wood are not yet known and are therefore likely to produce a new set of problems in the future (de Jong 1981). At the underwater sites in Loch Tay the timbers are not lifted but are recorded *in situ* and left in the water of the loch. Even this solution still poses problems, the reburial environment is not exactly as anaerobic as the original silty deposits.

Nigel Nayling, in his report to the Historic Buildings and Monuments Commission (HBMC), has made the recommendation that underwater marine timbers should not be lifted at all unless a site is under some dire threat (Nayling 1989); needless to say, this suggestion has not been received enthusiastically by marine archaeologists. At least it is obvious that the wood would not come to any very serious harm if left in its burial environment; wrecks in particular should perhaps remain unexcavated until such time as facilities for storage and conservation can be guaranteed. It is worth noting that the hull of the *Mary Rose* still awaits treatment. Scientists in Portsmouth are still working on the problem of how to get enough of the chosen consolidant into the remnant structure of the wood without total immersion (Squirrell & Clarke 1987). In view of the expense needed to maintain it in its waterlogged condition, perhaps the hull should have been kept in the harbour silt until research was complete.

Conservation during excavation

Wood has a cellular structure, mainly composed of cellulose and lignin. Burial in moist, aerated soils almost always results in the complete loss of wood. It is only in sealed, anaerobic deposits that bacterial activity is slowed down sufficiently to preserve wood. Even so, the softer, more soluble cellulose content is always depleted to some extent, leaving behind the harder structural substance, lignin (Jane 1956). If the waterlogging water is allowed to evaporate, the retreating front of the water through the pores brings about the surface tension effect of 'capillary tension collapse' and the cell walls themselves can also shrink, causing loss of dimension in all planes. Volumetric loss is usually up to 70% on drying (Cutler 1975). Partly degraded wood is just as susceptible as fully degraded; waterlogged wood is also very weak and soft, and vulnerable to physical damage. The aims of conservation, therefore, are to maintain the dimensions of the wood and also consolidate what remains.

The primary problem on site is that of keeping the wood wet enough, long enough either to complete recording and sampling or until it is ready to lift. This is usually done by spraying and covering. Conservators can help at this stage by advising archaeologists how to keep wood wet, how to expose pieces safely for recording, and how to record without damage. Samples for radiocarbon, dendrochronology, and species identification are usually taken at this stage. Another alternative to discarding or full conservation is making a mould of the structure, as in the case of the Graveney boat (Gregson 1975). The problem is to find a moulding compound that will set in damp conditions. Conservation research has led to the use of a 'Polysulfide' rubber which has been used successfully on sites in London and York, even on vertical surfaces (Brown & Peacock 1981).

If full conservation is chosen as an option, timbers have to be lifted and removed to a safer area for recording and washing. Conservators may supervise lifting operations, and design pallets and lifting gear to overcome specific problems. Specially curved cradles can be made to support shaped timber structures such as ships' timbers; they can be used also for future storage. Temporary storage tanks can easily be constructed on site or in the conservation laboratory. Timbers are first washed and labelled, and the smaller objects bagged in polythene. Some of the new types of storage tank can be taken down and constructed around the timbers themselves.

The choice of biocide can be problematic. It is generally agreed that biocides should not be used before samples are taken for radiocarbon dating. In addition, the reaction of biocides with wood or their treatment solutions is not fully understood (Baynes-Cope 1975). It seems to be most conservators' experience that, if the objects are carefully washed initially, if the tank is kept dark, and if the solution is regularly changed, there are no problems with mould growth in the short term. Running cold water is the best solution, as used at the *Mary Rose* conservation laboratories. There seems to be less of a problem with fungal growth on marine and estuarine sites than on inland and urban sites (Young 1988). It is useful to note that *Panacide* (orthophenylphenol) is not effective against bacteria and hence slime-moulds, which can form dense impenetrable layers on the surface of timbers.

Conservation: the choice of treatment

In the laboratory, the next task is to remove the waterlogging water (not the 'bound' water which is part of the wood structure itself) without causing shrinkage or cell-wall collapse. The water may be replaced with a bulking agent by a system of evaporation from a solution, or the wood can be chemically strengthened and the water removed in a way which will not damage the structure. Where wood is very degraded, the carbohydrate content has been washed out, leaving a lignin framework. Conservation therefore involves physically bulking out the framework with a hard material. With less degraded wood (where shrinkage can be just as extensive) there is a more difficult problem: cell material remains which needs to be kept in its swollen state to maintain the cell-wall structure, and there is less space into which the consolidant can penetrate (Tarkow *et al* 1966).

The choice of treatment, therefore, depends on several factors:

The size of the object. Few facilities are available to treat large objects, although many more laboratories have small freeze-driers or polyethylene glycol (PEG) treatment tanks.

Degree of degradation. The difference between the various remaining ratios of lignin to cellulose in wood determines the type of treatment. It is therefore important for the conservator to sample the wood to be treated fairly early in the process (Grattan 1982). Methods to be used include dissolving out lignin to determine the ratio of specific gravity, the use of infra red radiation, or tests which measure the resistance to pressure, using a needle, such as the *pilodyn*, a method which can also be used in the field (Clarke & Squirrell 1985).

Species of wood. Some woods such as alder, beech, and maple are very porous and easy to freeze-dry or impregnate, but oak and softwoods pose problems (Watson 1987).

Composite objects. There is frequently a problem with small items such as knives and other tools with organic handles; the problem also occurs with iron nails in ships' planking. PEG solutions are aqueous and also acidic which makes them aggressive towards metal. Non-aqueous methods are generally chosen within the constraints of health and safety rules for the solvents involved. Recently, research has been carried out into the use of corrosion inhibitors for use in PEG solutions, notably *Hostacor* and a new PEG-like substance which has an alkaline pH. These will undoubtedly extend the range of treatment options (Starling 1987).

Preservation of surface detail. Examples are inscribed Roman writing tablets or where there is evidence of carving or other toolmarks (Blackshaw 1974). PEG on the wood surface can often obscure details; the treatment process itself may result in loss of surface wood which would not be a major consideration on a very large timber with no features. Clearly other methods need to be used where detail exists.

Conservation: methods of treatment

Bulking agents for waterlogged wood in the past have included alum and various sugars, but PEG is probably the best known and most widely used, both as a pre-treatment for other drying techniques and on its own as a long-term impregnation treatment (Grattan 1988). The process is still not exactly understood, but research carried out by Per Hoffmann has determined which types of PEG can most successfully be used on different types and conditions of wood (Hoffmann 1981). PEG is a water-soluble wax-like polymer which can be made in different 'lengths' of molecule. The 'shorter' grades (*eg*, PEG400) are in liquid form, and as the chain length increases the substance becomes harder, until at grade 6000 it is a very hard wax. To summarise Hoffmann's conclusions, high molecular weight PEG is best for treating very badly degraded wood, mainly acting as a physical bulking agent for the lignin structure. The low-grade PEGs are excellent for treating very lightly degraded woods, since the 'short' molecule is small enough to enter the capillary system inside the cell walls. This also means that, if too much PEG of this type is used, the resulting wood may become hygroscopic. A lot of excavated wood, however, falls between these two categories and here Hoffmann recommends a dual system, using PEG of high and low grades. This system has recently been widely adopted with great success.

PEG is impregnated into the structure of the wood either by soaking or spraying with a heated solution and gradually raising the concentration over a long time, followed by air-drying, or by soaking for a shorter time, and removing the water safely by freeze-drying. Freeze-drying by-passes surface tension problems by removing the water from the object as vapour. For this to work, the object must be frozen and then the water vapour pressure on the ice surface has to be made lower than the saturation vapour pressure of the ice. This is brought about by carrying out the process under vacuum. A source of latent heat to the ice surface is also necessary to replace energy lost by removal of the water vapour (Rosenqvist 1975). Most freeze-driers comprise a drying chamber subject to vacuum and a refrigerated condenser. After pre-treatment lasting a few months, objects are frozen, then transferred to the freeze-drier. Progress is monitored either by repeatedly weighing the object or measuring its internal temperature with a thermocouple. It is usually necessary to consolidate the surface of freeze-dried objects after treatment.

Another method of water removal is the Acetone-Rosin system. Here wood is de-watered through baths of acetone, then soaked in a hot super-saturated solution of rosin. On evaporation of the solvent, the resin acts to bulk out the cell structure physically (Bryce *et al* 1975). It is quite a dangerous process, involving heating a solvent-resin system in a closed container. Most conservation laboratories which have the facility use this system twice a year on average. It is usually used for smaller items, composite objects, and in cases where detail cannot be sacrificed.

A recent development in Canada has been the experiment in 'natural' freeze-drying, using the effect of the Arctic winter (Grattan & McCawley 1978). The combination of intense cold and the dryness caused by the Arctic wind creates a freeze-dry system. Latent heat is supplied direct from the sun and the ice sublimes off.

It is also possible to air-dry in a temperate climate, providing it is carried out slowly and that loss of surface detail is not important. This method has proved successful with the Zuidersee boats in the Netherlands where other methods would have proved impractical. Even with this crude method, a great deal of difference can be made to the final results if a PEG solution is used to pretreat the timbers.

Summary

This paper attempts to show how conservators can give direct assistance to archaeologists on site by giving advice and taking on the organisation of storage, lifting, and sampling procedures. The great variety of types of conservation treatment, both on site and in the laboratory, serves to illustrate the contribution that conservation has made towards preserving and interpreting this important and vulnerable part of the archaeological record.

17 The development of Exeter Quay 1564–1701
C G Henderson

Abstract

Exeter did not possess a quay until the building of the Exeter Canal in the 16th century, the river below the city being un-navigable before that time. Lighters carried goods from sea-going vessels anchored in the Exe estuary to Exeter Quay via a series of locks. Excavation has revealed evidence for a number of successive quays and warehouses from the 1560s to the mid 18th century. The earliest waterfront was a wooden revetment of oak and wattle, soon replaced by a more substantial stone quay supplemented by a mole built to deflect large amounts of silt. Documentary and cartographic evidence for warehousing and a later quay to the south-east is presented. Development seems to have halted during the 17th century following a decline in trade with northern France and the Civil War. The woollen manufacturing industry expanded rapidly after the Restoration with a large volume of cloth exported to the Low Countries in particular. A new entrance basin was constructed and the canal extended. Further development of the quayside also took place, with extensive rebuilding and a new Custom House. The old Quay House was demolished and the new two-storey building erected on the same site is described. The Quay itself was enlarged and a new quay across the leat constructed for the landing and storage of timber and coal. The canal itself was subsequently deepened.

The Exeter Canal

Exeter lies on the east bank of the river Exe about 5km above the Exe estuary on the south coast of Devon. Although small craft were probably able to reach the city in the Roman and medieval periods, it is unlikely that the difficult river passage could have been relied upon for the regular carriage of goods. From at least the 12th century most of Exeter's trade passed through Topsham, near the head of the estuary, where there had probably also been a Roman port. After the late 13th century the river below Exeter was blocked by weirs, so that no vessels could pass between the city and the sea. In 1540, however, the citizens obtained an Act of Parliament permitting the clearance of all obstructions to navigation. Despite considerable efforts in the following years, it nevertheless proved impossible to make the river navigable even for small boats, and the City Council eventually decided to build a canal to bypass the most difficult sections of the channel (MacCaffrey 1975, 126–36; Jackson 1972).

The Exeter Canal or New Haven was built for use by lighters carrying goods between Exeter Quay and sea-going vessels anchored in the lower Exe estuary. These boats were hauled up the canal but had sails for use on the estuary and perhaps also on the Broad, the stretch of river between the head of the canal and the Quay. The canal was the first British waterway to be provided with pound locks and mitre sluice-gates, both in use earlier on the Continent (Skempton 1957, 450–6). It followed the west side of the Exe, starting from a point about 500m below Exeter Quay.

The canal was about 5m wide and less than 1m deep, with a fall of about 2m over a length of 2.82km. There were seven sluice gates, including one at the lower end which was opened by the incoming tide. The size of vessel capable of passing the entrance ranged from 8 tons on neaps to 16 tons on spring tides. Six gates formed three pound locks 1.7m deep and 57.6m long.

The two lower locks were 7m wide, allowing lighters to pass in opposite directions. The locks were long enough to permit groups of boats to pass through together, thereby taking advantage of favourable tidal conditions and reducing the time spent (and the water lost) in opening the sluices. The upper lock, at the head of the canal, was considerably wider than the other two. It probably served as a floating dock capable of holding a number of vessels on occasions when the river was in spate and the entrance gates could not be opened (Stephens 1957; Clark 1960, 27–32).

The late 16th and early 17th centuries

Construction of the Exeter Canal began early in 1564 and seems to have been completed by the end of 1566. No quay existed at Exeter before this time. The decision to build one, and to cut a new gate, the Watergate, through the city walls to give access to it, was taken by the City Council in July 1565. The site chosen lay within a bend of the Exe at the southern corner of the city walls (Fig 17.1). Above this point the river curves around a wide alluvial expanse known as Exe Island, a major part of which developed from around 1200 onwards in the lee of the medieval Exe bridge, about 250m above the Quay (Henderson 1981). The eastern side of Exe Island is defined by the Higher Leat, of medieval origin, which follows the edge of the floodplain beneath the walls to emerge just above the Quay. Below the Quay, the river originally flowed tight against low sandstone cliffs.

The earliest surviving buildings on Exeter Quay date from the late 17th century. Archaeological and historical research undertaken by Exeter Museums Archaeological Field Unit since 1985 has revealed evidence for a number of successive quays and warehouses dating between the mid 1560s and the mid 18th century. Our understanding of the form and chronology of these

Fig 17.1   Exeter: aerial view of Exeter Quay from the south-east, 6   March 1986. Photograph: F M Griffith, Devon County Council

structures is greatly enhanced by the survival of a number of early maps depicting the Quay and by the existence of a relatively comprehensive series of financial and administrative records, maintained by officials of the City Council throughout the period under consideration, which contain much material bearing on the Quay and the Exeter Canal.[1]

The recent excavations were concentrated mainly within or close to a standing building which has been identified as the Quay House, a transit shed built in 1680 at the same time as the Custom House. Beneath the floor of the Quay House are preserved deposits up to 4m deep (Fig 17.2). In the medieval period the river undercut the base of the sandstone cliff at this point to form a rock-cut shelf. Subsequently the channel gradually shifted away from the cliff, probably as a result of the continued growth upstream of Exe Island. At the same time deposits accumulated under the cliff in a roughly triangular alluvial bank whose outer margins were shaped both by the waters of the Higher Leat and by those of the river (Henderson *et al*, 1987, fig 4).

The earliest waterfront structure at the Quay took the form of a stout revetment of driven oak stakes and wattles erected along the margin of the alluvial bank. This stood up to a metre high and has been traced for 14m in excavation (Fig 17.2). River gravel was heaped inside the wattlework to create a broad, sloping wharf

whose full frontage is estimated to have been about 75m long (Fig 17.3). To judge by its undecayed state, this wharf could not have remained in use for long. It may have been erected in 1564 as a temporary provision for the stockpiling and dispatch of materials used in the construction of the canal. Whatever the case, the wattle-faced wharf was soon replaced by a much more substantial stone quay (Egan 1988, 205, fig 4). The revetment wall of the new quay stood about 3.2m high. A large volume of fill was required to raise up the level inside the wall. The obvious nearby source for this material was a sandstone bluff to the north-east of the new quay, part of the lands of Matthew Hull, who had acquired the former Greyfriars site next to the river after the Dissolution. The City Council requested Hull to sell them a piece of land 'for fyllynge of the ground atte and upon the Key newlye buylded', but he refused. The matter was resolved on 4 October 1565 when three justices directed Hull to convey to the Council a triangular plot of land adjoining the Quay. The deed of conveyance for this transaction, dated 18 April 1566, records that the plot had a 33ft (10m) frontage next to Quay Lane and that the other two sides measured 63ft (19.2m) and 51ft (15.5m) in length.

The south-west face of the new quay, flanked by the Higher Leat, was about 45.7m long, whilst its south-east frontage, called the Crane Quay, measured about

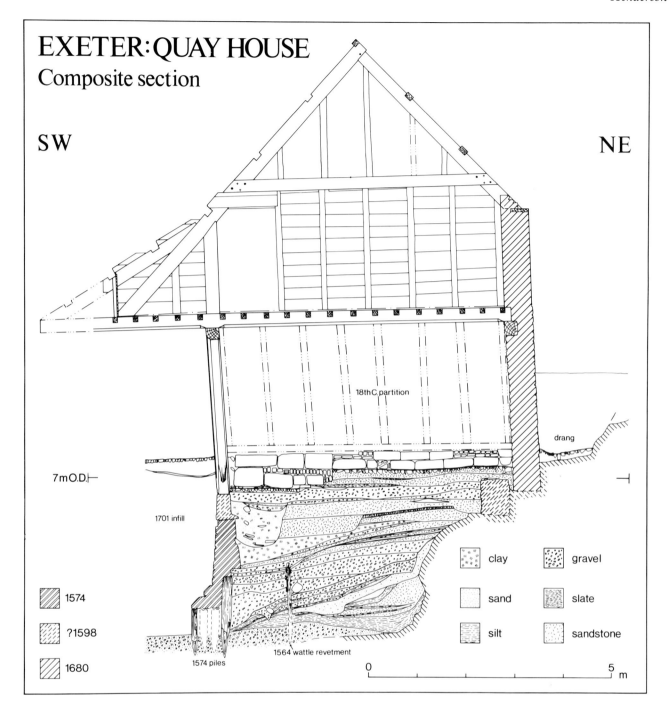

Fig 17.2 Exeter: composite section through the Quay House and underlying deposits

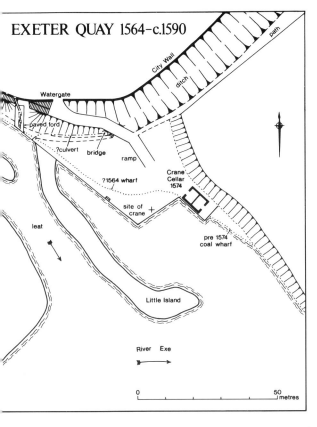

Fig 17.3 Exeter: plan of the Quay between 1564 and about 1590

18.3m in length. A crane was built early in 1567. A section of the original wattle-faced wharf adjoining the Crane Quay was retained for a few years as a landing place for coal.

Silting became a serious problem from the outset. In April 1567, the Council resolved that 'the earth before the key should be rydde as also a thwart weare there to be made for the keeping of the fylthe of the City from choking the Key'. The 'thwart weare' was probably constructed in 1567–8. It was a low protective mole designed to deflect the silt-laden waters past the Quay. It lay parallel with the south-west quay wall so as to enclose a long narrow dock, shown on the Hogenberg map of Exeter dating from the mid 1580s (Fig 17.4). The mole became known as the Little Island and seems to have served as an additional wharf for landing cargoes such as coal or timber. Coal was one of the staple commodities carried on the canal down to the arrival of the railways in the 19th century.

As far as is known, no warehouse existed on the Quay during the first few years of its operation. This suggests that initially the goods carried on the canal comprised cargoes not requiring secure or covered storage during transit. Following the opening of the canal most trade probably still passed through Topsham Quay, being carried to Exeter by road; but for bulky commodities such as coal, it was more economical to trans-ship into the city's lighters in the estuary and pay the tolls levied for the passage up the canal. The first documentary reference to a cellar (*ie* warehouse) on Exeter Quay occurs in a letter sent by the City Council to Lord

Burghley in 1577. This building can probably be identified with one labelled 'Crane Seller' on Hogenberg's map (Fig 17.4). The Crane Cellar was found in the recent excavations. It lay against the cliff at right-angles to the Crane Quay , overlying most of the residual wattle-faced coal wharf (Fig 17.3). The cliff had been cut back at this point to make room for the warehouse and to provide material for raising the level within the walls of a new quay built to accommodate it. These were founded on close-set oak piles driven into deep silt deposits choking the dock in front of the old wattle-faced wharf (Fig 17.2). Four piles dated by dendrochronology came from trees felled in 1574, which is likely to represent the construction date of the building.[2]

The Crane Cellar quay was 12.4m long by about 7m wide. The building stood close to the water's edge and measured about 5.2m by 7.8m externally; it possessed narrow stone footings which probably carried timber-framed walls (Fig 17.5). On its south-east side was a little stone-paved quay about 3.3m wide. Access to this quay must have been obtained by means of a passageway running between the Crane Cellar and the cliff, an arrangement common to both successor warehouses on the site (see below, p129). A timber partition divided the warehouse into two rooms (one with a cobbled floor – Fig 17.6) each measuring approximately 4.7m by 3.5m, an area of about 16.5m^2. These units were presumably used for storing goods in transit. The components of a cargo destined for a particular ship in the estuary would perhaps have been assembled here prior to shipment down the canal. The two warehouse units must have had separate entries: there would otherwise have been little point in partitioning so small a building. The Hogenberg map shows a door in the north-west end wall giving access to the main quay; probably a similar door permitted the south-east warehouse unit to be entered from the little quay adjoining it.

Hogenberg's map shows two small windows high in the side wall of the Crane Cellar (Fig 17.4). Hence although the building stood close to the edge of the quay, it apparently did not possess waterfront doors for the direct handling of goods between the warehouse units and the lighters. It is probable, however, that such doors were introduced late in the life of the building. Two sleeper beams let into the floor presumably performed the same function as a similar pair of sub-floor beams in the successor warehouse on the site, in which there was clear evidence for the presence of waterfront doors associated with a projecting roof canopy (see below). A conjectural reconstruction of the Crane Cellar incorporating these features is given in Figs 17.5 and 17.7. In view of the small size of the rooms, it is possible that single loading doors were provided rather than the double doors shown.

The surviving remnant of the wattle-faced coal wharf beneath the cliff next to the Crane Cellar was allowed to fall into decay after 1574, with the Little Island no doubt now being used for landing coal. Around 1590, the innermost section of the long dock between the Little Island and the main quay seems to have been filled in when a lime kiln was built in this area. The kiln is depicted on a map by Robert Sherwood (Fig 17.8) which is thought to have been drawn between 1600 and 1607. It may have been

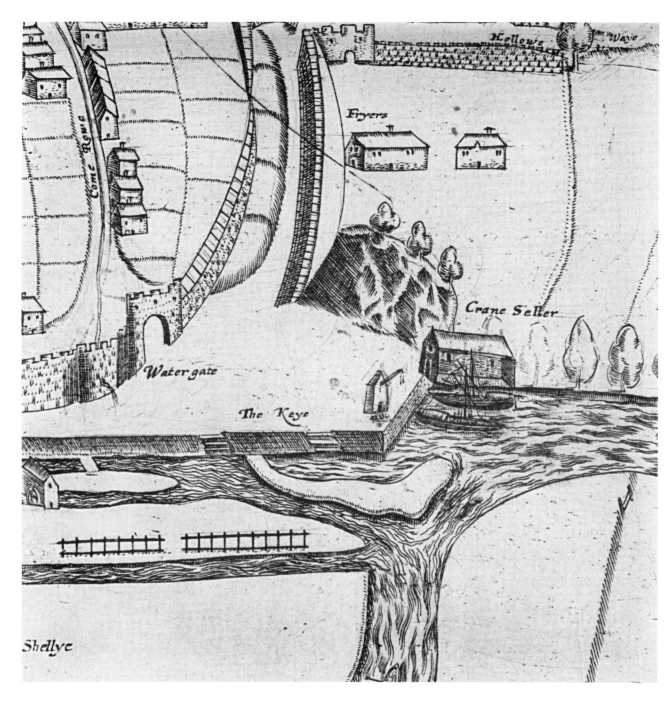

Fig 17.4 Exeter: detail from Hogenberg's map (state B) showing the Quay in the mid 1580s. Exeter City Council

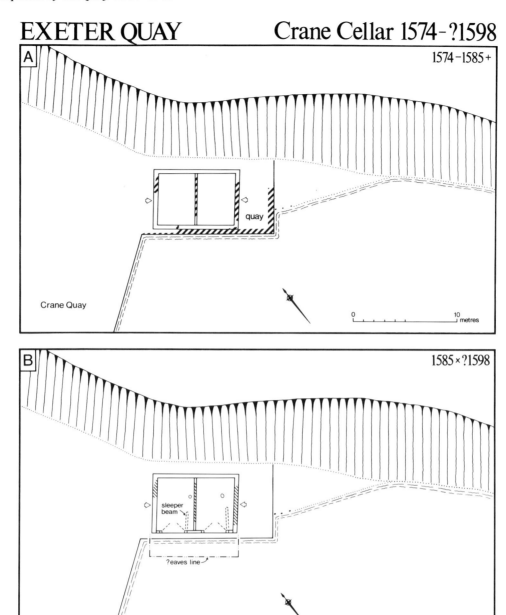

Fig 17.5 Exeter: plans of the Crane Cellar, 1574–?1598

constructed in 1589 when limestone first appears as a traded commodity in the Town Customs Rolls (Clark 1960, 82).

Some time between 1585 and 1600 the Crane Cellar was demolished to be replaced by a larger transit shed, which became known as the Quay House (Fig 17.9A). This was on essentially the same plan as its predecessor. Documentary evidence suggests that it may have been built in 1598, but this is not certain. The new warehouse measured 12.9m × 6m externally and occupied the whole of the stone quay built in 1574. As before, there were two warehouse units, separated by a timber partition, with average internal dimensions of 5.7m × 5.2m and floor areas of about 29.6m^2, almost twice the size of the rooms in the Crane Cellar. The rear and side walls were built of stone, whilst the front wall was

founded on a timber cill (which did not survive) set along the edge of the quay and supported on a narrow stone footing. The ends of two long, sub-floor beams were encased by this footing but connected vertically either with the overlying cill beam (possibly by means of a slip-tenon) or with upright posts in the timber-framed facade. The former alternative is the more probable, but the precise locations of the buried sleeper beams seem most readily explained if they are assumed to have corresponded fairly closely in position with major posts framing doorways, as reconstructed in Figure 17.9. The Sherwood map (Fig 17.8) clearly shows two wide waterfront doors and a projecting roof. The purpose of the sub-floor beams was presumably to anchor the structure so as to prevent the roof canopy from lifting in the wind.

Fig 17.6 Exeter: the interior of the Quay House looking north-west with, between the figures, the sloping cobbled floor of the Crane Cellar, and in the foreground the south-east wall of the first Quay House

Fig 17.7 Exeter: reconstruction of the Quay c 1595. Drawing by Jane Brayne

A large new quay known as the Quay Head was constructed on the south-east side of the Quay House. No trace survived of the primary revetment for this quay, but it was almost certainly built in timber, as indicated in Figure 17.9A, since a stone quay wall found in the excavation was evidently a secondary feature. The stone wall was probably built soon after June 1600, when the Council ordered that the Quay Head be rebuilt in stone. A stone wall is depicted in Sherwood's map (Fig 17.8). The length of the Quay Head can be calculated from measurements given in a survey of the Quay made in December 1676. It was 57ft (17.3m) long, its south-east limit corresponding exactly with that of the later Quay House built in 1680. Sherwood shows a number of small buildings on the Quay Head (Fig 17.8) as well as a gateway controlling access to the passageway

behind the Quay House (termed a *drang* in the 17th century documents). One side of this gate was located in excavation (Fig 17.9). The gate allowed the Quay Head to be made into a secure inner area cut off from the main quay, which appears to have been unenclosed at this period. The enclosed area was increased in 1607 when a walled compound, the Coal Court or Store Court, was built against the cliff on the north-west side of the Quay House (Fig 17.9B). The Quay House was later enlarged by the addition of a fore-building set with its long axis at right-angles to the primary warehouse. The added block is shown on a second Sherwood map (Fig 17.10) which probably dates from 1614 or later, since it shows the King's Beam hanging from the front of the fore-building: an order for the King's Beam to be hung up at the Quay was made by the Council on 9 June 1614. Sherwood also depicts a long open-fronted shed against a cliff at the back of the Quay Head.

As has been seen, the facilities at Exeter Quay were progressively upgraded over a period of about 60 years to 1625, around which time the crane was rebuilt. During this period the greatest part of Exeter's overseas trade was with northern France. From about 1625, however, the port's foreign trade entered a depression from which it had not fully recovered by the start of the Civil War (Stephens 1958). No major new developments are documented on the Quay in the half century between 1625 and 1675.

The late 17th century

Following the Restoration, Devon's woollen manufacturing industry experienced a period of great expansion, with prodigious quantities of serge cloth being exported, particularly to the Low Countries, through Exeter and Topsham, the two legal quays of the Exeter customs port. This increased volume of foreign trade

Fig 17.8 Exeter: detail of the Quay redrawn from a map of 1600–7 by Robert Sherwood. Devon Record Office

EXETER QUAY   Quay House ?1598-1614

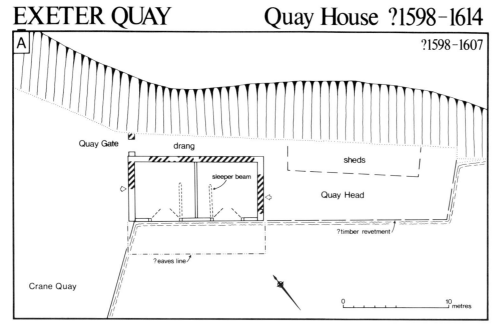

A   ?1598-1607

Quay Gate

drang

sheds

sleeper beam

Quay Head

?timber revetment

?eaves line

Crane Quay

0   10 metres

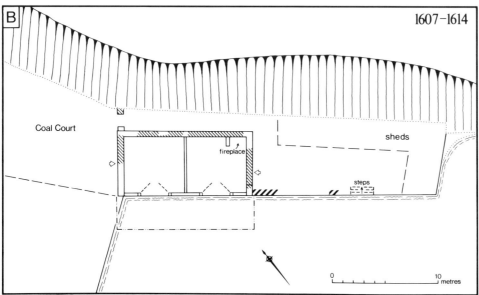

B   1607-1614

Coal Court

sheds

fireplace

steps

0   10 metres

*Fig 17.9 Exeter: plans of the Quay House between ?1598
and 1614*

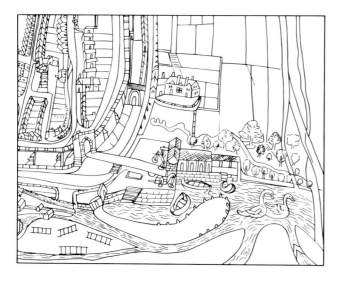

*Fig 17.10 Exeter: detail of the Quay redrawn from a map
by Robert Sherwood, ?1620s, in Devon Record Office*

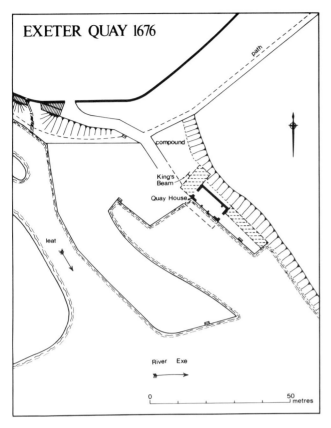

EXETER QUAY 1676

Fig 17.11 Exeter: plan of the Quay in 1676

At Exeter Quay, the Little Island was provided in 1676 with a stone revetment wall (Figs 17.11 and 17.12), increasing the full run of the stone quays to 483ft (147.2m), according to a survey made in December 1676. It was perhaps at this time that the Quay House was adapted to create an open transit shed, prefiguring the form of the much larger warehouse built to replace it in 1680. Wheel ruts in the floor (Fig 17.13A) indicate that the partition between the two primary warehouse units was removed to make a single room. This alteration was possibly made in response to a Council order, issued in February 1676, that a place should be prepared at the Quay for the receipt of pack goods. By analogy with the arrangement in the 1680 building, it is assumed that the waterfront loading doors were modified at this time to form a continuous run of three sets of double doors as shown in Figs 17.12 and 17.13A.

In 1680, the City Council commenced a programme of rebuilding at the Quay which saw the erection of the handsome group of buildings that stands there today. This included a large Custom House, the first to be provided at the Quay, and new warehouses. The dock between the Little Island and the main quay was filled in at this time, and a new lighter dock, 6m wide at its head and about 50m long, was built in front of the Quay House.

The old Quay House was demolished to be replaced by a two-storey transit shed, bearing the same name, which occupied the site of its predecessor as well as the whole of the former Quay Head (Egan 1986, 358, fig 3). The ground floor of the new Quay House functioned as a covered quay, about 6m wide and 30m long, with a floor area of around 149m^2 (a little over 1600sq ft). The building had a cobbled floor and was entered from the main quay (probably via a timber-framed fore-building) through a wide doorway in the end wall. It contained ten structural bays and was built of stone and brick except on the side facing the dock, where the middle eight bays were timber-framed. Here an oak cill

prompted the Council in 1676 to extend the Exeter Canal to Lower Sluice, a little above Topsham, enabling lighters to enter the waterway easily on all high tides. In addition, the new entrance basin was made large enough for small ships to moor within it and transfer their cargoes into lighters. The canal proper, however, was still deep enough only for vessels of up to 16 tons (Clark 1960, 32–4).

Fig 17.12 Exeter: reconstruction of the Quay in 1676. Drawing by Jane Brayne

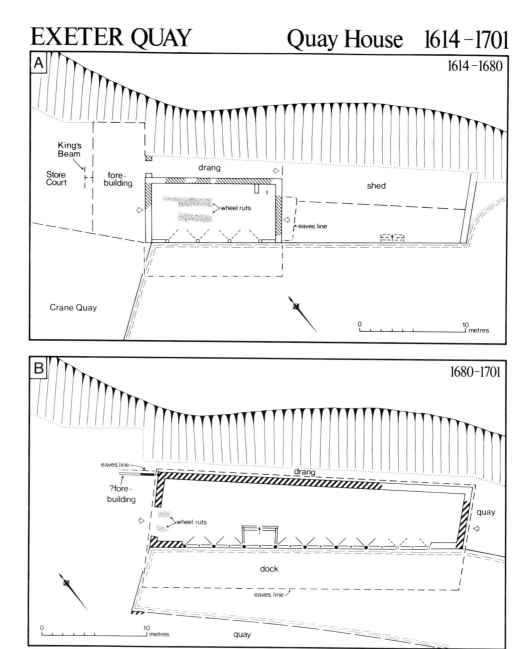

Fig 17.13 Exeter: plans of the first Quay House (after 1614) and the second Quay House, built 1680

beam (with iron mooring-rings attached) carried nine substantial oak posts framing a continuous series of eight doorways with ovolo-moulded surrounds. The openings were 2.6m square except in bay 4 where a doorway 3.3m high corresponded with a sunken loading well 0.45m deep. Each opening contained a removable intermediate post which fitted into mortices in the cill and top plate. In the sunken well the opening was closed by four removable panels held in place by two draw-bars. Each of the other doorways was fitted with four 'stable' doors which could be opened as necessary to provide access or light (Figs 17.13B–17.15).

The large upper room presumably served for the storage of goods delayed in transit. It must have been reached by means of stairs and a loading hatch at one or both ends of the building. The floor was carried on oak

beams up to 9.75m long which projected forward across the front wall-plate to support a cantilevered roof canopy extending about 3.8m over the lighter dock. The floor joists in the cantilevered area were set in open housings, indicating either that the flooring was secondary or that sections of it could be removed to permit direct loading into the lighters below. A narrow passageway at the back of the Quay House led to a new quay on its south-east side which replaced the old Quay Head. This was about 22m long by 6m wide. At the end of the quay a narrow slip about 2m wide sloped gently into the water (Fig 17.16). This may have served as the landing place for the Quay ferry, which is first documented in 1661 and still operates.

Much of the former main quay was now occupied by the Custom House and a two-storey warehouse at its

Fig 17.14 Exeter: reconstruction of the Quay c *1690. Drawing by Jane Brayne*

western end. This loss of space was compensated for by the infilling of a large area of the dock between the Little Island and the south-west side of the new lighter dock in front of the Quay House. In addition, a further sizeable open quay, called New Quay, was created in the 1690s on Shilhay, the adjacent portion of Exe Island on the other side of the leat. Reached via a bridge, this quay was used for the landing and storage of coal and timber (Figs 17.16 and 17.17).

In 1698–1701 the Exeter Canal was deepened to allow sea-going vessels of up to 14ft draught to reach the Quay. A single pound lock, the Double Locks, replaced the three original basins. At the Quay the lighter dock was filled in and the Quay House was eventually subdivided to form seven warehouse units, four upstairs and three on the ground floor (Henderson *et al* 1987, figs 16, 17). The building now became known

Fig 17.15 Exeter: reconstruction of the interior of the Quay House c *1690. Drawing by Jane Brayne*

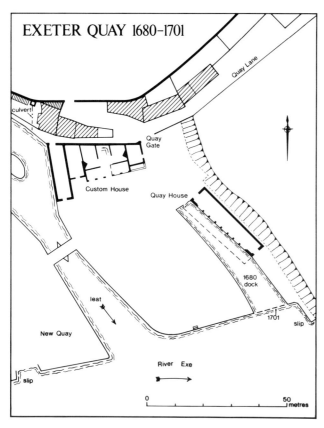

Fig 17.16 Exeter: plan of the Quay, 1680–1701

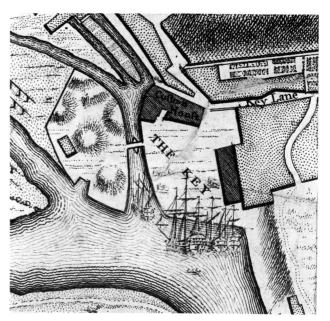

Fig 17.17 Exeter: detail of the Quay from Rocque's map of Exeter, 1744

as the Quay Cellars and the original name was forgotten.

The later history

The export trade in Devon cloth reached its height in the early 18th century. A French visitor in 1706 observed that ships of 200–300 tons came up to Exeter Quay. Soon, however, silting reduced the depth of the canal to 10ft and few vessels over 100 tons used the waterway (Clark 1960, 34–40). The Quay was further enlarged in the mid 18th century.

In 1825 work started on an extension of the canal to Turf Reach below Topsham. At the time of its completion in 1827, the improved Exeter Canal was the second largest man-made waterway in Britain (after the Caledonian Canal). Although ships of over 300 tons now came up to Exeter, the canal was too small for many of the vessels engaged in the coastal trade. At Exeter, a basin 900ft (275m) long was opened in 1830 at the head of the canal, and new warehouses and walled storage compounds were built on both sides of the river in the 1830s and 1840s. The City Council hoped this substantial investment would bring a revival in Exeter's mercantile fortunes, but this was not to be. The Great Western Railway reached Exeter in 1844, and from then on coal and other bulk commodities would increasingly be brought to the city by rail.

Commercial use of the canal, latterly for the carriage of timber and fuel oil, ceased in the mid 1970s. At the Quay, a core group of early buildings, including the 17th century Custom House and Quay House, remains as a monument to the Exeter merchants whose trading connections in the 17th and 18th centuries extended throughout the known world.[3]

Acknowledgements

Excavations and survey at Exeter Quay in 1985–9 were directed by the writer and supervised by John Dunkley and Mark Hall for Exeter Museums Archaeological Field Unit. Documentary research for the project was undertaken by Jannine Juddery, Andrew Pye, and Paul Staniforth. The drawings in this paper were prepared by Jane Brayne (reconstructions), Sandy Morris, Laura Templeton, and Mark Gardner; the photographs were taken by David Garner and Tony Ives; and the text was typed by Pam Wakeham. The Exeter Quay Project is supported by financial contributions from Exeter City Council, Devon County Council, MSC, Sidney Pratt Ltd, and the Exeter Canal and Quay Trust.

Notes

1 Notably the Chamber Act Books and the Receiver's Books, Rolls, and Vouchers, deposited in the Devon Record Office. The documentary evidence is cited at greater length in Henderson (1988), a fully referenced version of which appeared as Exeter Museums Archaeological Field Unit Report 88.18, obtainable from the Unit.
2 Dendrochronology by Coralie Mills of the Department of Prehistory and Archaeology, University of Sheffield.
3 Part of the Quay House is now an Interpretation Centre for the history of the Exeter Quay and Canal.

18 The medieval bridge and waterfront at Kingston-upon-Thames

G Potter

Abstract

Recent excavation has examined the structure of the medieval bridge together with associated waterfronts, the latter including reused boat material. The bridge was in existence by 1193 when it was repaired, and there are a number of documentary references to it from the 13th–15th centuries. Both archaeological and documentary evidence suggest frequent, often substantial, repairs. The piers of the first bridge were of masonry, those in the river being built within timber rings infilled with rubble. The superstructure would have been of timber, although precise details are lost. From the 13th century a solid masonry causeway incorporating the first two piers was constructed. This was closely followed by a series of timber waterfront revetments. The bridge and waterfront area have both been badly effected by erosion and silting. Rebuilding in the 15th century included the construction of stone arches and the consequent raising of the causeway. Further repairs followed with final replacement of the bridge in the early 19th century.

Introduction

Excavation took place on the Horsefair redevelopment, Kingston-upon-Thames, between June 1986 and January 1987, and again in April to May 1987. This preceded removal of all archaeological levels in the area. The site lay on the east bank of the Thames (at this point flowing roughly south to north), and to the north-west of Kingston town centre (Fig 18.1). Work concentrated on the eastern end of the medieval bridge, some 30m downstream from the present crossing built in 1828. Some 35m of the bridge was exposed, with phases of construction from the 12th to 18th centuries. Further trenches were excavated up and downstream, revealing a number of waterfront structures along some 50m of the medieval river-bank.

There was some investigation of buildings on the adjacent bridge approach road. These included a chalk-built undercroft (1300–1350), with partially extant vaulted roof, and other, timber-framed structures, dating from the 14th century to c 1700. This work concluded that undertaken by J S McCracken in 1985 (Youngs et al 1986, 142).

In conjunction with the excavation, parts of the masonry structure of the bridge, and the undercroft, were lifted en bloc and removed from the site, to be reinstated within the new development. A number of timbers, in particular sections of boat material, were also removed and sent for conservation.

Prior to the 1985–7 work some smaller-scale excavations had taken place, including trial work across the line of the bridge. Observations had also been made during contractors' work on the Middlesex bank (Cherry 1973, 117; Nelson 1983).

What follows in this paper is necessarily provisional, since there is much dating and analysis still to be done. The bridge itself forms a complex structure with numerous phases of rebuilding and alteration. Nevertheless, the major developments of both the bridge and the waterfronts appear to be contained within a quite short space of time, from the late 12th to the 15th century.

Kingston-upon-Thames

The first reference to Kingston is dated to AD 838. Thereafter it is recorded as the scene of a series of Saxon coronations. It appears that the Saxon town developed on a bank of higher ground, as represented by the present-day market place and church. Excavation has revealed the presence of an infilled natural channel up the east and north-east side of Kingston town centre. This probably began to silt up in the Roman period, but would have remained, even into late medieval times, as an area of low-lying, periodically flooded land (Penn et al 1984; Girardon & Heathcote 1988, 412).

The bridge

The first-known reference to Kingston Bridge, to the repair of an extant structure, comes in 1193 (Stenton 1927, 154). There is no direct reference to the building of the bridge, nor is there much in the present documentary or archaeological record to denote the nature of the contemporary town. Presumably by the mid 12th century, Kingston was well established, with a commercial life of some importance. However, political and strategic considerations may have been of equal importance: Kingston lies some 20 miles (32km) upstream of London Bridge, which until 1729 formed the only other crossing on this section of the Thames.

The siting of Kingston Bridge, offset from the medieval town centre, presumably reflects topographical features at the time of construction. The adjacent banks may have been particularly suitable at this point, or possibly there were shallower areas within the river

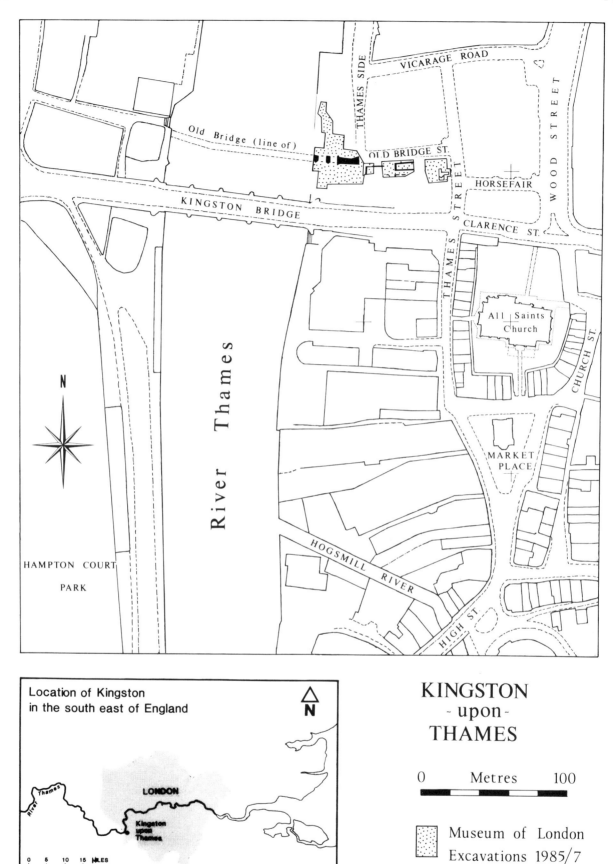

Fig 18.1 Kingston-upon-Thames: Museum of London excavations 1985–7

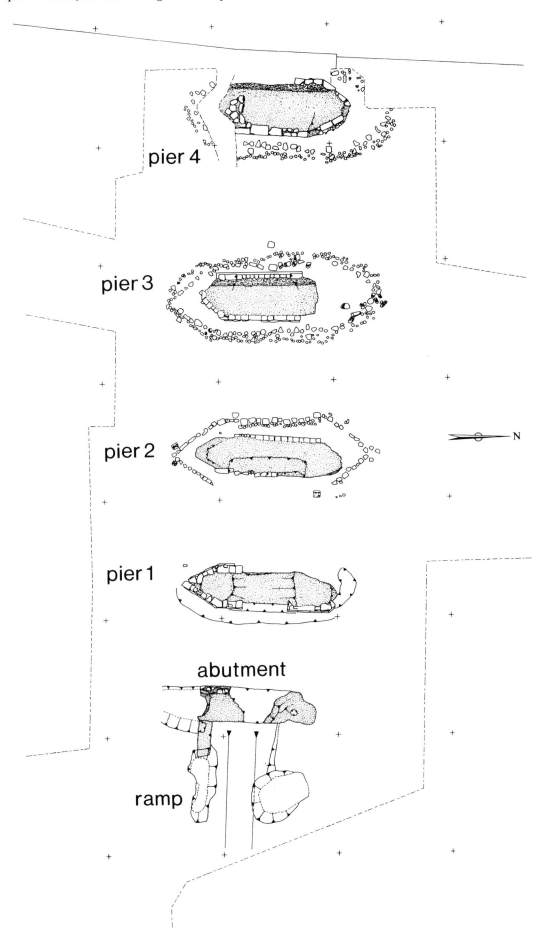

Fig 18.2 Kingston-upon-Thames: medieval bridge, earliest phase

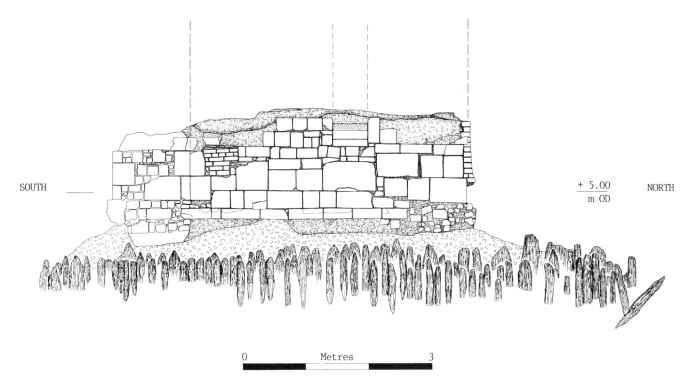

SOUTH

+ 5.00
m OD

NORTH

0   Metres   3

Fig 18.3 Kingston-upon-Thames: pier 3, landward elevation. South-east cutwater face (unshaded area) foreshortened by one third

itself. Plans made in the early 19th century clearly indicate a change in the bridge alignment as it approaches the Middlesex bank. This may reflect such topographical features (Horner 1813; Lapidge 1824).

From *c* 1200 to the mid 1400s there are a number of references to the bridge, mostly relating to repair or maintenance and often following flood damage. However, these are unspecific as to the nature or location of work undertaken. Later references are much more frequent: bridgewardens' accounts survive for the period 1527 to 1708, and go into some detail regarding expenditure (Powell 1935; Williams 1955; KBA 18/3/ 3). The cross-referencing of the written and archaeological record is generally tentative. Nevertheless, an attempt has been made to do this where it seems particularly relevant. It is at least clear from both sources that the bridge underwent quite frequent repair, and on occasion major reconstruction.

Construction of the bridge

There was no evidence in excavation of any activity definitely predating the bridge. A fairly large ditch, probably of 12th century date, was found in 1985 some 6m to the south of, and roughly parallel with, Old Bridge Street. The construction of the bridge itself is dated by preliminary dendrochronological work to *c* 1170. Excavation has revealed a construction of landward abutment and approach ramp and four free-standing piers belonging to the earliest phase (Fig 18.2). The standing structure was of dressed Reigate stone with a mortared flint-rubble core. The piers were fairly narrow, with a cutwater at each end. With facing intact, dimensions would have been some 2m × 7.5m. The foundations of all but the first pier had been embanked with timber piles. There was a progressive increase in

the span between each pier, from 3.4m at the landward end to 6.1m between piers 3 and 4. The principal elements of the bridge were:

The landward abutment and approach ramp

The abutment stood up to 0.8m above the contemporary land surface, retaining to the east a solid earth ramp. The ramp ran back some 6m, and was itself retained by flanking walls to the north and south, of similar construction to the abutment. However, the northern wall seems to represent a somewhat later rebuild, and probably contraction, of the original wall.

Pier 1

The first pier was built on the natural ground surface, just above normal river level. The basal course of Reigate stone facing was chamfered, and overlay an oak baseplate, now almost wholly decayed.

Pier 2

Just within the contemporary river stood a second pier which illustrates a construction intermediate between pier 1 and the outer piers. Oak piles embanked the western (river) face and cutwaters, retaining a base of unmortared flint. The larger piles had been driven on average 1m into the underlying ground. On its landward side the pier was open. The stone facing appears to have been constructed on a baseplate as pier 1.

Piers 3 and 4

The outer piers stood fully within the contemporary river, and were of similar construction. A ring of piles, principally beech with some elm, was set into the river bed. The third pier, which was fully excavated, had some 235 timbers, placed several deep in a ring measuring 3.8 × 9.5m (Fig 18.3). Originally the piles would have projected above normal river level by about 0.3–0.4m. The ring was infilled with unmortared flint rubble, as above, creating a low artificial island on which the stone pier was built.

At an early date some alteration took place to the landward abutment. A shallow robber trench showed where a projecting southern end had been removed. The abutment also underwent some refacing to the west, possibly as part of the same event.

The earliest construction raises several questions. There is no direct evidence to show whether the associated superstructure was of stone or timber. There were, however, occasional pieces of stone which could conceivably have come from an arch. A few such pieces were found within the first rebuild of pier 3, and one or two others were recovered from amongst fallen masonry. More significantly, it is suggested that the superstructure of the earliest bridge was considerably lower than that of the subsequent reconstruction. The evidence for this will be looked at below in the discussion of the causeway development (late 1200s), and in relation to a major reconstruction of the mid to late 15th century. However, it seems that at the second pier the original roadway would have been just above 6m above OD, in contrast to a suggested final form of *c* 7.5m above OD.

This evidence, in conjunction with the extant height of the earliest stone facing on piers 1 to 3, indicates that stone arches would not have fitted within the original construction. Either the superstructure would have been higher, or the arches would have sprung from a level at least equivalent to the base of extant stonework.

There is a further question relating to the original structure of the bridge outside the excavated area. There is a considerable contrast between the archaeological and historical record. Illustrations of the 18th and early 19th centuries show the bridge as an essentially timber structure.[1] A narrow roadway is supported by earthfast timber piles, the latter rather irregularly set in transverse rows across the river. These 'trestles' are braced individually, but there is no longitudinal support below the level of the superstructure. Such views are also reflected in the contemporary written record. The bridge was seen as an essentially timber structure, in which, except for 'frequent repairs, there had been no deviation from the plan on which it was originally built' (Manning & Bray 1804, 346). This view may be correct, but there is no real record of the bridge for the first 350 years, save that of frequent damage and occasional major repair.

Development of the causeway

In the 13th century, the landward abutment and the first and second piers were incorporated within a solid masonry causeway (Fig 18.4). Ultimately, this reached 16.3m in length by some 4–5m in width. The two outer piers remained freestanding but were largely rebuilt in the 14th and 15th centuries.

The development of the causeway falls into three main stages. The first stage saw the construction of blocking walls between the landward abutment and the first pier, on both sides of the bridge (B and C on Fig 18.5). This was probably a single development, dating to the second half of the 13th century. The southern blocking wall was wholly robbed out in the final demolition of the bridge *c* 1829. Finds of flint flakes on the adjacent construction surface would suggest a partially knapped flint facing. The northern wall survived as a mortared chalk and Reigate base, some 0.7m thick by 0.25m high. The wall appeared offset, but may have continued the line of the original flanking wall to the east of the landward abutment.

A further blocking wall was constructed on the downstream side between piers 1 and 2 (D on Fig 18.5). This was a very substantial construction of mortared chalk and Reigate stone, from 0.9m to 1.25m thick. The northern (outer) face was of ashlared Reigate stone, with knapped flint insets at its uppermost level, and was built with a marked outward batter. The wall sat on a base of mortared rubble, retained by timber to the north. There was no equivalent wall to the south, as there was to the east of pier 1 (*cf* B on Fig 18.5). The wall retained a substantial gravel bank, which presumably formed the roadway before dropping away as a simple embankment on the upstream side of the bridge.

The gravel bank sealed four posts dated to *c* 1275, at the upstream end of pier 2. Other factors would suggest a date before 1300. It is possible that the above construction is part of the 'costly rebuilding' referred to in a Royal Writ of 1286 (PRO C47 34/4 No 33).

Around 1300, the northern blocking wall between the landward abutment and first pier was rebuilt (E on Fig 18.5). This may have included the earliest ramp wall to the east. The two sections of wall appear to be of one build, mortared flint rubble with Reigate stone facing. This seems to have brought about a contraction of the causeway, best seen to the west of the landward abutment, where the new wall marginally overlaps the rear face (C on Fig 18.5) of the earlier structure. The enclosed area was infilled with clean gravel. Before this was done the central section of the landward abutment was robbed out.

It appears that the northern blocking walls described above survived to more or less their original height. The tops of both walls, as seen on their inner, protected face were at a constant level of 5.8-5.9m above OD (as was the surviving core of pier 2). This survival was also reflected in the gravel bank described above. Had this originally been higher there would have been more evidence for embanked deposits to the south of the bridge. As already suggested, these factors indicate that the early bridge superstructure was much lower than in subsequent reconstruction. The gravel bank and retaining walls in fact only make sense as a straightforward causeway forming a solid road base at *c* 6m above OD.

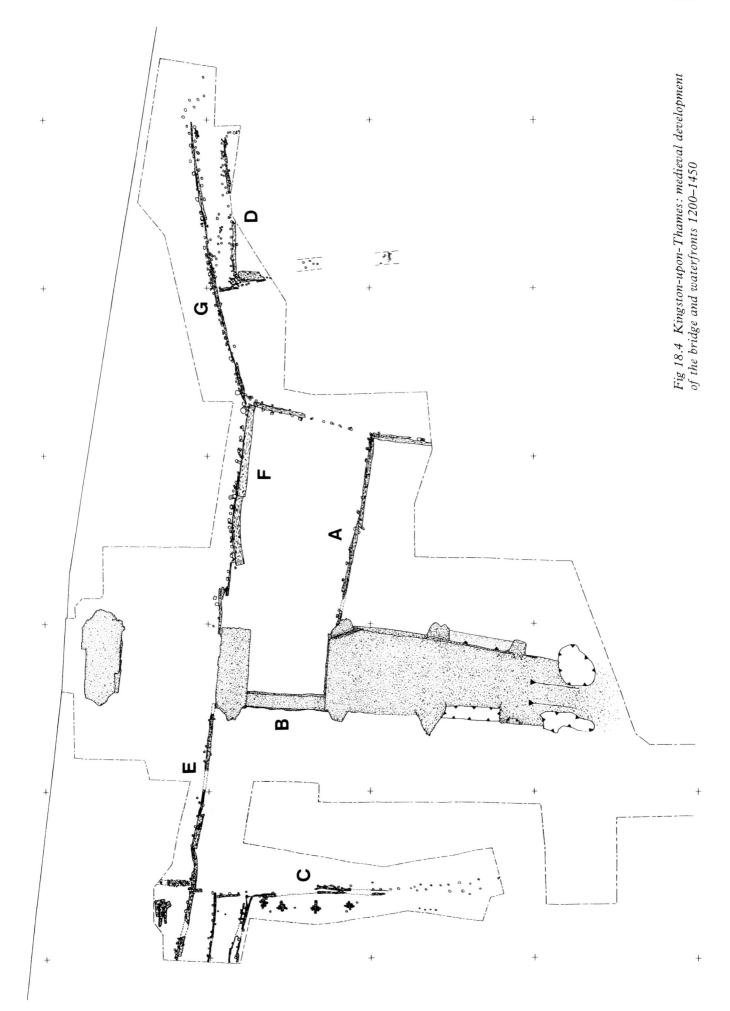

Fig 18.4 Kingston-upon-Thames: medieval development of the bridge and waterfronts 1200–1450

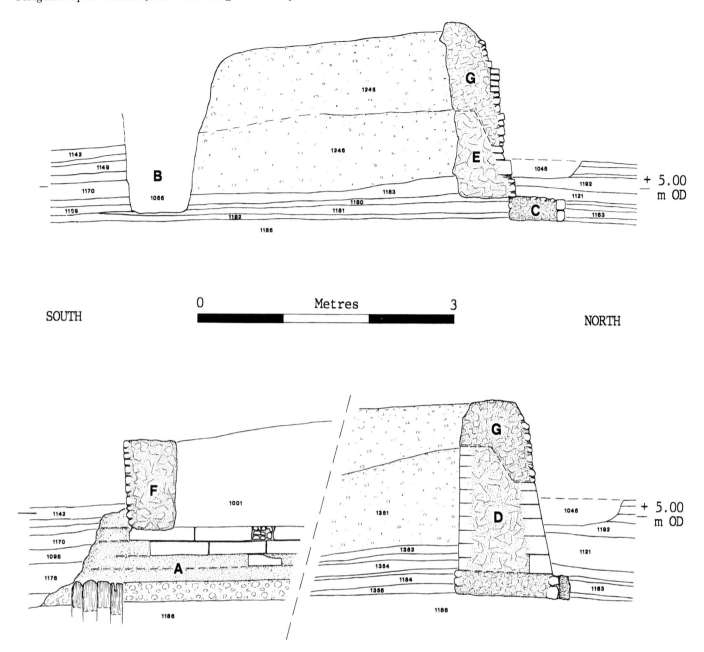

Fig 18.5 Kingston-upon-Thames: sections through causeway construction between (top) landward abutment and first pier, and (bottom) first and second piers with southern end cut back to show earliest phase of second pier (A)

Waterfront development

Work up- and downstream of the bridge revealed seven major phases of later medieval waterfront development (Fig 18.4). With one exception, the structures found were simple revetments, composed of roughly worked posts retaining timber and made ground up to a height of approximately 1m. The relatively low level of the waterfront reflects the medieval river regime. The tidal head would have been below Kingston, fluctuations in level being essentially seasonal. Today the river is locked downstream, ensuring a fairly constant level of *c* 4.5m above OD.

The first waterfront development, provisionally dated to 1300, appears to have been composed of two elements. Firstly, a timber revetment was built out from the north-west corner of the causeway (A on Figs

18.4 and 18.6). This revetment, some 11.5m in length, was constructed mainly from sections of clinker-built boat material (Goodburn this volume). It also included, on its upper edge, three substantial building timbers (1 and 2 on Fig 18.7). The second element was a substantial masonry blocking wall built between the south-west corner of the causeway and pier 3 (B on Fig 18.4). The wall was over 0.8m thick and was truncated at a height of 1m. The southern face, at its upper level, was finished with coursed Reigate stone blocks. It would appear that the purpose of this wall was to block off the direct flow of water, at least under normal conditions, into the area of downstream waterfront activity.

Some 10m upstream of the bridge was a further waterfront structure (C on Fig 18.4). This was quite elaborate with a back-braced double-thickness timber frame. The upper part of the structure had been lost to

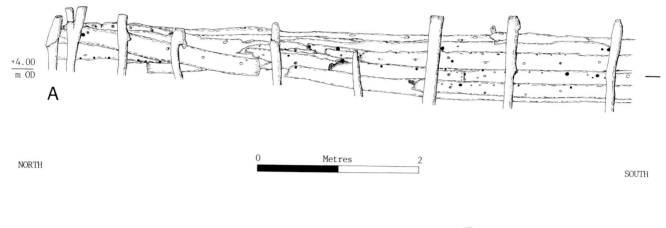

NORTH

0   Metres   2

SOUTH

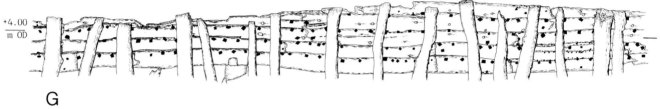

Fig 18.6 Kingston-upon-Thames: reused boat-timber revetments

decay. It is not accurately dated at present, although it may well predate the boat-timber revetment.

The above development of bridge and waterfronts can be seen to have initiated a cycle of silting and erosion, and structural damage leading to further development. This process was repeated several times from *c* 1300 to *c* 1600.

Heavy silting took place against the upstream face of the blocking wall between the causeway and pier 3, probably quite soon after construction. This extended over the whole excavated area to the south of the wall, and landward as far as the first pier. An initial consequence of silting was the riverward extension, by some 1.4–2m, of the back-braced revetment. With further deposition, a continuous upstream revetment was built, on a line with the western face of pier 3 (E on Fig 18.4). This structure was at least 15m in length (to the southern limit of excavation) and probably dates to the early 1300s. Construction was accompanied by some gravel infilling, particularly towards the southern end. The revetment itself was composed principally of reused building timbers (*eg* 3 and 4 on Fig 18.7).

Erosion and reconstruction

The above developments were interrupted by what appears to have been a single and quite dramatic erosion. Heavy scouring took place around the upstream cutwater and along the western face of the third pier, leading to the collapse and total rebuild of the latter. It appears that the downstream cutwater was also lost at this time, or perhaps slightly earlier. It is likely that the fourth pier also suffered damage. This pier was almost wholly rebuilt at an early date, possibly in two phases. Rebuilding of the upstream cutwater may well belong to this phase, that of the eastern face

and downstream cutwater could be slightly later (see below).

Heavy erosion seems to have been followed by rapid silting. The surviving unmortared rubble base at the northern end of pier 3 had silted over before rebuilding took place. Similar deposits also overlay fallen stonework to the west and north-east of the pier. Presumably such material would have been salvaged had it been accessible.

The western wall of the third pier was rebuilt from a level probably well below its previous base, and somewhat below contemporary river level. Presumably by now the upper level of the embanking timbers had rotted. Some of the stonework was reused, including several half-round moulded blocks with face reversed. The northern cutwater of the pier was not rebuilt. The end was simply blanked off on the line of the overlying roadway.

Further development of the waterfront

The revetment upstream of pier 3 evidently remained in use (E on Fig 18.4), although gradually silting up. Timber appears to have been stored here in this phase. Three roughed-out oak knees were found stacked just in front of the revetment. They were evidently contained within a wattle pen, the northern side of which was found built out at right-angles to the revetment. The knees may indicate boatbuilding in the vicinity, or simply the role of Kingston as a river port with a fairly extensive hinterland.

Heavy silting in the area to the north of the bridge led to the construction of a further revetment, provisionally dated to the second quarter of the 14th century. Silting, as the erosion which preceded it, probably owed much to the presence of the blocking wall upstream, and consequent interruption to the flow of water. The new

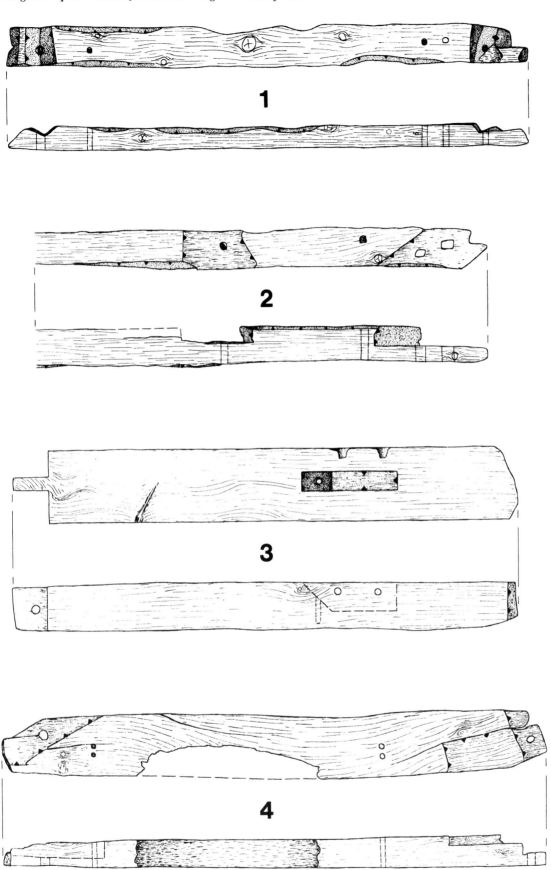

1

2

3

4

0   Metres   1

Fig 18.7 Kingston-upon-Thames: reused building timbers

waterfront consisted principally of a series of planks, running downstream from the western face of pier 3 for some 13.5m (F on Fig 18.4). Particularly notable was the use of three large sawn oak boards, one on the landward return and two forming parts of the river frontage. The latter measured in the region of 0.65m × 5.4m. This revetment appears to represent a more complex version of the process already seen upstream, in that there is little evidence of deliberate infilling. Possibly construction took place at the same time as the silting process; deposits may also have been cut away to the west to allow placement of the timbers.

Further downstream, some 20m north of the bridge, lay a further revetment (D on Fig 18.4). It is not securely dated, but may well precede the construction of revetment F. Structure D employed a variety of reused timber including fragmentary boat material.

Later erosion and reconstruction

The second major erosion probably took place in the mid 1300s. This did not affect the area upstream. However, a channel was scoured into deposits which had built up between piers 3 and 4. The adjacent downstream revetment (F on Fig 18.4) was undercut and slumped forward. Total collapse was only averted by the insertion of reinforcing posts, larger and more frequently placed than the originals. This appears to have been followed by deliberate dumping in front of and along the exposed base of the planking.

This phase of erosion may have necessitated the rebuild of the eastern face and northern cutwater of the fourth pier. There is an indication that reconstruction also took place at this time on the opposing western face of the third pier, with a slight change in wall alignment. It is possible that these events, or the problems preceding them, are reflected in a reference of 1375 to the bridge as 'gone to ruin and decay' (PRO C66 294 M26).

The final downstream waterfront appears to have closely followed remedial work on the planked structure. The revetment was extended a further 17m to the north, with the emplacement of two sizeable sections of articulated boat timbers (G on Figs 18.4 and 18.6). This material was from two different craft, somewhat heavier but of similar basic type to that of the first revetment (Goodburn this volume). A number of examples of this type of structure are known, including one recently found some 200m to the south of the bridge excavation.[2] Heavy abrasion on the face of the second boat-timber revetment would suggest that it took some time to silt up. However, it is likely that all the waterfronts had gone out of use by the early 15th century. The bank on both sides of the bridge reverted to shelving foreshore, gradually built up by further silting or dumping.

The rebuilding of the bridge

The bridge seems to have undergone a major rebuild, consisting of three main elements, dated provisionally to the mid or late 15th century (Fig 18.8). There is no specific reference to this event, although the background may be seen in records, in 1400 and again in 1435, of damage caused by flooding and measures to be

taken for repair (SuRO 33/1/5A and B; Wakeford forthcoming).

Stone arches were constructed between the causeway and pier 3, and from piers 3 to 4. These spanned, respectively, some 4.9m and 6.1m. The free-standing piers were largely rebuilt, in the case of the third pier from no higher than 5m above OD (Fig 18.3). The fourth pier lost its downstream cutwater at this time. Both piers retained arch springing, including elements of a chamfered rib on their downstream faces.

The northern causeway wall was reconstructed, with the addition along its length of a mortared rubble wall over the earlier build. The new wall was faced with flint and occasional Reigate stone, roughly coursed (G on Fig 18.5). The earlier wall had some damage on its outer face, but as already noted, probably survived to more or less its original height. On the inner face the rebuild line was quite constant, at 5.8–5.9m above OD.

On the upstream side of the bridge a new blocking wall (F on Fig 18.5) was constructed between piers 1 and 2, similarly faced to that on the north side of the causeway. The wall was set into the side of the existing gravel bank, which seems already to have suffered some erosion or slumping. The much higher level of construction relative to the early north wall is readily apparent in section. It is likely that the projecting upper sections of the southern cutwaters of piers 1 and 2 were removed at this time. It is also evident that there was some more general robbing of the earliest stonework. The inner face of the new blocking wall, for example, retained the impression of several facing courses from the demolished side of the second pier. Following this, and with the reconstruction of the northern wall complete, the intervening area was infilled with gravel to road level.

The upstream blocking wall between the landward abutment and the first pier was wholly robbed out (B on Fig 18.5). However, to the east of the abutment there remained a small section of flint-faced wall overlying the original ramp flanking wall. This was slightly offset to the south and retained made ground which sealed the earlier construction.

The above developments formed part of a substantial reconstruction of the bridge which involved a dramatic change in the form and level of the superstructure. Evidence for an earlier and lower causeway has already been discussed. The rise in level which now took place was a direct consequence of the construction of stone arches. Thus the causeway walls were raised, some 0.5m at the landward end, rising to a likely 1.5m at the western end. These developments created a structure which was to remain basically unchanged until 1828.

Later development of the bridge

A useful guide to the later development of the bridge is provided by an extensive deposit of water-laid silt on its upstream side. This is dated by remanent magnetism to 1520 ± 20 years. The silting is up to 0.55m thick, and reached a maximum height of *c* 5.95m above OD, which is very high in terms of the contemporary river level. It must derive from a relatively short period of major flooding. Such events are recorded as, for example, the flooding of the Market Place in 1570 (KBA P33/1/2).

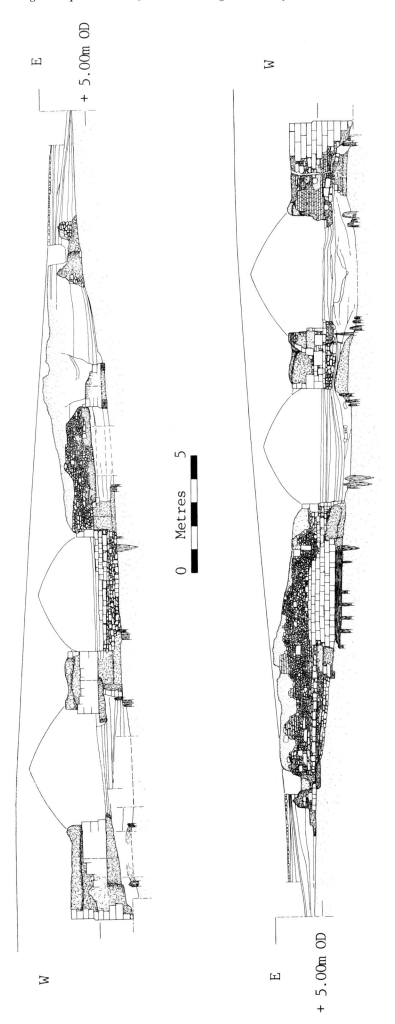

Fig 18.8 Kingston-upon-Thames: medieval bridge elevations, (top) upstream face, (bottom) downstream face

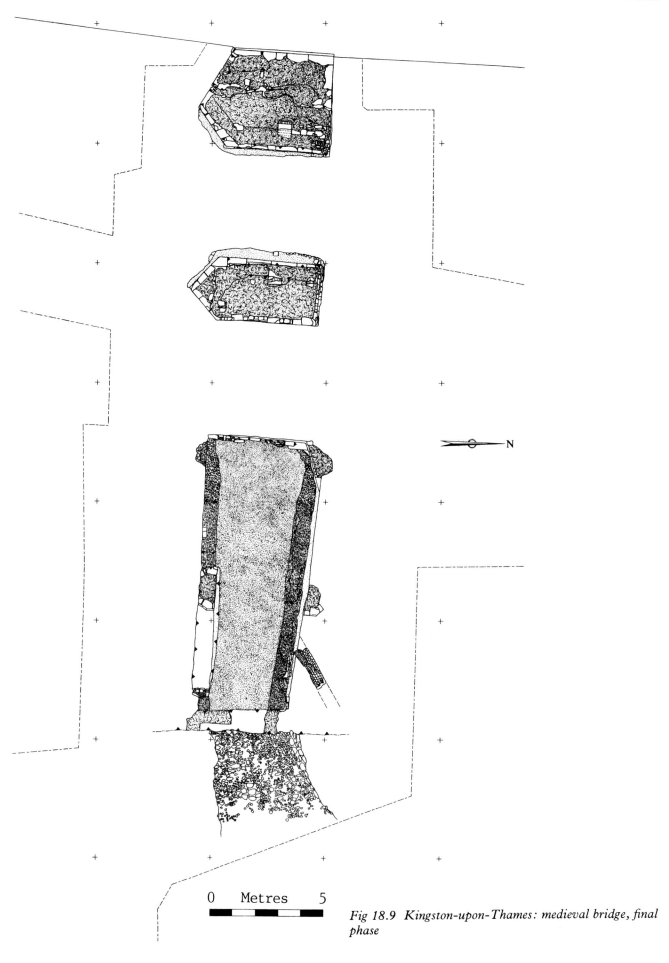

0   Metres   5

Fig 18.9 Kingston-upon-Thames: medieval bridge, final phase

The *c* 1520 silting may well have been accompanied by some damage to the bridge. There is some record of repair work, and the purchase of stone, in the early 1540s (Williams 1955, 31). In 1556 there was a further reference to the 'great burdens ... (of) repair and main-tenance', the bridge being in 'great ruin and decay' (Roots 1797, 78).

The outer arch, between piers 3 and 4, underwent reconstruction shortly after the silt was deposited. The supporting walls and most of the adjacent upstream cutwaters were rebuilt (Fig 18.9). The cutwater of the fourth pier had a particularly deep foundation, which must reflect earlier erosion. The new walls were built on, but in front of their earlier alignment, reducing the arch span from some 6.1m to 4.6m. The walls were faced, as before, with Reigate stone (much of it now robbed). However, within the foundations and wall core much roughly worked or unworked ragstone was used, the first appearance of this material on the bridge.

Subsequently, and probably following further erosion, the western (river) face of the fourth pier underwent reconstruction (Fig 18.9). The wall was extended 1m to the west, and refaced with substantial ashlared ragstone. This was the only use of ragstone in this form to be found. The best date for this construction comes from the extant Bridgewardens' accounts (Powell 1935). These describe major works in the period 1588–96, including the purchase and transporta-tion by river of much stone, and in one instance refer specifically to Kent as a source.

This represents the last major development of the bridge as seen in excavation, although it is evident from the documentary record that further quite extensive work was undertaken. The arches had become dry by the 17th century. Subsequently (*c* 1700) brick blocking walls were inserted on both faces of the bridge and the area thus enclosed was thereafter let out as storage space (Wakeford forthcoming).

At the landward end of the bridge, the causeway approach was progressively built up in the 16th and 17th centuries. A retaining wall of flint and brick was constructed from the north side of the causeway, running north-east and probably turning to the north (*c* 1700). There are a number of road surfaces associated with this final phase, of which one was cobbled (Fig 18.9).

By the late 18th century a combination of factors – growing traffic, deteriorating condition, and rising costs, and the example of new bridges under construc-tion elsewhere – brought growing pressure for the eplacement of the bridge. This was finally obtained in the Act of 1825 (6 *Geo IV cap cxxv*), the new bridge being opened in 1828. The old bridge was rapidly dismantled, the landward approaches levelled and much of the timber sold off at public auction.

Acknowledgements

I would like to thank all those colleagues and volunteers whose work on site made this paper possible. In particular, Bob Bazely, Tim Cawood, Margaret Darby, Phil Emery, Simon Mason, Rita Marson, Ken McDon-nell, Neil Price, Bill Smith, and Ian Tyrrell.

I would also like to acknowledge the work under-taken in connection with various aspects of the excava-tion and post-excavation work by Damian Goodburn, Scott McCracken, Valerie Saunders, and Ian Tyers.

Finally, I should like briefly to acknowledge the assistance received from many other quarters, in par-ticular from Marion Shipley and the staff of the Kingston Heritage Centre and from the Royal Borough Project Manager John Wolfenden.

Notes

1 There are a number of illustrations from the final years of the old bridge. Amongst the best of these are: Rowlandson *c* 1800 (Kingston Heritage Centre K1 937); Shepherd 1818, (the Suther-land Collection, Ashmolean Museum, Oxford); Ranyard 1828, (Kingston Heritage Centre K1 178); Watson 1828, (Kingston Heritage Centre K1 508). A reproduction of Rowlandson appears as a frontispiece in Williams (1955).
2 Excavated by R L Nielsen for the Museum of London

19 Vågen and Bergen: the changing waterfront and the structure of the medieval town
S Myrvoll

Abstract

During the 1980s, a series of rescue excavations has been undertaken in the area of the medieval town. This paper discusses projects centred on two areas of the waterfront and associated structures. The Finnegården sites, in the south, produced evidence for timber built houses and storage buildings erected in double rows. The sequence of reclamation and construction of these buildings from the 12th to the 17th century is described. At Domkirkegaten 250 m² were excavated close to the cathedral in an area assumed to be close to the water but without evidence for a harbour. Evidence for a medieval quay was recovered. Expansion in the northern area in the 13th century enabled construction of a deep harbour and the main focus of the town shifted northwards in response. The southern harbour was then filled in.

Bergen is situated on the west coast of Norway. Founded by King Olav Kyrre in AD 1070, the town grew to be of major importance in the Middle Ages, when it was one of four Hanse offices (*Kontor*) and, at one time, capital of Norway. The heart of the town, then as now, was the sheltered bay, Vågen, which provides excellent harbour facilities, particularly along the north-eastern shore, where it was protected from the prevalent northerly winds. The centre of the medieval town was located along the north-eastern shore and the southern part of the bay. The German wharf, Bryggen, with its standing buildings which date from 1702, is well-known for preserving the building traditions of the medieval waterfront, consisting of double tenements (*Dobbeltgård*) and passages from the quays to the street behind the buildings. The town's situation was ideal for trade, since it was connected to the fjords, the main communication network. Through its position as the main port on the coastal waterways, it became important as an intermediary between the western and northern parts of Norway and other countries, particularly around the North Sea.

When the northern part of Bryggen was devastated by fire in 1955, the ensuing archaeological excavations which took place during the period 1956–1979 under the direction of Asbjørn Herteig, initiated modern town archaeology in Norway (Herteig 1969; 1985a). These excavations are well known and are now the subject of a research project which is in the process of being published under the auspices of the University of Bergen.

In 1980 Riksantikvarens Utgravningskontor (the excavation unit of Bergen under the Central Office for Historic Monuments) was established to cope with any emergency excavations, mainly in the town centre. The unit was formed in response to the new Cultural Heritage Act of 1979 which placed the responsibility for archaeology in medieval towns on the Central Office, rather than the museums.

During the period 1980–7 this unit has been responsible for 20 emergency excavations in the town centre. Most of them were small, but some were of larger scale (although not on the scale of the Bryggen work) and there were several long-term trench observations. They cover, by pure chance, the major part of the medieval town and even though most of them are small in size, with a fixed time limit and strict budget, they may be characterized as effective sampling of the medieval town. Together with the background material provided by an archaeological survey of the town carried out by the excavation unit in 1982–5, they offer new information in several fields. Lack of grants and personnel have unfortunately made research into this material difficult and a large publication programme impossible.

To alleviate the situation and to make the information from the excavations accessible in the quickest possible way, either as a basis for further research into the town's development or to provide background information for future excavations, a research strategy has been established where the smaller sites are grouped together either by their position within the town or by their relationship to specific problems. Each of these groups of sites forms a small research project aimed at discussing the problems in question, rather than a total publication of all aspects of the site. This paper represents the results of this research strategy.

As this paper deals with the changing waterfront and town structure, the presentation of the recent Bergen excavations is limited to the most important sites to answer these problems, the Finnegården 3a and 6a excavations which form the basis for the 'Finnegården Project', and Domkirkegaten 6, the most recent site, excavated in 1987. To put these sites into proper perspective, it is necessary to touch on a few other sites which are important to an understanding of the town's development, mainly the churchyard of Korskirken (church of the Holy Cross) and the Svensgården stable building, as well as some sites in their vicinity (Fig

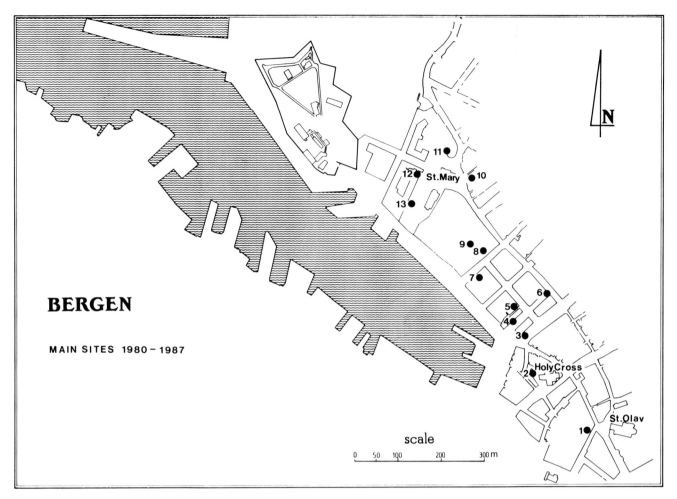

Fig 19.1 Bergen: principal excavated sites, 1980–7

19.1). As the town plan shows, these excavations fall into two main geographical groups. The southern group is of major importance for this paper.

The southern sites are found along the innermost shore of Vågen bay. In this part of the town the two churches, Korskirken and Domkirken, originally St Olav's, are presumably two of the three oldest and major churches, which may have served as unofficial parish churches in the town's earliest period: the parochial organisation was not established until the 14th century (Lidén 1985). Two of the sites excavated by the unit are located in the immediate vicinity of these churches, and the two Finnegården sites are found on the outskirts of the old Hansa Wharf.

Finnegården 6a (5 on Fig 19.1) was excavated by A R Dunlop in 1981 (Dunlop 1982) at the back of the Finnegården tenement (now the Hansa Museum). The site, which is some 100m from the present waterfront, yielded several phases of timber foundations for buildings, all of them conforming to a pattern still known today, a double row of buildings separated by a passage. Finds indicated a certain specialisation, with houses and storage buildings in separate rows. The oldest structures were clearly associated with harbour activities and consisted of foundations for piers and buildings on piles in the tidal belt.

Finnegården 3a (4 on Fig 19.1) was excavated by A Gołembnik in 1982 (Gołembnik 1983), and this site is presented by him in his own paper (Gołembnik this volume). As it is closely related to that of Finnegården 6a (5 on Fig 19.1), the two sites have been researched as one unit, and the phases correlated in six stages ('horizons') spanning the period between the 12th and 17th centuries (Myrvoll *et al* 1983). Together the two sites provide a longitudinal section of a 'double tenement' information on both the earliest shoreline and the land reclamation process. In many ways they parallel the site at Bryggen, although they are considerably smaller. Through these studies the following picture of the waterfront development for the Finnegården area emerges.

The first stage (Horizon A) is only known from Finnegården 6a, and includes two phases, both limited to the original beach zone. The earliest phase, dated to the middle of the 12th century, consists of a triangular timber structure (built partly of reused timbers) and a few larger piles, perhaps foundations for a quay (Fig 19.2). In the second phase these constructions were replaced by several large piles distributed through the whole site. Both phases were built within the upper part of the tidal belt, approximately 0.5m above sea-level, and they are obviously connected with harbour ac-

Fig 19.2 Bergen: Finnegården 6a, triangular harbour structure. Photograph: Riksantikvarens Utgravningskontor

tivities. Beach deposits from these activities were also located on the north-eastern part of the Finnegården 3a site. The end of this stage was marked by a fire in the second half of the 12th century, possibly the 1170s.

In the next stage (Horizon B), the waterfront was located under Finnegården 3a (Fig 19.3) as a row of timber boxes (caissons), each 1.5m square. These harbour structures were placed further out in the tidal belt, approximately 0.5m below sea-level, and presumably served as foundations for a pier or gangway. The caissons were corner-timbered, filled with stones, and the construction was strengthened by vertical lock bars placed through slots in the timbers (Fig 19.4). To judge by the length of these bars, the caissons must have had their surface at least 0.5m above sea-level. Three of these caissons were found close together on the site, in a line which indicated a very different shoreline from that of today. A wide, fairly shallow bay must originally have covered the present street, Vetterlidsalmenningen, as shown not only by the caissons, but also by the deposition of debris on the site and by the inclination of the piles caused by water pressure. The waterfront at this stage was associated with an expansion of building on dry land since stone foundations and posts in Finnegården 6a give an impression that the double tenement pattern may already have been in existence. (The dates of the phases are tentatively related to the dates of large fires which occurred in the town, but these should not be regarded as absolute.) This water-front was of two phases. The earliest covered the period between 1170 and the town fire of 1198, while the last, which was the final phase related to the tidal belt, ended

in the first quarter of the 13th century, in an historically unrecorded fire. The pottery assemblages from this and the succeeding phase suggest that the fire took place *c* 1230, confirmed by thermoluminescence dating of pottery burned in this fire.

With the third stage (Horizon C), covering the period between 1225/1230 and the town fire of 1248, the waterfront was extended into deep water, with large, cell-like timber constructions at least 5m × 5m, filled with earth and sand, as foundations for the new wharf (Fig 19.5). The boxes were held in place by large vertical timbers. By this time the bay had been filled in, and the actual quay frontage must have been located immediately south-west of the site. The area behind the quays was now taken up by dwellings, and perhaps storehouses, in a pattern which indicates a division of property corresponding to the double tenement known today in Finnegården.

After this first deep-water harbour had been devastated by a catastrophic fire in 1248, the new wharf was built and followed the same lines of construction, with only a slight modification of the front. The stage which covers the period 1248 to 1393/1413 (Horizon D) was marked mainly by a consolidation of the quay frontage and the structures of the earlier stage. The wharf on the eastern side of the harbour had now apparently acquired the shape which was functionally so effective that it has survived virtually unaltered up to the present day. The limited movement of the waterfront over the next 200 years is an indication that sufficient (or rather maximum) depth had been reached in this part of the harbour. In addition, the evenly sloping bottom in the

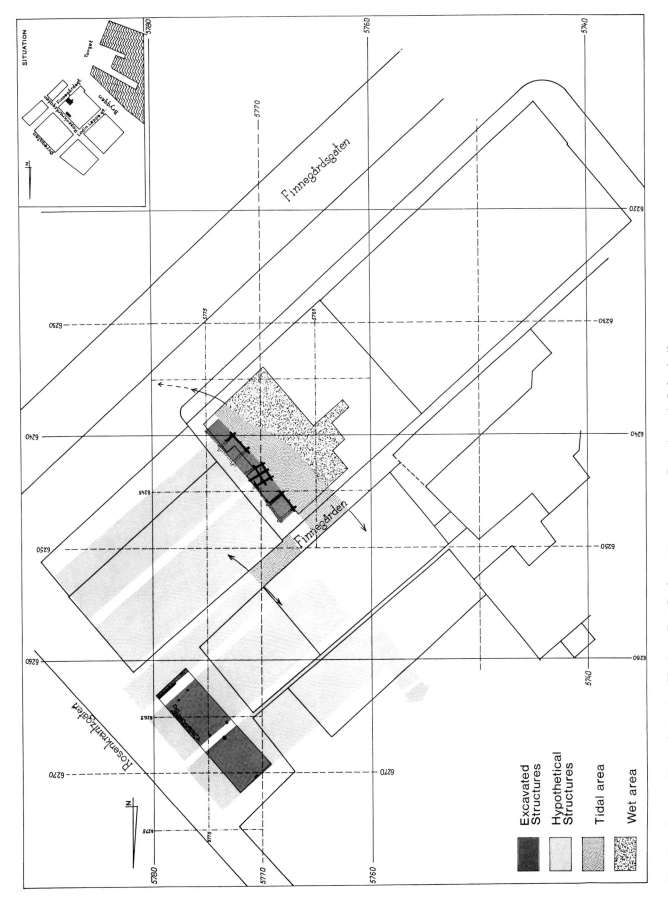

Fig 19.3   Bergen: Finnegården 3a, Horizon B. (Scale at 10m centres). Drawing: A Golembnik

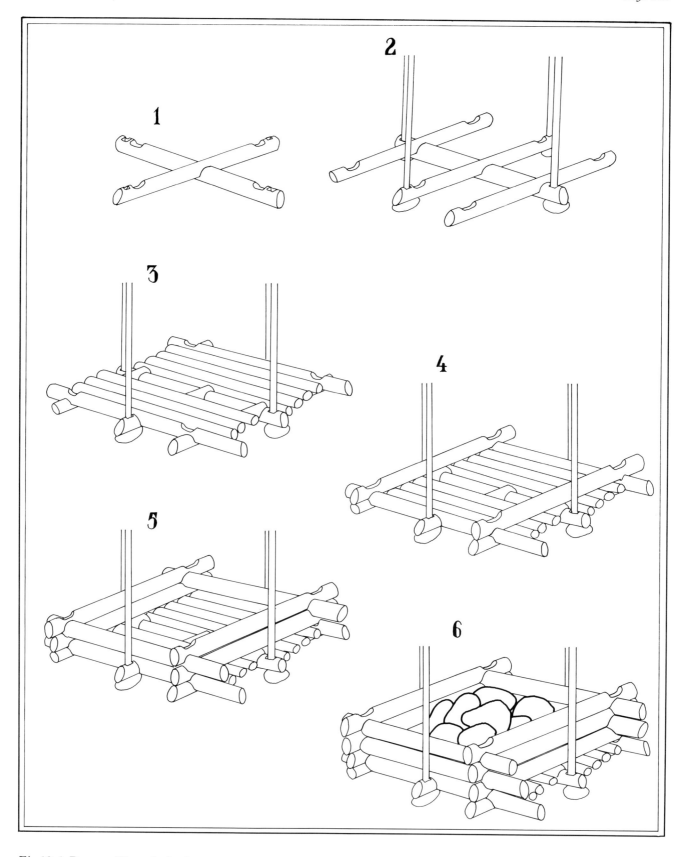

Fig 19.4 Bergen: Finnegården 3a, construction sequence of a caisson. These were made on dry land and sunk in the harbour with stones

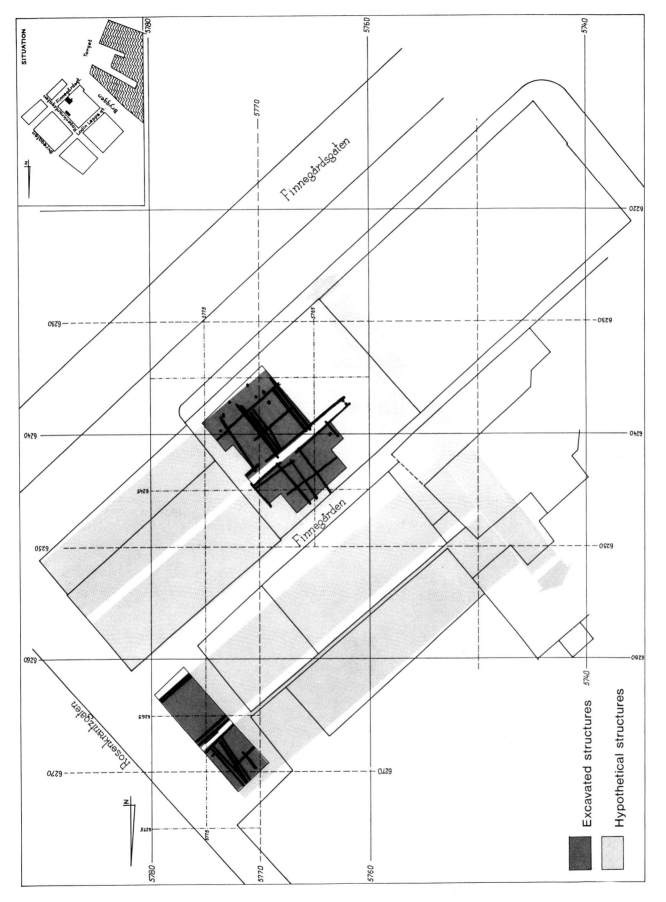

Fig 19.5 Bergen: Finnegården 3a, Horizon C. (Scale at 10m centres). Drawing: A Golembnik

southern part of Vågen, documented by geotechnical borings, gives a depth of approximately 3m at the quay front for the 14th and 15th centuries. Roughly the same depth is found in the inner part of Vågen today.

To sum up the Finnegården results, the earliest harbour activities, pre-1225/1230, were limited to the tidal belt. The major waterfront expansion took place immediately prior to the 1248 fire, with quays built out into deep water and with a building type characteristic of the Bergen waterfront, the double tenement, behind. During the following centuries this waterfront complex was consolidated, with only slight expansion into the bay (Fig 19.6). Presumably the mid 13th century expansion was an attempt to meet the steadily increasing sea traffic and a desire to increase the harbour capacity and improve harbour conditions.

On the other side of the original bay, close by Korskirken, a small site was excavated in 1983 (2 on Fig 19.1) on the outskirts of the churchyard (Dunlop 1984). The site yielded mainly churchyard remains, but the earliest phase provided information on the area's early topography. The original beach was located 0.5m above sea-level, and yielded deposits containing evidence of activity from the neighbouring district, including pieces of pottery. These deposits are dated earlier than 1220, and probably accumulated during the second half of the 12th century. There were no remains of harbour constructions, and the oldest churchyard goes back to 1220–30.

The last and largest site in this part of the town, Domkirkegaten 6 (1 on Fig 19.1), was excavated in 1987 by J Komber with the close cooperation of A R Dunlop (Komber *et al* 1988). The 250m² site was located near the Cathedral (Domkirkegaten 6), in the area assumed to be close to the water, but where any certain information on shoreline, depth, and possible existence of a harbour were lacking. The acquisition of knowledge on the natural topography was, therefore, one of the main purposes of this excavation.

The site had ten phases of activity. The late medieval period had left thick deposits of leather waste, slag, and the remains of a tanner's workshop. During this period the site had obviously been an open waste area closely connected with the leather workshops, whose presence is also known from written sources. The three earliest phases, however, differed strikingly from the later ones.

During the earliest phase (10), dated to the second half of the 12th century, a small corner-timbered caisson, 1m square, was built on the contemporary ground surface, the beach (Fig 19.7), approximately 1m above sea-level. In front of this structure, 0.9m above sea-level, a row of piles was placed in a north-west to south-east direction. The piles have been interpreted as a quay frontage following the natural shoreline, with an eastward passage up on to dry land. Three of the piles had features that suggested a special function. They have been tentatively interpreted as the foundation posts for an early hoisting spar, a type of construction used for the unloading and loading of cargo on the Bergen waterfront until the early 20th century.

In phase 9 (tentatively dated *c* 1180–*c* 1200), five large caissons were built on the beach at a level of 0.6–1m above sea level and filled with stones. They were positioned 1.5m apart in an east-west line (Fig

19.8). They were of the same type of construction as the ones found in the Finnegården phases of the same period (Fig 19.4), but larger, approximately 3.5m × 2.5m. The highest had the same constructional features as the Finnegården caissons, while the four others differ in having an extra strengthening of double lock bars to keep the structure together. The caissons are interpreted as foundations for a large quay built out into the bay, intended not for use as a passage, but for heavy-duty use such as loading and unloading cargo. Close by, the foundations for a triangular structure were also found. This construction was similar to the one from the beach in Finnegården 6a (Fig 19.2), but its function in this connection is uncertain.

In the early 13th century the pier was filled in and covered with logs (Fig 19.9) and a thick layer of soapstone debris. The resulting pathway or passage pointed towards the church, and can be interpreted as a transport ramp connected with construction work on the building. This phase covers the period between the early 13th century and 1276/80 after which the site was used for dumping waste mainly connected with leather crafts.

The development on the site Domkirkegaten 6 is obviously closely related to that of the neighbouring church. St Olav's church in Vågsbotn (Fig 19.1) is first mentioned in 1181, when it apparently functioned as a regular parish church (Lidén 1983). During the reign of King Håkon Håkonsson (1217-63) the church was taken over by the Franciscans who used it for their new monastery. The church may have been burnt in 1248, and was certainly consumed by fire in 1270. The first historical knowledge of shoemakers in the vicinity dates back to 1276/80 (Komber *et al* 1988).

The two earliest phases on the site, 9 and 10, correspond to the use of St Olav's as a parish church, prior to the early 13th century. At this time there was a harbour, with indications that heavy cargo was handled on this part of the waterfront. Phase 8, of the 13th century, may be related to the building of the monastery after which the harbour went out of use. This part of the town lost its importance and the site of Domkirkegaten 6 became a waste disposal area for the shoemakers.

In the old part of Bryggen to the north-west, the excavations under the Svensgården stable in 1981-2 (9 on Fig 19.1) gave important information on the early waterfront of Bergen (Dunlop *et al* 1982).The bedrock was found to occupy the eastern half of the site. On the beach in front deposits had formed of very similar character to the ones on the beach by Korskirken. The resulting layers indicated activity north-east of the beach (and of the outcropping rock) prior to the 1170s, the date of the earliest structural remains. These consisted of foundations placed close to the rock, either for a building or a gangway, belonging to the late 12th century and burnt in 1198. After this fire the rebuilding included the rock-covered part of the site. A passage ran up from the beach and there were buildings on either side, presumably the well-known double tenements. The expansion to the east, however, took some time, and the higher rock above the Svensgården stable was not built over until well into the 14th century (Dunlop 1985).

The development of the very northern part of

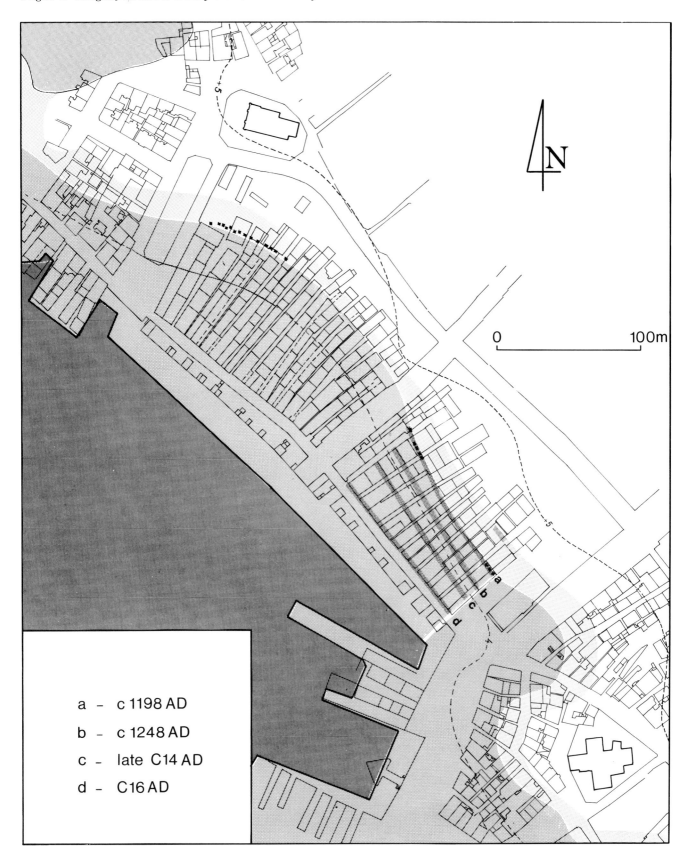

a – c 1198 AD

b – c 1248 AD

c – late C14 AD

d – C16 AD

Fig 19.6 Bergen: original shoreline and development of the waterfront. Drawing: A Gołembnik

Fig 19.7 Bergen: Domkirkegaten 6, early harbour structure, phase 10. Photograph: A S Herdlevær, Riksantikvarens Utgravningskontor

Fig 19.8 Bergen: Domkirkegaten 6, double caisson construction, phase 9. Photograph: A S Herdlevær, Riksantikvarens Utgravningskontor

Fig 19.9 Bergen: Domkirkegaten 6, transport ramp, phase 8. Photograph: A S Herdlevær, Riksantikvarens Utgravningskontor

Bryggen is known from the Bryggen excavations (Herteig 1985b). According to Herteig the early phases on this site belong to the 12th century and consist of primitive sheds, partly on dry land, partly in the tidal belt. By 1170/1 buildings on piles were found over the whole beach and small stone-filled caissons (of the Finnegården type) were built at the edge of the *marbakke* (submarine shelf) which is found on this part of the shore. During the period 1170-98 the quay frontage was extended into deep water with large earth-filled timber structures and yet another small extension made up prior to 1248. The largest expansions into the deep part of the bay, however, took place twice during the second half of the 13th century, when the quay frontage was moved, first 13m, and later a further 12m out into the harbour. At the same time the piers were made higher and deeper. The buildings behind these quays were definitely double tenements which certainly date back to the beginning of the 13th century or possibly earlier, but no documentation is as yet available. The unit's excavations in the vicinity of Bryggen (the Katarina Hospital in 1985 (12 on Fig 19.1), Kroken 3 in 1984 (11 on Fig 19.1), and Øvergaten 39 in 1982 (10 on Fig 19.1)) show, however, that the double-tenement pattern is particularly related to the waterfront (Myrvoll 1987). No double (or single) tenements are found within these other sites.

Adding this knowledge of the waterfront development to the information from the Bryggen excavations, the following sequence of the shoreline and early waterfront expansions in Bergen emerges (Figs 19.10 and 19.11).

The *marbakke* can now be shown to be limited to the northern part of the eastern shore, while the southern part was fairly shallow and had an evenly sloping bottom. In this southern part of Vågen, a promontory, where Korskirken was built, divided the shore into two natural harbours, one covering the present Vetterlidsalmenning, the other forming a bay near the old St Olav's church. The eastern shore was divided in two by the rock, and the building land must have been considerably less than previously assumed.

The earliest harbour activity is limited to the beach and the tidal belt, with small timber caissons built in shallow water at a depth of no more than 0.5m. These constructions are found all along the beach from Bryggen to St Olav's, with the exception of the area under the Svensgården stable and the beach in front of Korskirken. All were of roughly the same date, but the caissons on the beach by St Olav's were larger and of a stronger construction. The *marbakke* in the north provided a natural limit to the expansion of the harbour front in this tidal stage, while the southern part of the bay was apparently of greater importance as a harbour.

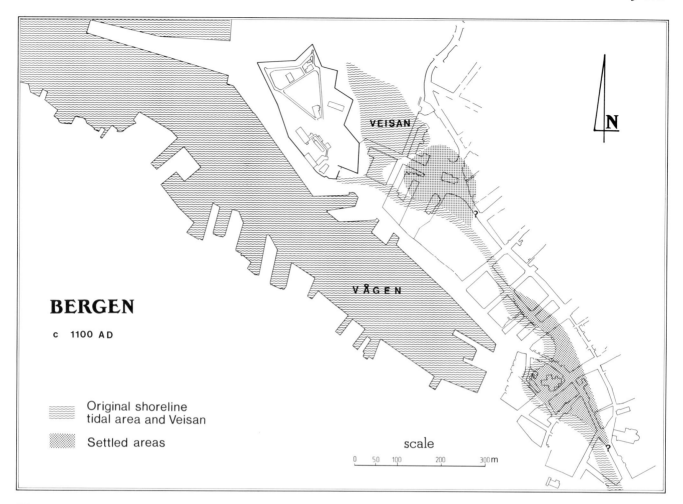

Fig 19.10 Bergen: settled areas c *1100*

It is here that the expansions took place and the area had not only the largest harbour structures but also works directly associated with the loading and unloading of cargo. The shallow bay must, however, have been a restriction on waterfront activity as maritime traffic increased, since the many large vessels needed depth, and a more effective arrangement of the loading facilities must have been desirable. In the years prior to the large fire in 1248 the main expansions took place under Finnegården, presumably as a result of infilling the bay, while the harbour by St Olav's went out of use. The church itself was taken over by the Franciscans, and the one-time harbour became a waste-disposal area. The parish of St Olav's then lost its importance as a harbour and centre.

In this early 13th century expansion the harbour frontage was moved out into deep water, by 20m out over the beach before 1230, and another 10m between 1230 and 1248. At the same time the first certain indications appeared of the double tenement as a building pattern. The expansion stopped, however, after the 1248 fire, when the maximum possible extent appears to have been reached due to the shallowness of the bay. During the ensuing centuries this part of the town underwent a period of consolidation and the further expansion of the harbour frontage took place in the

northern part of the town. The Bryggen excavations showed that the main harbour expansion here took place in two phases during the second half of the 13th century, pushing the frontage 25m further out into the harbour and increasing both the height and the depth of the wharf. This development was certainly related to the shape of the shoreline, since a really deep harbour is only possible on the northern half of the shore, where the marbakke allows an almost limitless expansion. The main centre of the town now moved northwards.

The excavations of the last decade in Bergen have shown that the land available for building was even less than previously assumed. The sites of Svensgården stable and the small site behind it (Dunlop 1984) also provide clear evidence that no continuous town centre existed in the 12th century and certainly no continuous waterfront before the mid 13th. Bergen must have in reality been two centres (Fig 19.10), one, Vågsbotn, located in the southern part of Vågen, surrounding the two shallow bays on either side of Korskirken and in close connection with St Olav's church, the other on the moraine terrace in the north, centred on St Mary's church. The evidence points to the southern part as the main centre, its harbour catering for the early trade. Steadily growing traffic and increasing trade led to a change in the town structure. The centre was gradually

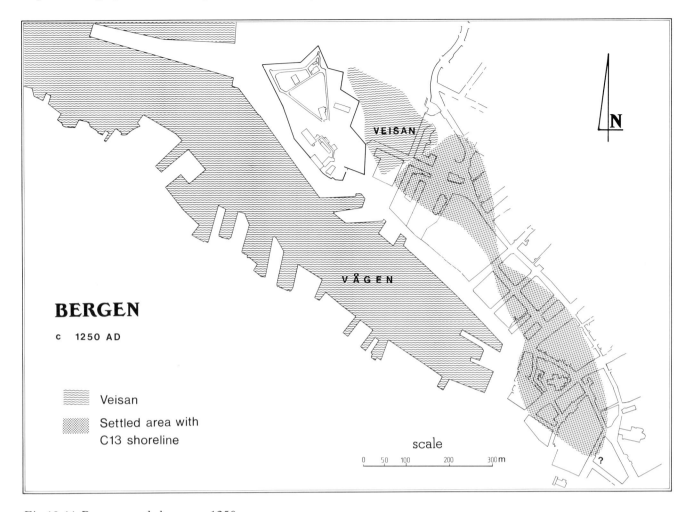

Fig 19.11 Bergen: settled areas c 1250

moved north until in 1248 the fire led to a complete rearrangement of the waterfront (Fig 19.11). The main harbour was now the eastern shore of the bay with a continuous frontage, and the buildings on the waterfront were tailored to the relevant trading activities with double tenements, a building pattern limited to the harbour area. St Olav's church now became a monastery, its harbour was filled in, and the town took the shape retained throughout the medieval period.

20 Some methodological aspects of the excavations at Finnegården 3a in Bergen

A Gołembnik

Abstract

In this paper the methods used to investigate the Bergen waterfront at Finnegården are discussed in detail. The methods used were developed in Bergen as a means of examining the complex structure of the double rows of medieval timber buildings which still, in part, line the former waterfront. Area excavation was limited by the presence of concrete floors but methods were devised for excavating and recording under these floors. The recording system adopted under these difficult conditions is described and assessed.

In early spring 1982, a large fire burnt down Finnegården 3a, which was part of a dense building complex erected at the beginning of the 18th century, and situated close to the wharf in the south-western part of medieval Bergen, in the lower part of the street Finnegårdsgaten (see Fig 19.1, 3). The rebuilding project allowed for two stages of archaeological investigation. The first included archaeological supervision of the foundation work. In the second stage methodical excavations were carried out at the same time as the rebuilding was taking place.

The first stage of the work confirmed the assumption that the houses erected in 1702 were representations of medieval buildings, originally constructed in a tidal area. The excavations provided evidence for seven phases which were associated with the use of the wharves in this part of medieval Bergen (Gołembnik 1983).

The natural sand was reached c 3m below the present-day street level, 0.5m below sea-level in the north-eastern part and 1.5m in the south-western part of the site. Fine-grained sand formed a slope towards the south-west. On top of it, the layers associated with the first phase were shown to have been deposited under water on the shallow bottom close to the sandy beach. They were associated with the erection and use of the first quay structure, found two years before in the upper part of Finnegården, at Finnegården 6a (Dunlop 1982). The thickness of these layers was approximately 4m, and in phase 2 they were covered by a deposit almost 1m thick connected with the construction of the new wharf. Three timber boxes filled with big stones, called *bolverk* (caissons) in Bergen, were found on the north-eastern part of the site. These constructions were placed along the shoreline, in direct contact with the water. During the investigation three main stages of deposition were distinguished in phase 2. The first group of layers was deposited during levelling and building activities and was divided into three in relation to the sequence of building the caissons. The next two groups were connected with their use and disuse. The same process was identified in the layers of the third phase, which had also accumulated in the sea but this time in the tidal

area. In this phase, seven stages of levelling, with three long interruptions, were recorded. The phase was associated with the building of a new structure. According to the new plan of the wharf, the quay front was moved towards the sea and the excavated area became dry land.

The next four phases contained the layers and timbers of foundations of double tenements, well known on the Bergen waterfront (Myrvoll this volume). The structures of phase 4 were the best preserved, and consisted of solid foundations built with huge timbers (Fig 20.1). The process of building was divided into 13 stages, with layers representing build-up as well as construction (Fig 20.2). The remaining three phases did not yield such detailed information. They contained the remains of foundations built in the same way as the structures of phase 4 but, having been partly destroyed by present-day building activities, were in a poorer state of preservation. In all, more than 450 cultural layers were distinguished, mainly associated with levelling undertaken in this part of the town during the Middle Ages.

As a result of recent building activities, the site was divided into three parts by concrete foundations. These were excavated as separate trenches. In the north-east and south-west new concrete floors limited the area available for investigation to 66m^2.

The excavation was carried out according to the method established for the excavation unit in Bergen by S Myrvoll. The main principle of this system is to excavate by following the original morphology of the layers and their stratigraphical sequence. This method was used throughout and a common level was kept in each of the three trenches. In addition to the many advantages for general field interpretation, this method also allowed the recognition of identical layers and allocation of the same numbers. It was not this stage, however, which made the excavation different from others. As mentioned above, the site was limited by concrete floors on both sides. Considering the importance of this area it was decided to excavate *below* the floors (Fig 20.3). This work was started when a depth of 1.8m had been reached in the main trenches. This method may be called successive sectioning (Fig 20.4).

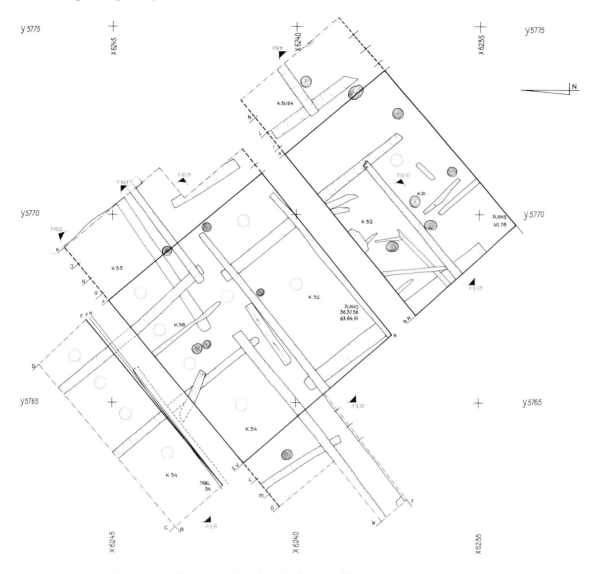

Fig 20.1 Bergen: Finnegården 3a, phase 4 timber foundations (grid at 5m centres)

Work was commenced from the top of the existing sections, removing the layers in succession to a horizontal depth of *c* 0.5m. When the extent of the layer had been ascertained, or there appeared to be a new one, it was recorded on a plan at a scale of 1:20 or on a sketch at a scale of 1:50. This made the basic drawings and their descriptions complete. The same method was also used for the elements of timber structures. The most arduous part was the need to cut horizontally lying timbers. Although difficult, this did not disrupt the progress of the excavation.

When all layers had been removed the new section was drawn, described, and photographed. After this had been completed, the section could be advanced a further 0.5m using the same method.

In this way, three sections were advanced, and the choice of sections was made according to research potential. By using this method, specific problems could be examined, the investigated area could be reduced, or unimportant parts of the site could even be given up, as actually happened during the excavation.

The emphasis was put on the north-eastern part of the site where two sections were progressed to solve the relevant problems. In contrast, on the opposite side of the area only one section was investigated. When all the sections had been examined, excavation was continued in the traditional way over the whole site.

In all, 13 sections were removed, which meant that every layer was examined in great detail. The layers were cleared horizontally while at the same time the position of each one could be observed in the successive sections. This excavation method gave good results during fieldwork and offered some advantages in report writing as well. By combining the series of sections, overall levels could be reconstructed with a high degree of accuracy, and presented in graphic form. Using this material in conjunction with the levelling grid from the plans it was also possible to use computer graphics. This was attempted during the final stages of excavation and considered to be a successful exercise.

Even though the method described was used at Finnegården as a necessity, excellent results were achieved.

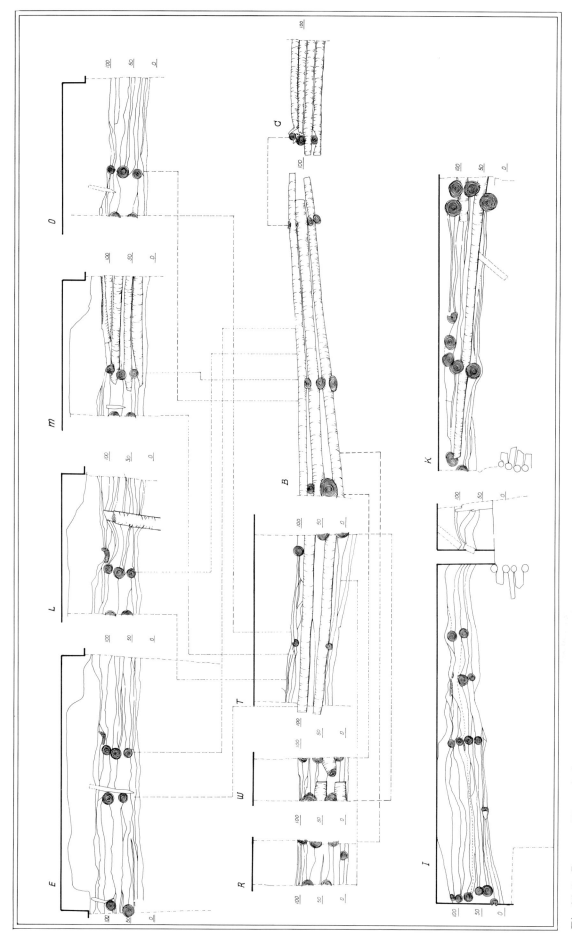

Fig 20.2 Bergen: Finnegården 3a, phase 4 stratigraphy

Fig 20.3   Bergen: Finnegården 3a, excavating below the concrete floor. Photograph: K Kristiansen, Riksantikvarens Utgravningskontor

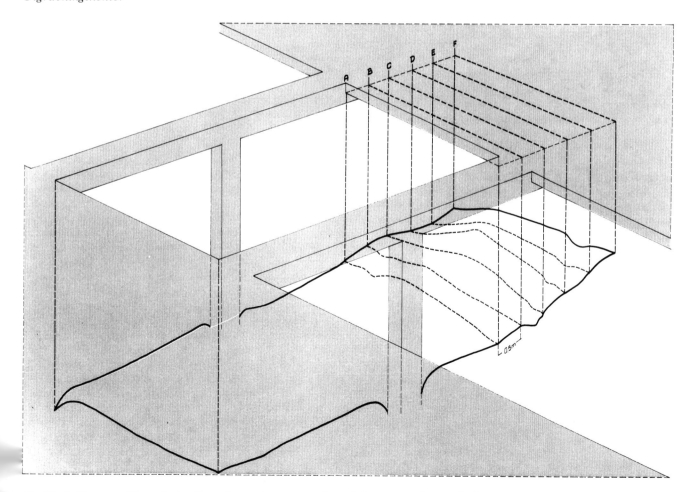

Fig 20.4   Bergen: Finnegården 3a, schematic presentation of the excavation method

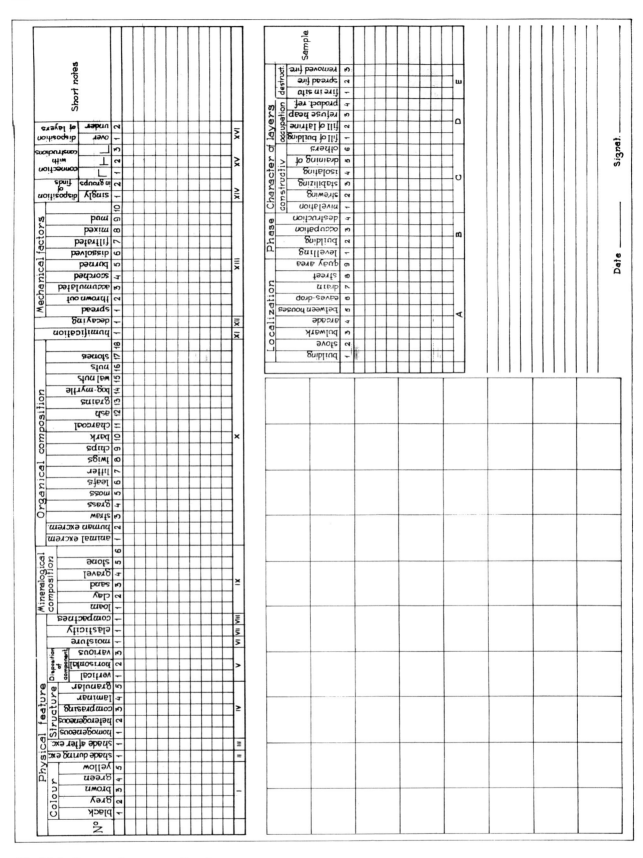

Fig 20.5 Bergen: layer recording form

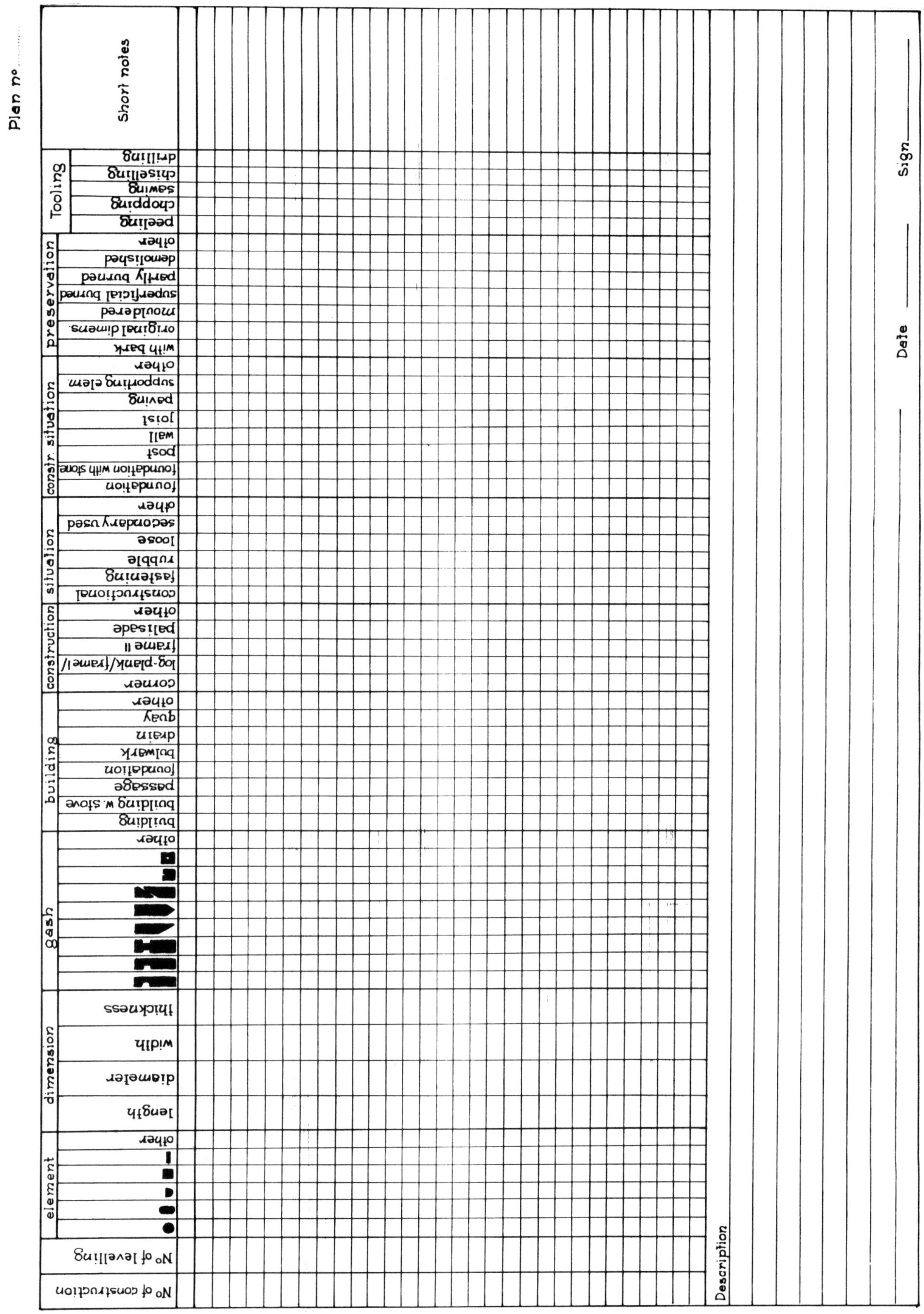

Plan n°

Short notes

Tooling: drilling, chiselling, sawing, chopping, peeling

preservation: other, demolished, partly burned, superficial burned, mouldered, original dimens., with bark

constr. situation: other, supporting elem, paving, joist, wall, post, foundation with stone, foundation

situation: other, secondary used, loose, rubble, fastening, constructional

construction: other, palisade, frame II, log-plank/frame I, corner

building: other, quay, drain, bulwark, foundation, passage, building w. stove, building

gash

dimension: thickness, width, diameter, length

element: other

N° of levelling

N° of construction

Description

Sign

Date

Fig 20.6 Bergen: timber documentation form

Carried out under very difficult conditions, the many sections made the interpretation more reliable and easier to corroborate. The method therefore would appear to be suitable not only for rescue excavations but would also give good results in normal conditions when used as a supplementary method in difficult, unexpected situations. It also has its didactic value, not only for students. On large, open-area excavations it would often be a salutary exercise for supervisors of excavations to cross-check their own decisions.

The recording system

The direction of excavations in three trenches at the same time also necessitated the use of a formalised system of descriptive recording. The introduction of forms and the requirement to complete all their blank spaces provided the opportunity to use the same criteria of description for all layers (Fig 20.5). It was also possible to compare different layers and even all levels. Since it was desirable to obtain uniform, detailed descriptions for similar layers found in different trenches, all layers were described by the same person. It is appropriate here to thank H Göhberg for his excellent work. He collected all the information from the field-workers and supplemented it with further details. The description of the layers should preferably be done with the aid of a sieve, but this was not always possible.

The basis for this system of description is the recognition of the single layer as a subject for investigation. It includes filling in a set form which allows for a versatile recording of the components and all the fractions. It provides a chance to ascertain the original location of the deposition of the layer. Such attempts were made regularly during the excavation, and it was often possible to decide if the layer was *in situ* or had been redeposited, under what conditions it had accumulated, and what had caused it to change. These attempts became a part of a research programme supervised by S Myrvoll.

The table of layer descriptions contains a list of common features, all of which are possible to distinguish without laboratory tests. The table is divided into three main parts. The description starts with the main physical features. In most cases, with the exception of colour, these have been adopted from geological terminology where the features have their own definition (Troels-Smith 1955), and are supplemented by archaeological data. The next part is a list of all components, mineralogical and organic, and a description of the degree of humification. Because mainly levelling layers were expected, the component's quantitative description is very superficial, and uses a five-point scale, ranging from hardly perceptible traces (1), to abundant

(5). Also included is brief information about the finds, as components of the cultural layers.

A detailed analysis of the structure of the layer and its composition offered a chance to determine the mechanical factors involved in the process of stratification. This part of the table was the starting point for the site interpretation. During the excavations at Finnegården 3a, efforts were made to determine some of these factors, such as the relationship between fractions of the layers, the difference between the positions of coarser and finer components, the state of preservation of the particles in each group of components, their size and traces of working, the relationship between organic and mineral elements, and the way different sand types accumulated. The results of all of these analyses, together with information obtained from the position of the layer in relation to timber structures, increased the precision of the final identification. An attempt was also made to ascertain the character of the layer as part of the investigated structures. In many cases, by using the method discussed, it is also possible to determine the original character of the layer. This aspect is of great importance for sites with large numbers of contexts where the process of stratification is the result of continuously repeated levelling.

As with the cultural layers, the elements of the timber structures survived in an excellent state, and their description was also formalised and tabulated (Fig 20.6). In addition to measurements, the table contained information about the state of preservation, traces of working and structural position, and information on elements of secondary use (Gołembnik 1982; 1985). In the case of the excavation at Finnegården 3a this information was added as remarks and comments to the plans. This method of description seems to be the simplest way to obtain a uniform catalogue of the timbers, and makes possible the use of statistics.

Both the layer and the timber tables offer considerable potential for report work and further research, in addition to their usefulness during fieldwork. This system of documentation supplemented the standard one used by the Bergen excavation unit, but during the report work it also became the basis for a different way of presenting the results of the excavations. The basic part of the report consists of tables, diagrams, and drawings. This makes it possible to understand the results without reading the text, which mainly consists of explanations for the conclusions presented in a formalised pattern. Each problem can be recognised and compared with the field documentation. This provides opportunities for a creative use of the report and for verifying the conclusions presented. It is thought that this system of documentation and presentation of the results facilitates the flow of information, enforces a certain discipline on research, and saves readers' time.

21   Lincoln's ancient docklands: the search continues
P Chitwood

Abstract

Recent archaeological and environmental research has added much to our understanding of the medieval waterfront in Lincoln. This paper presents a summary of information from sites excavated around the Brayford Pool. Environmental evidence shows that, in the later prehistoric and Romano-British periods, Lincoln lay close to the head of an estuary. From the Roman into the later medieval period the flow of water through the Pool was alternately slow and almost stagnant with peat formation, and faster flowing. This is indicative of periodic human interference with the channel upstream. Waterfront structures from the Roman and Saxon periods consist of hurdle and stake built fences or fishweirs. There was no well-defined port area until the 13th century. Excavations at Waterside North revealed a series of wattle fences, the foundations of a possible stone pier or slipway and a small jetty but not the hoped for sequence of successive waterfronts which have so far proved elusive. Bone-, leather- and antlerworking debris were recovered as well as some items of fishing equipment, coins, personal items of early medieval date and some Roman military equipment.

Introduction

Since the first International Conference on Waterfront Archaeology in London in 1979, considerable progress has been made in investigating various aspects of waterfront archaeology in the city of Lincoln. This paper includes information on the results of recent excavation and some associated environmental research.

The key to Lincoln's importance was its topographical situation, and an appreciation of this is necessary as a background to the river-front investigation. Lincoln lies near the junction of the Till and Witham rivers, in a Pleistocene gap through the Lincoln Edge, a ridge of Jurassic limestone running north to south (Fig 21.1). At the site of the junction is a lake, the Brayford Pool, which is presumed to be of natural origin, while to the east recent research has identified an estuarine creek system of prehistoric date (Wilkinson 1987; Darling & Jones 1988).

The sites discussed in this report all lay in or close to the area covered at one time by the Brayford Pool (Fig 21.2). Excavations have shown that the Pool and the river Witham were of much greater extent at the beginning of the historical period than in the present day. Although most of the Pool was marginal in terms of ancient port installations, waterfront structures have been identified which demonstrate reclamation of up to 100m on the north and east sides, while samples of environmental data have provided some evidence for river flow and (negligible) tidal influence. As yet no definite evidence for a Roman wharf has been discovered in Lincoln, although part of a possible Roman quay formed of huge stone blocks was noted in 1954 on the north side of the river Witham, east of the walled city. Remains of the medieval frontage of Brayford Pool were uncovered during rescue excavations in the 1970s, but the structures found were primarily concerned with local food supplies and of little significance in terms of long-distance trade.

A major new shopping centre, covering almost 200m of the waterfront, is planned for the area between Saltergate and the river Witham, its construction to commenced in 1989. Having undertaken a preliminary excavation in 1987, the City of Lincoln Archaeological Unit was, at the time of writing (late 1988), engaged in a major rescue excavation within this area. Because of deep-piled foundations and basements, the new development will involve the physical destruction of the buried evidence for a substantial proportion of the ancient riverside frontage. This will probably be one of the last opportunities to examine the crucial area east of High Bridge.

The potential here is enormous, as stated in the Lincoln contribution to the 1981 volume (Jones & Jones 1981). The work should provide important new information about the area of waterfront adjacent to the city walls. The line of successive waterfronts can be investigated as well as buildings such as riverside warehouses which are preserved by the waterlogged nature of the site. The excavations should also yield more information about river conditions such as salinity and tidal influence, while sea-level and flow conditions can all be studied, as well as fluctuations in climate and environmental conditions. There may be other incidental rewards such as traces of boats, either abandoned in the channel or reused in later revetments, and evidence for goods traded and trade links.

The environment of the river

The Brayford Pool lies on the river Witham at the point where the river, flowing northwards towards the southwest corner of the ancient walled city, turns eastward through the gap. The Pool also forms the junction between the river and the Foss Dyke, the former Roman canal linking the Witham with the river Trent to the west. Between the Brayford Pool, the west side of

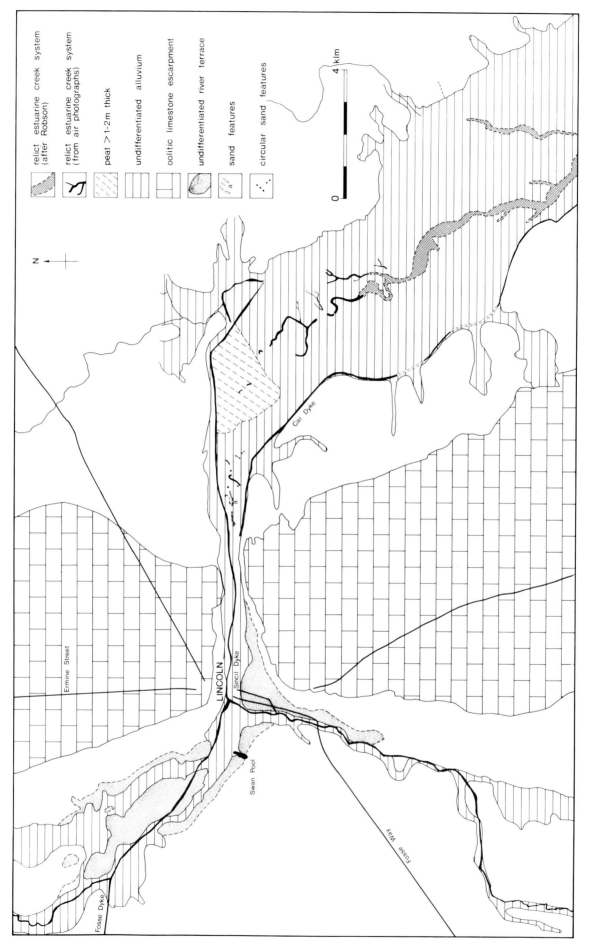

Fig 21.1 Lincoln: geology and topography, including the prehistoric estuarine creek system

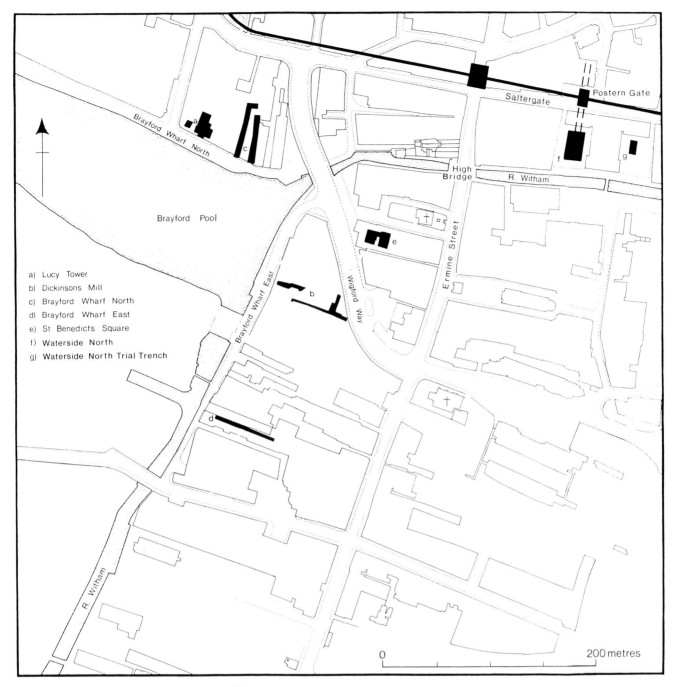

Fig 21.2 Lincoln: location of excavated sites

the Witham, and the 'Swan Pool' to the south (Fig 21.1), lay water meadows or areas of low-lying ground amidst the marshes, known as holmes (*holmi*) (Cameron 1985, 25).

The present course of the river at and below Lincoln, as well as its canal-like appearance, is partly man-made. It seems likely that modification of the Witham course was carried out in the Roman period. In prehistoric times, the Witham between Lincoln and Boston probably took a meandering course nearer the centre of the valley rather than the present course very close to the north side.

Some detective work and research by T Wilkinson, the unit's environmental consultant, has led him to

suggest that in the late prehistoric and Romano-British periods Lincoln was sited not far from the head of an estuary. A classic estuarine creek system is indicated on air photographs extending up to a point approximately 8km east of Lincoln (Fig 21.1). Upstream of this, channel features are obscured by deposits of peat 1–2m or more in thickness, often separated by channels containing sand rather than the coarse silt and fine sand characteristic of estuarine sediments (Wilkinson 1987).

The earliest sedimentary deposits examined so far in the city, which appear to be Fen Clays at Brayford Wharf East, are probably of Bronze or Iron Age date.[1] Unfortunately, the lack of diatoms and molluscs from these sediments made it difficult to establish whether they were deposited in brackish or fresh-water conditions. These data imply that, during the late prehistoric period, still-water deposits accumulated in what was to become the Brayford Pool. They were approximately at their contemporary sea-level and may well have been connected directly with it. The abundance of *Phragmites* and other rushes indicates an environment of pools choked with rushes.

By the Roman period the water level at Brayford Wharf East appears to have risen 1–2m above the high water mark as indicated from sites on the coast. Molluscan examination and particle-size analysis showed that sediments within the Roman channel were dirty, poorly sorted, included some small lenses of silt and peat, and contained bone, artefacts, and other settlement debris. They are likely to have been deposited in a turbid body of fresh water of variable flow velocity. This increase in velocity, along with the rise in water level, suggests that man was influencing flow conditions. Dredging and the addition of lock and sluice gates, as well as clearance of woodland within the Witham basin upstream, may have increased run-off, thus raising the water level. It is therefore evident that Lincoln occupied a primarily riverine, as opposed to an estuarine, site.

Between the 4th and 9th centuries there was a stagnation in flow conditions resulting in the accumulation of thick layers of peat. This might have been caused by extensive silting and lack of channel maintenance downstream. Water levels at this time remained at approximately the same level as during the late Roman period, but possibly fell in the 10th or 11th century. Flow velocities increased. In the same period, as seen at St Benedict's Square in 1985, and in later medieval times as indicated by redeposited river sands, visible as lenses above Roman deposits.

Waterfront excavations before 1987

At Brayford Wharf East and St Benedict's Square (d and e on Fig 21.2) there seems to have been an attempt to revet the waterfront in the mid to late 2nd century, perhaps to prevent flooding. This was followed by later Roman land reclamation through the dumping of building debris. Whether the waterfront was advanced at the same time along its whole length is unclear, but the possibility of a coordinated operation cannot be ruled out. A record of early vertical piles, noted in a late 19th century manuscript (Drury n d), implies that the Romans had bridged the Witham south of the city gate along Ermine Street (High Street) at High Bridge. Therefore coastal traffic may have docked below and east of the bridge.

The remains of hurdles or stake-built structures built successively out into the shallow part of the river during the 3rd century AD were found at the Brayford Wharf East site. A succession of similar structures was erected in the shallow water near the riverside during the period *c* 900–*c* 1200. All structures had been set up roughly parallel to the shore and may be the remains of fishweirs put up to funnel the fish into areas of still water near the shore. At the St Benedict's Square site a series of wicker fences of *c* 975–*c* 1025 were found; these

were part of a rather more elaborate structure or series of enclosures, possibly indicating a fish farm.

The clearance of the river may have coincided with the extensive commercial development of the lower town from the late 9th or early 10th century. The evidence from the Brayford sites at least suggests that the waterways at or near Lincoln were cleared during the period *c* 875–*c* 975.

The most dramatic event during this period at the Brayford Wharf East site was the rapid migration of the waterfront as a result of the construction of hurdle structures in the shallows. These resulted in variable-flow conditions, with sands being deposited in the fast flow on the channel side of hurdles, and peats in weedy or rush-choked ponds on the bank side, suggesting that the hurdles were set near the main channel. It is possible, however, that the peat accumulation was at least partly man-induced. By the time the present waterfront was fixed during the 19th or 20th century, the water's edge had migrated some 45m west in approximately 1000 years.

On the north side of the Brayford Pool, excavations at the Lucy Tower Street site (a on Fig 21.2) showed that the north bank of the pool had more or less reached the modern street Brayford Wharf North by *c* 1250, after which it remained largely unchanged, at least until the 18th century (Colyer 1975). A watching brief in 1982 at Waterside South, downstream and across the river, indicated that the area to the south-east of the High Bridge was either within the river channel or was marshland. A thick layer of peaty material may represent the silting up either of a pool or a widening of the river, and its return to a marsh lagoon as a result of neglect following the Roman period. This wider stretch of river would have been suitable for the mooring of river traffic serving the city to the north. The river-bank here appears to have lain at least 30m south of the present line. No evidence of revetments or river frontages of any kind was encountered in this area, which had silted up by the late 11th or 12th century. The area, together with the original arm of Sincil Dyke, a channel cut across the river terrace, probably in the Roman period, was finally filled in and levelled off in the late 15th or 16th century.

The evidence from these sites seems to suggest a piecemeal approach regarding the use of land upstream around the Brayford, as well as downstream, and the absence of a recognisable coherent plan for much of the time. There is, so far, no well-defined port area with wharves and warehouses until the 13th century; remains of a vertical wharf, made partly out of a reused boat hull, were uncovered at Dickinson's Mill (b on Fig 21.2), east of the Brayford (Jones 1981). It is possible that the boats used were of a type that could be beached or, perhaps, did not require substantial structures for the transfer of goods.

Excavation at Waterside North

An unrepeatable opportunity to throw light on this problem was provided by the plans for the large development scheme east of the High Bridge. A trial excavation in 1987 in the car park east of the Cannon Cinema (g on Fig 21.2) showed that the Roman river-

Fig 21.3 Lincoln: Waterside North excavation, probable 11th century wattle fencing

front lay several metres to the south of the Roman city wall which is beneath the north side of modern Saltergate (Miles 1988). This was corroborated by analysis of recent bore-hole tests, which seemed to indicate that there had been a considerable movement of the river frontage towards the south. The river-bed was discovered *c* 5m below modern sea-level. By the 4th century AD deliberate reclamation had begun to move the river-front south. Following an undefined period of abandonment, this movement continued from the late 9th to at least the early 11th century, partly as a result of natural silting or seasonal flooding. It was interrupted by episodes of activity: a limestone beach retained by wattle fences was set into the water's edge and the river channel was dredged clean. Successive silting and reclamation continued until the area eventually became dry land.

The artefacts recovered from the trial excavation indicated activity on or near the site from the Roman period into the medieval and post-medieval periods. Commercial activity during the Roman period may be indicated by a steelyard balance of copper alloy with adjustable counterbalance weight, and scale pan and suspension hook positions. Roman coins of the 4th century were also recovered. Later commercial activity is indicated by a lead cloth seal.

Work on the larger-scale investigation of this area commenced in June 1988 (f on Fig 21.2) and included excavation along the south side of Saltergate, as well as some investigation to the west below Woolworth's department store adjacent to the High Street. It was hoped to locate the Roman, Saxon, and later medieval waterfronts, associated reclamation deposits, riverside buildings, and possible bridge footings. Additionally, traces of a lane leading from a Roman postern (Fig 21.2), still visible beneath the Royal Bank of Scotland, and extending down to the landing stage, might be uncovered. This may have been the forerunner of the medieval lane, *Watergangstigh*, on roughly the same alignment. Any structures immediately west of this track or lane would be of great interest.

On the basis of previous work it was concluded that the Waterside North excavation might produce evidence for merchant docks of the Roman and medieval towns and for the postulated *wic* – the mid Saxon trading settlement which is presumed to have lain close to the river.

The normal water problems were compounded by the very wet weather of July 1988; a blow-hole (a natural fissure in the subsoil) caused serious flooding. This meant a serious delay to the investigation and a change in excavation strategy. A cofferdam, approximately 6m × 10m with a potential depth of about 6–8m, was created around the west portion of the area to combat the water problem.

The excavation was undertaken in two areas, Area A (cofferdam), and Area B (stepped). Work in the cofferdam uncovered four double lines of possible wattle fencing running east-west, not earlier than the 10th century and probably 11th century in date (Fig 21.3).

Fig 21.4 Lincoln: Waterside North excavation, possible stone pier or slipway foundation

Fig 21.5 Lincoln: Waterside North excavation, vertical wooden posts set in stone foundations

These appear to be associated with reclamation of the area by rapidly dumping sand, peat, and stones between these features. The third and fourth fences seemed to contain material more of a silty nature than man-made dump and it is possible that they were erected for a different purpose. Through these levels had been dug several pits and a 10th or 11th century well, circular at the top, changing several courses below to a square structure set on an oak plank foundation. At the time of writing, this area primarily included dump deposits that would appear to be part of the early land reclamation and which have yielded a large amount of Roman material.

Below the substantially mixed series of redeposited Roman dumps, a potential foreshore of well-worn limestone and coarse sand of mid to late Roman date was encountered. This was confined primarily to the south of a north-east to south-west line of vertically set piles. The equivalent layer was located in the trial trench at c 1.5m above OD. A linear channel, running north-west to south-east at right-angles to the line of set piles, about 1.5m wide and infilled with a large amount of miscellaneous wood fragments, leather, and coarse silt, may suggest some form of drainage network within this marshy area of the river Witham.

In Area B the excavators have had the opportunity to look quickly at the post-medieval to Roman periods. Below the modern concrete rubble there was a build-up of soil. This sealed the foundations of a possible stone pier or slipway used to launch river craft (Fig 21.4). The foundations were much disturbed by wood- and straw-

lined pits of late medieval date, probably connected with some industrial function. A series of vertical wooden posts packed with smaller stones was added to the stone structure (Fig 21.5). There seems to have been a chronological gap before a horizontal beam and stone pier-like structure was added to its southern end. A series of overlapping planks running c 7.5m north-south on the east side of the stone pier has been uncovered. They appear to be part of a revetment for the channel into which the slipway was set. The planks, possibly reused from a boat, were held in place by a series of upright posts to which they may have been nailed. As yet there is no evidence that they existed to the west of the pier. There was a possible stone buttress or small jetty jutting out from the pier-like structure. Below this series of structures was a build-up of dump material interspersed with wooden posts or fencing, again showing evidence of land reclamation.

At the lowest level investigated, various plant remains and large pieces of wood were encountered, sealed by deposits containing 3rd century pottery. The wood may be from a structure pushed or fallen into the river, or the material may have been deliberately deposited in the more marshy area at the edge of the river as initial reclamation or as a simple pathway through a wet area. On the other hand, evidence gleaned from the trial trench in 1987 suggests that this wood may be of late Saxon date.

A programme of environmental sampling has been carried out. Bulk sieving of soil samples from an agreed column has given a representative stratigraphic

Fig 21.6 Lincoln: Waterside North excavation, Roman child's shoe

sequence from the Roman to medieval periods. Other contexts, particularly those that are poorly understood, have also been sampled. The soil will be analysed for pollen and parasites as well as allowing for radiocarbon samples to be obtained. A careful timber recording procedure in conjunction with a dendrochronological sampling process has also been undertaken in order to determine dates of wooden features and the species of the timbers. With the help of the Lincoln Metal Detector Club and a systematic 'context-controlled' use of metal detectors, a large number of datable and historically important small finds have been recovered. These provide evidence for several industries on or near the site, as well as commercial activities. Objects of a domestic and personal nature have also been found.

Leatherworking, bone- and antlerworking, and possibly fishing are the best represented of the industries. Numerous fragments of leather footwear (*eg* Fig 21.6) have been found, including over twenty near-complete Roman shoes with hobnails in the soles, several Roman sandals, one of which has an exceptionally fine cut-out and punched design, and several almost complete medieval shoes. Numerous offcuts and trimmings from hides being prepared for shoe manufacture, and possible fragments of cobblers' waste all indicate an active leatherworking and shoe-repair industry. Other leather objects include two fragments of dagger sheaths with incised linear decoration.

Evidence for bone- and antlerworking occurred in the form of several fragments of sawn and chopped antler and an unfinished bone pin dropped or lost before the final touches were added. The most important find, however, was a motif piece or practice run of a design on a fragment of waste bone. This is the first such piece recovered from excavations in Lincoln. The high standard of craftsmanship possible with this basic material is demonstrated by 15 beautiful bone pins, all probably used for securing clothing, and a carved object with an interlace and linear design of Saxon date.

The artefactual evidence for a fishing industry is perhaps slightly more tenuous, being based on a few lead weights, probably net or line sinkers, and at least one iron fish-hook.

During the Roman period, this area would appear to have been quite commercially active as shown by the recovery of over 300 coins, largely of 3rd and 4th century date. One coin of the House of Constantine with a *chi rho* on the reverse is of a type not recovered before from excavations in Lincoln.

A few finds of a domestic nature have been recovered, for example tools and implements such as bronze needles, almost certainly of medieval date, knives, a fine awl or reamer with part of the wooden handle still intact (although this may be associated with leatherworking), and bone and pottery spindle whorls. A few whetstone fragments have been recovered, including one piece of probably Norwegian ragstone, a stone commonly used for hones during the late Saxon and later periods.

Several very fine personal objects, largely jewellery, have been found, including an 11th century twisted silver wire brooch, bracelet fragments of jet and silver, a bead and a triangular pendant, both of jet, a bronze signet ring of Roman date, and, perhaps most notably, part of a glass finger ring. This is of green glass with an extremely high lead content which gives it the appearance of steel. Similar rings were being manufactured at Flaxengate (Bayley *et al* forthcoming).

Other notable finds include a bone gaming piece, several iron *styli*, various finds of military significance including a spearhead, two arrow heads, a *ballista* bolt head, and fragments of chain mail. A very fine decorative bronze stud was also found, with a domed head and long, bent shank. Such studs are believed to have been used for the decoration of large objects such as furniture or saddles. A wooden 'paddle' has been recovered, with a perforated leaf-shaped blade and split shaft secured by nails. It is not known at present whether this is a paddle from a river craft or a domestic implement. Finally, wet-sieving of the spoil has produced several pieces of very fine Roman glass.

This paper is based on a relatively small amount of material compared with that which is likely to become available for study in the next few years, and so is offered in the form of an interim report which will be extended by further research. Only time will tell if this area contained the main wharves of the Roman, Saxon (Anglo-Scandinavian), and later medieval city, or if they perhaps lay further downstream.

Acknowledgements

The author would like to thank the following for their help: the excavation crew and staff; Lisa Donel, site field officer, for great patience, advice, and understanding while running the site; Mike Jarvis, assistant field officer, for comments and moral support; Chris Guy, field officer (post-excavation), for help and direction while reading the report; John Wilford, unit administrator, for skill and persistence in helping to organise; Mick Jones, director, for guidance and useful expertise in all archaeological matters. The pottery was processed by Caroline Kemp and provisionally dated by Jane Young. Small finds were organised by Jenny Mann and Val Williams. Also thanks to David Watt for illustrations and public relations; Keith Smith for conservation; Tony Wilkinson and David Schofield for the environmental work; and to John Hockley for remote sensing.

Note

1 The conclusions in this part of the paper are based on Wilkinson's interpretation of the results of various recent excavations (in Gilmour and Guy forthcoming).

22 The waterfronts of York
R A Hall

Abstract

The presence of the Roman Ninth Legion in York is reflected in the erection of grain storage buildings on the riverfront outside the fortress. A possible Roman jetty with crane-base is also recorded on the river Foss. Roman inscriptions name merchants trading between the colonia and the continent. Road and building sequences from sites along the waterfront within the colonia are described.

Recent excavations at Fishergate, at the confluence of the Ouse and Foss, have located what seems to be the missing wic of the 8th-9th centuries, though the river frontage itself could not be examined. Evidence for Anglo-Scandinavian river frontages is also very slight but the Coppergate site produced bone skates, fish-hooks and a large assemblage of fresh and saltwater fish bones. The later history of the Foss and King's Fishpool is briefly described. The later medieval period saw much reclamation of the Ouse banks with river walls being erected in the 15th century. York became an important berth for international traders until the port's role was eclipsed by the development of Hull. The role of York's religious houses in the development of the waterfront is discussed.

York's location at the confluence of the river Ouse with its tributary the Foss, some 60km (38 miles) from the head of the Humber estuary and a further 60km from the present Humber mouth, was probably the single most important reason why Roman military surveyors first chose the site for a legionary fortress in c AD 71. Not only did the neck of land between the two rivers offer a readily defensible site, but the Ouse allowed the passage of manpower and supplies from the North Sea coast and beyond. These same characteristics in turn made the place attractive to Anglo-Saxon, Scandinavian, and Norman invaders, and helped to ensure York's continuing pre-eminence in northern England.

There is a range of evidence for the importance of the rivers through the greater part of York's 1900 year history, although until recently archaeology had made hardly any contribution to understanding their role in the city's development. This position is now beginning to change, and there is likely to be a growing number of further opportunities for excavation and analysis over the next few years as the river frontages become increasingly attractive to developers. This paper offers a concise survey of the present sparse archaeological evidence for the waterfronts and puts it in the context of historical and other sources.

In c AD 71, when some 5500–6000 men of the Ninth Legion arrived at York, one of the problems initially confronting the Roman military machine was the supply of this new base. A solution, recognised in excavations at 39–41 Coney Street, between the fortress and the Ouse (1 on Fig 22.1), was the erection of store-buildings close by the river and the importation of grain supplies from the south of England or the continent; the evidence for the source of the grain comes from the species of weeds represented (Kenward & Williams 1979, 62). The earliest buildings, dated c AD 70–90, were identified as shallow gullies and trenches, which had been cut into the natural clay, filled with dark organic material (Fig 22.2). After a decade or so the

store was overwhelmed by an infestation of grain beetles; the threat posed to the military supply line was overcome by dismantling the buildings and sealing the pests underneath a dump of clay 0.45m thick upon which a near identical successor structure was erected. This remained in use for some years, but was apparently the last such building, for the area was replanned and eventually sealed by a roadway (Hall 1986); possibly the stores had been made redundant by the provision of locally grown supplies.

This outline sequence, gleaned from a single trench measuring 5m × 1.8m, remains all that is known at present about the Romans' use and development of the Ouse waterfront in the vicinity of the fortress; the extent and nature of the military use of the river remains almost wholly unknown, although the altar dedicated by Marcus Minucius Mudenus, a river pilot of the Sixth Legion, seems to confirm this use (RCHM 1962, 116).

The Roman military may also have made use of the Foss. Excavation in Hungate in 1950–2 (2 on Fig 22.1) exposed a small area of substantial gritstone blocks, interpreted at the time as a Roman crane-base on a jetty (Richardson 1959, 54–6), and traces of what may also have been Roman wharves and jetties have been encountered in Walmgate and Piccadilly (3 and 4 on Fig 22.1; RCHM 1962, 64–5). Yet the precise course of the Foss in the Roman period remains unknown; its present course is the product of major Norman and early modern alterations (below). Excavations directed by M Stockwell in St George's Field (5 on Fig 22.1), near the current confluence of the Ouse and Foss, exemplify the difficulties encountered in attempting to solve this problem, for they took the excavators well below the present level of the river-bed. A stratigraphic succession of deposits 8m in depth, laid down in the river or on its margin, was examined. This succession is believed to date to the 10th–20th centuries, and when fully analysed should provide some evidence on the hydrology of the Foss in that period. Currently,

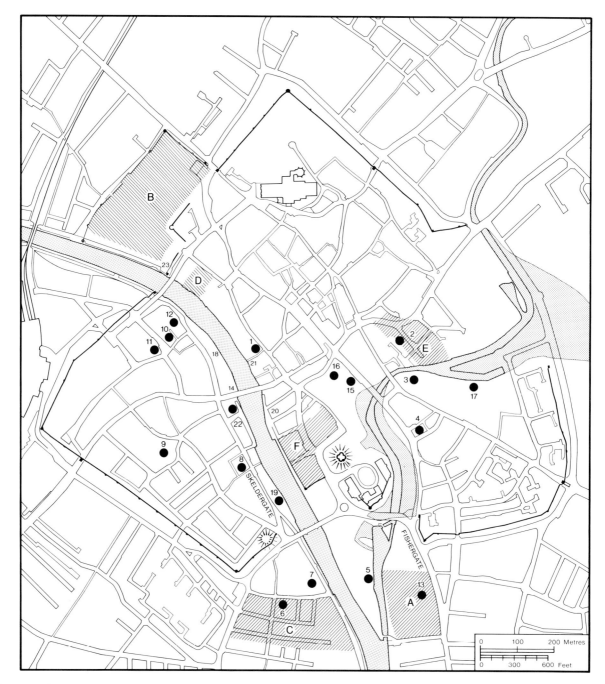

Fig 22.1 York: position of sites referred to in the text. Hatched areas show the location of medieval monastic houses with waterfronts: A Gilbertines; B Benedictines; C Benedictine Nuns; D Augustinians; E Carmelites; F Franciscans. The stippled area on the right shows the King's Fishpool, diminished from its earlier medieval extent, as mapped by Horsley in the late 17th century

however, the Roman use of the Foss remains largely enigmatic.

The south bank of the Ouse held the Roman civilian town of *colonia Eboracensis*. There is a number of inscriptions which imply or refer to the presence of merchants in this centre, trading with continental Europe. Among them is one recovered in Trust excavations on a site at Clementhorpe (6 on Fig 22.1), just east of the medieval walls which themselves may follow a Roman circuit. It refers to L Viducius Placidus, *negotiator*, who dedicated an arch and a gate in AD 221 (Fig 22.3) (Brinklow & Donaghey 1986, 63–7). Whether or not Placidus erected his arch and gate in Clementhorpe,

there is as yet no evidence there of a quayside from which he could have operated; a trench cut in the low-lying riverside area here at Terry Avenue (7 on Fig 22.1) in 1982 under the direction of A Davison failed to recover any ancient structural evidence, but rather suggested that this vicinity remained as 'ings', or water meadows, until beyond the late medieval period (*cf* Dobson & Donaghey 1984, 20).

Another inscription, from Bordeaux, dated to AD 237, records M Aurelius Lunaris, a *sevir* at both York and Lincoln, and one from York refers to M Verecundius Diogenes, *moritex*, a 'shipper' (Birley 1966, 228; Hassall 1978, 43). Together, these inscriptions provide

Fig 22.2 York: sequence of Roman river-side activity at 39–41 Coney Street. Foundation slots for an early storehouse cut the natural clay, and were sealed by a dump of clay into which similar slots for a replacement storehouse were cut. Above the thin dark band representing decayed grain is a layer of fire debris and then a succession of road surfaces

evidence for a *floruit* of commerce at York in the early 3rd century, in the early days of the *colonia*.

Until the 1980s the development of the entire *colonia*, let alone its waterfront, was almost completely unknown. The only evidence for possible riverside features came from an excavation at 58–9 Skeldergate (8 on Fig 22.1) in 1973–5 which revealed what was either a riverside road or hard (Donaghey 1978). L P Wenham's excavations at the church of St Mary Bishophill Junior (9 on Fig 22.1) in 1961–3 and 1967 uncovered traces of what may have been a late Roman fish-sauce emporium (Jones 1988), but the small herrings or sprats recovered there were presumably imported up the Ouse, for they are a marine or estuarine catch.

More recently, a concentrated series of excavations carried out near the waterfront in the north-western sector of the *colonia*, close to the Roman bridgehead, has brought a wealth of new material to light. A trench excavated at 5 Rougier Street (10 on Fig 22.1), under

the direction of P J Ottaway, shows well the influence of the waterside environment (Ottaway forthcoming). Among the earliest Roman features on the site was a ditch draining the relatively steep valley slope above; it was subsequently infilled and replaced by a timber-lined channel dated to the late 2nd century. In turn this was truncated at the riverward end of the trench by a substantial wall of gritstone blocks. The area was eventually covered by a deposit of burnt debris including timbers, daub, wall-plaster, and grain, suggesting that the wall may have formed part of a warehouse destroyed by fire. Following this, the area within the excavation had been reorganised; a new road was laid down near and parallel to the river Ouse and a substantial building erected, which stood on a series of stone columns. Each of the three excavated columns comprised three large superimposed blocks of millstone grit, with a socket in the top surface of the uppermost block. These sockets were presumably to take timber members, and it is suggested that this structure can be

Fig 22.3 York: the dedication stone from Clementhorpe, with the title [N]EGOTIATOR *three lines from the bottom*

interpreted as another warehouse, raised on these foundations to take it well above flood level. The building continued in use into the mid 4th century, although deposits of red and yellow ochre in the upper levels may indicate that it became a painter's or decorator's workshop in its later life.

Nearby, some 25m further back from the river at 24–30 Tanner Row (11 on Fig 22.1), N F Pearson has excavated a complementary sequence (Pearson forthcoming). Here too the earliest Roman activity includes a ditch running towards the Ouse. This is probably a continuation of the feature recorded at 5 Rougier Street, and both its position and alignment, close beside and parallel to the main road through the *colonia* leading towards the bridge, suggest that it was constructed as an integral part of the drainage of the road. It ran at the base of a dump created from mixed material including peat and turves, evidently raised to provide an elevated and water-free terraced platform upon which timber buildings could be erected in the third quarter of the 2nd century. These were the first in a sequence which included further timber and then stone buldings. Other relevant non-structural evidence includes, for example from late 2nd century levels, good evidence for the

presence of the black rat (*Rattus rattus*), an unintentional ship-board importation and something of a testimony to the contacts of the *colonia*. The site has also produced specimens of the garden dormouse (*Eliomys quercinus*), a north Gaulish animal, perhaps deliberately imported as an acceptable substitute for the fat or edible dormouse (*Glis glis*), a well-attested Roman delicacy which, however, lives further south and west in Europe (O'Connor 1988, 105–10). There is, too, an important series of small objects, including many in organic materials; they include military tent panels with official stamps and unofficial graffiti, and other leather items which may have originated in the clearance of a *fabrica* (Hooley forthcoming).

The most recent excavation in this vicinity, again directed by Ottaway, is nearest of all to the Ouse, and immediately west of the main road to the Roman bridgehead (12 on Fig 22.1). The road has been located and investigated; its earliest surface lay over vestigial timber features which may have formed part of an early causeway or *agger*. As might be expected so close to the river, there is evidence for river silts at this point. Inundation continued to pose problems, for the first road surface too was eventually sealed by a deposit up to 0.25m deep, again interpreted as the result of flooding. These silts are currently being studied by Ms C Batt of Sheffield University in an attempt to extend archaeomagnetic dating techniques to deposits of this type.

Further west a composite cross-section across the area at 90° to the river has shown that virtually all the area was available for use, at least at the end of the Roman period, and that there is no evidence for medieval reclamation here. At the time of writing, excavation in an area immediately adjacent to the main road to the bridge is revealing remains of a substantial stone structure near the water's edge, which, on the basis of its form and position, may well have been built as a warehouse, perhaps in the late 2nd century. It apparently remained in use, albeit in altered form, into at least the late 4th century; a precise chronology for subsequent events remains elusive at present.

In the 'dark ages' of the 5th or 6th centuries, there is no sign of any flooding of lower lying areas of the city, as has sometimes been suggested. In the Anglian period there is hardly any evidence available to complement the late 8th century description by Alcuin of 'Ouse, its waters teeming with fish' (Godman 1983). Indeed, on the river frontages discussed so far the only piece of possibly relevant information is the sequence of silting which accumulated against the Roman wharf at Hungate, and which might date, in part at least, to this era.

Recent work directed by R L Kemp at a site on the Foss at 46-54 Fishergate (13 on Fig 22.1) at its confluence with the Ouse, has at last located what is interpreted as the missing *wic* or commercial settlement of the period c 700–c 850, but evidence for the river-front itself was not forthcoming. At least, however, these discoveries point to the general area where further search must be directed in any attempt to find tangible traces of the trade conducted by the late 8th century Frisian merchants mentioned in passing by Altfrid in his *Life of St Liudger* (Whitelock 1955, 725).

The pre-Norman coin sequence at the Fishergate site ended in the 850s, and there is evidence that in the mid 9th century there was a movement of settlement back to the area within and immediately around the Roman defences. It is likely that this period saw the creation of the Ouse crossing at its enduring position, Ouse Bridge (14 on Fig 22.1), some 250m downstream from the Roman bridge, although this has yet to be proved. Structural evidence for the Anglo-Scandinavian period or Viking Age (mid 9th to mid 11th century) on the banks of the Ouse is as yet limited to one site, at 58–9 Skeldergate (8 on Fig 22.1), where the function of buildings of the late 9th/early 10th century is likely to have been the reason for their position, although data to support this are missing (Donaghey & Hall 1986).

Rather more is known about the Foss at this period. Pearson's necessarily limited work in 1987 at 22 Piccadilly (15 on Fig 22.1) located what is thought to be the 11th century river's edge with associated revetments. These discoveries will be placed in a wider context when seen in conjunction with the evidence from the immediately adjacent landward site at 16–22 Coppergate (16 on Fig 22.1), where the organically rich soil conditions are, in part, a product of the drainage pattern. The artefacts and environmental material from the Coppergate excavation also shed some light on the rivers and their margins. Numerous bone skates in 10th–12th century layers suggest not only somewhat harsher winters than those of today, but also wider, shallower, slower-moving rivers more prone to freeze over, with larger stretches of contiguous ings which would also provide a frozen highway. Fish-hooks point to a degree of piscatory self-sufficiency; the relative and fluctuating importance of different species in the catches has been charted by the work of A K G Jones (in prep; O'Connor 1989). An interesting sidelight on river pollution, probably to be linked directly to the growing size of York's population at this time, is the disappearance in the 10th century of species such as grayling (*Thymallus thymallus*), barbel (*Barbus barbus*), and shad (*Alosa* sp/spp), which tolerate only the cleanest conditions: they were presumably driven out by the dumping of debris in the rivers (O'Connor 1989).

The arrival of the Normans changed the face of York in many ways, but notably in the river regime, for William dammed the Foss to flood his castle ditches. He thereby created *stagnum regis*, the King's Fishpool, which remained an (albeit gradually diminishing) element of the city up to the 18th century. It seems possible that the rise of water-level behind the dam encouraged property owners along the pool to take steps to safeguard their holdings. The 'embankment' found near the Roman wharf in the Hungate excavations of 1950–2, and attributed to the Viking Age (Richardson 1959, 59*ff*), would logically fit into this late 11th century context. Certainly, the late 11th and early 12th centuries saw a rapid rise of up to 2m of soil at the riverward end of the 16–22 Coppergate site, some of which might have been the product of deliberate dumping. The damming of the Foss and the creation of the King's Fishpool barred access to the Ouse and led to the creation of a new environment around the Foss margins. Goods could still be brought downstream, but the sole archaeological evidence for this aspect of the river-fronts is the causeway and piles seen in a watching brief at Hungate (2 on Fig 22.1) in 1952, which could be part of the friars' landing, where building materials for the Carmelite Friary were unloaded in the early 14th century (Richardson 1959, 66–7).

Downstream of the dam, an island at the far end of St George's fields, between the Foss and the millstream, was known in 1376 as the Otter Holmes (Tillot 1961, 507). This attractive-sounding name belies the generally unpleasant nature of the waters above the dam. A succession of reports from the early 14th century had condemned the sewage, filth, and silt which accumulated in the Pool (*ibid*, 510), a picture enhanced by the discovery of what is probably late medieval debris, particularly from leatherworking, seen in investigations by N J Oakey at 76–82 Walmgate (17 on Fig 22.1) in 1987. Near the castle, Thomas Baskerville reported in 1677, 'dead standing water ... corrupts the air, of which they make a strong, heavy, sluggish ale, so that I could not digest it' (Palliser & Palliser 1979, 25).

The more recent history of the Foss and King's Fishpool includes the creation of the Foss Navigation Company in 1792, but the canal upstream of York was abandoned when the Foss was purchased by the City, drained, and a system of sewers installed in the mid 19th century. What was once described as 'a great elongated cesspool for a great part of this city' was finally reclaimed (Whellan & Co 1857, 373). In 1856 the Castle Mills were demolished, a new wharf was built nearby, and as late as 1895/6 Leetham's Mill was built between the Foss and Wormald's Cut (a relic of the canalization). There is still a little commercial traffic today, with news-print coming up by barge to a new printing works in Walmgate which backs on to the Foss.

Having dealt with the later developments of the Foss and the Fishpool it remains to discuss the Norman and later evidence from the Ouse. There is a number of contemporary historical records. In the late 11th century William of Malmesbury mentioned three Irish ships meeting German vessels in York (Hamilton 1870, 208). There is a further reference to York's Irish connection in the name *Divelinestaynes* (Dublin stones) given to a quay and the lane leading to it off North Street (18 on Fig 22.1; Palliser 1978, 9). First recorded in 1233–9, it may, like William of Malmesbury's reference, reflect the persistence of what originated as pre-Norman contacts. Other contemporary documentary references include one from the early 12th century concerning the archbishop's riverside interests in the Fishergate area (Leach 1891, 195–6), and the charter of 1189–1200 which provides the earliest in the series of records of Ouse Bridge (14 on Fig 22.1) (Tillot 1961, 515ff), which remained the only bridge across the Ouse in York until the 19th century. The account of Archbishop William's triumphal entry into the city in 1154, when the timber structure of Ouse Bridge gave way beneath the crowd gathered to greet him, comes from a mid 14th century source, and cannot be considered wholly reliable.

The only archaeological evidence for the Norman river-front here is a substantial stone wall of the late 12th or early 13th century seen in a short, isolated length at 39–41 Coney Street (1 on Fig 22.1), on the lip of a steep drop away towards the Ouse. This may represent a riverside wall, or could have been part of a riverside building, perhaps one of those referred to in the early 19th century as surviving 'till very lately' (Hargrove 1818, 411).

It was the 13th–16th centuries which seem to have been the main period of reclamation and attendant constriction of the Ouse. This in turn was to lead to the awful devastations wrought periodically by the down-river surge of abnormal amounts of rainfall or meltwater (Radley & Simms 1970).

There is one well-known documentary reference to this reclamation process. This is a petition to the king by property owners on the south bank of the Ouse in Skeldergate, who objected to the deleterious effects of works undertaken on the opposite bank by the Franciscan Friars. They asked for, and in 1305 were given, permission to undertake remedial action on their river frontage (Raine 1955, 239–40). New light has been shed on these historical references by two adjacent excavations towards the southern end of Skeldergate (19 on Fig 22.1), next to the site of the city's common crane, which have produced evidence for a sequence of activity extending from *c* 1200 to the present day. In *c* 1200 waterborne alluvium extended to within 3m of the

modern street line, but successive reclamations extended the properties a total of some 28m into the river. The most substantial gains were made in the 15th century, when the erection of a double line of limestone walls, running parallel to the river, allowed the reclamation of 20m of the riverside on each tenement. On the landward side a flight of steps led to an arch through the inner wall which gave access to a vaulted passage leading to the outer wall (Fig 22.4). Unfortunately, evidence for contemporary occupation on the newly reclaimed land has been largely destroyed, although at the Skeldergate street frontage new buildings were erected in the 14th/15th centuries (Oakey forthcoming).

Although York's role as an important berth for international traders was eclipsed by the rise of Hull, the city remained a major regional commercial and distribution centre, as the importance of the city's Merchant Adventurers shows. From 1357, based in their hall beside the Foss, they regulated trade; their members were active along the European littoral from Spain to the Baltic, as well as in Iceland. The contemporary river-fronts must have presented the sort of busy scene recognised in London, Hull, and so many other places, but archaeological details in York are few. It may be conjectured that the city's water lanes, which gave access to the main quays, go back at least to this period, if not before. Those leading to the principal quay at King's Staith (20 on Fig 22.1), described as newly built in 1366, were replanned in the 19th century; others which once existed have been either lost or downgraded, for example Sywinlending (Swine Landing), between Coney Street and the Ouse (21 on Fig 22.1), mentioned in 1300 (Palliser 1978, 15). Limited trial excavations on the opposite bank of the Ouse, behind the present Queen's Staith (22 on Fig 22.1), have also revealed what may be a previously unsuspected medieval lane there too (although other interpretations are possible).

As a footnote to this brief introduction to York's medieval commercial role, it is worth pondering for a moment on the number of religious houses which occupied lengths of the river frontages. They include St Mary's Abbey, founded in the 1080s immediately beyond the city walls; St Clement's Nunnery, founded 1125-33 only slightly further away from the defences at the opposite end of the city; St Andrew's Gilbertine Priory, approximately opposite St Clement's, but on the Foss, founded 1195; the Franciscan Friary, on the Ouse, founded *c* 1230 and expanding in the 1240s; the Augustinian Priory, further up the Ouse within the walled area, founded by 1272; and the Carmelite Friary, which was granted its new site beside the King's Fishpool in 1293. Some of these, such as the Clementhorpe nunnery, may well have had their own staithes at the waterfront (Dobson & Donaghey 1984, 19). Others, such as St Mary's, do not seem to have utilised their river frontages (Tillot 1961, 357), while there is uncertainty about several other sites. Yet these river frontages were potentially most valuable commercial assets; does their granting away demonstrate the extreme, self-denying piety of the donors, or is it an indication that the city's waterfront trade could be adequately served by the stretches of river bank remaining in secular hands?

The continuing fluctuations of riverborne commerce

Fig 22.4 York: excavation of the 15th century steps, arch, and inner river-side wall at City Mills, Skeldergate

into the Tudor era and beyond have been traced from the documentary evidence (*cf* Tillot 1961; Palliser 1979); complementary archaeological data for the Ouse has come from just two sites. At 39–41 Coney Street (1 on Fig 22.1) excavation against the inner part of the extant riverside wall, which contained a blocked gateway to the river, demonstrated that a stone-lined passage leading towards the gate had been constructed *c* 1575. This may have served as a slipway where small craft could be beached, but whatever its purpose it was apparently redundant by *c* 1700, when the passage was backfilled. It was rather earlier, in the late 16th or early 17th century, that the stairway and arch on the opposite bank of the river at Skeldergate (19 on Fig 22.1), noted above, were backfilled and blocked respectively, although the passage itself may have remained open and in use, perhaps as a slipway, until the early 18th century. At this site there was also archaeological evidence for the sugar refinery which is known to have operated here between 1681 and 1719, sited to take advantage of waterborne transport (Brooks 1983; Oakey forthcoming).

In addition to its commercial functions, the Ouse was used for a variety of other purposes. It was always a convenient waste-disposer, as exemplified in the building in 1367 of *novae latrinae, Anglice, les New Pryves* in an arch of Ouse Bridge under the Maison Dieu there (Raine 1955, 213). Some 300 years later, in the 16th and 17th centuries, the river-bank downstream of Ouse Bridge was the site of 'the Pudding Holes', a public washing place where not only clothes but also the innards of animals for use in black puddings were washed; contemporary exhortation and bye-laws about rubbish dumping in the river suggest that this was not the cleanest and most hygienic of places (Raine 1955, 224–5). It is therefore not surprising that when, in 1616, there was a first, ultimately unsuccessful attempt to draw water from the Ouse and to distribute it throughout the city by a series of pipes, the extraction point chosen was at the upstream boundary of the city's defences, at Lendal Tower (23 on Fig 22.1). A new beginning was made in 1677, and the tower continued to house machinery for the waterworks until 1836.

The modern history of the Ouse includes the creation of a 'New Walk' beside the river in the 1730s, but also continuing commercial interest, with the opening of Naburn Lock in 1757. Nevertheless, the Ouse's days as a great transport artery were numbered, the coming of the railways sounding the death knell. Only now does it seem that the river-fronts are to be re-invigorated once again, this time on an unprecedented scale, and offering in some cases the last opportunity to enhance an understanding of the skeletal framework outlined above.

Post-script

Since this paper was submitted, a number of small-scale excavations on either side of the Ouse off Clifford Street and Skeldergate, downstream of Ouse Bridge, have brought to light pieces of 7th–9th century Anglian pottery. These suggest that Anglian waterside activity was not restricted to the Fishergate extramural site, although its scale and nature in the central area remain uncertain. See A J Mainman forthcoming in *The Archaeology of York* 16/6.

Acknowledgements

I am grateful to all those of my colleagues at York Archaeological Trust and the Environmental Archaeology Unit at York University who have contributed to the writing of this paper by discussing the results of their excavations and research, and particularly to Terry Finnemore for providing the plan and to Simon Hill for the photographs. The responsibility for any errors is, of course, my own.

Bibliography

Armstrong, P, 1977   Excavations in Sewer Lane Hull, 1974, *E Riding Archaeol*, **3**

Artsikhovsky, A V, & Kolchin, B A, 1959   *Materials and researches on the archaeology of the USSR*, **65**

Aston, M (ed), 1988   *Medieval fish, fisheries and fishponds in England*, Brit Archaeol Rep, **182**

Aston, M, & Dennison, E, 1988   Fishponds in Somerset, in Aston 1988, 391-408

Aston, M, & Leech, R, 1977   *Historic towns in Somerset*

Atkin, M W, 1985   Excavations at Alms Lane (Site 302N), in Excavations in Norwich, 1971-78, part II, (M Atkin, A Carter, & D H Evans), *E Anglian Archaeol*, **26**, 144-260

Atkin, M W, Ayers, B S, & Jennings, S, 1983   Thetford-type ware production in Norwich, *E Anglian Archaeol*, **17**, 61-104

Ayers, B S, 1987a   Excavations at St Martin-at-Palace Plain, Norwich, 1981, *E Anglian Archaeol*, **37**

——, 1987b   *Digging deeper: recent archaeology in Norwich*

——, forthcoming a   Excavations at Fishergate, Norwich, 1985, *E Anglian Archaeol*

——, forthcoming b   Building a fine city: the provision of flint, mortar and freestone in medieval Norwich, in *Proceedings of Loughborough 1988 conference* (ed D Parsons)

Ayers, B S, & Murphy, P, 1983   A waterfront excavation at White-friars Street car park, Norwich, 1979, *E Anglian Archaeol*, **17**, 1-60

Baildon, J (ed), 1914   *Calendar of the manuscripts of the Dean and Chapter of Wells Cathedral*, **2**, HMSO

Bain, J (ed), 1887   *Calendar of documents relating to Scotland*, vol 3

Baker, D A, Baker, E, Hassall, J, & Simco, A, 1979   Excavations in Bedford 1967-77, *Bedfordshire Archaeol J*, **13**

Bates, E H, 1887   Leland in Somersetshire; 1540-1542, *Somerset Archaeol Natur Hist*, **33**, 60-136

Bathgate, T D, 1948   Ancient fish-traps or yairs in Scotland, *Proc Soc Antiq Scot*, **83**, 98-102

Bayley, J, Foley, K, & White, R, forthcoming   in *The archaeology of Lincoln*

Baynes-Cope, A, 1975   Fungicides and the preservation of water-logged wood, in Oddy 1975, 31-4

Beachcroft, G & Sabin, A (eds), 1938   *Two compotus rolls of St Augustine's Abbey, Bristol*, Bristol Rec Soc **9**

Biddle, M, 1967   Excavations at Winchester 1966: fifth interim report, *Antiq J*, **47**, 251-79

——, 1968   Excavations at Winchester 1967: sixth interim report, *Antiq J*, **48**, 250-84

——, 1969   Excavations at Winchester 1968: seventh interim report, *Antiq J*, **49**, 295-329

——, 1970a   Excavations at Winchester 1969: eighth interim report, *Antiq J*, **50**, 277-326

——, 1970b   Winchester: the Brooks, *Curr Archaeol*, **20**

——, 1972   Excavations at Winchester 1970: ninth interim report, *Antiq J*, **52**, 93-131

Bickley, F B (ed), 1900   *The Little Red Book of Bristol*

Binding, H, 1983   *Old Minehead*

Birley, E, 1966   Review, of The Roman inscriptions of Britain I: inscriptions on stone, *J Roman Stud*, **56**, 226-31

Black, G, 1976   Excavations in the sub-vault of the misericorde of Westminster Abbey, *Trans London Middlesex Archaeol Soc*, **27**, 135-78

Blackshaw, S M, 1974   The conservation of the wooden writing-tablets from Vindolanda Roman fort, Northumberland, *Stud Conserv*, **19**, 244-6

Blake, J B, 1967   The medieval coal trade of north-east England: some 14th century evidence, *Northern Hist*, **2**, 1-26

Blanchard, I S W, 1981   Lead mining and smelting in medieval England and Wales, in *Medieval industry* (ed D W Crossley), CBA Res Rep **40**, 72-84

Blomefield, F, 1806   *An essay towards a topographical history of the County of Norfolk*

Bond, C J, 1988   Monastic fisheries, in Aston 1988, 69-112

Book of Fees (Testa de Nevill), **1**, HMSO (1920)

Boon, G C, 1949   A Claudian origin for Sea Mills, *Trans Bristol Gloucestershire Archaeol Soc*, **68**, 184-8

Bown, L, 1988   The Queen Street pottery, in O'Brien *et al* 1988, 41-77

Braekman, W L (ed), 1980   *The treatise on angling in the Boke of St Albans*, 1496, Brussels

Brendalsmo, J, 1986   *Innberetning over de arkeologiske utgravingene i Baglergaten 2-4, Tønsbereg 1981-1982*, Tønsberg

Bridger, J P, *et al*, 1981   *Glossary of UK fishing gear terms*

Bridgwater, 1977   West Quay, Bridgwater 1973, a report by members of the Bridgwater and District Archaeological Society, *Somerset Archaeol Natur Hist*, **121**, 101-5

Brinklow, D A, & Donaghey, S, 1986   A Roman building at Clementhorpe, in Brinklow *et al* 1986, 55-74

Brinklow, D A, Hall, R A, Magilton, J R, & Donaghey S, 1986   *Coney Street, Aldwark and Clementhorpe, minor sites, and Roman roads, The archaeology of York* (ed P V Addyman), **6/1**

Brooks, C M, 1983   Aspects of the sugar-refining industry from the 16th to the 19th century, *Post-Medieval Archaeol*, **17**, 1-14

Brown, C E, & Peacock, E E, 1981   Smooth-on flexible mould compounds for wet site conditions, *Conserv News*, **15**, 8-9

Brown, P (ed), 1984   *Domesday book, 33: Norfolk*

Bryce, T, McKerrell, H, & Varsanyi, A, 1975   The Acetone-Rosin method for the conservation of waterlogged wood, and some thoughts on the penetration of PEG into oak, in Oddy 1975, 35-44

Buchanan, R A, & Cossons, N, 1969   *The industrial archaeology of the Bristol region*

Budd, P, forthcoming   The examination of ironworking slag and other technological material, in Ayers forthcoming a

Cameron, K, 1985   The place-names of Lincolnshire, part 1: the place-names of the county of the city of Lincoln, *Eng Place-Name Soc*, **58**

Campbell, J, 1975   Norwich, in *The atlas of historic towns: vol 2* (eds M D Lobel & W H Johns)

Carr, R D, Tester, A, & Murphy, P, 1988   The Middle Saxon settlement at Staunch Meadow, Brandon, *Antiquity*, **62**, 371-7

Carter, A, 1978   The Anglo-Saxon origins of Norwich: the problems and approaches, *Anglo-Saxon Engl*, **7**, 175-204

Carter, A, & Roberts, J P, 1973   Excavations in Norwich, 1972: the Norwich Survey second interim report, *Norfolk Archaeol*, **35**, 443-68

Carus-Wilson, E M, 1967   *Medieval merchant venturers*

Cherry, J (ed), 1973   Post-Medieval Britain in 1972, *Post-Medieval Archaeol*, **7**, 100-17

Chevenix-Trench, C, 1974   *A history of angling*

Christensen, A E, 1985   Boat finds from Bryggen, in *Bryggen Papers, Main series vol I* (ed A E Herteig), Universitetsforlaget, Oslo

Clark, E A G, 1960   *The ports of the Exe estuary, 1660-1860*

Clark, J G D, 1965   *Prehistoric Europe: the economic basis*

Clark, P, 1983   *The English alehouse*

Clarke, R W, & Squirrell, J P, 1985   The Pilodyn: an instrument for assessing the condition of waterlogged wooden objects, *Stud Conserv*, **30**, 177-83

Clay, P, 1986   Castle Donington, *Curr Archaeol*, **102**, 208-11

Clay, P, & Salisbury C R, forthcoming   A Norman mill dam and other sites at Hemington Fields, Castle Donington, Leicestershire, *Archaeol J*

Coles, J M, 1984   *The archaeology of wetlands*

Colyer, C 1975   Excavations at Lucy Tower Street, in Excavations at Lincoln 1970-1972: the western defences of the lower town. An interim report (C Colyer), *Antiq J*, **55**, 259-66

Coppack, G, 1986   The excavation of an outer court building, perhaps the Woolhouse, at Fountains Abbey, north Yorkshire, *Medieval Archaeol*, **30**, 46-87

Corcos, N J, 1983   Early estates on the Poldens and the origin of settlement at Shapwick, *Somerset Archaeol Natur Hist*, **127**, 47-54

Craig, H, 1954   Carbon 13 in plants and their relationships between carbon 13 and carbon 14 variations in nature, *Journ Geol*, **62**, 115-149

Cramp, R J, & Daniels, R, 1987   New finds from the Anglo-Saxon monastery at Hartlepool, Cleveland, *Antiquity*, **61**, 424-32

Craster, H H E, 1907   *A history of Northumberland: vol 8, the parish of Tynemouth*, Northumberland County Hist Comm

Crumlin-Pedersen, O, 1985   Cargo ships of northern Europe AD 800-1300, in Herteig 1985, 83-93

Cutler, D F, 1975   The anatomy of wood and the processes of its decay, in Oddy 1975, 1-8

Daniel, W E, 1895   The churchwardens accounts of St John, Glastonbury, *Somerset Dorset Notes Queries*, **4**

Daniels, R, 1986a   The excavation of the church of the Franciscans, Hartlepool, Cleveland, *Archaeol J*, **143**, 260-304

——, 1986b   The medieval defences of Hartlepool, Cleveland: the results of excavation and survey, *Durham Archaeol J*, **2**, 63-72

——, 1988   The Anglo-Saxon monastery at Church Close, Hartlepool, Cleveland, *Archaeol J*, **145**, 158-210

——, forthcoming   *Early medieval occupation and medieval tenements at Church Close, Hartlepool*

Daniels, R, & Robinson, P, forthcoming   *Hartlepool: Barker Place, Borough Buildings and Middlegate: three sites around the medieval harbour*

Darling, M J, & Jones, M J, 1988   Early settlement at Lincoln, *Britannia*, **19**, 1-57

Davies, J Conway, 1953   Shipping and trade in Newcastle upon Tyne, 1294-1296, *Archaeol Aeliana 4 ser*, **31**, 175-204

——, 1954   The wool customs accounts for Newcastle upon Tyne for the reign of Edward I, *Archaeol Aeliana 4 ser*, **32**, 220-308

Davis, F M, 1958   *An account of fishing gear of England and Wales*, Fishery Investigations Ser II, **21**, 8

Daynes, J N, 1965   *A short history of the Ancient Mistery of the Dyers of the City of London*

Dean, M, 1980   Excavations at Arcadia Buildings, Southwark, *London Archaeol*, **3.14**, 367-73

de Boe, G, & Hubert, F, 1977   Une installation portuaire d'époque romaine à Pommeroeul, *Archeologica Belgica*, **192**

de Jong, J 1981   The deterioration of waterlogged wood and its protection in the soil, in *Conservation of waterlogged wood: international symposium on the conservation of large objects of waterlogged wood* (ed L H de Vries-Zuiderbaan), Amsterdam 1979, UNESCO

Dent, J G, 1984-5   Fish spears and eel glaives - some notes on development and design, *Folk Life*, **23**, 105-15

Dilks, T B (ed), 1933   Bridgwater borough archives 1200-1377, *Somerset Rec Soc*, **48**

Dobson, R B, & Donaghey, S, 1984   *The history of Clementhorpe nunnery, The archaeology of York* (ed P V Addyman), **2/1**

Donaghey, S, 1978   Riverside structures and a well in Skeldergate, in *Riverside structures and a well in Skeldergate and buildings in Bishophill* (M O H Carver et al), *The archaeology of York* (ed P V Addyman), **4/1**, 4-29

Donaghey, S, & Hall, R A, 1986   58-9 Skeldergate, in *Anglo-Scandinavian settlement south-west of the Ouse* (J Moulden & D Tweddle), *The archaeology of York* (ed P V Addyman), **8/1**, 37-52

Donaldson, A M, Jones, A K G, & Rackham, D J, 1980   Barnard Castle, Co Durham, a dinner in the great hall: report on the contents of a 15th century drain, in Barnard Castle, Co Durham. Second Interim Report: excavation in the inner ward 1976-8: the later Medieval period (D Austin), *J Brit Archaeol Assoc*, **133**, 86-96

Doubleday, H A, 1901   *Victoria history of the counties of England, Worcester*, **1**

Drury, M, n d   *Notes on the excavations for the sewer works at Lincoln*, 19th century unpublished manuscript in Lincoln Library Local Collection

Dulley, A J F, 1967   Excavations at Pevensey, Sussex 1962-6, *Medieval Archaeol*, **11**, 209-32

Dunlop, A R, 1982   *Finnegården 6A, 1981*, Riksantikvaren, Bergen

——, 1984   *Report on the excavations at BRM200 Korskirken, 1984*, Riksantikvaren, Bergen

——, 1985   *Report on the excavations at BRM202 Nikolaikirkealmenningen, 1984*, Riksantikvaren, Bergen

Dunlop, A R, Göthberg, H, & Christensson, A, 1982   *Stallen 1980-1982*, Riksantikvaren, Bergen

Dur Acct Rolls   Durham Account Rolls I, Surtees Society, **99**, 1898. Durham Account Rolls II, Surtees Society, **100**, 1898

Dyson, A G, 1981   The terms 'quay' and 'wharf' and the early medieval London waterfront, in Milne & Hobley 1981, 37-8

Egan, G, 1979   A shearman's hook from London, *Trans London Middlesex Archaeol Soc*, **30**, 190-2

——, 1985   *Leaden cloth seals*, Finds Research Group Datasheet 3

——, (ed), 1986   Post-medieval Britain in 1985, *Post-Medieval Archaeol*, **20**, 333-60

——, (ed), 1988   Post-medieval Britain in 1987, *Post-Medieval Archaeol*, **22**, 189-231

Ellmers, D, 1972   *Frümittelalterliche Handelsschiffahrt in Mittel- und Nordeuropa*, Neumünster

Endrei, W, & Egan, G, 1982   The sealing of cloths in Europe, with special reference to the English evidence, *Textile Hist*, **13**, 47-75

Eriksson, J E G, 1986   Tønsberg. Tre norske middelalderbyer i 1970årene, *Riksantikvarens rapporter*, **12**, Oslo

Farmer, P G, 1979   *An introduction to Scarborough ware and a reassessment of knight jugs*

Farr, G E, 1939   Sea Mills Dock, Bristol, *Mar Mirror*, **25**, 349-50

——, 1977   *Shipbuilding in the port of Bristol*, Nat Maritime Mus Monogr Rep 27

Fenwick, V (ed), 1978   *The Graveney boat*, Nat Maritime Mus Greenwich Archaeol Ser, **3**; Brit Archaeol Rep, **53**

——, 1984   Insula de Burgh: excavations at Burrow Hill, Butley, Suffolk, 1978-1981, *Anglo-Saxon Stud Archaeol Hist*, **3**, 35-54

Fernie, E C, & Whittingham, A B, 1972   *The early communar and pitancer rolls of Norwich Cathedral Priory with an account of the building of the cloister*, Norfolk Rec Soc, **41**

Finberg, H P R, 1964   *The early charters of Wessex*

Firman, R J, & Firman, P E, 1967   A geological approach to the study of medieval bricks, *Mercian Geol*, **2.3**, 299-318

Fisher, F J, 1950   London's export trade in the early seventeenth century, *Econ Hist Rev 2 ser*, **3.2**, 151-61

Fraser, C M, 1961   Medieval trading restrictions in the North East, *Archaeol Aeliana 4 ser*, **39**, 135-50

——, 1962   The North East coal trade until 1421, *Trans Architect Archaeol Soc Durham Northumberland*, **11**, 209-20

—— (ed), 1966   *Ancient petitions relating to Northumberland*, Surtees Society, **176**

—— (ed), 1968   *The Northumberland lay subsidy roll of 1296*, Soc Antiq Newcastle upon Tyne Record Ser, **1**

——, 1969   The pattern of trade in the north-east of England, 1265-1350, *Northern Hist*, **4**, 44-66

—— (ed), 1981   *Northern petitions illustrative of life in Berwick, Cumbria and Durham in the 14th century*, Surtees Society, **194**

—— 1987   *The accounts of the Chamberlains of Newcastle upon Tyne 1505-1511*, Soc Antiq Newcastle upon Tyne Record Ser, **3**

Frost, H, 1963   From rope to chain: on the development of anchors in the Mediterranean, *Mar Mirror*, **49**, 1-20

Gaimster, D R M, Margeson, S, & Barry, T, 1989   Medieval Britain and Ireland in 1988, *Medieval Archaeol*, **33**, 161-241

Gelling, M, 1984   *Place names in the landscape*

Gibson, W S, 1846   *The history of the Monastery at Tynemouth in the Diocese of Durham*, vol 1

Gillespie, R, & Polach, H A, 1979   The suitability of marine shells for the radio-carbon dating of Australian prehistory, in *Radiocarbon dating: proceedings of the ninth international conference, Los Angeles and La Jolla 1976* (eds R Berger & H E Suess), 404-21

Gilmore, K, 1973   *The Keeran site*, Texas Historic Commission, Office State Archaeol Rep **24**, Austin, Texas

Gilmour, B J J, 1982   Brayford Wharf East, *Archaeology in Lincoln 1981-82. Tenth annual report of Lincoln Archaeological Trust*, 20-4

Gilmour, B J J, & Guy, C, forthcoming   *Excavations around Brayford Pool, The archaeology of Lincoln*, **8/1**

Girardon, S, & Heathcote, J (eds), 1988   Excavation round-up 1987: part 2, London Boroughs, *London Archaeol*, **5**, 410-15

Gjessing, H, 1913   *Tunsbergs historie i middelalderen til 1536*, Kristiana

Godman, P (ed), 1983   *Alcuin. The bishops, kings and saints of York*

Golembnik, A, 1982   Medieval wooden stronghold in Pultusk. Organization of investigation and documentation system of archaeological findings, in *Dokumentasjon ved bygravninger i Norden* (eds Ø Lunde, L Marstrander, & S Myrvoll), *Riksantikvarens Rapporter*, **3**, Øvre Ervik

——, 1983   *Finnegården 3A, 1982*, Riksantikvaren, Bergen

——, 1985   The excavations on the castle hill in Pultusk - new directions in archaeological research, *ISKOS*, **5**, Helsinki

Good, G L, 1987   The excavation of two docks at Narrow Quay,

Bristol, 1978-9, *Post-Medieval Archaeol*, **21**, 25-126

Good, G L, & Russett, V E J, 1987   Common types of earthenware found in the Bristol area, *Bristol Avon Archaeol*, **6**, 35-43

Goodburn, D M, 1986   Do we have evidence of a continuing Saxon boat-building tradition?, *Int J Naut Archaeol Underwater Explor*, **15**, 39-47

——, 1988   Recent finds of ancient boats from the London area, *London Archaeol*, **5**, 423-8

——, 1989   Toolmarks on the logboat, in Marsden 1989, 97-103

Goodburn, D M, & Redknap, M, 1988   Replicas and wrecks from the Thames area, *London Archaeol*, **6**, 7-10, 19-22

Gough, J W, 1930   *Mendip mining laws and forest bounds*, Somerset Rec Soc, **45**

Gras, N S B, 1918   *The early English customs system*

Grattan, D W, 1982   A practical comparative study of several treatments for waterlogged wood, *Stud Conserv*, **27**, 124-36

——, 1988   Summary of the results of the International Comparative Waterlogged Wood Treatment Project, in *ICOM Committee for Conservation. Working Group on Wet Organic Archaeological Materials*, Newsletter ,**16**

Grattan, D W, & McCawley, J C, 1978   The potential of the Canadian winter climate for the freeze-drying of degraded waterlogged wood, *Stud Conserv*, **23**, 157-67

Gray, M, 1969   *The archaeology of Redditch New Town* Progress rep **1** Feb

Green, B, & Young, R M R, 1981   *Norwich: the growth of a city*

Greeves, I S, 1980   *London Docks 1800-1980*

Gregson, C W, 1975   Progress on the conservation of the Graveney boat, in Oddy 1975, 113-4

Griffin, K, 1984   Botanisk prøvemateriale. Analyseresultat Bilag, in Lindh 1984

Griffith, F M, 1986   Salvage observations at the Dark Age site at Bantham Ham, Thurlestone, Devon, *Proc Devon Archaeol Soc*, **44**, 39-57

Hack, B, 1988   A mooring stone from Rackley, *Somerset Dorset Notes Queries*, **32**, 672-3

Hall, A, & Tomlinson, P, 1984   A dyeing art, *Interim*, **10**, 1, 21-5

Hall, R A, 1984   *The Viking dig*

——, 1986   Roman warehouses and other riverside structures in Coney Street, in Brinklow *et al*, 1986, 5-20

Hamilton, J R C, 1956   *Excavations at Jarlshof, Shetland*

——, 1968   *Excavations at Clickhimin, Shetland*

Hamilton, N E S A, (ed), 1870   *De gestis Pontificum Anglorum*, Rolls Ser

Hancock, F, 1903   *A history of Minehead*

Hargrove, W, 1818   *History and description of the ancient city of York*

Harkness, D D, 1985   The extent of natural ^{14}C deficiency in the coastal environment of the United Kingdom, in *Proceedings of the 1st International Symposium Radiocarbon & Archaeology, Groningen, 1981* (eds W G Mook & H T Waterbolk), 351-64

Harland, J, 1984   *Seamanship in the age of sail*

Harvey, P D A, 1980   *The history of topographical maps: symbols, pictures and surveys*

Hassall, M W C, 1978   Britain and the Rhine provinces: epigraphic evidence for Roman trade, in *Roman shipping and trade: Britain and the Rhine provinces* (eds J Du P Taylor & H Cleere), CBA Res Rep, **24**, 41-8

Hasslöf, O, 1949   *Svenska västkustfiskarna*, Göteborg

Heath, P, 1968   North Sea fishing in the fifteenth century: the Scarborough fleet, *Northern Hist*, **3**, 53-69

Henderson, C G, 1981   Exeter, in Milne & Hobley 1981, 119-22

——, 1988   Exeter quay in the sixteenth and seventeenth centuries, *Maritime South-West*, **4**, 5-17

Henderson, C G, Dunkley, J A, & Juddery, J Z, 1987   Archaeological investigations at Exeter Quay, *Exeter Archaeology 1985/6* (eds C G Henderson & S R Blaylock), 1-19

Herteig, A E, 1969   *Kongers havn og handels sete*, Oslo

——, 1975   Borgund in Sunmore. Topography, history of construction, state of research, in *Archaeological contributions to the early history of urban communities in Norway* (eds A E Herteig, H Liden, & C Blindheim), 23-48, Oslo

——, 1985a   Details from the Bergen medieval waterfront, in Herteig 1985c, 69-78

——, 1985b   The archaeological excavations at Bryggen, 'The German Wharf' in Bergen 1955-68, in *The Bryggen Papers, Main Series, vol 1* (ed A E Herteig), Universitetsforlaget, Oslo

—— (ed), 1985c   *Conference on waterfront archaeology in north*

European towns No 2, Bergen 1983

Hewett, C A, 1969   *The development of English carpentry 1200-1700: an Essex study*

——, 1980   *English historic carpentry*

Hinchliffe, J, forthcoming   Excavations in Church Walk, Hartlepool, Cleveland, 1972, *Durham Archaeol J*

Hobley, B, 1982   Roman military structures at 'the Lunt' Roman fort: experimental simulations, in *Structural reconstruction: approaches to the interpretation of the excavated remains of buildings* (ed P J Drury), Brit Archaeol Rep, **S110**, 223-74

Hoffmann, P, 1981   Chemical wood analysis as a means of characterising archaeological wood, *Proceedings of the ICOM Waterlogged Wood Working Group Conference, Ottawa*, 73-83

Hoffmann, R C, 1985   Fishing for sport in medieval Europe: new evidence, *Speculum*, **60.4**, 877-902

Holdsworth, E W H, 1874   *Deep sea fishing and fishing boats*

——, 1883   *The sea fisheries of Great Britain and Ireland*

Hooley, D, forthcoming   *Roman finds from the General Accident site Tanner Row and other sites, The archaeology of York* (ed P V Addyman), **17/7**

Horner, T, 1813   *Plan of Kingston-upon Thames*, Surrey Record Office Q9.2408

Horsey, I P, 1981   Poole, in Milne & Hobley 1981, 145-6

——, forthcoming   The town cellars, in *Excavations in Poole 1973-1983*, Dorset Natur Hist Archaeol Soc Monog Ser

Horsman, V, Milne, C, & Milne, G, 1988   *Aspects of Saxo-Norman London: I, building and street development near Billingsgate and Cheapside*, London Middlesex Archaeol Soc Spec Pap, **11**

Hübner, J, 1913   A contribution to the history of dyeing, *J Soc Dyers Colourists*, **29**, 12

Hudson, W H (ed), 1889   *The streets and lanes of Norwich: a memoir by J Kirkpatrick*

——, 1892   Leet jurisdiction in the City of Norwich, *Selden Society*, **5**

Hudson, W H, & Tingey, J C, 1910   *The records of Norwich II*

Hurry, J B, 1930   *The woad plant and its dye*

Hurum, H J, 1977   *A history of the fish hook and the story of Mustad, the hook maker*

Jackson, A M, 1972   Medieval Exeter, the Exe and the earldom of Devon, *Rep Trans Devonshire Assoc*, **104**, 57-79

Jane, F W, 1956   *The structure of wood*

Jenkins, J G, 1974   *Nets and coracles*

Jenkins, R, 1942   The copper works at Redbrook and at Bristol. *Trans Bristol Gloucester Archaeol Soc*, **63**, 145-67

Johnsen, O A, 1929   *Tønsbergs historie I*, Oslo

Jones, A K G, 1988   Fish bones from excavations in the cemetery of St Mary Bishophill Junior, in O'Connor 1988, 126-30

——, in prep   *Fish bones from York sites, The archaeology of York* (ed P V Addyman)

Jones, J, & Watson, N, 1987   The early medieval waterfront at Redcliffe, Bristol: a study of environment and economy, in *Studies in palaeoeconomy and environment in south-west England* (eds N D Balaam, B Levitan, & V Straker), Brit Archaeol Rep, **181**, 135-62

Jones, M J, & Jones, R H, 1981   Lincoln, in Milne & Hobley 1981, 138

Jones, P E, 1955   The guilds of the City of London with special reference to the Worshipful Company of Dyers, *J Soc Dyers Colourists*, **71**, 9

Jones, R H, 1981   Dickinson's Mill, in Excavations at Lincoln. Third interim report: sites outside the walled city 1972-1977 (ed M J Jones), *Antiq J*, **61**, 88-90

——, 1986   *Excavations in Redcliffe 1983-5*

Jope, E M, 1963   The regional cultures of medieval Britain, in *Culture and environment* (eds I Ll Foster & L Alcock), 327-50

Keene, D, 1985   *Survey of medieval Winchester*

Kelly, S, 1983   The economic topography and structure of Norwich c1300, in *Men of property: an analysis of the Norwich enrolled deeds 1285-1311*, 13-39

Kent, E A, 1932   The houses of the Dukes of Norfolk in Norwich, *Norfolk Archaeol*, **24**, 73-87

Kenward, H K, & Williams, D, 1979   *Biological evidence from the Roman warehouses in Coney Street, The archaeology of York* (ed P V Addyman), **14/2**, 45-100

Ketteringham, L L, 1976   *Alsted: excavation of a thirteenth-century sub-manor house with its ironworks in Netherne Wood, Merstham, Surrey*, Res Vol Surrey Archaeol Soc, **2**, 1-68

Knight, F A, 1902   *The seaboard of Mendip*

188

Bibliography

Kolsrud, K, 1984   Fishermen and boats, in *The Northern and Western Isles in the Viking world: survival, continuity and change* (eds A Fenton & H Pálsson), 116-28

Komber, J, Dunlop, A R, & Sigurdsson, J, 1988   *Domkirkegaten 6*, Riksantikvaren, Bergen, unpubl MS

Lahtiperä, P, 1984   Osteologisk prøvemateriale. Analyse Bilag, in Lindh 1984

Landon, L, 1926   *Somersetshire pleas from the rolls of the itinerant justices*, Somerset Rec Soc, **41**

Lapidge, E, 1824   *Plan for the proposed New Bridge*, SuRO Q56/8/106

Latimer, J, 1900   *The annals of Bristol in the seventeenth century*

Leach, A F, 1891   *Visitations and memorials of Southwell minster*, Camden Society, N S **48**

Leach, P J, 1982   *Ilchester volume 1 excavations 1974-1975*, Western Archaeol Trust Excavation Mono, **3**

Lidén, H-E, 1983   Domkirken, historisk oversikt, in *Norges Kirker. Bergen, vol II Norske Minnesmerker* (H-E Lidén & E M Magerøy), Riksantikvaren, Oslo

——, 1985   Middelalderens Bergen - kirkenes by, in *Middelalderbyen 1* (ed I Øye), Bryggens Museum, Bergen

Lindh, J, 1980   *Rosenkrantzgaten 4; rapport efter de arkeologiska utgrävningarna, maj 1978-maj 1979*, unpubl rep, Bryggens Museum, Bergen

——, 1984   *Innberetning over de arkeologiske utgravningene i Stortgaten 24-26, Tønsberg 1979*, Tønsberg

Lloyd, T H, 1977   *The English wool trade in the Middle Ages*

Lobel, M D & Carus-Wilson, E M, 1975   Bristol, in *The atlas of historic towns: vol 2* (eds M D Lobel & W H Johns)

Locker, A, 1977   Animal bones and shellfish, in Excavations at the Palace of King's Langley, Hertfordshire 1974-6 (D S Neal), *Medieval Archaeol*, **21**, 160-2

Losco-Bradley, P M, & Salisbury, C R, 1979   A medieval fish weir at Colwick, Nottinghamshire, *Trans Thoroton Soc Nottinghamshire*, **83**, 15-22

——, & ——, 1988   A Saxon and a Norman fish weir at Colwick, Nottinghamshire, in Aston 1988, 329-51

McAvoy, F, 1986   Excavations at Daw's Castle, Watchet, 1982, *Somerset Archaeol Natur Hist*, **130**, 47-60

MacCaffrey, W T, 1975   *Exeter, 1540-1640*

McGrail, S, 1983   The interpretation of archaeological evidence for maritime structures, in *Sea studies* (P G W Annis *et al*), Nat Maritime Mus, 33-46

——, 1989   Boatbuilding characteristics, in Marsden 1989, 103

Major, A F, 1911   Report on excavation work at Brinscombe, Weare, *Somerset Archaeol Natur Hist*, **57**, 110-13

Mangerud, J, 1972   Radiocarbon dating of marine shells, including a discussion of apparent age of Recent shells from Norway, *Boreas*, **1(2)**, 143-72

Manning, O, & Bray W, 1804   *The History and Antiquities of the County of Surrey*, vol 1

Marsden, P, 1971   Archaeological finds in the city of London 1967-70, *Trans London Middlesex Archaeol Soc*, **23.1**, 1-14

——, 1981   Early shipping and the waterfronts of London, in Milne & Hobley 1981, 10-16

—— (ed), 1989   A late Saxon logboat from Clapton, London Borough of Hackney, *Int J Naut Archaeol Underwater Explor*, **18**, 89-111

Martin, C J M, 1978   The *Dartmouth*, a British frigate wrecked off Mull, 1690: 5, the ship, *Int J Naut Archaeol Underwater Explor*, **7**, 29-58

Miles, P R, 1988   Waterfront North, in *Archaeology in Lincolnshire 1987-8* (fourth annual report of the Trust for Lincolnshire Archaeology), 32-3

Miller, L, Schofield, J, & Rhodes, M, 1986   *The Roman quay at St Magnus House, London: excavations at New Fresh Wharf, Lower Thames Street, London 1974-8* (ed T Dyson), London Middlesex Archaeol Soc Spec Pap , **8**

Milne, G, 1979   Medieval riverfront revetment construction in London, in *The archaeology of medieval ships and harbours in northern Europe* (ed S McGrail), Brit Archaeol Rep, **S66**, 145-53

——, 1981   Medieval riverfront reclamation in London, in Milne & Hobley 1981, 32-6

——, 1985a   *The archaeology of medieval waterfront installations in London*, unpublished M Phil thesis, Univ London

——, 1985b   *The port of Roman London*

——, 1987   Waterfront archaeology in British towns, in *Urban archaeology in Britain* (eds J Schofield & R Leech), CBA Res Rep, **61**, 192-200

——, forthcoming   Saxo-Norman house construction and the introduction of the box-frame building in London, in *Domestic architecture in Europe 500-1100* (ed P Wallace)

——, & Hobley, B (eds), 1981   *Waterfront archaeology in Britain and northern Europe*, CBA Res Rep, **41**

——, & Milne, C, 1978   Excavations on the Thames waterfront at Trig Lane, London, 1974-76, *Medieval Archaeol*, **22**, 84-104

——, & ——, 1979   The making of the London waterfront, *Curr Archaeol*, **66**, 198-204

——, & ——, 1981   Medieval buildings iat Trig Lane, *London Archaeol*, **4**, 31-7

——, & ——, 1982   *Medieval waterfront development at Trig Lane, London*, London Middlesex Archaeol Soc Spec Pap, **5**

Mitchell, N C, 1965   The lower Bann fisheries, *Ulster Folk Life*, **11**, 1-32

Molaug, S, 1980   Lasten i Bamblevraket, *Norsk Sjøfartsmuseum Arsberetning*, Oslo

Morris, C, 1981   *Anglo Saxon and medieval woodworking crafts*, unpubl PhD thesis, Univ Cambridge

Murphy, P, 1987   Discussion of the environmental evidence, in Ayers 1987a, 131-3

Mynard, D C, 1979   Stone weights from the rivers Great Ouse, Ouzel, Nene, & Tove, *Rec Buckinghamshire*, **21**, 11-28

Myrvoll, S, 1987   Archaeological investigations in Bergen 1980-1986: some new aspects on the development of the town, *Norwegian Archaeol Rev*, **20**, 2

——, Golembnik, A, & Dunlop, A R, 1983   *The Finnegården Project*, Bergen, unpublished MS

Nayling, N T, 1989   *The archaeological wood survey*, Ancient Monuments Lab Rep, **62/89**

Neale, W G, 1968   *At the port of Bristol Volume 1. Members and problems 1848-1899*

Nelson, S, 1983   Recent work at the Old Bridge at Kingston, *London Archaeol*, **5**, 15, 412-3

Nicholls, J F, & Taylor, J, 1881   *Bristol past and present*

Nielsen, C, 1980   *Wooden boat designs*, Stanford Maritime Press (translation)

NIV, 1966   *Hydrobiologiske undersøkelser i resipienter ved Tønsberg. Rapport 0-38/62*, Norsk institutt for vannforskning, Oslo

Oakey, N J, forthcoming   *Riverside development at City Mills, Skeldergate*, The archaeology of York (ed P V Addyman), **9/1**

O'Brien, C, Bown, L, Dixon S, Nicholson, R *et al*, 1988   *The origins of the Newcastle quayside: excavations at Queen Street and Dog Bank*, Soc Antiq Newcastle upon Tyne Monogr Ser, **3**

——, ——, ——, Donel, L, Gidney, L J, Huntley, J P, Nicholson, R, & Walton, P, *et al*, 1989   Excavations at Newcastle quayside: the Crown Court site, *Archaeol Aeliana 5 ser*, **17**, 141-205

O'Connor, T P, 1988   *Bones from the General Accident site, Tanner Row*, The archaeology of York (ed P V Addyman), **15/2**, 61-136

——, 1989   *Bones from Anglo-Scandinavian levels at 16-22 Coppergate*, The archaeology of York (ed P V Addyman), **15/3**, 137-207

Oddy, W A (ed), 1975   *Problems of the conservation of waterlogged wood*, Nat Maritime Mus Monogr Rep, **16**

Olsen, T, 1987   *Båt og fiske*, unpubl rep, Riksantikvaren, Tønsberg

Ottaway, P J, forthcoming   *5 Rougier Street*, in General Accident site, Tanner Row, and other sites (P Ottaway *et al*), The archaeology of York (ed P V Addyman), **4/2**

Owen, D M, 1979   Bishop's Lynn: the first century of a new town?, in *Proc Battle Conf Anglo-Norman Studies* (ed R Allen Brown), **2**, 141-53

Palliser, D M, 1978   The medieval street names of York, *York Historian*, **2**, 2-16

——, 1979   *Tudor York*

——, & Palliser, B M, 1979   *York as they saw it*

Pannett, D J, 1988   Fish weirs of the river Severn with particular reference to Shropshire, in Aston 1988, 371-89

Patterson, R, 1979   Spinning and weaving, in *A history of technology, vol II* (eds C Singer *et al*), reprint

Pearson, N F, forthcoming   General Accident site, Tanner Row, in *General Accident site, Tanner Row and other sites* (P Ottaway *et al*), The archaeology of York (ed P V Addyman), **4/2**

Penn, J, Field, D, & Serjeantson, D, 1984   Evidence of Neolithic occupation in Kingston: excavations at Eden Walk 1965, *Surrey Archaeol Collect*, **75**, 207-24

Penn, K J, 1980   *Historic towns in Dorset*, Dorset Natur Hist

Archaeol Soc Monogr Ser, 1

Philpots, J R, 1890 *Oysters and all about them*, XIX (publ John Richardson)

Platt, C, & Coleman-Smith, R, 1975 *Excavations in medieval Southampton 1953-1969*

Ponsford, M W, 1981 Bristol, in Milne & Hobley 1981, 103-4

——, 1985 Bristol's medieval waterfront, 'the Redcliffe project', in Herteig 1985c, 112-121

Powell, D L, 1935 *Bridgewardens' Accounts 1568-1603*, unpubl transcript, Kingston Heritage Centre

Power, E (ed), 1928 *The Goodman of Paris*

Preece, R C, Burleigh, R, Kerney, M P, & Jarsembowski, E A, 1983 Radiocarbon age determinations of fossil *Margaritifera auricularia* (Spengler) from the river Thames in west London, *J Archaeol Sci*, **10**, 249-57

Priestley, U, 1985 'The fabric of stuffs': the Norwich textile industry, c1650-1750, *Textile Hist*, **16.2**, 183-210

Prior, M, 1982 *Fisher Row*

Pritchard, F, n d *Swan Lane building material level 3 report*, unpubl archive rep, Mus London, Dept Urban Archaeol

Radley, J, & Simms, C, 1970 *Yorkshire flooding*

Raine, A, 1955 *Mediaeval York*

Ramsay, G D, 1982 *The English woollen industry, 1500-1750*

RCHM, 1962 *An inventory of the historical monuments in the city of York*, 1, *Eburacum: Roman York*, Royal Commission on Historical Monuments (England)

Richardson, E, 1977 Excavation round-up 1976, *London Archaeol*, **3.2**, 36-9, 53

Richardson, K M, 1959 Excavations in Hungate, York, *Archaeol J*, **116**, 51-114

Rickwood, D L, 1967 *The origin and decline of the Stranger community of Norwich 1565-1700*, unpubl MA dissert, Univ East Anglia

Robberstad, K (transl), 1923 *Magnus Lagabøters bylov*, Kristiania

Robertson, R H S, 1986 *Fuller's earth: a history of calcium montmorillonite*

Rogerson, A, 1976 Excavations on Fullers Hill, Great Yarmouth, *E Anglian Archaeol*, **2**, 131-245

Roots, G, 1797 *Charters of Kingston-upon-Thames*

Rosenqvist, A M, 1975 Experiments on the conservation of waterlogged wood and leather by freeze drying, in Oddy 1975, 9-24

Ross, C D, 1955 Bristol in the Middle Ages, in *Bristol and its adjoining counties* (eds C M MacInnes & W F Whittard), 179-92

Rule, M, 1982 *The Mary Rose*

Rulewicz, M, & Zajdel-Szczyrska, L, 1970 Materiały do wczesnośredniowiecznego rybołostwa w Wolinie, *Materiały Zachodniopomorskie*, **16**, 325-82, Szczecin

Russett, V, 1987 Wedmore, Sharon Farm, in Somerset Archaeology 1987 (ed E Dennison), *Somerset Archaeol Natur Hist*, **131**, 223

Salisbury, C R, 1981 An Anglo-Saxon fish-weir at Colwick, Nottinghamshire, *Trans Thoroton Soc Nottinghamshire*, **85**, 26-36

——, 1983 An early Tudor map of the River Trent in Nottinghamshire, *Trans Thoroton Soc Northamptonshire*, **87**, 54-9

——, 1985 The taming of the Trent, *E Midlands Archaeol*, **1**, 5-12

——, Whitley, P J, Litton, C D, & Fox, J L, 1984 Flandrian courses of the River Trent at Colwick, Nottingham, *Mercian Geol*, **9.4**, 189-207

Salzman, L F, 1923 *English industries of the Middle Ages*

——, 1952 *Building in England down to 1540: a documentary study*

Schofield, J, & Harrison, M, 1975 London: Seal House and Trig Lane, *Curr Archaeol*, **49**, 54-9

Seebohm, F, 1884 *English village community*

Sharp, C, 1816 *A History of Hartlepool*

Sherborne, J W, 1965 *The port of Bristol in the Middle Ages*, Bristol Branch Hist Ass, **13**

Shiercliff, E, 1793 *Bristol and Hotwell guide*, 2 edn

Silvester, R J, 1981 An excavation on the post-Roman site at Bantham, South Devon, *Proc Devon Archaeol Soc*, **39**, 89-118

Skempton, A W, 1957 Canals and river navigation before 1750, in *A history of technology* III (eds C Singer *et al*), 438-70

Smith, P D E, Allen, J P, Hamlin, A, Orme, B, & Wootton, R, 1983 The investigation of a medieval shell midden in Braunton Burrows, *Proc Devon Archaeol Soc*, **41**, 75-80

Somerset House, 1977 *London and the Thames: paintings of three centuries*, exhibition catalogue, Somerset House

Squirrell, J P, & Clarke, R W, 1987 An investigation into the condition and conservation of the hull of the Mary Rose. Part 1: assessment of the hull timbers, *Stud Conserv*, **32**, 153-62

Starling, K, 1987 *The conservation of wet metal/organic composite archaeological artefacts at the Museum of London*, MS of paper presented to ICOM Waterlogged Wood Working Group Conference, Fremantle 1987

Steane, J M, 1985 *The archaeology of medieval England and Wales*

Steane, J M, & Foreman, M, 1988 Medieval fishing tackle, in Aston 1988, 137-86

Steers, J A, 1964 *The coastline of England and Wales*

Stenton, D M (ed), 1927 *Pipe Roll for the fifth year of the reign of King Richard I, Michaelmas 1193*, Pipe Roll Soc, N S, **3**

Stephens, W B, 1957 The Exeter lighter canal 1566-1698, *J Transport Hist*, **3**, 1-11

——, 1958 *Seventeenth century Exeter*

Sutermeister, H, 1973 A note on the historical evidence for Westwick Street, North, in Carter & Roberts 1973, 464-7

Tamm, L, 1988 *The treatment of the Boys' School timbers*, unpubl dissert, Inst Archaeol, London

Tarkow, H, Feist, W C, & Southerland, C F, 1966 Interaction of wood with polymeric materials, penetration versus molecular size, *Forest Products Journal*, **16**, 61-5

Tatton-Brown, T, 1974 Excavations at the Custom House site, city of London, 1973, *Trans London Middlesex Archaeol Soc*, **25**, 118-219

Taverner, J, 1600 *Certaine experiments concerning fish and fruite*

Taylor, J N, 1974 *Fishing on the lower Severn*

Tesch, F W, 1977 *The eel*

Thomas, R, 1982 Stone weights from the Thames, *Oxoniensia*, **46**, 129-33

Tillot, P M (ed), 1961 *The Victoria history of the counties of England. The city of York*

Tillyard, M, 1987 The documentary evidence, in Ayers 1987a

——, forthcoming The documentary evidence, in Ayers forthcoming

Toller, T N, & Bosworth, J, 1976 *An Anglo-Saxon dictionary*

Troels-Smith, J, 1955 Karakterisering a løse jordarter, *Geological survey of Denmark, 4 ser*, **3.10**, 40-62, Copenhagen

Tyers, I, 1989 Dating by tree-ring analysis, in Marsden 1989, 104

Unger, R W, 1980 *The ship in the medieval economy 600-1600*

Upham, N E, 1983 *Anchors*, Shire publ, **110**

Vanes, J, 1977 *The port of Bristol in the 16th century*, Bristol Branch Hist Ass, **39**

Veale, E W W (ed), 1933 *The Great Red Book of Bristol (Pt 1)*, Bristol Rec Soc, **4**

——, 1950 *The Great Red Book of Bristol (Pt 3)*, Bristol Rec Soc, **16**

Verrey, 1788 Map of Cheddar, LoRO

Vilkuna, K, 1975 Unternehmen lachsfang. Die geschichte der lachsfischerei in Kemizolii. Studia Fennica. *Rev Finnish Linguistics & Ethnology*, **19**, Helsinki

Vince, A G, 1985 The processing and analysis of the medieval pottery from Billingsgate Lorry Park 1982, in Herteig 1985c, 157-63

von Brandt, A, 1984 *Fish catching methods of the world*, 3 edn

Wakeford, J E, forthcoming *Kingston's past rediscovered*

Wallace, P F, 1981 Dublin's waterfront at Wood Quay: 900-1317, in Milne & Hobley 1981, 109-18

Walton, P, 1988 Caulking, cordage and textiles, in O'Brien *et al* 1988

Waterman, D M, 1959 Late Saxon, Viking and early medieval finds from York, *Archaeologia*, **97**, 59-105

Watson, J, 1987 Suitability of waterlogged wood from British excavations for conservation by freeze-drying, in *Recent advances in the conservation and analysis of artefacts* (J Black), 273-6

Weber, B, 1981 Heita, feita pylsa!, *Viking bd XLIV*, Oslo

Wedlake, A L, 1984 *Old Watchet*

Went, A E J, 1945 Fishing weirs of the river Erne, *J Roy Soc Antiq Ir*, **75**, 213-23

——, 1946 Irish fishing weirs, *J Roy Soc Antiq Ir*, **76**, 176-94

——, 1956 Historical notes on the fisheries of the river Suir, *J Roy Soc Antiq Ir*, **86.2**, 192-202

——, 1969 The ancient 'sprat' fishing weirs in the south of Ireland, *Ind Archaeol*, **6**, 254-60

Wheeler, A, 1979 *The tidal Thames*

Whellan, T, & Co, 1857 *History and topography of the city of York and the North Riding of Yorkshire I*

White, A J, 1984   Medieval fisheries in the Witham and its tributaries, *Lincolnshire Hist Archaeol*, **19**, 29-35

——, 1988   Medieval fisheries in the Witham and its tributaries, in Aston 1988, 309-27

Whitelock, D (ed), 1955   *English historical documents I*

Wilkinson, T J, 1987   Palaeoenvironments of the Upper Witham Fen: a preliminary view, *Fenland Research*, **4**, 52-6

Williams, A F, 1962   Bristol port plans and improvement schemes of the 18th century, *Trans Bristol Gloucestershire Archaeol Soc*, **81**, 138-88

Williams, B, 1981   *Excavations in the medieval suburb of Redcliffe, Bristol, 1980*

——, 1982   Excavations at Bristol Bridge, 1981, *Bristol Avon Archaeol*, **1**, 12-15

Williams, M, 1970   *The draining of the Somerset Levels*

Williams, N J (ed), 1955   *Kingston-upon-Thames Bridgewardens' Accounts 1526-1567*, Surrey Rec Soc, **22**

Wilson, B, 1980   Animal bone and shell, in A Beaker burial and medieval tenements in the Hamel, Oxford (N Palmer), *Oxoniensia*, **45**, Fiche E04-F11

Wilson, D M, & Hurst, D G, 1964   Medieval Britain in 1962 and 1963, *Medieval Archaeol*, **8**, 231-99

Winder, J M, 1985   Oyster culture, in Milne 1985b, 91-5

——, forthcoming The marine mollusca, in Horsey, I P, *Excavations in Poole 1973-1983*, Dorset Nat Hist Archaeol Soc Monogr Ser

Woodward-Smith, N, & Schofield, J, 1977   A late 15th century account for a wharf at Vauxhall, London, *Trans London Middlesex Archaeol Soc*, **28**, 278-91

Young, A, 1988   Microbial activity in waterlogged wood, *Conservation today: papers presented at the UKIC 30th Anniversary Conference 1988* (ed V Todd), 123-7

Young, G A B, 1987   Excavations at Southgate, Hartlepool, Cleveland, 1981-2, *Durham Archaeol J*, **3**, 15-55

Youngs, S M, Clark, J, & Barry, T B, 1983 Medieval Britain and Ireland in 1982, *Medieval Archaeol*, **27**, 161-229

——, ——, & ——, 1985 Medieval Britain and Ireland in 1984, *Medieval Archaeol*, **29**, 158-230

——, ——, & ——, 1986 Medieval Britain and Ireland in 1985, *Medieval Archaeol*, **30**, 114-98

Index
by Barbara Hird

Figures in italic refer to pages on which
tables or illustrations occur

191

17th century 61; Newcastle, medieval 39; Viking Age consumption, York 177, 181; *see also individual types of fish and*: fishing; fishweirs

fish-sauce emporium, Roman; York 179

fish traps 83, 97, *99*, 100; *see also* basketware

fishing; fleets 88, 101; Hartlepool 43, 47, 48-50; Iceland; Scarborough and 48; Mesolithic 89, 94; methods 88-93; hand *77*, *78*, 88; harpooning 89; line 89-93; Neolithic 88; Norwich *1, 2, 3*, 6-7; regional traditions *99*, *100*; Tønsberg, Norway 73-5; *see also*: fishing tackle; fishweirs

fishing tackle 88-101; lack of typological change 88; Lincoln 169, 175; Neolithic 88; Tønsberg, Norway *74*, *75*; *see also individual items*

fishweirs 76-87, *99*, 100; catching devices 76, *77*, *78*, 80, *81*; for eels 76, *79*; Eire 76, *79*, *80*, 83, *84*; *hacwer* (hedge weir) 76; Lincoln, Roman or Saxon 169, 172; Montford, Shropshire *79*, 80; Neolithic 76, 83, *84*; Severn *78*, *79*, 80, *81*, 87, 100; Thames 100; Tyne, medieval 36; types 76, *77*; *see also*: Colwick; Hemington Fields

FitzHerbert, William (St William of York) 182

Flanders,; Baltic trade, medieval 39; invasion via Hartlepool (1171) 44; Newcastle; medieval trade 39, *41*, 42; sack of Norwich (1174) 3

flatfish, fishweirs to trap *77*, *78*; York finds 92

flax 1, 8n

fleets, fishing 88, 101

flint mining, Norwich 1, 6

floats, fishing line and net 90; bark 88, *95*, 96; cork *93*, 96, 97; 16th century, *Mary Rose* 92, *93*, 97; Neolithic; Traun, Switzerland 88, net *74*, 94; Tønsberg, Norway *74*; willow 97; Wolin, Poland *95*, 96; wood *93*, *95*, *99*

flooding; Bristol 23; Kingston 146; Lincoln; and migration of waterfront 173; York; Roman 180-1; medieval, after engineering works 182

flounder fisheries; Tønsberg, Norway 73

fly pupae, medieval; Bristol 21

Forthhere (bishop of Sherborne 709-737) 63

Foss, R, York 177-8, 181-2

Foss Navigation Company, York 181

Foster, John (fl 1583, citizen and plumber of London) 7

frame, hand, for fishing line 89, 92, *93*

frame elements, ship's; 17th century, London *113*, *114*

France; anchors, stone 83; trade: with

Exeter 124, 131; with Newcastle 39, *41*, 42; with Poole 51, 53, 104; with York, Roman 180

Franciscan order; Bergen; St Olav's monastery *151*, 156; Hartlepool 43, *44*

Franklyn, Joshua (18th century, Bristol merchant) 32

freeze-drying, conservation by 122, 123

Frisian merchants, late 8th century; York 181

fuller's earth; London, Swan Lane 12, *13*, 15, 16; Newcastle; medieval trade 39; use in brewing 18n7

fulling; Bristol 19, 25, 26; dyeing combined with, 16th century 18n9; London, Swan Lane 12, *13-15*, 16; mills 4, 18n8; Newcastle 39; Norwich *2*, 4, 5, 6

furnaces; dyer's: Italian, 16th century 15; Norwich 4; iron smelting, Norwich 3

Galfrid le Teinturer (fl 1257, of Norwich) 4

gaming piece, bone; Lincoln 176

gangion (fishing lines) 90

garderobes *see* privies

garfish fisheries, Tønsberg, Norway 73

gates *see under*: lock; sluice

Gateshead, Tyne and Wear *36*, 39

Gerard, William (fl1359/60, of Norwich) 4

Germany; trade with England 39, *41*, 182; *see also individual towns*

Gilbert of Cowgate (13th century, Newcastle merchant) 39

gilding, imitation of; 17th century, London 113, *115*

glaive 89

glass; Bristol industry 23, 26; Lincoln; Roman 176

Glastonbury, Somerset, Abbey 60, 62, 63, 64; possible medieval waterside structure 65; St John's Church 62

Gloucester, fishing tackle collection, Folk Museum 88, *96*

goose; use to tow troll line 90

gorges (fish-hooks), medieval *90*

gouge, driven; Saxon use 108

gouge adze; Saxon use *107*, 108

Gournay family of Weare, Somerset 64

grain; import to York, Roman 177; medieval export from Bridgwater 62; Poole; late medieval trade 53

grass on river islands, mowing of 7

Graveney, Kent 111, 122

grayling 181

Great Western, SS 32

Great Western Railway Company 34

Great Yarmouth, Norfolk, fish bones 94; iron fishing hooks *91*, 92; medieval trans-shipment for Norwich 6

grindstones; medieval export from

Newcastle 40; *see also*: millstones; querns; whetstones

gripes, bow and stern 105-6, *107*

Gypsy, SS; wrecked in Avon (1878) *32*

hacwer (Anglo-Saxon, hedge weir) 76

haddock 73, 92

Hadrian, Emperor of Rome 36

hair, tarred; caulking, 13th century, Kingston no 1 boat *109*, 111; 17th century, City of London Boys' School boat *114*

Håkon Håkonsson, King of Norway 71

halibut 73, 92

Ham Green, Avon; medieval pottery 64

Ham Hill, Somerset; stone distributed by river 62

Hamburg, Germany 39, 41

Hamworthy peninsula, Dorset 102

Hanse 150

hards; Poole, Dorset 102, 103; York, Roman 179

hare pelts, medieval trade in 39

harpooning of fish 89

Hartland, Robert (fl 1743, of Langport, Somerset) 62

Hartlepool, Cleveland 43-50; Anglo-Saxon monastery 43; boom chain 47; Brus family 43, 48; 19th century revival of docks 43, 50; coal trade 43, 50; coastal trade 47; cobbles *48*; communications with hinterland 43; and Durham 43, 48; Durham Street 43, *44*; fair 43; Fish Quay 47; fish-hooks 92; fishing industry 43, 47, 48-50; Flemish invasion (1171) 44; friary 43, *44*; harbour, medieval 43, *44-6*, 47; High Street 43, *44*; Middlegate 43, *44*, 49, 50; murage grants 48; and Norman conquest 43; Northgate 43, *44*; oven complexes 47; pier, late 15th century 48; post-medieval decline 43, 50; quay walls *44-6*, 47; railways 43, 50; reclamation 43, 47, 50; refuse 45, 47; Sandwell Gate 48; sea defences *44*, 45, *46*, 47; Southgate 43, *44-6*, 47; St Hilda's Church 43; tombstone, hogback 43;trade with continent, medieval 47; Victoria Dock 50; and Vikings 43; walls, town *44*, 47-8; wars, Anglo-Scottish 43, 47, 50; wharf, medieval *46*, 47; wool trade 47

hatch coamings; 17th century carvel-built craft, London 113

hatch grating beam; 17th century carvel-built craft, London *113*

hawthorn posts in fishweirs 76

Hawton, river, Devon; fishweir *77*, 78

hazel wattles in fishweirs 76, 81

hearths, medieval industrial; London, Swan Lane; cloth finishing 9, 12, *13-15*; Norwich; ironworking 3; Tønsberg, Norway; shipbuilder's 73; Winchester; dyeing 14